# Ecotourism

## THEMES IN TOURISM

Series Editor: Professor Stephen J. Page, Scottish Enterprise Forth Valley Chair in Tourism, Department of Marketing, University of Stirling, Stirling, Scotland FK9 4LA.

The Themes in Tourism Series is an upper level series of texts written by established academics in the field of tourism studies and provides a comprehensive introduction to each area of study. The series develops both theoretical and conceptual issues and a range of case studies to illustrate key principles and arguments related to the development, organisation and management of tourism in different contexts. All the authors introduce a range of global examples to develop an international dimension to their book and an extensive bibliography is complemented by further reading and questions for discussion at the end of each chapter.

Books published in the Themes in Tourism Series

S.J. Page *Transport and Tourism*

C.M. Hall *Tourism Planning*

Forthcoming titles

*Tourism in the Less Developed World*

*Recreational Geography*

*Heritage Management*

# Ecotourism

Stephen J. Page and Ross K. Dowling

*An imprint of* **Pearson Education**

Harlow, England · London · New York · Reading, Massachusetts · San Francisco · Toronto · Don Mills, Ontario · Sydney
Tokyo · Singapore · Hong Kong · Seoul · Taipei · Cape Town · Madrid · Mexico City · Amsterdam · Munich · Paris · Milan

**Pearson Education Limited**
Edinburgh Gate
Harlow
Essex CM20 2JE

*and Associated Companies throughout the world*

*Visit us on the World Wide Web at:*
www.pearsoneduc.com

© Pearson Education Limited 2002

ISBN 0 582 35658 X

**British Library Cataloguing-in-Publication Data**
A catalogue record for this book is available from the British Library

**Library of Congress Cataloging-in-Publication Data**
Page, Stephen, 1963-
    Ecotourism / Stephen J. Page and Ross K. Dowling.
       p.   cm. -- (Themes in tourism)
    Includes bibliographical references (p. ).
    ISBN 0-582-35658-X (pbk.)
    1. Ecotourism.   I. Dowling. Ross K.   II. Title.   III. Series.

  G156.5.E26 P35 2001
  338.4'791--dc21                                  2001032890

10  9  8  7  6  5  4  3  2  1
05  04  03  02  01

Typeset in 11/12pt Adobe Garamond by 35
Printed and bound in China
SWTC

# Contents

# Preface

This is the third book in the Themes in Tourism Series and focuses on the fast-growing and often used buzzword – ecotourism. The growing interest in environmental issues in tourism from the consumer and industry perspective, has raised the awareness of the natural world as an attribute to be understood, valued, observed and conserved. An entire industry has developed around the theme of ecotourism, seeking to extend many of the principles of ecotourism to the burgeoning interest in experiences which harness ecological elements. At the same time, ecotourism has become a vigorously debated and contested domain of interest among academics, managers and the tourism industry – in relation to its identification, characteristics and impact. This is reflected in the popular literature and rhetoric surrounding ecotourism through to the philosophical reviews of ecotourism in relation to tourism.

This book seeks to offer a synthesis of the burgeoning literature on ecotourism, with a necessarily selective approach to the key debates, issues and prospects for ecotourism. What is apparent from this burgeoning literature is that a very extensive range of academic and non-academic and professional reports are being produced for this area. Yet distilling down the elements of the debates and issues associated with the worldwide growth in ecotourism has not made this an area easy for the student or novice researcher to grapple with. Indeed, some excellent material is being produced through leading research efforts in countries such as Australia (see Higginbottom *et al.* 2001) through research agencies such as the Centre for Sustainable Tourism (http://www.crctourism.co.au) which provide good overviews of the situation in one country and yet are not as accessible or immediately evident to students or other researchers. It is hoped this book will make a valid contribution to the literature on ecotourism, offering analysis, commentary and insights to make this complex area understandable to its readers. The book also aims to provide a degree of intellectual challenge for more advanced researchers who may use this as a springboard for further research, given the complexity of the tourism–environment relationship and debates surrounding how it should be conceptualised, interpreted and managed. Although primarily designed for more advanced level students, the book will also have interest for planners, managers, communities and operators. Inevitably, the space constraints imposed by a publisher mean that some of the book will be limited to the key points, leading the reader to other sources. Nevertheless, the authors have sought to provide a systematic overview of ecotourism with a balanced argument, synthesis, analysis of good practice and discussion of the central issues in ecotourism. While a range of authoritative sources have begun to be published in the area of ecotourism and nature-based tourism, no one source seeks to provide a holistic assessment of the area. Readers do not need any prior knowledge of ecotourism, but an implicit assumption made by the authors is that readers will be familiar with the nature of tourism. While some of the findings and debates may prove controversial, the authors hope the book will engage students and practitioners to consider the ecotourism phenomenon and to critically evaluate its value, meaning and significance in relation to tourism.

*Stephen J. Page*
*Stirling*
*Scotland*

*Ross Dowling*
*Perth*
*Australia*

*April 2001*

# Acknowledgements

Stephen Page would like to thank the support staff in the Department of Marketing, University of Stirling for the assistance with scanning, compiling tables and figures. In particular, Lynne, Lynsey, Sheila and Sharon for their help and very quick turnaround. A number of organisations have kindly consented to the use of their material and illustrations including: the RSPB Scotland and the Hebridean Dolphin and Whale Trust. The kind provision of illustrations by Mark Orams at Massey University Albany, Auckland, New Zealand was invaluable in illustrating many of the themes discussed in the book. Also no mention would be complete without acknowledging the help and assistance provided by Jo Connell at the University of Stirling who made various editorial suggestions, helped with the provision of material and the rewriting of some of the chapters. Lastly, a special mention needs to be made to Matthew Smith at Pearson Education for his forbearance with the project and to Karen Mclaren for her help with the project.

Ross Dowling would like to thank a number of people for their support of this project. Firstly I wish to thank my coauthor and the series editor, Stephen Page, for his unfailing support of this book and also of my work over numerous years. I owe him a huge debt of gratitude. I also wish to thank Matthew Smith and the team at Pearson Education for their encouragement throughout the many years of gestation of the book.

Several colleagues at Edith Cowan University have encouraged me in my career and I would like to thank them for their ongoing professional support throughout the duration of writing this book. They are John Wood (Pro Vice Chancellor, Research) and Thandarayan Vasudavan (Lecturer in Tourism). In addition Research Assistants Sarah Parkin (formerly McNee) and Rebecca Lovitt also added immensely to the project and I wish to thank them for their enthusiastic research and personal interest in the book.

I also wish to thank a number of others who have in some small way contributed to my own thoughts on ecotourism through discussion, debate and dialogue over time. They are Pat Barblett (FACET, Western Australia), Tony Charters (Tourism Queensland), Paul Eagles (University of Waterloo, Canada), David Fennell (Brock University, Canada), Michael Hall (University of Otago, New Zealand), Jim Sharp and Phil Smeeton (Department of Conservation and Land Management, Western Australia), Dallen Timothy (Arizona State University, USA), Peggy Webb (Rottnest Island Authority, WA) and Betty Weiler (Monash University, Australia).

Finally I wish to thank my wife Wendy, my children and grand children for their support and encouragement of my endeavours in ecotourism over a long number of years. I truly appreciate your contribution to my life.

# Publisher's Acknowledgements

The publishers wish to thank the following for permission to reproduce the following copyright material:

Channel View Publications for figure 1.1, reprinted from D. Newsome, S.A. Moore and R.K. Dowling (2001), *Natural Area Tourism: Ecology, Impacts and Management*; tables 5.3–5.8, reprinted from R. Burton (1998) Maintaining the quality of ecotourism: ecotour operators' responses to tourism growth, *Journal of Sustainable Tourism*, 6(2), pp. 117–42; for tables 6.8–6.11, reprinted from C. Chin, S. Moore, T. Wallington and R.K. Dowling (2000) Ecotourism in Bako National Park, Borneo: visitors' perspectives on environmental impacts and their management, *Journal of Sustainable Tourism*, 8(1), pp. 20–35; for tables 6.12–6.14, reprinted from J. Obua (1997) Environmental impact of ecotourism in Kibale National Park, Uganda, *Journal of Sustainable Tourism*, 5(3), pp. 213–23; for figure 7.2, reprinted from R. K. Dowling (1993) An environmentally based planning model for regional tourism development, *Journal of Sustainable Tourism*, 1(1), pp. 17–37; for table 8.2, reprinted from B. McKercher and B. Robbins (1998) Business development issues affecting nature-based tourism operators in Australia, *Journal of Sustainable Tourism*, 6(2), pp. 173–88; for tables 9.1–9.3, reprinted from V. Palacio (1997) Identifying ecotourists in Belize through benefit segmentation: a preliminary analysis, *Journal of Sustainable Tourism*, 5(3), pp. 234–43, all by permission from Channel View Publications.

McGraw-Hill Book Company for figures 1.3 and 7.3, and table 7.3 from C.M. Hall, J. Jenkins and G. Kearsley (eds) (1997), *Tourism Planning and Policy in Australia and New Zealand: Cases, Issues and Practice*, by permission of McGraw-Hill Book Company.

Congizant Communication Corporation for figure 3.1 from N. Beaumont (1998) The meaning of ecotourism according to . . . is there now consensus for defining this 'natural' phenomenon? An Australian perspective, *Pacific Tourism Review*, 2(3/4), pp. 239–50.

Routledge for figures 3.2 and 3.7, and table 3.1 from D. Fennell, *Ecotourism* (1999); and figure 6.2 from S. Page, *Urban Tourism* (1995).

Tourism Queensland for table 3.2 from *Queensland Ecotourism Plan* (1997), www.tq.com.au/ecotourism

CAB International for figure 4.1 from A. Poon, *Tourism, Technology and Competitive Strategies* (1993), CABI Publishing.

Dept of Geographical Sciences, University of Plymouth, for table 4.1 from M. Mowforth, *Ecotourism: Terminology and Definitions* (1993).

Sage Publications, Inc. for tables 4.2 and 4.3 from P. Eagles, The travel motivations of Canadian ecotourists, *Journal of Travel Research*, 31(2), pp. 3–7, © 1993 by Sage Publications; for figures 5.5, 9.2 and 9.4 from P. Wight, Ecotourism: ethics or eco-sell, *Journal of Travel Research*, 31(3), pp. 3–9, © 1993 by Sage Publications. All reprinted by permission of Sage Publications, Inc.

Conservation International Foundation for table 5.1 from K. Ziffer, *Ecotourism: The Uneasy Alliance* (1989).

Elsevier Science for table 5.2, reprinted from *Tourism Management*, 17(1), A. Holden and H. Kealy, A profile of UK outbound 'environmentally friendly' tour operators, pp. 60–4, © 1996, with permission from Elsevier Science; tables 5.9 and 5.10, reprinted from *Journal of Rural Studies*, 13(4), D.A. Fennell and D. B. Weaver, Vacation farms and ecotourism in Saskatchewan, Canada, pp. 467–75, © 1997, with permission from Elsevier Science; for tables 6.3, 6.4 and 6.5, reprinted from *Tourism Management*, 17(4), J.G. Laarman and H.M. Gregersen, Pricing policy in nature-based tourism, pp. 247–54, © 1996, with permission from Elsevier Science; for table 6.7, reprinted from *Tourism Management*, 20(2), R. Scheyvens, Ecotourism and the empowerment of local communities, pp. 245–9, © 1999, with permission from Elsevier Science; for figure 8.1 and table 8.1, reprinted from *Tourism Management*, 20(1), S. Ross and G. Wall, Ecotourism: towards congruence between theory and practice, pp. 123–32, © 1999, with permission from Excerpta Medica Inc.

The Tourism and Environment Forum and Scottish Natural Heritage for table 6.2 from D. Masters, *Marine Wildlife Tourism: Developing a Quality Approach in the Highlands and Islands of Scotland* (1998).

The International Ecotourism Society for tables 8.3 and 8.4 from A. Drumm, *New Approaches to Community-based Ecotourism Management* (1998), courtesy The International Ecotourism Society.

Pearson Education Limited for tables 9.4, 9.5 and 9.6 from C.M. Hall and A. Lew (eds) *Sustainable Tourism: A Geographical Perspective* (1998).

RSPB Images for plates 6.1, 6.2, 6.3, 6.4, and 6.5.

If any unknowing use has been made of copyright material, owners should contact the author via the publishers as every effort has been made to trace owners and obtain permission.

# Chapter 1

# Introduction: from the environment–tourism nexus to ecotourism

The growing concern for conservation and the well-being of our environment is now firmly in the wider public arena. There has been a corresponding upsurge in tourism all over the world leading to the phenomenon referred to as 'mass tourism' (Krippendorf 1987). With this unparalleled growth of mass tourism as a consumer of the natural environment, concern has been voiced over the relationship of the natural environment with tourist activities (Hunter and Green 1995) and the potentially synergistic and yet conflicting relationship which may exist between these two phenomena. According to Page *et al.* (2001: 293):

> In the 1960s, the effects of mass tourism and increasing awareness of the human impact on the environment led to a general realisation that nature is not an inexhaustible resource which was embodied in the seminal study by Young (1973) *Tourism: Blessing or Blight?* This was a notable turning point in the analysis of tourism's impact on the natural and built environment, questioning the validity of uncontrolled growth.

In the natural environment, where tourism either exists or is proposed there is the potential for both beneficial and adverse environmental and socio-cultural impacts to occur. Thus there are two streams of thought regarding the environment–tourism relationship. The first is that the natural environment is harmed by tourism and hence the two are viewed as being in conflict. The second is that the two have the potential to work together in a symbiotic manner where each adds to the other.

The environment–tourism relationship has been the subject of academic (and popular) debate for the last three decades (for an overview see Dasmann *et al.* 1973; Budowski 1976; Bosselman 1978; Mathieson and Wall 1982; Pearce 1985; Romeril 1985a, 1989a, b; Farrell and McLellan 1987; Smith and Jenner 1989; Ross and Wall 1999b; Holden 2000). In the popular literature, seminal studies such as Wood and House's (1991) *The Good Tourist* epitomise the growing concern of tourist activity and the need to tread carefully on the environment as LaPlanche's (1995) *Stepping Lightly on Australia* emphasised. Within the academic community, tourism–environment relationships have attracted a growing interest from researchers in environmental science, geography, planning and other cognate areas which has also meant that research findings are very fragmented and dispersed across a wide array of

1

subject areas. One consequence is that researchers have found it difficult to assess the totality of the debate and arguments now emerging on the tourism environment relationship due to the wide range of interest groups involved.

The International Union for the Conservation of Nature and Natural Resources (IUCN; now known as the World Conservation Union) first raised the nature of the relationship when its director-general posed the question in a paper entitled 'Tourism and environmental conservation: conflict, co-existence, or symbiosis?' (Budowski 1976). Thirteen years later the question appeared to remain unanswered when Romeril (1989a) posed a similar question: 'Tourism and the environment – accord or discord?' What Romeril (1989a) achieved was the wider dissemination of the key debates over the tourism–environment relationship in terms of two standpoints – that is, either conflict or symbiosis. Either point of view may be adopted and defended, but it is argued here that no matter which standpoint is espoused the way to reduce conflict or increase compatibility is through understanding, planning and management which is grounded in environmental concepts and allows for sustainable development.

The environment–tourism relationship is grounded in the concepts of the sustainable use of natural resources as fostered by the World Conservation Strategy (IUCN 1980) and the sustainable development strategy of the World Commission on Environment and Development (WCED) (WCED 1987). This environmental–development link often includes tourism as a bridge. The base of this partnership is resource sustainability, so that tourism is fully integrated within the resource management process. This requires the adoption of resource conservation values as well as the more traditional develop-ment goals. Central to the goals of environmental conservation and resource sustainability are the protection and maintenance of environmental quality. To achieve this primary goal requires an awareness which is grounded in environ-mental protection and enhancement, yet fosters the realisation of the potential of tourism. Therefore, to understand how this debate has contributed to a greater emphasis on the potential value of the environment for specific forms of tourism, such as ecotourism, it is useful to explore a number of fundamental concepts such as the term 'environment'; and how human values towards the environment have shaped the philosophy behind forms of tourism that are environmentally dependent, which have been variously termed nature-based tourism and ecotourism in a more generic sense.

## The environment

The terms 'environment', 'tourism' and 'ecotourism' are open to many inter-pretations. The environment is defined as 'a concept which includes: all aspects of the surroundings of humanity, affecting individuals and social group ings (see O' Riordan 2000 for more detail). Environmental investigations are concerned, therefore, with people and their present and future activities in the surrounding atmosphere, water bodies and landscape' (Gilpin 1990: 65). The term 'environment' is often used interchangeably with the physical environment which Pearce (1989: 185) outlined as 'soil, vegetation, relief, aspect, fauna, climate – and the dynamics of the relationships between these elements'. The physical environment is defined by Mieczkowski (1995: 8) as the 'combination of non-living, i.e. abiotic, physical components, with biological resources, or the biosphere, including flora and fauna'.

Within the tourism and environmental management literature, much of the interest in tourism and the environment has focused on the resource base for tourism in specific locations, where resources can be defined in 'cultural, economic and ecological terms. Resources may be classified as renewable or non-renewable' (Fernie and Pitkethly 1985: 3). In other words, resources are recognised and exploited based on the qualities they may hold for tourist activity (Hall and Page 2002). The exploitation of resources and the environment in which they are located is not a new theme, since the history of Western civilisation and the urban–industrial culture has been dependent upon the exploitation of resources as raw materials and their processing into products for consumption. In the case of tourism, it is the use of environments for tourism which has caused a great deal of concern due to the impacts this may cause.

## Human values and environmental worldviews: how the environment and resources are perceived

People differ over the use of resources and the degree to which environmental problems exist due to their worldviews. Worldviews exist in many forms but the two most common vary according to whether or not they are human-centred as opposed to environment-focused (Miller 1994). These worldviews can be seen as two opposing paradigms along a continuum with the two main strands summarised in Table 1.1. Key principles within the human-centred

Table 1.1   The dominant worldview (anthropocentrism) and ecocentric view

| Dominant worldview | Ecocentric view |
| --- | --- |
| Dominance over nature | Harmony with nature |
| Natural environment as a resource to be exploited by humans | All elements of nature have intrinsic worth |
| Economic growth is necessary for human development | Humans have simple material needs |
| The reserves of resources are plentiful | The earth's resources are finite |
| Technology will provide solutions to environmental and resource-related problems | Appropriate technology is needed which is in balance with nature |
| Consumerism | Recycling |
| National/centralised community | Minority tradition |

worldview are that humans are the planet's most important species and are in charge of the rest of nature. It assumes the earth has an unlimited supply of resources to which we gain access through use of science and technology. In contrast are more environmentally grounded views which recognise inherent or intrinsic value to all forms of life regardless of their potential or actual use. This is a life-centred or ecocentric worldview in which humans believe that it is useful to recognise biodiversity as a vital element of earth for all life. The ecocentric worldview believes that nature exists for all of earth's species and humans are not apart from or in charge of the rest of nature. In simple terms it implies that humans need the earth, but the earth does not need them. It also suggests that some forms of economic growth are beneficial while other forms are harmful. Where these divergent views are most pronounced is in their attitude towards environmental problems resulting from human activity such as tourism.

## Environmental solutions: towards an environmental ethic

If one accepts the underlying premise that the earth's resources and environments are finite resources and that global environmental problems exist as a result of man's actions (including tourism), then one valuable approach within the ecocentric paradigm is to understand how individuals can minimise their environmental effects. This will involve developing an environmental ethic. Wearing and Neil (1999: 11) summarise the two opposing views in terms of how humans value and attach an ethic to the environment in terms of

> An ethic of 'use' – this is the normative or dominant mode of how human beings relate to nature: where nature is viewed predominantly as a set of resources which humanity is free to employ for its own distinct ends. It is an instrumental and anthropocentric view. An ethic 'of' nature – holds that non-human entities are of equal value with the human species. It is broadly intrinsic and ecocentric (Wearing and Neil 1999: 11).

Consequently, the human attitude to the environment and global environmental problems encompasses a variety of methods or approaches focused on the 'ethic of use' or 'ethic of nature' and to live in a sustainable manner involves a move towards the 'ethic of nature'. This is a precondition for developing a personal environmental ethic to understand the geographic area where one lives as part of a natural region or bioregion. A bioregion is a unique life territory with its own soils, landforms, watersheds, microclimates, native plants and animals, and other distinctive natural characteristics. Bioregional living is an attempt to understand and live sustainably within the natural cycles, flows, and rhythms of a particular place. What it means in terms of an individual's use of their leisure time for recreation or tourism, is to think more carefully about how their actions can minimise environmental damage. There are a number of steps one can take in order to foster a personal environmental ethic as Table 1.2 suggests.

**Table 1.2**   Developing a personal environmental ethic: guidelines

---

- First, we should evaluate the way we think about how the world works and sensitise ourselves to the local environment
- Secondly, we need to become ecologically informed (see Dowling 1993c). We should specialise in one particular area of environmental knowledge and awareness and share our knowledge and understanding with others by networking
- Thirdly, we should become more intimately involved in caring for the earth by experiencing nature directly
- Fourthly, to adopt an environmental ethic it is important that we become actively involved in an environmental cause. This will help us develop an awareness of the earth and its problems
- Finally, we must remember that the environment begins at home. Before starting to try to convert others we must begin by changing our own living patterns

---

## Principles of ecological ethics

The major principles underlying the ecocentric or earth-centred view are associated with ecological ethics (Yeoman 2000) and include interconnectedness, intrinsic value, sustainability, conservation, intergenerational equity and individual responsibility. The principle of interconnectedness focuses on the principle that humans are a valuable species, but humans are not superior to other species. The principle of intrinsic value is that every living thing has a right to live, or at least to struggle to live, simply because it exists; this right is not dependent on its actual or potential use to humans. Part of this principle includes the notion that it is wrong for humans to cause the premature extinction of any wild species and the elimination and degradation of their habitats. This focuses on the need for the preservation of wildlife and biodiversity principle.

Sustainability means that something is right when it tends to maintain the earth's life-support systems for humans and other species and wrong when it tends otherwise (Miller 1994). Conservation is a generic concept which is generally understood by most people in simple terms. It recognises that resources are limited and must not be wasted. The principle of intergenerational equity suggests that one must leave the earth in as good a shape as one found it, if not better. Inherent in the notion is that one must protect the earth's remaining ecosystems from human activities, rehabilitate or restore ecosystems that have been degraded, use ecosystems only on a sustainable basis, and allow many of the ecosystems that have been occupied and abused to return to a wild state. The final principle is one of individual responsibility. To carry this out, one must ensure that humans do not do anything that depletes the physical, chemical and biological capital which supports all life and human economic activities; the earth deficit is the ultimate deficit. All people must be held responsible for their own pollution and environmental degradation.

However, as Yeoman (2000: 316) argued, tourism is an activity that has largely been associated with the dominant worldview. Devall and Sessions

(1985) suggest that humans differ from and dominate all other creatures, such as through wildlife-based tourism. Humans also control their own destiny by developing forms of tourism that have control over the environment (i.e. types and forms of development that appeal to humans). In fact tourist operators associated with the mass market and more niche markets are always looking for destinations which are undiscovered, untouched and seemingly pristine in environmental terms. This is compounded by the thought processes of tourist operators and destinations that by introducing new forms of tourism which are less damaging to the environment, the problems of mass tourism have been resolved. For this reason, attention now turns briefly to the issue of tourism – what it is, how it can be conceptualised and its significance as a global activity.

## Tourism: what is it?

The late twentieth century and the new millennium have witnessed the continued growth of the leisure society where people value the significance of holidays, travel and the experience of going to see new societies and their cultures. This growth has been associated with the consumer society and is a characteristic of the dominant worldview, with its emphasis on discretionary spending on leisure activities in the developed world since the 1950s. It reflects the increased availability of disposable income to engage in leisure pursuits and holidays. Although this leisure society was traditionally the remit of the Western developed world, during the 1990s, trends have emerged where a greater propensity of the world's population are now travelling and engaging in holidays in their new-found leisure time. Tourism is increasingly being recognised as a part of a global process of change and development (known as globalisation). It is no longer confined to the developed countries that traditionally provided the demand for world travel. In this respect, understanding the pace of change in tourism is now a complex process, as the development of tourism throughout the world is a function of complex factors that coalesce to generate a process of change that needs to be understood in its local context. Therefore, understanding how these changes occur and how patterns of tourism affect the environment they are developed in now serves as a major question for researchers, governments, planners and local societies.

To understand tourism as a global and dynamic form, it is important to distinguish between three interrelated terms: tourism, leisure and recreation. The interrelationships among the three have been discussed by Boniface and Cooper (1987) and more recently by Hall and Page (2002) and more detail can be found in these sources. Although there is great deal of ambiguity about these terms, leisure can be defined as the time available to an individual when work, sleep and other basic needs have been met, and recreation as any pursuit engaged upon during leisure time. In contrast, Mathieson and Wall (1982: 1) argued that tourism is the temporary movement of people to destinations outside their normal home and workplace, the activities undertaken during the stay and the facilities created to cater for tourist needs. Mathieson and

Wall (1982) also argued that if leisure is a measure of time, and recreation embraces the activities undertaken during that time, then tourism is simply one of those activities which often is identified as a holiday; also other forms of tourism exist such as business travel and pilgrimages which have a tourist travel component but are not solely related to rest and relaxation. However, a central part of the tourism experience usually focuses on leisure and recreational activities. One of the most useful concepts used to understand how tourism functions as a phenomenon and as a business/activity is that known as the tourism system (Page 1994, 1999).

## The tourism system

The concept of the tourism system has been described and modelled from several different perspectives. Each perspective includes elements of demand and supply linked by the interconnecting strand of travel. Gunn (1988) proposed a simple approach called the *functioning tourism system* which comprises a number of interrelated components. Demand consists of the tourist market and incorporates people's interest in and ability to travel. Supply components include transportation, attractions, services and information/ promotion. Transportation consists of the volume and quality of all modes of transport. Attractions are the quality resources which have been developed for satisfying visitors. Services include the variety and quality of food, lodging and other products, and information/promotion is essential to entice the tourist to visit the products offered. Other writers have described the components of the tourism system in a similar manner with only minor differences in functions. For example, Mill and Morrison (1985) combine attractions and services into a 'destination' component, whereas Pearce (1989) separates accommodation from services and replaces information/promotion with infrastructure. An origin–destination approach emphasises the interdependence of the generating and receiving environments (Leiper 1981). Mathieson and Wall (1982) argued that tourism should be divided into three general components including a dynamic dimension (consisting of demand and travel), a static element (characteristics of tourists and destinations) and consequential component (impacts).

A tourism system model which embraces many of the elements of the existing models but which focuses on tourism's environmental aspects is outlined in Figure 1.1. It is based on the traditional view of a system incorporating inputs, processes, outputs and feedback. The inputs include elements of demand or markets, that is, the prospective tourist's motivation for and ability to travel, as well as supply, that is, the destination resource with its attractions, services, information and hosts. Processes include economic, social and environmental interactions which may have positive and/or negative outputs (impacts). Feedback allows for the planning of appropriate controls, capacities, policies and strategies for tourism growth while minimising adverse impacts. It is this model which serves as a backdrop for the examination of environmental aspects of existing tourism planning approaches.

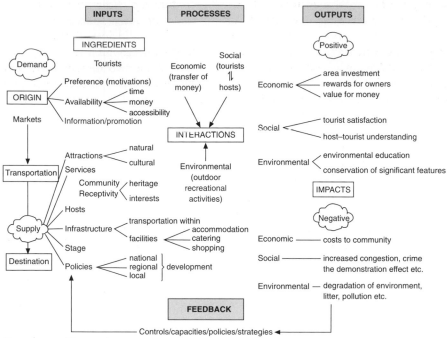

**Figure 1.1**   The tourism system
*Source*: Newsome *et al.* (2001)

## Tourism as a global economic activity

In 1991 the international tourism industry employed 112 million people worldwide and generated over $2.5 trillion at 1989 prices. In 1996, 593 million tourists travelled abroad (WTO 1997). In global terms, the expansion of international tourism continues to generate an insatiable demand for overseas travel. Europe remains the most visited of all regions of the world, where half of all global tourist receipts and almost two-thirds of international arrivals occurred in 1996. In 1996, almost 352 million arrivals and US$215.7 billion in receipts were received. Eastern and Central Europe were among the fastest growing areas to benefit from Western European tourism flows. In contrast, the East Asia Pacific region remains the area experiencing the highest growth rates, with total arrivals increasing by 9.3 per cent in 1996 to over 87 million with receipts of US$1 billion. Therefore, it is not surprising that many of the estimates of tourism's significance as a global activity leads many analysts such as the World Travel and Tourism Council (WTTC) to argue that it is the world's largest industry, though seeking evidence to substantiate this claim is difficult.

According to the WTTC, tourism is now the world's largest industry generating 6 per cent of the global gross national product and employing one in 15 workers worldwide. Globally, tourism is expected to grow at around 4 per cent per year. Global tourist arrivals are also forecast to reach 1 billion by 2010 and 1.6 billion by the year 2020, a more than threefold increase over the arrivals of the 1990s. This implies that a larger proportion of the world's population will travel, especially in developing countries in the twenty-first century. People will also holiday more often, perhaps two to four times per year. Travellers in the twenty-first century will also journey further afield and one out of every three trips will be long-haul journeys. Long-haul travel is expected to increase from 24 per cent of all international journeys to 32 per cent by the year 2020.

The WTO's (1999) *Tourism: 2020 Vision* forecast that the 1.6 billion tourists visiting foreign countries annually by the year 2020 will be spending more than US$2 trillion or US$5 billion every day. Tourist arrivals are also forecast to rise by an average 4.3 per cent a year over the next two decades, while receipts from international tourism will climb by 6.7 per cent a year. At the same time, this indicates that tourism will impact on the environment at a scale not previously considered possible, as the dominant worldview still drives the private and public sector arguments for economic benefits from tourist activity for national and local economies. The economic argument is a consistent strand that negates an ecocentric paradigm, although there is evidence that the environmental lobby is forcing the tourism industry to take more responsibility for its extensive impacts – not only its economic impact, but also its impact on the environment. What is of concern for the ecocentric view is that the WTO (1999) *Tourism: 2020 Vision* indicates that the volume of long-haul travel is forecast to increase from 18 per cent in 1995 to 24 per cent in 2020, spreading the impacts of tourism geographically.

To understand tourism as a global activity, it is useful to understand the essential features of tourism, since other studies (e.g. Leiper 1990) examine the meaning and definitions of tourism. From the diversity of definitions of tourism the common elements are that (Hall 1991: 6):

1. Tourism is the temporary, short-term travel of non-residents, along transit routes to and from a destination.
2. It may have a wide variety of impacts on the destination, the transit route and the source point of tourists.
3. It may influence the character of the tourist.
4. It is primarily for leisure or recreation, although business is also important.

What these four characteristics highlight are that tourism is a dynamic activity which is ever-changing and that a range of problems may result from the interaction of tourism with the environment. For this reason, it is useful to outline the way in which natural areas and the environment have been viewed as resources for tourism.

## Tourism and natural areas as tourism attractions

Within the tourism and environmental science literature, it is recognised that tourism activities are dependent upon the concept of attractivity: without this element in a given context, it is unlikely that tourist visitation will occur. Although the concept of attractivity has not been studied in its own right to understand the motivation, behaviour and response of tourists from different cultural backgrounds, most visitors have rated natural environments highly in simple surveys of what they like about particular places. Although a substantial literature exists on the complexity of developing scales, adjectives and measures to assess landscape attractiveness for tourists (see Hall and Page 1999 for a review), the natural environment has emerged as a particular focus for tourism research. Although Hall and Page (2002) point to the artificial division of the use of natural environments into tourist and recreationalist activities, in practice, use of the same resource base often blurs the distinction between these groups with different motives, behavioural traits and demand on the resource. To understand the natural environment as a tourist resource, one needs to recognise the continuum of the resource base from the urban, man-made environment through to the urban fringe, rural areas to wilderness areas. In addition one should also not overlook the significance of specific tourism attributes which can run through the continuum of resources, such as rivers and waterways, marine and coastal areas that also comprise distinct environments. While specific models of the resource base for tourism and recreation have been used since the 1950s and 1960s (see Pigram 1983 and Hall and Page 1999 for a review), the research paradigm guiding research on the natural environment has undergone profound changes over the last decade. It has moved from a primary focus on the resource base, use and problems of monitoring and evaluating impacts to a new conceptualisation of different tourist typologies and their differential impact on the environment. In particular, new philosophical stances have developed to show how tourist use of the natural environment may be beneficial for wildlife conservation and preservation, rather than simply condemning tourism for its negative environmental impacts. Yet this has to be set against the context of growing problems of global tourism activity which poses significant problems for natural areas.

## The problems of tourism as a global activity

Tourism is in many ways a new type of industrial revolution for many countries with the main difference being that it is a smokeless industry that has provided service sector employment, revenue and impacts. Like any form of economic activity it has impacts on the environment (see Hunter and Green 1995 for more detail) but as Fennell (1999: 7) recognises, 'Tourism has been both lauded and denounced for its ability to develop and therefore transform regions into completely different settings.' In the former case, tourism is seen to have provided the impetus for appropriate long-term development; in the latter the ecological and sociological disturbance to transformed regions can be overwhelming. The problems associated with mass tourism have been parodied by Lodge (1992) in his novel *Paradise News*, and have been documented by tourism practitioners and scholars since the 1970s, most notably Turner and Ash (1975), MacCannell (1976), Krippendorf (1987) and Urry (1990).

Their concerns focus on the sheer number of tourists now travelling around the world, the adverse impacts on the natural, cultural and social environments and whether or not the perceived economic benefits are real. Yet even if tourism does not generate some of the economic benefits which are widely heralded by policymakers, from the impact perspective ecotourism, with its sustainable, conservation approach, still fails to face the issue of the continuing growth of numbers. This has also been examined by Wheeller (1992a: 104) in terms of 'the diametrically opposed and widening divergence that exists between the slow, steady, self-less, cosy, back to nature, sustainable, eco-friendly, controlled small-scale solution to tourism problems and the realities of globally, a capitalist society with inbuilt growth dynamics'. Again, much of the debate focuses on the philosophical underpinning of tourism as a global activity: the anthropocentric versus the ecocentric view which perhaps is embodied in the growing categorisation by some commentators of tourism as either comprising mass tourism or alternative tourism. The former is characterised by large numbers of people seeking replication of their own culture in institutionalised settings with little cultural or environmental interaction in authentic settings. Alternative tourism, however, is usually taken to mean alternative forms of tourism which place emphasis on greater contact and understanding between hosts and guests as well as between tourists and the environment (Smith and Eadington 1992).

The development of alternative options began in the early 1980s and is associated with the emergence of what has been described as the adaptancy platform. According to Jafari (1990: 35) the 'adaptancy platform favoured new forms of tourism responsive to host communities and their natural environments and man-made (heritage) environments' (Sofield 2000: 47). What this means is that adapted tourism must be more community-focused, utilise local resources and not be destructive and is the antithesis of mass tourism since it has been variously labelled as 'green tourism', 'alternative tourism', 'soft tourism', 'appropriate tourism' and 'ecotourism'. Influenced by the negative attitudes towards mass tourism, this new perspective argued that large-scale tourism was problematic, and that small-scale alternatives were therefore more desirable in most cases. The associated options, generalised under the umbrella term of alternative tourism, were conceived as alternatives to mass tourism specifically, rather than other types of tourism (see Weaver and Oppermann 2000: 366–7 for more detail).

As a result, 'Alternative tourism can be broadly defined as forms of tourism that set out to be consistent with natural, social and community values and which allow both hosts and guests to enjoy positive and worthwhile interaction and shared experiences' (Wearing and Neil 1999: 3) and has a clear relevance for natural areas since tourism needs to fit within the capacity and ability of the environment to accommodate visitors. Consequently, one type of alternative tourism which is based on natural areas is tourism in natural settings (Figure 1.2). Examples can include nature-based tourism, in which viewing nature is the primary objective, and adventure tourism, in which the focus is on the activity, for example, white-water rafting or scuba diving – an

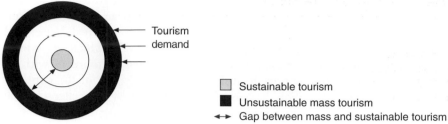

Figure 1.2     The sustainable – unsustainable tourism continuum

active use of the environmental resources. Indeed, many forms of adventure tourism are focused on natural areas as Table 1.3 indicates. According to the Ministry of Commerce (1996), adventure tourism is defined as commercially operated activities involving a combination of adventure and excitement pursued in an outdoor environment. In the case of New Zealand, over 10 per cent of all visitors undertake some form of adventure activity (New Zealand Tourism Board 1993) and recent research by Bentley *et al.* (2000) examined the nature of such activities from a tourism operator's perspective (see Table 1.4). What is apparent from the definition of alternative tourism is that it is a generic term that encompasses a whole range of tourism strategies (e.g. appropriate, eco, soft, responsible, controlled, small-scale, cottage and green tourism), all of which are supposed to be preferred alternatives to conventional mass tourism (Weaver 1991).

Fennell (1999: 25) suggests that 'Although mass tourism may be said to be predominantly unsustainable, more recently new and existing developments in the industry have attempted to encourage more sustainable practice through various measures, some of which include the controlled use of electricity, a rotating laundry schedule, and the disposal of wastes' (Figure 1.2). However, Fennell (1999) also observed that most forms of alternative tourism are theoretically sustainable in nature. The alternative tourism sphere comprises both sociocultural tourism and ecotourism. The former alternative tourism includes, for example, 'rural or farm tourism, where a large portion of the tourist's experience is founded upon the cultural milieu that corresponds to the environment in which farms operate' (Fennell 1999: 26). What is important in Fennell's (1999) argument is that ecotourism is described as involving a type of tourism that is dependent upon nature (Whelan 1991) and natural resources as the primary component or motivator of the trip. Hence Fennell (1999: 26) regards ecotourism as an alternative form of tourism but expounds 'the belief that ecotourism is distinct from mass tourism and various other forms of alternative tourism'. There is also a growing debate over alternative tourism, particularly distinct forms such as ecotourism which are natural area dependent, as to whether they contribute to the concept of sustainable development within a tourism context.

Table 1.3   A typology of adventure tourism activities

*Aviation-related*

- Ballooning
- Hang gliding
- Gliding
- Heli-bungy jumping
- Parachuting
- Paragliding
- Scenic aerial touring (small aircraft/helicopter)

*Marine*

- Black-water rafting
- Caving
- Charter sailing
- Diving/snorkelling
- Jet boating
- Parasailing
- Rafting
- River kayaking/sea kayaking
- Canoeing
- River surfing/river sledging
- Water skiing
- Wind surfing
- Fishing

*Land-based*

- Cross-country skiing
- Downhill skiing
- Heli-skiing
- Ski touring
- Trekking/tramping
- Vehicle safaris
- Flying-fox operations
- Bungy jumping
- Mountain biking/cycling
- Guided glacier trekking
- Horse trekking
- Hunting
- Mountain guiding
- Rap jumping/abseiling
- Rock climbing

*Source*: Based on Page (1997) and Bentley and Page (2001).

Table 1.4   Activities of adventure tourism operators

| Environment in which activity is undertaken | Activity of operator | No. of operators | Years in business |
|---|---|---|---|
| Land-based | All terrain vehicles (ATV) | 5 | 7.6 |
| | Adventure education | 4 | 7 |
| | Bungy jumping | 5 | 5 |
| | Caving | 2 | 2.5 |
| | Cycle touring | 5 | 7.4 |
| | Eco tours | 9 | 9.3 |
| | Guided walking | 15 | 8.7 |
| | Horse riding | 10 | 12.9 |
| | Mountain recreation | 11 | 12.1 |
| | Quad biking | 3 | 2.7 |
| Water-based | Black-water rafting | 3 | 12.7 |
| | Diving | 4 | 9.6 |
| | Fishing | 2 | 7 |
| | Jet boating | 5 | 6.2 |
| | Kayaking | 24 | 10.9 |
| | Marine encounter (dolphins/seals) | 7 | 8.4 |
| | Wind surfing | 3 | 7.4 |
| | White-water rafting | 10 | 12.8 |
| Aviation | Ballooning | 3 | 7.7 |
| | Skydiving/parasailing | 3 | 6.7 |
| | Scenic flight | 9 | 15.3 |
| Subtotal | | 15 | |
| Total | | 142 | |

*Source*: Modified from Bentley *et al.* (2000) and Bentley *et al.* (2001b).

## Sustainability as a concept

Since the introduction of the World Conservation Strategy (IUCN 1980) with its emphasis on 'ecodevelopment' there has been a strong move towards recognising the interdependencies that exist among environmental and economic issues. This led to the Brundtland Commission's (WCED 1987) 'sustainable development' concept which equates development with environmental and social responsibility.

The momentum for global action continued to mount, with the United Nations Conference on Environment and Development being held in June 1992. The conference, also referred to as the Earth Summit, was hosted by

Rio de Janeiro and was attended by 178 countries. The Summit covered three fundamental areas (Harris and Leiper 1995: xviii):

1. the Declaration – a detailed blueprint for implementing sustainable development;
2. a framework convention on biological diversity;
3. a framework convention on climate change.

This approach was advanced over a decade ago by Travis (1980) who suggested that taking actions which ensure the long-term maintenance of tourist resources (be they natural or human-made) is good economics, as it can mean long-term economic returns from their use. This was endorsed by Romeril (1985a: 217) as 'tourism's strong dependence on quality natural resources makes such a goal (of sustainable development) not just a desired ideal but an economic necessity'. There was also a growing recognition that 'the environment should no longer be viewed primarily in negative terms as a constraint, but as a resource and an exciting opportunity for compatible human use' (Pigram 1986: 2).

There are a multitude of definitions for the term 'sustainability'. Often the descriptions or explanations include characteristics such as: long-term maintenance of natural resources; minimal adverse environmental impacts; appropriate and adequate economic benefits to local communities; optimal production with minimal negative outputs; and satisfaction and provision for human social, political and economical needs (Jordan 1995). The WCED established a definition for sustainability that encompasses and applies to all resources. Sustainable development is development that meets the needs of the present without compromising the ability of future generations to meet their own needs (Jordan 1995: 166). Three principles are fundamental to ecological sustainability, which also have the capability and potential to be applied to all resources and activities (after Harris and Leiper 1995):

1. Do not use non-renewable resources faster than renewable substitutes can be found.
2. Do not use renewable resources faster than they can be replenished.
3. Do not release pollutants faster than the biosphere can process them to be harmless.

In the anthropocentric paradigm, development is frequently equated with economic growth and progress as well as an escalation in material consumption. If the definition of sustainability is acknowledged as 'the existence of ecological and social conditions necessary to support human life at a certain level of well-being through future generations' (Harris and Leiper 1995: xix), then the definition of sustainable development which Harris and Leiper (1995: xx) use as 'a form of managed economic growth that occurs within the context of sound environmental stewardship' modifies many of the tenets of the anthropocentric logic. The objective of such stewardship should be to pass on to future generations a stock of natural resources no less in quantity and quality than that inherited by the present generation. Therefore, in a tourism context this has a great deal of validity because it calls into question the logic of unfettered tourism growth based on mass numbers without any concern for the impact on the environment, particularly in natural areas.

## Tourism and sustainability

Among the first advocates of a sustainable development approach to tourism were Mathieson and Wall (1982) who had compiled their treatise on tourism's economic, physical and social impacts since 'planning for tourist development is a complex process which should involve a consideration of diverse economic, environmental and social structures' (Mathieson and Wall 1982: 178). The same conclusion was drawn by Murphy (1985) in his advocacy of a community approach to tourism planning, concluding that tourism planning needs to be restructured so that environmental and social factors may be placed alongside economic considerations. Getz (1986) approached the situation from his investigation of tourism planning models and indicated that reference to theoretical models will remind tourism planners not to act in isolation from other forms of social, economic and environmental planning.

During the late 1980s the sustainable development approach to tourism planning was advanced by a number of authors including (Inskeep 1987, 1988; Gunn 1987, 1988; Pearce 1989; Romeril 1989a, b). Inskeep (1988) suggested that tourism planning cannot be carried out in isolation but must be integrated into the total resource analysis and development of the area with possible land and water conflicts resolved at any early stage. Inskeep (1988) noted that recently prepared tourism plans gave much emphasis to socio-economic and environmental factors and to the concept of controlled development.

Pearce (1989) indicated that the recognition of tourism's composite nature and multiplicity of players involved in its development are critical in planning for tourism. This was endorsed by Romeril (1989a) who stated that a strong emphasis of many strategies is their integrated nature where tourism is one of a number of sector and land-use options. In deciding national and regional policies, a matrix of all sectors of activity are assessed and evaluated – positive and negative economic effects, positive and negative social effects, positive and negative environmental effects. Thus tourism and environmental resource factors are not taken in isolation, nor at the remote end of a decision-making process.

The underlying concept of sustainable tourism development is the equating of tourism development with ecological and social responsibility. Its aim is to meet the needs of present tourists and host regions while protecting and enhancing environmental, social and economic values for the future. Sustainable tourism development is envisaged as leading to management of all resources in such a way that it can fulfil economic, social and aesthetic needs while maintaining cultural integrity, essential ecological processes, biological diversity and life support systems.

One of the early attempts to develop an action strategy for sustainable tourism emerged from the Globe 90 conference in British Columbia, Canada in 1990 (Fennell 1999) which identified the goals of sustainable tourism (after GLOBE '90 1990: 2):

1. to develop greater awareness and understanding of the significant contributions that tourism can make to environment and the economy;

2. to promote equity in development;
3. to improve the quality of life of the host community;
4. to provide a high quality of experience for the visitor;
5. to maintain the quality of the environment on which the foregoing objectives depend.

Achieving the fifth goal of environmental conservation includes providing for intergenerational equity in resource conservation (Witt and Gammon 1991). It also includes avoiding all actions that are environmentally irreversible, undertaking mitigation or rehabilitation actions where the environment is degraded, promoting appropriate environmental uses and activities, and cooperating in establishing and attaining environmentally acceptable tourism. As a result, 'The concept of sustainability has become a mediating term in bridging the ideological and political differences between the environmental and development lobbies, a bridge between the fundamentally opposed paradigms of eco- and anthropocentrism' (Wearing and Neil 1999: 15).

## Sustainable tourism development: towards a sustainable tourism paradigm

Sustainable development is vital for the continued survival and viability of the tourism industry and for the protection and nurturing of the natural and cultural environment on which tourism depends (Hall and Lew 1998). Protecting environments for the principal reason of sustaining tourism is not an ideal nor responsible objective. A more appropriate and conscientious approach would be to use tourism as a means to protect the environment and in turn sustain biodiversity (Harris and Leiper 1995). Sustainable tourism denotes all types of tourism (whether natural or human-made resources) that contribute to sustainable development (de Kadt 1990). Sustainability has emerged as a popular term which has become widely used in the academic and popular literature on tourism, planning and development studies. There has been little agreement among researchers on the precise definitions, focus and methodology by which sustainable tourism can be implemented in different contexts. In fact sustainable tourism suffers from the same problem as ecotourism, where operationalising the concept poses numerous problems (Bottrill and Pearce 1995).

In 1992 the Global Conference on Business and the Environment held in Vancouver, British Columbia, established a challenge statement for the global tourism sector, identifying the measures necessary for the industry to become environmentally sustainable (Manning and Dougherty 1995: 30). The document addressed a number of areas deemed essential in sustaining tourism including (after Manning and Dougherty 1995: 30):

1. create a nationwide institutional framework for sustainable tourism;
2. protect the resource base central to the industry's success;
3. develop better inventory and monitoring systems for both the resource base and the actions of tourists;

4. use improved technology and design to minimise negative impact;
5. take advantage of market opportunities for a greener tourism product;
6. develop standards for the industry and encourage collaboration at all levels in the development and implementation of effective regulatory mechanisms.

The above action items have the potential to collaboratively establish a more sustainable tourism industry through more efficient and enhanced planning, management and cooperative efforts. Within a planning context, Getz (1987) has observed that there are four traditions to tourism planning: boosterism, an economic-industry approach, a physical-spatial approach and a community-oriented approach, none of which are mutually exclusive. More recently, a fifth approach has been added – sustainable tourism planning, with a concern for the long-term future of resources, the effects of economic development on the environment and its ability to meet present and future needs. While Dutton and Hall (1989) recognise that there are certain preconditions for achieving a sustainable approach to tourism planning (e.g. cooperation, industry coordination, consumer awareness of sustainable and non-sustainable options, strategic planning and commitment to sustainable objectives), it does require the tourism industry and the public sector planning agencies to radically rethink both the way they operate and the effects of tourism. However, Ashworth (1992: 327) argues that the emergence of the sustainability debate is leading the tourism industry to tackle

> criticisms being made of it, not the problems that cause the criticisms. If there is no resource or environmental problem, then it does not need to be defined nor do solutions need to be found. The problem is seen as one of promotion, and promotion is what the tourism industry is especially good at. Buying off the grumblers with 'commitments' and 'mission satements' . . . is easier than the alternative [of sustainable tourism planning].

In fact, Ashworth (1992) rightly acknowledged that for the tourism industry to embrace sustainable tourism means that it will need to set goals for environmentally damaging activities, sustainable targets for specific activities, sites, towns or regions and could actually 'require potential tourists to engage in other forms of activity, or in extreme cases it could ask tourists: "please go somewhere else"' (Ashworth 1992: 327). Therefore, for sustainable tourism planning to exist, it may require the tourism industry to take a hard look at its future to assess its own capability in accommodating growth and development and to make some difficult decisions on the future scope and scale of tourism activity in specific locations. Yet this approach presupposes that tourism planning exists as a well-defined and focused activity within the public and private sector. In reality, 'planning for tourism occurs in a number of forms (development, infrastructure, promotion and marketing), a number of structures (different government organisations) and a number of scales (international, national, regional and local level)' (Hall 1991: 98). However, even this assumes that tourism is either the focus of a separate planning process or integrated into the normal planning process, especially at regional and local levels, to anticipate and regulate change in 'a system, to promote orderly development so as to increase the social, economic and environmental benefits of the development process. To do this, planning becomes an ordered sequence of operations, designed to lead to the achievement of either a single goal or to balance between several goals' (Murphy 1985: 156).

In most countries, tourism planning exists as a component of public sector planning, and its evolution as a specialist activity has been well documented (Gunn 1988; Inskeep 1991). As a component of public sector planning it is recognised that 'the development of tourism will not be optimal if it is left in the hands of private sector entrepreneurs, for they are motivated by the profit and loss accounts. But on the other hand, if tourism development is dominated by the public sector then it is unlikely to be developed at the optimal rate from the economic point of view' (Cooper *et al.* 1998: 130). The implication here is that a balance of private and public sector involvement in tourism planning is vital to ensure a suitable balance is reached and for principles of sustainability to be incorporated into development plans and scenarios. For the public sector, their main task is the coordination of public and private sector interests and the preparation of the tourism element in the statutory planning process.

Ceballos-Lascurain (1998: 8) argues that 'though the concept of ecotourism is still often used synonymously with that of sustainable tourism, in reality, ecotourism fits within the larger concept of sustainable tourism. As our millennium draws to a close, it is imperative that all forms of human activity become sustainable – and tourism is no exception.' In contrast, Harrison and Husbands (1996) describe what they call 'responsible tourism' which is not a tourism brand or product but rather an approach to tourism that delivers benefits to tourists, host populations, investors and governments. As a consequence, responsible tourism acknowledges that there is a place for well-conceived ecotourism products but also for mass tourism if it can be undertaken in a responsible manner.

A scrutiny of the term 'sustainable tourism' reveals a number of difficulties. Some critics suggest that the term is an oxymoron, with 'sustainability' (with its steady-state implications) and 'development' (with its growth implications) being mutually exclusive. The widespread support that the term enjoys, therefore, may simply reflect the ease with which it can be appropriated by the supporters of various ideologies to perpetuate and legitimise their own views (McKercher 1993). Another common criticism is that the theory is extremely difficult to translate into action when subject to the actual complexities of both the natural and social environments (Weaver and Oppermann 2000: 353). Accompanying the more intellectual development of tourism development and planning in relation to the sustainability paradigm, has been a trend inherent in the tourism sector which has been described as 'the greening of tourism'. This is a useful trend to consider because if the tourism sector develops the products which tourists consume, then this is a natural precursor to the emergence of ecotourism.

## The greening of tourism

Wight (1993a) argued that there is no question that the marketplace is becoming 'greener', or more environmentally sensitive, both in terms of awareness and in its desire to contribute through its efforts a more sensitive approach to numerous activities and purchases. Some 85 per cent of the industrialised world's citizens believe that the environment is the number one public issue, while Burr (1991: 3) stated that over 76 per cent of Americans considered themselves environmentalists. This greening of the marketplace should not be taken as some sort of fad, or fashionable interest in environmental interests but an undercurrent that is now pervading many business sectors including tourism. In tourism terms there is considerable collective power resting within the hands of the individual tourist, regarding the impact on the places visited, the nature of the tour operation they select, and the attitudes which tourists bring with them on return home. Chalker (1994: 90) argued that

> a degree of personal unease must be expressed at the 'green' stamp of approval being given to one sector only of the global tourism industry. The key issue for the industry is to make all tourism sustainable. Ecotourism must not be an excuse to ignore the potential for all forms of tourism to have an impact on the environment and become unsustainable.

McLaren (1998) uses the term 'ecotravel' to encompass all forms of ecotourism, conservation-focused tourism, and other types of nature travel that market the earth. The popular term, 'ecotourism', is not limited to visits to natural areas. The number of tourists who travel solely to view natural surroundings or wildlife is actually quite modest. A majority of travellers also want an opportunity to experience a culture different from their own. Cultural activities and lifestyles are featured prominently in travel brochures. Ecotravel programmes cover a wide variety of experiences – from spartan, hard-core, bury-your-own-poop backpacking in special conservation zones to the purely hedonistic, luxury vacations at typical resorts. They offer a participatory experience in the natural environment. At its best ecotravel promotes environmental conservation, international understanding and cooperation, political and economic empowerment of local populations, and cultural preservation. When ecotravel fulfils its mission, it not only has a minimal impact, but the local environment and community actually benefit from the experience and even own or control it. At its worst ecotravel is environmentally destructive, economically exploitative, culturally insensitive, 'greenwashed' travel (McLaren 1998: 97).

Academic study programmes with an environmental twist have boomed. Indeed, ecotourism courses in academic institutions have also expanded rapidly since the 1990s. As Robertson *et al.* (1996) found, some 21 programmes on ecotourism or nature-based tourism had emerged in the period 1990–95, all of which focused considerable attention on environmental carrying capacity and the preparation of managers to balance the conservation principles with the demand for ecotourism products. University research expeditions, the

School for International Field Studies, Earthwatch expeditions, the Sierra Club travel programmes, and other programmes deliver thousands of new-breed ecostudents to tag turtles, bag leeches and count plants in the wilds (McLaren 1998: 100). What is clear is that the demand and supply for products and experiences with an 'eco' label have expanded in line with the 'greening' of the consumer and its permeation of the tourism sector, where new business opportunities have been recognised.

## Ecotourism: towards a definition

According to Weaver (1998: 1) 'terms such as sustainable tourism, alternative tourism and ecotourism, which were not even in the lexicon 20 years ago, are now the objects of intense scrutiny, debate and controversy. At present, there is no consensus at all surrounding the use of the term ecotourism', a feature poignantly emphasised by Orams (1995). Not surprisingly, the question of semantics now appears to be occupying a significant portion of the research agenda as researchers seek to debate its meaning and value and a number of studies have debated this term. For example, Jaakson (1997) explored the epistemology of ecotourism, a feature expanded and developed by Malloy and Fennell (1998) in relation to ethical issues. 'Further confusion results from the use of related terms, such as sustainable tourism and alternative tourism, to name only two of the more prominent ecotourism affiliates' (Weaver 1998: 1). As emphasised earlier, ecotourism has been recognised as a subset of alternative tourism (i.e. an alternative to mass or large-scale tourism) where the major motivation for travel is to use, see and experience the natural environment (Cater and Lowman 1994). The seminal study of this area is widely acknowledged as Boo's (1990) *Ecotourism: The Potential and Pitfalls* which widely popularised the area where passive and active forms of activity patterns among tourists have been observed (Woods and Moscardo 1998). Among the other notable, accessible and comprehensive overviews of this growth area for research are the syntheses by Weaver (1998), Fennell (1999) and Wearing and Neil (1999). Other notable studies in report or book form in this growing area of research are by Honey (1999), Beeton (1998), Liddle (1997) and the review of the area by the WTO (1999).

Hawkins (1994) suggested that the major factors contributing to the boom in ecotourism included an international awareness of global ecological realities, the desire among a rapidly growing and relatively affluent segment of the industrialised world's tourists to have nature-based experiences, and the developing world's conviction that natural resources are finite and must be conserved for future generations. What Hawkins (1994: 263) observed was that ecotourism is growing rapidly and is influencing the overall tourism industry both as a special interest form of travel (see Weiler and Hall 1992) and a 'greening' influence on the tourism field in general, stressing environmentally friendly approaches to tourism product development, operations and consumption.

**Plate 1.1**  Visitor interaction with wildlife and the natural environment is an integral part of the visitor experience of ecotourism, as shown with this example of visitors holding a koala bear in an Australian wildlife park.

**Plate 1.2**  Humpback whales migrate close to the coastline making them accessible for whale watching and a rewarding encounter between visitors and mammals (Source: M. Orams).

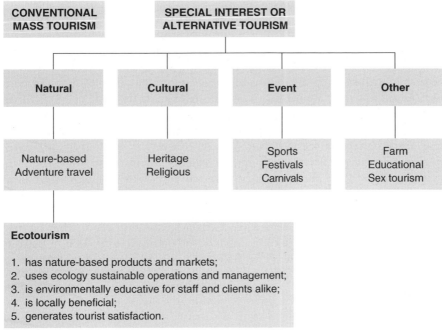

Figure 1.3   An overview of tourism
*Source*: Dowling (1997a: 100).

There is considerable confusion among the terms 'sustainable tourism', 'nature-based tourism' and 'ecotourism'. All three terms are neither synonymous nor mutually exclusive. All tourism comprises either mass tourism or alternative tourism (Figure 1.3). The former is characterised by large numbers of people seeking replication of their own culture in institutionalised settings with little cultural or environmental interaction in authentic settings. Haenn (1994) notes that the mass tourism industry is successful because it intervenes between the tourist and their destination in order to free the tourist from as many obligations as possible. The tourism industry replaces the social relationships of friends, family and neighbours with financial relationships. Haenn (1994) argued that the mass tourist does not seem to have adapted to his/her destination and instead they appear to want their destination to adapt to them. An interesting study by Diamantis and Ladkin (1999) highlighted the linkage between sustainable tourism and ecotourism, particularly the coexistence and common themes. This coexistence, however, has led other commentators such as Ross and Wall (1999b) to argue that the linkage of protected areas, people and resources in the context of North Sulawesi may offer mutual benefits, but they have not been linked together so that the sustainability principles and ecotourism products are able to create a realistic form of alternative tourism. Nevertheless, it has been recognised that the use of economic techniques such as willingness to pay highlights that environmental protection makes economic sense if it harnesses the sustainability and ecotourism linkages for community and environmental benefits. One indication of the scale of ecotourism development was illustrated by Jie *et al.* (2000) in relation to the development of 874 forest parks in China of 7.48 × $10^6h^2$ by the Chinese State Forestry Administration up to 1997. The improved usage has in part been attributed to the development of ecotourism where over 50 million visits are made a year. This highlights the scale of impact that may be achieved even though one might argue that this is not necessarily the intended use or meaning of ecotourism. This is endorsed by Fennell (1999) who argued that his thesis is not that ecotourism is some form of 'pure' tourism which will in the long term challenge mainstream tourism. It is unashamedly a niche form of tourism which comprises one segment of the range of alternative forms of tourism, which by assumption, is alternative to traditional mass tourism.

Honey (1999: 13) notes that while Ceballos-Lascurain claims that he first coined the term *ecotourism* in 1983, other experts claim it originated in Kenton Miller's (1978) pioneering work on national park planning in Latin America. Miller argued that development must integrate biological considerations with economic, social and political factors to meet both environmental and human needs. Miller contended that the potential for national parks to contribute to 'ecodevelopment' had grown during the 1970s as greater numbers of well-trained personnel were able to work with larger budgets on more parklands. Kenton's concepts of ecodevelopment and ecotourism quickly entered the debate on sustainable development.

## Hector Ceballos-Lascurain

Hector Ceballos-Lascurain is a Mexican architect and environmentalist who is frequently attributed with first coining the term 'ecotourism' in 1983. In 1983, he was the founding president of PRONATURA, a Mexican conservation non-governmental organisation. PRONATURA was involved in conserving wetlands as breeding and feeding habitats for birds such as the American flamingo. Ceballos-Lascurain noted that there was the presence of an ever-growing number of tourists, especially North Americans, interested mainly in birdwatching. He believed such people could play an important role in boosting the local rural economy, creating new jobs and preserving the ecology of the area, and began using the word 'ecotourism' to describe this phenomenon.

Ceballos-Lascurain stated that ecotourism was tourism that involved travelling to relatively undisturbed natural areas with the specific object of studying, admiring and enjoying the scenery and its wild plants and animals, as well as any existing cultural aspects (both past and present) found in these areas. He added that the term also implies a scientific, aesthetic or philosophical approach although the ecotourist is not required to be a professional scientist, artist or philosopher. Ceballos-Lascurain suggested that the main point is that the person who practises ecotourism has the opportunity of immersing him/herself in nature in a way that most people

**Plate 1.3** Hector Ceballos-Lascurain, the acknowledged 'father of ecotourism', at the 7th Australian Ecotourism Conference, Fraser Island, Queensland, 14th October 1999.

cannot enjoy in their routine, urban existences. This person will eventually acquire a consciousness and knowledge of the natural environment, together with its cultural aspects, that will convert him/her into somebody keenly involved in conservation issues.

In 1993 Ceballos-Lascurain's earlier definition was revised to 'Ecotourism is environmentally responsible travel and visitation to relatively undisturbed natural areas, in order to enjoy and appreciate nature (and any accompanying cultural features – both past and present) that promotes conservation, has low negative visitor impact, and provides for beneficially active socio-economic involvement of local populations.' This definition was officially adopted by the IUCN during its First World Conservation Congress held in Montreal in October 1996.

## Towards a universal definition of ecotourism?

Given the relative recency with which ecotourism has been used in the wider academic and industry contexts, what is surprising is the general lack of agreement on a universal definition which is compounded by the inclusion of different criteria, perspectives and philosophical standpoints. For this reason, it is pertinent to examine a number of the ways in which researchers and practitioners have defined the term ecotourism (for more detail see the *Encyclopedia of Tourism* by Jafari 2000 and *Encyclopedia of Ecotourism* by Weaver 2001), although the concept of ecotourism is also subject to a greater discussion in Chapter 3. Laarman and Durst (1987: 5) in their early reference to ecotourism, defined it as nature tourism in which the 'traveller is drawn to a destination because of his or her interest in one or more features of that destination's natural history. The visit combines education, recreation, and often adventure.' In essence ecotourism is an industry in which elements of outdoor recreation and the environmental movements come together at the consumer level (Shoup 1989 cited in Backman *et al.* 1994). Ziffer (1989: 6, cited in Fennell 1999: 38–9) suggests that nature tourism, while not necessarily ecologically sound in principle, concentrates more on the motivation and the behaviour of the individual tourist. Conversely, ecotourism is much more difficult to attain owing to its overall comprehensiveness (the need for planning and the achievement of societal goals). As a result, Ziffer (1989) defined ecotourism as a form of tourism inspired primarily by the natural history of an area, including its indigenous cultures. It also implied a managed approach by the host country or region which commits itself to establishing and maintaining the sites with the participation of local residents, marketing them appropriately, enforcing regulations, and using the proceeds of the enterprise to fund the area's land management as well as community development.

An early definition suggested that the fundamental functions of ecotourism are the protection of natural areas, production of revenue, education and local participation and capacity building. In fact the Canadian Environmental Advisory Council (1991: 25) suggested that ecotourism should embrace the following characteristics:

1. It must promote positive environmental ethics.
2. It does not degrade the resource.
3. It concentrates on intrinsic rather than extrinsic values. Facilities never become attractions in their own right.
4. It is ecocentric rather than anthropocentric in orientation.
5. It must benefit the wildlife and the environment (socially, economically, scientifically, managerially or politically).
6. It is a first-hand experience with the natural environment.
7. It includes a component of education and/or appreciation.
8. It has a high cognitive and affective experiential dimension.

These characteristics have been repeated in research by Butler (1992) and Wight (1993a). The Council added that theoretically, ecotourism experiences will encourage protection by developing awareness, insight, knowledge, understanding, appreciation and respect for participants for the local environment (Canadian Environmental Advisory Council 1991: 27). However, as Ballantine and Eagles (1994) observed, an extensive, eight-point scale is quite difficult to operationalise. What is clear is that ecotourism contrasts markedly with other forms of tourism due to its unique ecocentric focus along with environmental education, personal growth and other intrinsic values underlying the travel motivation of ecotourism participants (Wearing and Neil 1999).

Wight (1993a: 3) suggested that

> ecotourism is an enlightening nature travel experience that contributes to conservation of the ecosystem, while respecting the integrity of host communities . . . two views seem to prevail on ecotourism. One sees that public interest in the environment may be used to market a product, the other sees that this same interest may be used to conserve the resources upon which this product is based. What is required is an effective integration of both views so that the industry and the resource may be sustained over the long term.

Thus, ecotourism is a subset of natural area tourism and may combine elements of both nature-based tourism and adventure travel. However, it is also characterised by a number of other features, notably its educative element and conservation-supporting practice. According to Boeger (1991) the tourism potential to natural areas is vast. Boeger (1991) promoted ecotourism within the context of environmentally sound tourism respecting the dignity and diversity of other cultures, as well as concern for the earth's renewable resources. Citing a Standford Research Institute study, Boeger (1991) recognised the real potential of ecotourism globally, forecasting an 8 per cent annual growth in worldwide tourism but a staggering 30 per cent growth in ecotourism. Boeger (1991) also pointed to the estimated US$4 billion spent annually on birdwatching tours as well as to the millions of people trekking in the Himalayas, hiking in Central America and cycling in China. This highlights a clear relationship with the forms of tourism which Boo (1992) observed in the early growth of ecotourism.

Boo (1992) suggested that ecotourism is nature travel that contributes to conservation through the generation of funds for protected areas, the creation of employment opportunities for communities surrounding protected areas, and by providing environmental education for visitors. Another early view by Rymer (1992) described ecotourism as a sub-branch of tourism centred on the tourist's desire for immersion in a relatively natural environment in which they and their support facilities have low impact upon the environment. Rymer (1992) added that the critical factor that differentiates ecotourism from other more traditional forms of tourism is the conscious effort to minimise tourism's negative environmental impacts.

In a similar vein, The Ecotourism Society (TES) defined ecotourism as purposeful travel to natural areas to understand the cultural and natural history of the environment, taking care not to alter the integrity of the ecosystem while producing economic opportunities that make the conservation of natural resources financially beneficial to local citizens (TES 1993). It placed emphasis on responsible travel to natural areas, conservation of the environment, and the well-being of local people. The Ecotourism Society defines ecotourism as 'responsible travel to natural areas which conserves the environment and improves the welfare of local people' (Western 1993: 8). In contrast, Wall (1994: 5) stated that ecotourism is usually defined on the basis of one or more of three criteria: the characteristics of the destination, the motivations of participants and the organisational characteristics of the trip. He argues that a strong case can be made for classifying specific trips rather than specific individuals as being examples of ecotourism, as tourists may take different trips of different types.

The definition of ecotourism advanced by the Australian *National Ecotourism Strategy* is that 'ecotourism is nature-based tourism that involves education and interpretation of the natural environment and is managed to be ecologically sustainable'. The definition recognises that 'natural environment' includes cultural components and that 'ecologically sustainable' involves an appropriate return to the local community and long-term conservation of the resource (Australian Department of Tourism 1994: 17).

Zeiger (1997) suggested that ecotourism is about preserving the natural environment and giving the locals fair employment so that it empowers the local population to take an active role in environmental programmes and that it is more important to educate the tourist than to make a profit. Khan (1997b), however, argued that ecotourism is purposeful travel to natural areas to understand the culture and natural history of the environment, taking care not to alter the integrity of the ecosystem, while producing economic opportunities that make the conservation of natural resources beneficial to local people. Lindberg and McKercher (1997: 66) considered that the term 'ecotourism' struck a chord with the tourism industry in the 1990s when it became a buzzword that pushed this sector into a crisis. As a term, 'ecotourism' had been hijacked and, by the early 1990s, had become a positioning statement and a politically correct form of mass tourism, and as such, virtually any type of tourism activity could claim to offer an ecotourism experience. Several changes had occurred in the development of ecotourism in the previous decade. First, there was a desire for more educative and challenging vacations, combined with an increased awareness of and interest in the natural environment, and this has led to a growth in visitation at many natural areas, particularly developing countries. In addition many development professionals had increasingly viewed natural areas as an avenue to provide employment in regions that had experienced decline. Many conservation and resource management professionals increasingly viewed natural area visitation as an avenue for enhancing protected area finance and providing conservation-related benefits. Finally, increased attention was paid to improving the sustainability of all tourism activities, including those occurring in natural areas. Lindberg and McKercher (1997: 67) postulated that by the mid-1990s, ecotourism as a concept had begun to enter a period of maturity, arguing that many of the claims made in earlier years had begun to be disputed, and the legitimacy of many ecotourism products was increasingly being challenged.

According to the World Tourism Organisation (WTO 1999) ecotourism is one of the fastest-growing segments within the more than $425 billion worldwide tourism industry. It has been identified as a way for developing countries to achieve self-sufficiency without losing autonomy (Nixon 1999) and is likely to be of increasing significance for developing nations (Cater 1994).

Lindberg *et al.* (1998a: 12) reported that although estimates of ecotourism's growth are rare, due to the problem of defining it, most observers feel that ecotourism has grown faster than tourism generally during the past several years. Based on a survey of ecotourism operators in the region, Lew (1998a) found that average annual growth rates have been steady at 10–25 per cent over the past few years, and many are projecting higher growth in coming years. This may in part be a reflection of the diverse motives associated with the development of ecotourism experiences. While McLaren (1998: 98) pointed to the different motives (e.g. conserving the environment, providing nature-based and adventure travel, and serving the growing tourist demand for more 'authentic' experiences), ecotourism is generally perceived as a form of alternative tourism distinguished in three main ways from other types of tourism:

- Ecotourism emphasises the natural environment, or some component thereof, as the focus of attraction, with associated cultural attractions being recognised as a secondary component (Boo 1990).
- The resulting interaction with nature is motivated by a desire to appreciate or learn about the attraction in terms of its intrinsic qualities.
- Qualifying activities should be carried out in a sustainable way (Blamey 1997).

Within these parameters there are a number of activities that can be placed under the ecotourism umbrella. Activities such as birdwatching and stargazing can be placed entirely within ecotourism, while pursuits such as safaris, trekking and nature photography overlap with the nature-based components of adventure tourism, 3S tourism and/or sociocultural alternative tourism (Weaver and Oppermann 2000: 369).

Helleiner (1997) stated that the attitude which defines the ecotourist is one of personal responsibility both for their own safety as well as for the sustainability of the natural and cultural environments being visited. Thus Helleiner's (1997) view of an ecotourist is someone who undertakes travel which combines elements of adventure and the conservation ethic. An essential ingredient of ecotourism, which is often overlooked, is the need to provide ecotourists with a sense of adventure and the need for challenge. As Helleiner argued, operators are often tempted to maximise the comfort level of the ecotourists at the expense of the element of adventure. Helleiner advocated the need for balance but argued that 'for the long-term sustainability of ecotourism, the wise strategy is to err on the side of providing adventure, not comfort' although that has to be provided with a safe and meaningful manner (see Bentley *et al.* 2000, 2001 for more detail on tourism and safety issues). Yet there are also protagonists who question the validity of ecotourism and for that reason it is useful to review some of their arguments.

## Arguments against ecotourism

A number of commentators feel that the definition of ecotourism has become a catch-all term which is now meaningless (see Oppermann 1997; Ryan 1999; Fennell 1999: 181 for a discussion of this argument). Some commentators actively deride the term 'ecotourism'. For example, Wheeller (1994) questioned the logic and validity of such attempts to disguise mass tourism under a new guise. When poorly planned, unregulated and overhyped, ecotourism, like mass tourism or even traditional nature tourism, can bring only marginal financial benefits but serious environmental and social consequences (Honey 1999: 54), as has been seen in Nepal and other fragile tourism environments. All too often, ecotourism has been hailed as a panacea: a way to fund conservation and scientific research, protect fragile and pristine ecosystems, benefit rural communities, promote development in poor countries, enhance ecological and cultural sensitivity, instil environmental awareness and a social conscience in the travel industry, satisfy and educate the discriminating tourist, and, some claim, build world peace. Although 'green' travel is being aggressively marketed as a 'win-win' solution for the less developed world, the environment, the tourist and the travel indus-try, close examination shows a much more complex reality (Honey 1999: 4).

Haenn (1994) stated that an ecotourist's visit to a natural environment changes it unequivocably and that their mere presence challenges a destina-tion's claim to being a pristine unaltered environment as even a small number of ecotourists can have a large adverse impact and that they inevitably spoil the place for the future ecotourists. Haenn (1994) suggests that ecotourism relies on a place to look and feel pristine and that once it is degraded ecotourists will search for the next pristine undiscovered destination, so that ecotourism acts against the goals of environmental protection. Haenn (1994) suggests that rather than offer a new relationship between people and places, ecotourism is simply a new way of travelling and an attention getter for environmental causes. Thus, ecotourism has not only changed tourism but is a market diversi-fication technique to broaden the tourist: ecotourism does not change tourists but has merely allowed them to maintain different expectations while travelling.

Ecotourism has been defined and redefined as many times as there have been conferences or articles written on the topic, since most definitions have been broad; ecotourism is not so much a 'word' but a philosophy which has evolved from the environmental consciousness of the 1960s to be included in what is now a way of life for many people. Cater (1993) suggested that there is a very real danger of viewing ecotourism as the universal panacea, and the ecotourist as some magic breed, mitigating all tourism's ills. Cater (1993) recognised that when business is the principal motivation behind ecotourism it is not surprising that it may serve to alienate, rather than benefit local communities. Hall and Butler (1995) suggested that many government agencies and tourism academics have been caught up in the 'new' forms of tourism such as ecotourism and cultural tourism in the mistaken belief that these forms of tourism are ethically superior. However, it has been advanced that ecotourism and cultural tourism are often used merely as marketing tools, whereas in fact they are sometimes ethically inferior (Thomlinson and Getz 1996).

An ardent chronicler of ecotourism's negative facets is Wall (1994, 1997, and Ross and Wall 1999b). Wall (1994: 4) suggested that much ecotourism may be little more than 'old wine in new bottles' and therefore it raises fundamental questions concerning the forms which tourism might take if it is to be ecologically sustainable, culturally sensitive and economically viable. The lack of a clear definition means that the word 'ecotourism' conjures up vivid images, but it is evident that the images are not consistent among users. Indeed, Wall (1997) argued that ecotourism is not automatically sustainable: if it is to be sustained and contribute to sustainable development, it must be economically viable, environmentally appropriate and socioculturally accept-able. Thus if ecotourism is not economically viable, then the facilities and services required by ecotourists will not be provided and ecotourism's poten-tial economic benefits for owners, operator and residents will not be achieved.

Wall (1997) noted that the literature on ecotourism is growing rapidly and that its meaning is becoming increasingly varied to the extent that ecotourism is becoming discredited, arguing that ecotourism as an instigator of change in areas previously seldom visited by outsiders will place new demands upon the environment associated with new actors, new activities and new facilities. Several years later Ross and Wall (1999b) were more scathing, arguing that 'despite the existence of substantial literature highlighting its potential benefits, there is a growing amount of case-study research reporting the failure of ecotourism to achieve the ideal goals upon which it should be founded. In other words, ecotourism theory has often not been successfully put into practice' (Ross and Wall 1999b: 123). Ross and Wall (1999b) added that it has become clear that ecotourism ultimately relies on the availability and quality of natural areas, and therefore must be considered alongside strategies for maintaining and protecting nature.

Pretty and Primbert (1995) argued that when people (i.e. local indigenous people) are excluded from conservation the goals of conservation are at risk and that some pristine rainforests assumed to be untouched by human hands, are now known to have once supported thriving agricultural communities. They postulated that the 'pristine' concept of the wilderness is a modern myth that is not substantiated in reality. In a similar vein, McKercher (1998: 203) argued that 'ecotourism has gained such a high profile that it has come to mean almost any form of non-urban tourism. The term has been hijacked by marketers who do not understand its concepts, by destinations that are clearly not ecotourism destinations and by businesses that are capitalising on a trend.' This divergence of opinion is reflected in Addison's (1996: 298) sentiments as the

> recent literature on the subject is generally divided between those who see ecotourism as a positive trend (Choy 1991, Millman 1989) and those who see it either as no better (and possibly worse) than what it purports to replace – that is, mass tourism (Butler 1990, Munt 1994, Wheeller 1991, 1992a) – or as cynical marketing 'hype' (Wight 1993a). Many who view ecotourism as generally positive are aware that it is far from a panacea for community development (Cater 1993, Hughes 1995, Jones 1992).

Many commentators are now beginning to doubt whether alternatives to mass development are genuinely sustainable (Butler 1990; Wheeller 1991, 1994; Shackley 1996; Wall 1997). For example, Wall (1997) raises the question of whether or not forms of mass tourism development can be environmentally benign, in a paper entitled 'Is ecotourism sustainable?' On the other hand some authors contend that ecotourism cannot be sustainable if it is regarded as only a market segment. Thus the whole concept of ecotourism is now under intense scrutiny. In a critical manner, Wight (1993a) outlined how ecotourism has been seized upon by opportunistic tour operators who merely relabel their tourism products as ecotourism ones in order to capitalise on its market advantages. Wight (1993a) listed the many forms of tourism which have been relabelled as ecotourism. These include ecotour, ecotravel, ecoadventure, ecovacation, ecocruise, ecosafari to name a few. Cater (1994: 2) concluded that ecotourism thus interpreted, may be ecologically based but not ecologically sound.

Campbell (1999) found that one of the most insidious elements of ecotourism is when affluent travellers embark on ecotours largely to 'tick off' another exotic destination which they can 'brag about', a phenomenon Campbell refers to as 'ego tourism'. This represented a form of ecocolonialism which is certainly in the same vein as the neocolonialism concept discussed by Britton (1982) in the context of Pacific Islands. In the Pacific Islands this led to a route for tourism development in the post-colonial era which has seen colonial patterns of behaviour replicated in tourist behaviour and in the control of tourism afforded by multinational corporations (see Hall and Page 1996 for a discussion).

## Structure of the book

This book is not intended to be a comprehensive review of ecotourism in view of the objectives of the new Themes in Tourism Series. It is designed as an introduction to the subject of the environment–tourism relationship so the reader can gain a feel for the scope of, complexities arising from, and possibilities of undertaking successful tourism developments in natural areas. One objective of the book is to overcome the existing perception that tourism developments in environmentally sensitive areas are inherently adverse and that rather it offers a view that with adequate foresight, planning and management such developments represent vehicles to bring about increased awareness and conservation. While the actual built tourism developments in natural areas obviously change the naturalness of the area it is through the design, interpretation and education that environmental awareness may be fostered.

This book offers a number of useful points for further research on the environment and tourism. One underlying theme is that ecotourism is an appropriate medium to bring about greater environmental understanding. For this reason ecotourism separates itself out from other forms of tourism in natural areas. If people in the developed world seek to ascribe some form of legacy to the earth then one of the best ways of doing this is by gaining an understanding of our environment leading to its appreciation which inspires action for the environment. This book reviews the environment–tourism relationship through the context of ecotourism, a niche form of tourism. It will involve the clarification and definition of terms and concepts such as sustainable tourism, nature-based tourism, wildlife tourism and ecotourism. The book focuses on ecotourism's principles and characteristics and illustrates these by way of numerous examples of ecotourism such as natural attractions and ecotourism's organisations, accommodations and tours. In addition issues related to the planning, development and management and marketing of ecotourism will also be examined.

Chapter 2 reviews the relationship between tourism and the environment. It takes the debate forward from the traditional relationship being viewed as being in either coexistence, conflict or symbiosis to the integration of the two where all states may occur at the same time. The chapter defines and characterises environmental tourism and illustrates the various types of tourism carried out in, about and for the environment. Chapter 3 describes ecotourism as being a subset of environmental tourism, combining elements of both nature-based tourism and adventure travel. It is characterised by a number of other features including its educative element, conservation-supporting practices and local benefits.

In Chapter 4 the concept of whether or not there is such a thing as an ecotourist is discussed. Comparisons are made between the characteristics of ecotourists in several parts of the world. This is followed in Chapter 5 by an overview of the ecotourism industry. A review is made of the industry at different levels, including the local, regional, national and global scales. Public and private ecotourism is outlined and different types of businesses are examined in relation to touring operations, attractions and accommodation. Case studies are included to illustrate each type of business. In Chapter 6 the focus is on ecotourism's impacts. Various beneficial or adverse impacts of ecotourism are described and classified according to whether they are environmental, social, economic, political and cumulative.

Ecotourism planning and development principles are explained in Chapter 7. The need for environmentally friendly principles is outlined and best-practice ecotourism is described at a range of levels. An environmentally based approach to tourism planning is described and illustrated through the case study of the Gascoyne Region of Western Australia. Issues of ecotourism development in environmentally sensitive areas are presented and reviewed. Chapter 8 examines the principles of management in relation to ecotourism. Case studies of management practices are given at various levels for countries, regions and individual businesses. The need for ethics is propounded and the importance of education and interpretation is stressed. Issues related to marketing are reviewed in Chapter 9. Marketing techniques, selling the environment and influencing attitudes are addressed. The final chapter articulates the future of ecotourism by way of examination of its past growth as well as the present situation. By extension, the future development of the ecotourism industry is cast in the context of the growth of tourism generally and the projected increase in environmental stringencies. Completing the book is a comprehensive list of references and websites.

## Questions

1. Is it appropriate to use the word 'environment' as a simple descriptor for 'our surroundings'?
2. In what ways is the environment–tourism relationship viewed?
3. To what extent is environmental tourism viewed as part of mass tourism?
4. What are the main features of tourism?

## Further reading

The following references provide a guide to key reading which supports the material examined in this chapter.

## The environment and environmental values

Devall, B. and Sessions, G. (1985) *Deep Ecology: Living as if Nature Mattered*, Utah: Gibbs Smith.

Yeoman, J. (2000) 'Achieving sustainable tourism: a paradigmatic approach', in M. Robinson, J. Swarbrooke, N. Evans, P. Long and R. Sharpley (eds), *Reflections on International Tourism: Environmental Management and Sustainable Tourism*, Sunderland: Business Education Publishers, 311–26.


## Tourism and the environment

A number of seminal studies which examine the tourism–environment relationship include:

Mathieson, A. and Wall, G. (1982) *Tourism: Economic, Physical and Social Impacts*, Harlow: Longman.

Whelan, T. (ed.) (1991) *Nature Tourism: Managing for the Environment*, Washington, DC: Island Press.


## Ecotourism

Beeton, S. (1998) *Ecotourism: A Practical Guide for Rural Communities*, Collingwood, Victoria: Landmark Press.

Boo, E. (1990) *Ecotourism: The Potential and Pitfalls*, Washington, DC: World Wildlife Fund for Nature.

Ecotourism Society (1993) *Ecotourism Guidelines for Nature Tourism Operators*, North Bennington, Vt: The Ecotourism Society.

Fennell, D.A. (1999) *Ecotourism: An Introduction*, London: Routledge.

Wearing, S. and Neil, S. (1999) *Ecotourism: Impacts, Potential and Possibilities*, Oxford: Butterworth-Heinemann.

Weaver, D. (1998) *Ecotourism in the Less Developed World*, Wallingford: CAB International.

Weaver, D. (ed.) (2001) *The Encyclopedia of Ecotourism*, Wallingford: CAB International.

# Chapter 2

# Tourism and the environment

The relationship between tourism and the environment has assumed a significant position through the development of tourism studies over the last 50 years (Hudman 1991). The debate on this relationship has been reinvented and redeveloped under different guises during this period, most recently with the sustainability debate (e.g. Hall and Lew 1998). As Hall (1998) argued, the historical antecedents of the sustainability debate can be traced back to the nineteenth century which highlights the significance of historical analysis to understanding the tourism–environment relationship. This is a feature also emphasised by Hviding and Bayliss-Smith (2000) in relation to logging and ecotourism development in the Solomon Islands and by Kousis (2000) in terms of local environmental mobilisations against tourism in Greece, Spain and Portugal. Dowling (1992a: 33) encapsulates the essence of this debate on the tourism–environment relationship since

> In the 1950s it was viewed as being one of coexistence ... However, with the advent of mass tourism in the 1960s, increasing pressure was put on natural areas for tourism developments. Together with the growing environmental awareness and concerns of the early 1970s, the relationship was perceived to be in conflict. During the next decade this view was endorsed by many others ... at the same time a new suggestion was emerging that the relationship could be beneficial to both tourism and the environment.

This chapter examines this transition in tourism thought since the 1950s, particularly the development of the shift from a philosophical stance described as coexistence to conflict and symbiosis embodied in the work of Budowski (1976), Pigram (1980), Romeril (1989a), Gunn (1988) and Farrell and Runyan (1991). This contributed to a focus on the concept of integration and a new paradigm that is associated with the sustainability perspective (Dowling 1992a). A critical understanding of these changes in environmental philosophy and their application to tourism is fundamental to any analysis of ecotourism because it highlights how research has provided a renewed focus on tourism as a human activity in natural areas, if it is appropriate to the environmental base and resources in specific locations. In many respects the emergence of ecotourism as a specific form of tourism which is environmentally dependent has arisen from the sustainability debate and therefore to understand ecotourism, one needs to recognise how this has emerged over the last 50 years. This is

followed by a discussion of the issues which the environment–tourism debate
has highlighted as appropriate to the analysis of a tourism activity such as
ecotourism which directly and indirectly impacts upon global, regional and
local ecosystems and environments.

## Evolution of environmental thought on tourism and the environment: coexistence

Over 40 years ago the prevailing view was that tourism had few impacts on
the natural environment, enshrined in the comments by Zierer (1952: 463)
that 'A notable characteristic of the tourist industry and recreation industry is
that it does not or should not lead to the destruction of natural resources.'
However, tourism's professional body, the International Union of Official
Travel Organizations (IUOTO – the predecessor of the World Tourism
Organisation, WTO), did recognise the possibility of adverse impacts. In
1954 it introduced into its General Assembly a section on the preservation
of tourist heritage which focused on the protection of tourism 'capital' or
resources from potentially adverse physical and social effects. The advent of
mass tourism, which characterised the 1960s and was associated with greater
mobility and access to package holidays, led to research on tourism and the
environment. IUOTO demonstrated that natural tourism resources were the
primary attraction for tourists even in countries with an outstanding cultural
heritage, which led to a concern with the ecological impacts of tourism (e.g.
Beed 1961). Concern was expressed that the tourist invasion could induce
ecological imbalance within an island's ecosystem if tourism was not carefully
managed. A subsequent study examined the impact on fragile sites by visitors
destroying vegetation, collecting souvenir rock specimens, and causing trail
erosion (Darling and Eichhorn 1967). Conversely, other studies asserted that
tourism was beneficial for the environment. Later in the decade the IUCN
began its first study of tourism and conservation when it met for its Tenth
Technical Meeting, *Ecology, Tourism and Recreation* (IUCN 1967).

The advance of international tourism fostered high expectations regarding
its potential role in economic growth and overall development for many
countries. However, environmental concerns that were beginning to arise
at this time, gained greater credence. On occasion the two would overlap, an
early example being in the Caribbean where a strong rationale for conservation of nature and historical sites was fostered as an integral part of tourism
(Carlozzi and Carlozzi 1968). Carlozzi and Carlozzi (1968) argued that bringing tourism development and conservation together would provide a major
opportunity for achieving a measure of economic self-sufficiency in the Lesser
Antilles.

During the 1960s, mass tourism was accompanied by a growing public
awareness of environmental issues epitomised by the studies of the human
impact on the environment and the deterioration of the resource base for human
habitation (e.g. Ehrlich *et al.* 1970) and the consequences for environmental
deterioration (Nicholson 1970). This awareness, which had already embraced

the tourism industry, was highlighted by Akoglu (1971) in the same year in which the IUOTO adopted an environmental tourist policy. Central to it was the recommendation that at the national level countries should establish an inventory of natural tourist resources. Implicit in the policy directive was the concept of classifying or zoning whereby areas with a particularly sensitive or fragile environment would be developed on a small scale, if at all. These policies were shared at the United Nations Conference on the Human Environment at Stockholm in 1972. During this meeting an important concept was formulated which would have far-reaching implications for the future. It was the birth of the ecodevelopment strategy which suggested that economic development should only take place if it was linked to environmental protection. This was the first major attempt to involve all countries in environmental issues through an international dimension. Yet in reality this achieved very little in practical terms beyond awareness raising and as a catalyst for the establishment of the UNEP. A corollary to this strategy was the notion that any resulting natural area tourism development should be entirely compatible with local values and culture. These views were also endorsed by the World Bank (1972) which concluded that tourism planning should avoid disparities in the standards of amenities for visitors and the local population.

## Conflict and symbiosis

Although the environment–tourism relationship was viewed as one with problems, it was also recognised that tourism could be an agent of conservation as studies in East Africa (e.g. Pollock 1971; Myers 1972) indicated. Mishan's (1969) *The Costs of Economic Growth* and the example of Lake Tahoe and the impact of resort development also embodied these views. Negative environmental impacts resulting from tourism were also identified in England (Beck and Bryan 1971), the Great Barrier Reef, Australia (Clare 1971), the rural environment in Germany (*Der Spiegel* 1972), desert oases in the Sahara (Blake and Lawless 1972) and in Africa in relation to wildlife (Myers 1973a, b). By 1973 the environment–tourism debate had gained increased attention. Europa Nostra and the European Travel Commission (ENETC) met in Copenhagen at a conference entitled 'Tourism and Conservation Working Together'. Both positive and negative factors were examined in relation to the interdependent relationship between tourism and the environment, and conclusions were that:

1. The environment is the indispensable basis, and the major attraction, for tourism. Without an attractive environment, there would be no tourism.
2. The interests of tourism demand the protection of the scenic and historic heritage.
3. Tourism can directly assist active conservation and can prompt people to contribute towards conservation.

Despite these positive links, many conservationists and economists argued that tourism presented a major threat to the environment (ENETC 1973: 14). These views were also endorsed in Dasmann *et al.*'s (1973) seminal work

*Ecological Principles for Economic Development,* in which a chapter was devoted specifically to the development of tourism based on environmental considerations. This addressed regional planning issues especially in regard to the nature and role of tourism within parks. The problems of mass tourism's adverse impacts on the natural environment were also outlined by Forster (1973) and Ovington *et al.* (1973).

In the mid-1970s, a number of divergent themes on the environment–tourism relationship emerged which argued both for and against tourism developments in natural areas. Some argued that tourism creates unacceptable costs – due to pollution (Young 1973; Goldsmith 1974) and impacts on fauna (Mountfort 1974, 1975; Crittendon 1975) or flora (Liddle 1975; Edwards 1977; McCabe 1979). Other studies examined environment–tourism conflicts, including the adverse impacts of off-road vehicles on the ecology in New Zealand and the USA (Massachusetts – Godfrey and Godfrey 1980; Utah – Kay 1980; Alaska – Slaughter *et al.* 1990) with a general overview by Webb and Wilshire (1982), the impact of mountain climbers and hikers on the Mt Everest region of Nepal (Jefferies 1982; Pawson *et al.* 1984; Karan and Mather 1985; Cullen 1986; Weber 1986), disturbance of African wildlife (Curry 1982, 1985; Sindiyo and Pertet 1984) and the effects of tourism on coral reefs (Dahl and Lamberts 1977; Gajraj 1981; Rogers 1981; Wells 1981). Other studies included the impacts of the ski industry on the Rio Hondo watershed in the USA (Rodriquez 1987), the effects of recreationists on picnic sites in Hong Kong (Jim 1987) as well as general statements – for Malaysia (Hong 1985), Canada (Butler 1986) and the Caribbean (Holder 1988).

Conversely, other studies indicated that tourism provided the incentive for the conservation of natural and cultural resources (e.g. Gunn 1973; Agarwal and Nangia 1974; Dower 1974; Nelson 1974). In addition two tourism professionals provided the strongest support for acknowledgement of the link between tourism and the natural environment. Haulot, the Commissioner-General of Tourism in Belgium, and Krippendorf, the Director of the Swiss Tourism Association, both highlighted the tourism–environment connection (Haulot 1974; Krippendorf 1975). Their books concluded that tourism developments in natural areas must embrace conservation. The year 1976 was a landmark year in the environment–tourism debate with Budowski (1976), the Director-General of the IUCN, exploring the relationship between nature conservation and tourism. This was critical in establishing that the relationship is particularly important when tourism is partly or totally based on values derived from nature and its resources, adding that the relationship could be one of *conflict, coexistence* or *symbiosis*; it is worth reiterating the discussion of these concepts from Chapter 1 since they are fundamental to the discussion in this chapter.

In this context, *conflict* is understood to mean that the tourism–environment relationship is not compatible and that tourism is the cause of conflict. *Coexistence,* on the other hand, is meant to imply that although tourism and the environment are not necessarily compatible, there are certain circumstances where the two elements may coexist for each others' benefit. Lastly, *symbiosis* is a more complex relationship where the environment is directly affected by tourism: it can be used to enhance the environment in terms of protection, management and the implementation of principles such as sustainability because of the intrinsic benefits and advantages of tourism–environment interactions if carefully managed and integrated.

Budowski stated that conflict occurs when tourism induces detrimental effects on the environment and that the two are in coexistence particularly when there is little contact and each remains in isolation. The environment and tourism are in symbiosis when each derives benefits from the other, that is, natural attributes are conserved while tourism development is attained. Budowski indicated that the environment–tourism relationship was more often one of conflict than coexistence, challenging both conservationists and tourism developers to change their attitudes and work together, suggesting that this would lead to the environment–tourism relationship becoming symbiotic. Budowski suggested that if this approach were followed then conservation and tourism would benefit mutually as 'tourism helps by lending support to those conservation programmes which will "develop" educational, scientific, and recreational resources, with the objective that they in turn will attract more, and different kinds, of tourists' (Budowski 1976: 29).

The symbiotic approach was subsequently fostered in the Mediterranean where tourism was having a visible effect on the natural, human-made and sociocultural environments especially in the coastal areas (Tangi 1977). To protect and preserve the region's environmental quality the United Nations Environment Programme (UNEP) sponsored a Mediterranean Action Plan and Regional Seas Programme which devised a number of tourism development strategies to overcome the adverse impacts of mass tourism. The approaches were described as alternative development strategies and included the following spatial, temporal and educational aspects (Tangi 1977: 340–1):

1. land-use zoning for a range of uses from environmental protection to tourism development;
2. fostering the dispersal of tourists by developing inland areas as tourist nodes;
3. encouraging home-host and other forms of tourist accommodation;
4. staggering holidays in order to lengthen the tourist season and reduce the concentration of tourist numbers;
5. establishing environmental protection laws for tourist developments;
6. encouraging nature-oriented tourism with environmentally trained guides;
7. establishing a 'tourism code of conduct' applicable to both tourists and the tourism industry.

The problem is that such strategies may only be a partial solution because they are applied in a limited geographical context, after development has already begun, and development pressures may limit the widespread application of such principles.

In the late 1970s, there was an attempt to systematically assess the environmental impacts of tourism (Cohen 1978) which 'the physical environment' as containing both natural and cultural components and impacts classified as being either positive or negative. The factors leading to environmental impacts from tourists were dependent upon the intensity of tourist site use, the resiliency of the ecosystem, the time perspective of developers, and the transformational character of tourist developments. An evolutionary phase was proposed for natural areas in which the original tourist destinations become environmentally degraded through intensive use. Cohen also stated that the environment–tourism relationship could be viewed in two ways, either as protecting the environment *for* tourism or *from* tourism; the latter approach was particularly important in developing countries.

Bosselman's (1978) study for the American Conservation Foundation compiled case studies of tourism in natural areas in eight developed countries. It outlined many of the problems associated with tourism's impacts on natural areas but concluded that tourism can be most beneficial if it makes the tourist more aware of the special qualities of places. While both Cohen and Bosselman pointed out the potential environmental risks posed by tourism, the tourism–environment alliance was proposed by Gunn (1978) who endorsed Budowski's view that the environment–tourism relationship had evolved from coexistence to potential for conflict or symbiosis. This relationship had synergistic possibilities. To explore these further, Gunn advocated the need for an international alliance of tourism, recreation and conservation. A practical project in North Auckland, New Zealand illustrates a situation where increasing recreational and tourist pressure was used to justify the establishment of a marine park (Ballantine and Gordon 1979). The 1970s can be best summarised as a decade in which the potential conflicts of tourism and the natural environment were realised. Parallel with this was an associated interest in the relationship between the social and cultural environment and tourism. Research focused on the tourist, the host and the tourist–host relationship (Affeld 1975). Case studies were drawn from East Africa (Ouma 1970), Spain (Greenwood 1972), the Caribbean (Bryden 1973; Lundberg 1974; Perez 1975), Bali (Francillon 1975; McKean 1976), the Pacific Islands (Farrell 1977; Finney and Watson 1977) and Mexico (Hudman 1978). General overviews were provided by Young (1973), Jafari (1974), Turner and Ash (1975), Smith (1977), Pizam (1978) and de Kadt (1979). This social empowering of tourism ushered in an awareness that tourism development, with its predominantly economic emphasis and incipient environmental aspects, also had to embrace its social consequences which could be either negative (Thomason *et al.* 1979) or positive (Cohen 1979).

The 1980s saw a new wave of interest in tourism and conservation issues, with 1980 a landmark year for the environment–tourism debate. The importance of the stewardship of resources and the inclusion of community views were both advocated for tourism development planning. In March UNEP and the WTO formally signed an agreement on tourism and the environment. In September at the World Tourism Conference in the Philippines the 'Manila Declaration on World Tourism' was generated. The philosophy of the declaration with respect to environment and tourism issues was made quite clear.

Tourism resources available in the various countries consist at the same time of space, facilities and values. These are resources whose use cannot be left uncontrolled without running the risk of their deterioration, or even their destruction. The satisfaction of tourism requirements must not be prejudicial to the social and economic interests of the population in tourist areas, to the environment or, above all, to natural resources which are the fundamental attraction of tourism, and historical and cultural sites. All tourism resources are part of the heritage of mankind. National communities and the entire international community must take the necessary steps to ensure their preservation (WTO 1980: 2).

In 1980 the Organisation for Economic Cooperation and Development (OECD) also published the results of a three-year investigation by a 'Group of Experts on Environment and Tourism' (OECD 1980). The publication characterised the environment and tourism as in conflict due to the adverse environmental impacts caused by tourism. The study forecast that 'tourism is involving more and more people and is becoming a virtual mass phenomenon whose uncontrolled expansion can be seriously damaging for the environment' (OECD 1980: 41). While such environmental initiatives were undertaken by tourism (WTO) and development (OECD) organisations, the world's environmental organisations, the IUCN, UNEP and the World Wildlife Fund (WWF; later to be known as the World Wide Fund for Nature), combined to present a global conservation plan – The World Conservation Strategy (IUCN 1980). The strategy argued that development can only be sustained by conserving the living resources on which it depends as well as by the integration of development and conservation. This policy took the earlier concept of 'ecodevelopment' linking environment and development and added the notion of the 'integration' of the two in order for the earth to be able to continue supporting humankind in the future. This was to shape the future direction of conservation for the remainder of the decade, and the Brandt Commission Report on North–South relations stated that development must also include the care of the environment (Brandt Commission 1980). A number of contributions were also made to the environment–tourism debate by geographers, including the interdependency of the relationship (Pearce 1980) and the symbiotic link (Pigram 1980; Holmes 1980).

In 1982 UNEP and the WTO issued a joint declaration formalising interagency cooperation for the purpose of protection, enhancement and improvement of the environment for the harmonious development of tourism (UNEP/WTO 1982). It suggested that the rational management of tourism could contribute to the protection and development of both the physical environment and cultural heritage as well as improving the overall quality of life. In contrast, a major survey of the environmental impacts of tourism reached a different conclusion (Mathieson and Wall 1982). Taking up Budowski's (1976) theme of coexistence, conflict or symbiosis, Mathieson and Wall (1982) explored the latter two views and concluded that more often than not the two were in conflict as 'there is little evidence to indicate the widespread existence of a symbiotic relationship between tourism and the environment' (Mathieson and Wall 1982: 101).

Mathieson and Wall (1982) offer a number of insights into the environmental problems associated with tourism since they identified the scope and nature of tourism impacts in an environmental context including impacts related to:

- architectural pollution due to the effect of inappropriate hotel development on the traditional landscape;
- the effect of ribbon development and urban sprawl in the absence of planning and development restrictions;
- the resort infrastructure becoming overloaded and breaking down in periods of peak usage;
- tourists becoming segregated from local residents (though this may not necessarily be a problem);
- good quality agricultural land being lost to urban tourist development due to the inflationary effect on land prices which encourages landowners to sell to developers;
- traffic congestion resulting in urban resort areas;
- pollution of the local ecosystem from sewage, litter and too many visitors in the peak season also posing serious problems for the destination.

By the 1980s, the environment–tourism debate was being widened to include the sociocultural aspects which had been the focus of separate research in the 1970s. A social-theory base for tourism was advanced by Travis (1982) and a community-based environmental approach advocated by Murphy (1983). It was argued that tourism is essentially resource-based and by ignoring social, as well as ecological implications, the industry was in danger of undermining its very existence. It was suggested that benefits would accrue for the industry and the destination community from the development of a mutually symbiotic relationship.

UNEP and the WTO held a jointly sponsored workshop on 'The Environmental Aspects of Tourism' in Madrid in July 1983. This meeting canvassed the wider view of tourism and the environment but it also took a significant step forward in its systematic identification of specific issues requiring the attention of the two world bodies. This was further advanced by UNEP in the following year in a special issue of its newsletter (Industry and Environment 1984). In addition, a tourism and conservation workshop in Nova Scotia, Canada in June 1984 stressed the interrelatedness of tourism and the environment and argued for their better planning and management (Young 1985).

## From idealism to realism

By the mid-1980s the environment–tourism relationship was beginning to be more clearly understood, as a review of the literature by Duenkel (1984) and the Organisation of American States (1984) argued for more positive benefits from tourism. The importance of the environment to any aspect of development had been asserted through the World Conservation Strategy and close cooperation between the environment and tourism had been advocated (UNEP/WTO 1983) and initiated (Mlinaric 1985). Cooperation between conservation and tourism was advocated at a European Heritage Landscapes Conference held in 1985 by the Director of the Countryside Commission in the United

Kingdom. He stressed the interrelationships between tourism and conservation, and pointed to the need for their future cooperation as there were three reasons why conservation should seek the support of tourism: tourism provides conservation with an economic justification; is a means of building support for conservation; and can bring resources to conservation (Phillips 1985). A special edition of the *International Journal of Environmental Studies*, **25** (4) 1985 focused on the 'symbiotic ideal (being) much more a reality now than it was in 1976' (Romeril 1985a: 217). The view that tourism can be a major agent for landscape conservation was also endorsed by Murphy (1986a) and Leslie (1986). At the same time the integration of the relationship was also being advanced for its benefits to both business (Murphy 1986b) and regional development (Pearce 1985). These studies continued a long tradition of examining the biological impacts of the environment both by and on tourists (see Edington and Edington 1986 for an excellent review), as well as aspects of the environmental carrying capacity of tourism (Industry and Environment 1986) based on the recreational literature in the USA which is considered in more detail later in this chapter. By the end of 1986 it was clear that the idealism of the environment–tourism relationship as advocated through symbiosis, was being tempered by the realism that in actual fact the underlying conflicts were still ever-present. This was demonstrated during a symposium held in Canada in March 1986 by the Alberta Chapter of the Canadian Society of Environmental Biologists. The symposium theme of 'Tourism and Environment: Conflict or Harmony?' was debated by leading Canadian researchers and academics, with arguments being presented for both the viewpoints of conflict (e.g. Landals 1986) and harmony (e.g. Mackie 1986).

## Towards integration

By the middle of the 1980s, the environment–tourism relationship had embraced aspects of the three states of coexistence, conflict and symbiosis. Since then it has been argued that all three relationships exist simultaneously depending on location and issue (Hall 1991; Dowling 1992a). While the symbiotic relationship has been sought as the 'ideal', in reality it has been largely one of conflict (Smith and Jenner 1989). Therefore a new orientation for the relationship has been advanced in which both the environment and tourism are viewed a unified whole (Dowling 1990). This state of integration exists where the possibilities of coexistence, conflict and symbiosis are recognised, and environmentally appropriate tourism opportunities are advanced (Figure 2.1). Such activities and developments are fostered if they are environmentally compatible, minimise adverse impacts and maximise beneficial ones. This was the essence of sustainable development which was advocated by the World Commission on Environment and Development (WCED 1987) as discussed in Chapter 1. Entitled *Our Common Future*, and generally referred to as 'The Brundtland Report', it examined the world's critical environmental and development problems and concluded that only through the sustainable use of environmental resources will long-term economic growth be achieved

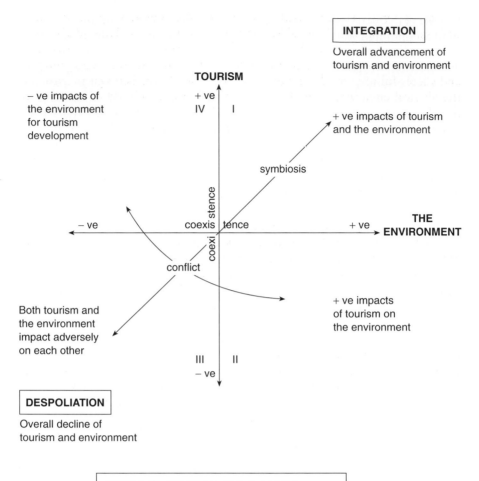

Figure 2.1   The integration of tourism and the environment

(Brundtland 1987). Hence the term 'sustainable development', which had previously been coined as discussed in the previous chapter, was now brought into wider use and the concept began to shape the nature of the future debate on the environment–tourism relationship. As a result the Brundtland Report not only popularised the term and the ideals of sustainability, but also the key principles of the report in enshrined in the argument that we have not inherited the earth from our parents but borrowed it from our children'. What this embodies is the need to understand the natural environment's ability to sustain certain types of economic activity such as tourism.

This approach was proposed by a number of people writing on the theme of 'Tourism and the Physical Environment' (e.g. Special Issue of *Annals of Tourism Research* Vol. 14(1), 1987) which suggested that the environment and tourism must be integrated in order to maintain environmental integrity and successful tourism development where 'A symbiosis between tourism and the physical environment is the second strand of a dual braid of concern, the first being the contextual integration of both physical and social systems' (Farrell and McLellan 1987: 13). This reasoned approach advanced the need for the integration of community concern and involvement in tourism development as argued by Travis (1982), Murphy (1983, 1985), Farrell (1986) and Miller (1987). This integrative approach was viewed as one in which the 'resource assets are so intimately intertwined with tourism that anything erosive to them is detrimental to tourism. Conversely, support of environmental causes, by and large, is support of tourism' (Gunn 1987: 245). This view had begun to shape natural area tourism development by the late 1980s with aspects of environment–tourism planning incorporated in some of the resulting tourism plans (Gajraj 1988), thereby reflecting a wider environmental concern of that time which might be described as a second environmental wave following the 1960s and 1970s. Thus the late 1980s saw a renewed concern for the environmental aspects of tourism. Further research was advocated on the role of national parks and protected areas in relation to regional planning and development, indigenous people and tourism (Nelson 1988). A popular study found that although tourism brings substantial economic benefits it is damaging to the world's environment (Smith and Jenner 1989). Specific problems identified and described included pollution of beaches, damage to coral reefs, disturbance of wildlife, degradation of historic sites, air pollution, congestion, and negative social impacts on local culture and customs. This study concluded that 'the tourism industry in its widest sense needs to take a lead in becoming more environmentally sensitive before it becomes one of the main targets of accusation that it is environmentally irresponsible' (Smith and Jenner 1989: 68).

Similar concerns were also expressed by Romeril (1989a, b). Whereas just four years before Romeril had championed Budowski's environment–tourism symbiotic relationship (Romeril 1985), he now concluded that 'the goal is to maintain a profitable and viable tourism industry without detriment to the environment, an objective which must surely become the norm in the 1990s' (Romeril 1989a: 208). Romeril (1989a, b) suggested the increase of alternative or 'green' tourism as a possible future way towards environment–tourism integration, a proposal also suggested by the Centre for Advancement of Responsible Tourism (CART) (Millman 1989). However, alternative tourism is often used as a synonym for 'appropriate' tourism, but questions were later raised as to whether or not this was the case (Cohen 1989; Pigram 1990; Farrell and Runyan 1991; Järviluoma 1992). Butler (1990) stated that the assumption is often made that alternative forms of tourism will have fewer and less severe negative effects on destination areas and their populations without diminishing the positive economic effects.

**Plate 2.1** Visitor impacts on fragile natural environments such as coastlines pose many problems for environmental management. In this example from Wenderholm Regional Park, Auckland, New Zealand, regeneration through planting grasses and prevention of visitor use may inhibit further erosion of the very delicate sandy coastline.

**Plate 2.2** Visitor impacts on fragile natural environments such as coastlines pose many problems for environmental management. In this example of the coastline at Wenderholm Regional Park, Auckland, New Zealand, regeneration through preventing visitor use may inhibit further erosion.

By the late 1990s, the goal of integration of tourism and the environment had occurred, ranging from small-scale projects (e.g. the Northern Mariana Islands – School of Travel Industry Management 1987; the Galápagos Islands – Kenchington 1989; Yankari Game Reserve, Nigeria – Olokesusi 1990) to large-scale projects (Lake Baringo, Kenya – Burnett and Rowntree 1990), and some projects included conservation (Brake 1988), cultural (Gale and Jacobs 1987), heritage (Millar 1989), social (Brockelman and Dearden 1990) and spatial benefits (Jansen-Verbeke and Ashworth 1990). At a global scale this integrative approach was fostered by principles of both conservation (McNeely and Thorsell 1989; McNeely 1990a, b) and development (GLOBE '90 1990; Whelan 1991) and a range of organisations now exist with a significant focus on the tourism–environment relationship (see Appendix 2.1).

## Critical research issues in the tourism–environment relationship: implications for ecotourism

It is clear from the previous discussion that a wide range of philosophical perspectives have shaped the way in which researchers and planners approach the tourism–environment relationship and in spite of this growing interest, Butler (2000: 338) argued that 'The relationship between tourism and the environment is often taken for granted and rarely researched to any depth', questioning the commonly held premise that 'One among the many myths is that tourism is dependent upon a healthy or pristine environment' (Butler 2000: 338). Yet as Hall and Page (1999: 131–2) argued, 'the environment is the foundation of the tourist industry. The relationship between tourism and the environment is site and culture dependent and will likely change through time and in relation to broader economic, environmental, and social concerns.' In the case of natural area based tourism and certain forms of ecotourism, Butler (2000: 339) rightly identified the need to acknowledge that 'certain forms of tourism are very much, or almost entirely dependent upon an apparently pristine environment, and intensive research is needed to identify critical elements of the relationship such as limits, carrying capacity, impacts, aspects of environmental change'. For this reason this section examines some of these themes in more detail as a basis for a more cohesive understanding of the key relationships of ecotourism and the environment in conceptual and practical terms.

What is clear from the discussion in this chapter so far is that 'Over the past two decades, in particular, there has been considerable research dealing with the environmental effects of tourism. The articulate and conceptually important work of Mathieson and Wall (1982) not only provides a superb review of the literature on that topic up to around 1980 but an excellent conceptual base' (Butler 2000: 341). As Mathieson and Wall (1982) found, there are a number of significant methodological problems which need to be addresssed in undertaking research on the environmental effects of tourism (Mathieson and Wall 1982: 94 cited in Hall and Page 1999):

**Plate 2.3** Footpath and trail hardening is a necessary tool used by planners to reduce further erosion on popular areas in the natural environment. The aesthetic problem this poses is that the environment has a definite human management feel and may detract from the experience of a natural environment where one can be at one with nature.

- 'the difficulty of distinguishing between changes induced by tourism and those induced by other activities;
- the lack of information concerning conditions prior to the advent of tourism and, hence, the lack of a baseline against which change can be measured;
- the paucity of information on the numbers, types and tolerance levels of different species of flora and fauna; and
- the concentration of researchers upon particular primary resources, such as beaches and mountains, which are ecologically sensitive'.

In studying the tourism–environment relationship there is certainly no substitute for 'a proper understanding of biological, or more specifically, ecological factors which can significantly reduce the scale of environmental damage associated with recreational and tourist development' (Edington and Edington 1986: 2). The main problem which researchers in tourism face in environmental analysis is in assigning cause and effect to tourism. Whereas environmental scientists can conduct experiments on the environment at specific sites based on controlled settings, this is rarely possible in terms of tourism. The independent variable is the tourist who cannot easily be controlled or manipulated to conform with such experiments so easily. Further it is hard to distinguish tourism effects from recreation (Hall and Page 1999). Yet as Butler (2000: 344) suggested, 'The basic impacting processes, namely fire, pollution (litter, human waste, fuel waste), consumption (collecting, hunting, fishing), and trampling (soil and vegetation compaction) along with habitat modification through development, such as water modification are common to most forms of human activity in the natural environment.' Much of the ecological research in tourism and recreation (e.g. Edington and Edington 1977, 1986; Liddle 1997) demonstrates the effects of many of these human processes which have led to short-term environmental change. The existence of a large research literature within the recreational management field and within National Parks in Canada and the USA (e.g. Lucas 1964; Wagar 1964) has explored many of these relationships in natural settings and generated a good deal of information which would benefit the ecotourism planner and researcher. The real problem which research consistently raises in this field is the way in which one quantifies and monitors the impact of tourism on the environment.

## Monitoring tourism impacts on the natural environment

One of the most controversial and widely cited attempts to establish the impact of recreationalists on the natural environment was the use of carrying capacity as a technique. Although the recreational literature (e.g. Wagar 1964) was primarily concerned with rudimentary analysis of the effects of human trampling on trails with a limited number of attempts to establish perceptual carrying capacity (i.e. what is termed social carrying capacity below), it has been modified and referred to in tourism contexts and caused considerable debate and disagreement among researchers. As Hall and Page (1999: 132) suggest,

> The majority of research has been undertaken on the effects of tourism and recreation on wildlife and the trampling of vegetation, with relatively little attention being given to impacts on soils and air and water quality (Wall and Wright 1977; Mathieson and Wall 1982; Edington and Edington 1986; Parliamentary Commissioner for the Environment 1997). The majority of studies have examined the impacts of tourism and recreation on a particular environment or component of the environment rather than over a range of environments.

According to Mathieson and Wall (1982: 94): 'there has been little attempt to present an integrated approach to the assessment of the impacts of tourism'.

### Carrying capacity
Mathieson and Wall (1982: 21) describe carrying capacity as 'the maximum number of people who can use a site [or area] without an unacceptable alteration in the physical environment and without an unacceptable decline in the quality of the experience gained by visitors'. Such a concept has been used to measure the capacity for tourism in natural and man-made tourism environments. While the literature on carrying capacity has been extensively reviewed in other studies and need not be reiterated here (see Pigram and Jenkins 1999; Hall and Page 2001), three principal elements can be discerned. According to van der Borg and Costa (1993: 7) the tourist carrying capacity comprises three elements:

- *the physical (or ecological) carrying capacity*, which is the limit at which the number of visitors can be accommodated at maximum stress. Beyond this threshold, the cultural, historical, natural and built environment is irreparably damaged by tourism;
- *the economic carrying capacity*, which is the limit beyond which the quality of the tourists' experience falls and makes it less attractive to visit as a destination;
- *the social carrying capacity*, which is the number of visitors an area can absorb without adversely affecting the other social and economic activities which underpin its rationale for existence.

These components of the carrying capacity of sites or areas have become notoriously difficult to calculate, although it has raised important debates on the limits of the natural environment to sustain activities (e.g. Butler 1991, 1992) such as ecotourism, particularly as new research techniques such as geographical information systems have been developed to monitor the diverse range of variables that impact upon the ecological systems in natural areas. Therefore, if measuring elements of change in the natural environment proves difficult, then monitoring change which occurs as a result of tourism impacts (e.g. ecotourism) are equally difficult to operationalise. What environmental monitoring requires is an audit of the resource base prior to tourism and then ongoing monitoring. Although techniques such as environmental assessment (EA) (see Wathern 1990 for example) have been widely cited as the potential solution to such difficulties, as Page (1992) has shown, this is mainly used for large projects (e.g. the impact of the Channel Tourism project on the natural environment) and even then post-impact monitoring of impact rarely occurs. As Page (1992) found in the case of the Channel Tunnel EA, there were no real measures of the impact of tourism on the environment due to the focus on the project as a transport infrastructure development that would generate tourism but was not perceived as a tourism-related project. As a consequence, efforts have been directed at managing visitor impacts on the natural environment.

## The management of visitor impacts on the natural environment

The principles of visitor management have largely evolved from the 1960s thinking in relation to carrying capacity and the need to intervene in the management of specific sites and areas to ensure environmental degradation does not directly destroy the resource base for future generations. One method, again developed in a recreational context, was the limits of acceptable change method (Stankey *et al.* 1984) which recognised that a single carrying capacity figure was unrealistic and that change is inevitable, so determining the acceptable level of change was necessary. Butler and Waldbrook (1991) modified these ideas to propose a tourism opportunity spectrum in a similar vein. However, what are widely used in tourism environments are specific techniques to control and minimise environmental impacts using planning techniques such as zoning. Zoning segregates incompatible recreational and tourism activities. This introduces the necessity of appropriate site and spatial design principles and in extreme cases, the introduction of regulations and controls (e.g.

Manyani 1998) to modify visitor behaviour to reduce pressure on key habitats and ecosystems as well as mechanisms to ensure local people benefit from such strategies (e.g. Sindiga 1999). Techniques such as visitor concentration or dispersal are widely used as well as techniques associated with pricing, codes of conduct (Malloy and Fennell 1998a) and management regimes. While many of these techniques offer theoretical solutions to the long-term sustainability of environmental resources for tourism, implementation is dependent upon the willingness of tourism operators, landowners and destinations to agree effective management regimes. The main concerns are usually associated with management mechanisms which may lead to a decline in visitor numbers and associated revenue. In the case of designing sustainable ecotourism projects, some trade-off between visitor numbers against higher quality experiences and additional revenue may be one possible option in natural environments. For this reason, some of the key questions and research needs raised by Butler (2000) with his synthesis of tourism and the environment are interesting to consider since it helps focus attention on the implications of this chapter for the development, analysis and philosophical approaches adopted towards ecotourism as a user of the natural environment.

## Questions and research needs for the tourism–environment debate: implications for ecotourism

- Research needs to address conceptual issues such as the relationship between different forms of tourism and the natural environment, such as ecotourism. This research needs to understand the potential linkages and interactions between the environment, the tourist and the consequences for local ecosystems.
- The relationship between the attractiveness of the natural environment and forms of tourism such as ecotourism need to be fully investigated to understand which elements in the natural environment have specific conservation needs for the long-term sustainability of ecotourism activities.
- The linkage between environmental science research, tourism management and planning of destinations and ecosystems is needed so management can be more biocentric rather than anthropocentric. This would assist in a more holistic approach to tourism and the environment.
- A greater emphasis is needed on the causes of impacts rather than the outcome.
- A greater use of quantitative measures such as carrying capacity are needed for sites and environments which are designed for ecotourism so that planners and developers have realistic targets and goals to work to.

## Summary

One direct result of tracing the evolution of environmental thought in relation to tourism is that the environment appears a dynamic and ever-changing phenomenon which is difficult to gauge and measure. Changing philosophical approaches are also reflected in the tools and techniques which researchers have adopted to assess tourism impacts in natural environments. While Muller (1994) recognised the growing environmental consciousness in tourism ranging from industry greening initiatives (e.g. Diamantis 1999) to the sustainability debate (see Hall and Lew 1998), there is also a prevailing tendency to use sustainability as the latest 'buzzword' and environmental anlysis has been subsumed under this new bandwagon without a growth in methodologies to measure, monitor and assess the direct and indirect impact of tourism activities on the natural environment. As Page *et al.* (2001: 307) argued,

> Research is at a relatively early stage of development and there is still much work to be undertaken to establish clear knowledge of cause, effect, systems and interactions. Wider uptake of auditing procedures and improvements in corporate environmental management through legislation and consumer demand will invoke a higher degree of environmental consciousness in tourism-based enterprises.

Yet this is unlikely to ameliorate the direct effects of tourism on the environment. A philosophical shift is needed by both the tourist and the tourism industry as the facilitator of tourist impacts, to recognise that an ecocentric approach to both the environment and the way the environment is valued is necessary. This is vital if the goal of tourism–environment integration is to be achieved in a context where impacts are minimised and genuine principles of sustainability can be nurtured through developments which are ecotourism related.

## Questions

1. What are the main features of the tourism–environment debate in the period since the 1950s?
2. Why has the sustainability debate altered the nature of the way tourism researchers and environmentalists think about the way tourism uses the natural environment?
3. How important was the evolution of the 'integration' paradigm in environmental thought?
4. Why should ecotourism development need to consider environmental values and philosophy?

## Further reading

The following studies are a good overview of the tourism–environment debate:

Farrell, B. and Runyan, D. (1991) 'Ecology and tourism', *Annals of Tourism Research*, **18** (1): 26–40. This is a good literature review and discussion of many of the concepts covered in this chapter.

Hall, C.M. and Lew, A. (eds) (1998) *Sustainable Tourism: A Geographical Perspective*, Harlow: Addison-Wesley Longman. This is a good edited collection of papers on sustainable tourism which contains chapters on environmental issues in tourism and a critical debate throughout the book on sustainability.

Hall, C.M. (1998) 'Historical antecedents of sustainable tourism and ecotourism: new labels on old bottles', in C.M. Hall and A. Lew (eds), *Sustainable Tourism: A Geographical Perspective*, Harlow: Addison-Wesley Longman, 13–24. This a very good chapter which deals with the origins and issues associated with sustainability and tourism.

Mathieson, A. and Wall, G. (1982) *Tourism: Economic, Physical and Social Impacts*,
   Harlow: Longman.
This is now a classic study that develops many of the early interests in the tourism–
environment debate and covers the classic studies in the field. It is still a very readable,
articulate and popular book to consult as a basic introduction to the subject.

## Appendix 2.1    Environment–tourism organisations

There are a number of Non-Government Organisations (NGOs) and public
bodies which are concerned with the tourism–environment relationship and
among the more prominent are the following.

### The World Tourism Organisation (WTO)

The WTO, which has its offices in Spain, was set up in 1975 as a United
Nations intergovernmental organisation, amid increasing awareness of the growing impacts of tourism. Some 134 nations are members of the WTO, as well
as more than 300 affiliates, including private companies, regional and local
government bodies. Though its critics argue that, possibly because of its linkages
with the private sector, it is overly concerned with the promotion of tourism,
and the lowering of trade barriers, it has increasingly become concerned with
environmental issues, especially as they affect poorer countries, and has helped
promote projects and programmes aimed at making the industry more environmentally sustainable.

   In harness with the World Travel and Tourism Council and the Earth
Council, the WTO has prepared a report, *Agenda 21 for the Travel and Tourism
Industry: Towards Environmentally Sustainable Development*. It attempts to
translate the Rio Agenda 21 document into an action plan for the industry.

### The World Travel and Tourism Council (WTTC)

The World Travel and Tourism Council is a 'global coalition' of chief executives
from travel and tourism companies – mostly major firms, including international
airlines, hotel and holiday groups – which was set up in 1990 to promote the
tourism industry. Its goals are 'to convince governments of the strategic and
economic importance of travel and tourism, to promote environmentally compatible development and to eliminate barriers to growth of the industry'. The
WTTC has been responsible for a series of environmental initiatives, such as
the Green Globe programme and more recently the EcoNETT system. Needless
to say, the inherent possibility for contradiction is evident. The interests of an
expanding industry, calling for greater free trade and generally lower taxation,
are not necessarily the same as those of the natural environment.

#### Green Globe and Green Flag
WTTC has developed, together with the Earth Council, the Green Globe
programme. Its objective is to provide a low-cost practical means for travel

and tourism companies to improve their environmental practice. Good environmental practice is not only morally right; it makes sound business sense and
can lead to significant cost savings. It defines 'low cost' as follows: in 1994,
annual membership fees were as low as $200 for companies with a turnover of
under $1 million rising to $7,500 for those corporations with yearly turnovers
in excess of $50 million. The Green Globe scheme, suggested by Maurice
Strong, is designed to give participating companies advice in changing their
environmental practice, as well as the means of evaluating them and the
information about cost-saving techniques and technologies.

## World Wide Fund for Nature (WWF)

For more than 35 years WWF has been (directly or with partner organisations)
involved in practical project work around the world aimed at safeguarding
vulnerable natural species and ecosystems by supporting efforts by people
everywhere to live in harmony with nature (Neale 1998). Of particular relevance
to travel and tourism has been its portfolio of projects aimed at conserving
coral reefs and other marine ecosystems, and its collaborations with the World
Conservation Union (IUCN), TRAFFIC and other partners in relation to
international trade in endangered species of wild fauna and flora, including
illegal trade in tourist curios.

## Campaign for Environmentally Responsible Tourism (CERT)

The Campaign for Environmentally Responsible Tourism marks an attempt
to evaluate, through customers' reports, how well individual holiday companies
perform from an environmental perspective (Neale 1998). Under the CERT
environmental kitemark scheme, companies must have a published environmental policy, ensure that their staff are aware of it, and distribute CERT
literature and a questionnaire to customers. In addition, the company includes
a one pound donation to conservation projects in its holiday prices, and
undertakes to match every donation itself. CERT is trying to encourage good
practice within the industry, and help it contribute to the ideas of conservation and sustainability.

# Chapter 3

# Ecotourism: concepts, definitions and issues

Within the recent growth in tourism research, ecotourism has certainly emerged as one of the least clearly defined areas of study, with a lack of any common agreement on what it is, how it should be defined, and more importantly how it interacts with the physical environment. The term has entered into the language of tourism (see Dann 1996 for a sociological analysis of the language of ecotourism) as one of the key terms now used to denote the interaction of tourism with ecologically sustainable forms of tourism in its purest form. Paradoxically, it is also used to refer to more environmentally related tourism activities which purists often decry as a commodification and inappropriate use of the term. Thus, ecotourism is certainly one of the most contested, debated and controversial areas of tourism research in the new millennium even though the area is beset with conceptual fuzziness and tautological arguments that do little to advance knowledge and our understanding of its conceptualisation. The result is a plethora of case studies and research outputs that have provided descriptive depth but limited debate on this seemingly amorphous phenomenon. This has meant students are faced with a vast array of studies, many of which reinvent the wheel, seek to rehearse well-worn arguments and do not establish new domains for research based on conceptual clarity.

One example which serves to illustrate this point can be found in McKercher's (1998) *The Business of Nature Based Tourism*, which cited Litvin's (1996) description of the scope of nature-based tourism as encompassing adventure tourism, ecotourism, alternative tourism, educational tourism, anti-tourism, sustainable tourism, responsible tourism and many other forms of outdoor-oriented, non-mass tourism: in other words it is an all-embracing term – almost an umbrella for a wide range of environmentally related tourism themes. McKercher (1998) argued that it has been common practice to put these activities under one label – ecotourism: therein lies the problem of defining the nature and scope of ecotourism. It groups different types of tourism activity under one generic heading due to the link with the resource base it uses – the natural environment. This chapter seeks to distil the very essence of ecotourism by outlining some of its antecedents, the problem of defining it, what might be used to characterise ecotourism as well as some of the forms of ecotourism which are subsumed under this heading, particularly nature-based tourism.

Travel to natural areas can be categorised in a number of ways according to the relationship between specific tourism activities and nature. Wearing and

Neil (1999: 4) included activities or experiences for which the natural setting is incidental, those that are dependent on nature, and those that are enhanced by nature. These three dimensions of environmental tourism equate to the environmental education equivalents of education – in, about and for the environment (Dowling 1976). However, prior to examining some of the propositions and arguments on how to define ecotourism, it is useful to commence with a short review of the way in which the term evolved.

## The evolution of ecotourism

The history of ecotourism has been discussed by Lindberg and McKercher (1997) and Fennell (1999), who described the convergent evolution of ecotourism. Both researchers suggest that it was only in the 1980s that ecotourism sought to find common ground due to the expansion of global tourism, and the increasing interest in the natural environment. The phenomenon known as ecotourism was in existence long before the terminology began to be used within tourism studies even though it was often called other things. This is reiterated by Beaumont (1998: 240) as

> Ecotourism is not new to Western society. It has been around since at least the 18th century but by a different name. The early geographers who toured the world in search of new lands, species and cultures were ecotourists . . . The establishment of National Parks – Yellowstone in the US in 1872 and Banff in Canada in 1885 – is further evidence of the early interest in nature tourism . . . African wildlife safaris and Himalayan treks in the 1960s and 1970s were also part of this trend.

Even so Fennell (1999: 34) argued that 'given the ambiguity associated with the historical origins of ecotourism' there is a clear need to focus on definitions of ecotourism. It was not until the 1980s that the term 'ecotourism' entered into common usage and was associated with the work of Hector Ceballos-Lascurain in 1983 and subsequently in 1987. There is also some debate as to whether the term was used first by a Costa Rican tour operator in 1983 (see Hummel 1994 for more detail). However, Fennell (1999: 31) has traced one of the origins of the term 'ecotourism' to the work of Hetzer (1965), who used it to explain the intricate relationship between tourists, the environments and cultures in which they interact. Hetzer identified four fundamental pillars that needed to be followed for a more responsible form of tourism. These include:

- minimum environmental impact;
- minimum impact on – and maximum respect for – host cultures;
- maximum economic benefits to the host country's grass roots; and
- maximum 'recreational' satisfaction to participating tourists.

The development of the concept of ecotourism grew, according to Hetzer (D. Fennell, personal communication, October 1997), as a culmination of dissatisfaction with governments' and society's negative approach to development, especially from an ecological point of view.

According to Beaumont (1998: 240), Hall (1984) was one of the earliest writers to use the term 'ecotourism' in a paper published in *New Scientist* and was closely related to natural area-based tourism. This was closely followed by Ceballos-Lascurain (1987: 14) who defined ecotourism as 'travelling to relatively undisturbed or uncontaminated natural areas with the specific object-ives of studying, admiring, and enjoying the scenery and its wild plants and animals, as well as any existing cultural manifestations (both past and present) found in these areas'. Subsequently, a rapid growth in interest within tourism and environmental science has led to it arguably becoming one of the most frequently published areas of research in tourism journals (see Page 2000). A search of the literature up to 2000 on *Leisure, Recreation and Tourism Abstracts* for the 1990s yielded over 500 articles of relevance which attests to the multidisciplinary nature of much of the research when one considers the type of research and outputs generated. Much of the early literature on ecotourism naturally sought to debate the issue of semantics, definitions and the very essence of this new term which rapidly became a buzzword and trendy area to research. For this reason, the next section reviews the complexity of trying to define the term 'ecotourism'.

## Defining ecotourism: an impossible task?

### Philosophical concerns: what's in a name?

One of the most used terms in the modern tourism literature is the word 'ecotourism'. In fact it had been used so much that to some commentators it is almost meaningless in its present usage. First, part of the problem arises from an external set of circumstances in that it is confused with a plethora of terms used to describe types of alternative tourism. Secondly, when used on its own it has been accorded a variety of meanings, some of which are merely tautological. Ceballos-Lascurain (1998: 7) suggested that 'a lingering problem in any discussion on ecotourism is that the concept of ecotourism is not well understood, therefore, it is often confused with other types of tourism development'. This is further explained by Harrison (1997: 75) in that

> in recent years ecotourism has become something of a buzzword in the tourism industry. To put the matter crudely, but not unfairly, promoters of tourism have tended to label any nature-oriented tourism product an example of 'ecotourism' while academics have so busied themselves in trying to define it that they have produced dozens of definitions and little else.

Harrison also indicated that if sustainable tourism development is to occur, trade-offs are inevitable and often nature will be the loser, since ecotourism cannot solve all the problems of mass tourism and may in fact, generate problems of its own. Harrison continued that it should not be considered as a stepping stone to large-scale tourism, though it often proves to be so. In this respect, ecotourism is an ideal, but one worth working towards, because at best ecotourism fosters environmental conservation and cultural understanding.

Cater and Lowman (1994: 1) ask the question 'is ecotourism a product or principle?', concluding that it is a variant of alternative tourism with the attributes of ecological and sociocultural integrity, responsibility and sustainability. However, these qualities may, or unfortunately may not, pertain to ecotourism as a product. Cater (1994) also asserted that the first essential element of ecotourism is its embrace of ecological principles. Any form of ecotourism must be carried out in an environmentally sensitive manner and as Rees (1990) suggested by way of a business analogy, ecotourism only uses the interest and not the capital stock. This approach encompasses the conservation ethic and ecotourism is viewed as an inextricable component of fostering conservation. This is by its very nature not protectionist but caring in approach. Thus, ecotourism does not necessarily protect the environment: instead it fosters the wise use of the environment. Cater (1994: 6) described the range of interests involved in ecotourism as being loosely grouped into four categories. These are tourist guests, tourism organisations, the host population and the natural environment. Chalker (1994: 99) argued that ecotourism must take into account three interconnecting issues – the need to be ecologically sound, respect for the local traditions, and ensuring benefits for local residents.

## Definitions of ecotourism

Beaumont's (1998) approach to ecotourism (see Figure 3.1) suggested that ecotourism is a subset of nature tourism which is a subset of tourism and that three principles define it: a natural setting, ecological sustainability, and an environmentally educative or interpretive element. These elements are common to a number of definitions. The Ecotourism Society (now the International Ecotourism Society), for example, approaches ecotourism as 'responsible travel to natural areas, which conserves the environment and improves the welfare of local people' (Lindberg and Hawkins 1993). The Australian definition is that ecotourism is nature-based tourism that involves education and interpretation of the natural environment and is managed to be ecologically sustainable (Australian Department of Tourism 1994). This definition recognised that 'natural environment' includes cultural components and that 'ecologically sustainable' involves an appropriate return to the local community and long-term conservation of the resource. According to this definition, ecotourism involves three components or dimensions: nature-based, environmentally-educated and sustainable management. Finally, the IUCN (World Conservation Union) definition, cited in Ceballos-Lascurain (1996), that ecotourism is environmentally responsible travel and visitation to relatively undisturbed natural areas, in order to enjoy and appreciate nature (and any accompanying cultural features – both past and present) that promotes conservation, has low visitor negative impact and provides for beneficially active socio-economic involvement of local populations.

Many of these definitions emphasise a number of key components of ecotourism which are focused on the natural environment (see Diamantis

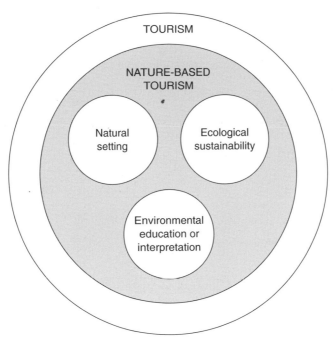

**Figure 3.1** An inclusive approach to defining ecotourism using three key principles
*Source*: Beaumont (1998: 24).

(1999) for a useful and recent review of the area). If one examines Beaumont's (1998: 241) review of ecotourism, it was recognised that

> most definitions that subsequently emerged insist that ecotourism must have minimal impact on the environment and host communities and contribute to conservation of the natural resources . . . consequently it should have a nonconsumptive use of wildlife and natural resources. Others specify that ecotourism should foster appreciation of the natural environment by providing education or interpretation to participants . . . Many definitions also include a cultural component . . . [so that it] . . . provides net benefits to indigenous and local communities, as well as the local environment.

This emphasised the natural environment as an enduring theme and much of this can be traced to the early work by Laarman and Durst (1987) who emphasised the nature tourism elements where the 'traveller is drawn to a destination because of his or her interest in one or more features of that destination's natural history. The visit combines education, recreation, and often adventure.' They also highlighted a vital distinction between the hard and soft dimensions of nature tourism based on both the physical rigour and level of interest in nature as shown in Figure 3.2. A subsequent conceptualisation of the area by Laarman and Durst (1993) made a fundamental distinction between ecotourism and nature tourism but also highlighted the ensuing debate over the differences between each form of tourism. Nature tourism was viewed in precise operational terms as operators providing nature-oriented tours and

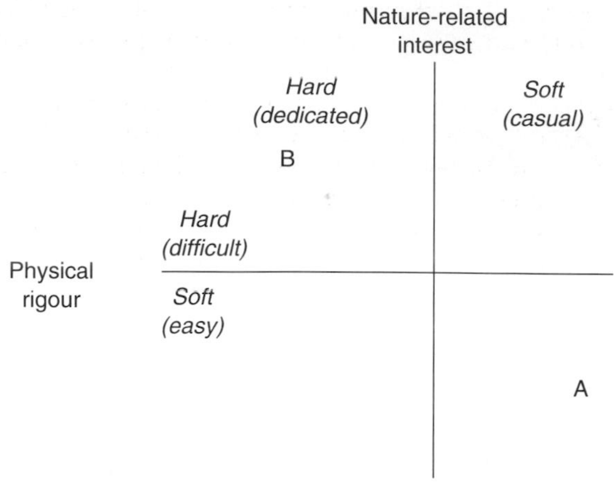

Nature-related
interest

*Hard*
*(dedicated)*

*Soft*
*(casual)*

B

*Hard*
*(difficult)*

Physical
rigour

*Soft*
*(easy)*

A

**Figure 3.2**  Hard and soft dimensions of ecotourism
*Source*: Fennell (1999).

yet also in a broad manner as 'tourism focused principally on natural resources such as relatively undisturbed parks and natural areas, wetlands, wildlife reserves and other areas of protected flora, fauna and habitats' (Laarman and Durst 1993: 2). In this respect, ecotourism was one element of nature-based tourism, a feature which Goodwin (1996: 287) examined in terms of nature tourism which

> encompasses all forms of tourism – mass tourism, adventure tourism, low impact tourism, ecotourism – which use natural resources in a wild or undeveloped form – including species, habitat, landscape, scenery and salt and fresh-water features. Nature tourism is travel for the purposes of enjoying undeveloped natural areas or wildlife.

In contrast, ecotourism was defined by Goodwin (1996: 288) as

> Low impact nature tourism which contributes to the maintenance of species and habitats either directly through a contribution to conservation and/or indirectly by providing revenue to the local community sufficient for local people to value, and therefore protect, their wildlife heritage area as a source of income.

Blamey (1995) acknowledged that the feature which distinguished ecotourism from nature-based tourism is an educative and sustainability component as well as the ethical nature of the tourism experience provided (Wight 1993b; Wallace and Pierce 1996). However, even though nature-based tourism is recognised as a distinctive form of tourism, there is no universal agreement over the term 'ecotourism', with many new papers and publications seeking to review this state of apoplexy and lack of clarity with some writers emphasising nature tourism (e.g. Boo 1990; Eagles 1995; Lindberg 1991; Valentine 1992) which is biological and ecologically grounded. One interesting attempt to overcome these problems was evident in a hybrid definition by Ziffer (1989: 6) which emphasised the standards which a destination or programme had to meet to be defined as ecotourism related, thus:

Ecotourism: a form of tourism inspired primarily by the natural history of an area, including its indigenous culture. The ecotourist visits relatively undeveloped areas in the spirit of appreciation, participation and sensitivity. The ecotourist practices a non-consumptive use of wildlife and natural resources and contributes to the visited area through labour or financial means aimed at directly benefiting the conservation of the site and the economic well-being of the local residents. The visit should strengthen the ecotourist's appreciation and dedication to conservation issues in general and the specific needs of the locale. Ecotourism also implies a managed approach by the host country or region which commits itself to establishing and maintaining the sites with the participation of local residents, marketing them appropriately, enforcing regulations, and using the proceeds of the enterprise to fund the area's land management as well as community development.

This is a departure from the nature-based versus environmental tourism debate and also introduced an implicit concern for sustainable management of the resource base through the commercial use of the area for ecotourism activities.

## Ecotourism: definition to application

In contrast, Orams (2000: 316) argued that ecotourism as a term is a continuum of paradigms bounded by polar extremes as shown in Figure 3.3. What Orams (2000) identified was a view whereby ecotourism (and for that matter all forms of tourism) had negative impacts and influences on the natural world, indicating ecotourism is impossible. Conversely, at the other extreme is the view that humans do not have a responsibility to consider other living organisms and that all forms of tourism are possible, being an extreme conceptualisation of the anthropocentric view of the world (see Chapter 1). In other words, the earth's resources are limitless and there to be used by humans. The result is that the conditions where ecotourism can exist largely reside within these polar extremes. In this respect, Orams (1995) argued that definitions of ecotourism can be classified as to whether they had a high or low level of human responsibility, with more passive approaches associated with lower levels of responsibility. The more active approaches had a higher level of human responsibility. Consequently, Orams (1995) is a useful approach by which to classify definitions, so that those by Ziffer (1989), Valentine (1992) and Richardson (1993) are within the 'active' category with a high degree of human responsibility. In contrast, Orams (2000) pointed to more passive definitions by the Ecotourism Association of Australia. Yet even Orams (2000: 318) admitted

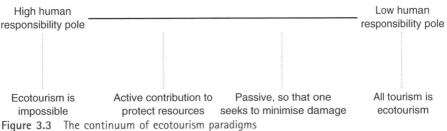

Figure 3.3  The continuum of ecotourism paradigms
*Source*: Modified from Orams (2000: 316).

Table 3.1   Comparisons of selected ecotourism and nature tourism definitions

| Main principles of definition[a] | Definitions | | | | | | | | | | | | | | |
|---|---|---|---|---|---|---|---|---|---|---|---|---|---|---|---|
| | 1 | 2 | 3 | 4 | 5 | 6 | 7 | 8 | 9 | 10 | 11 | 12 | 13 | 14 | 15 |
| Interest in nature | ✓ | ✓ | | | ✓ | ✓ | ✓ | ✓ | | ✓ | ✓ | | | ✓ | ✓ |
| Contributes to conservation | | | ✓ | | ✓ | ✓ | ✓ | ✓ | ✓ | ✓ | | | ✓ | ✓ | ✓ |
| Reliance on parks and protected areas | ✓ | | ✓ | | ✓ | ✓ | | ✓ | ✓ | | | | ✓ | ✓ | ✓ |
| Benefits local people/long-term benefits | | | ✓ | | ✓ | ✓ | ✓ | | ✓ | | | | ✓ | ✓ | ✓ |
| Education and study | ✓ | ✓ | ✓ | | | ✓ | | | | | ✓ | | | ✓ | ✓ |
| Low impact/non-consumptive | | | | | ✓ | | | | | | | ✓ | ✓ | ✓ | ✓ |
| Ethics/responsibility | | | | ✓ | | | | | ✓ | ✓ | | | | | ✓ |
| Management | | | | | ✓ | | | ✓ | | | ✓ | | | | ✓ |
| Sustainable | | | | | | | | ✓ | | | ✓ | | | ✓ | ✓ |
| Enjoyment/appreciation | ✓ | | | | ✓ | | | | | | | | | ✓ | |
| Culture | ✓ | | ✓ | | ✓ | | | | | | | | | ✓ | |
| Adventure | | ✓ | | | | | | | | | | | | | |
| Small scale | | | | | | | | | | | | ✓ | | | ✓ |

1 Ceballos-Lascurain (1987); 2 Laarman and Durst (1987)[b]; 3 Halbertsma (1988)[b]; 4 Kutay (1989); 5 Ziffer (1989); 6 Fennell and Eagles (1990); 7 CEAC (1992); 8 Valentine (1993); 9 The Ecotourism Society (nd); 10 Western (1993); 11 Australian National Ecotourism Strategy (nd); 12 Brandon (1996); 13 Goodwin (1996); 14 Wallace and Pierce (1996); 15 The present study.

[a] Variables ranked by frequency of response.
[b] Nature tourism definitions.

*Source*: Fennell (1999: 41).

> This plethora of definitions does little to clarify what is meant by the use of the term ecotourism . . . this review of the variety of ecotourism definitions shows that, at a minimum, ecotourism is tourism which is based on the natural environment and seeks to minimise its negative impact on that environment. However, many definitions argue that ecotourists should attempt to do more than simply minimise impacts . . . It may be that one of the challenges for the ecotourism industry is to assist in moving ecotourists from a minimal 'passive' to a more active contribution to the sustainability of eco-attractions.

This would certainly counter the concerns of commentators such as Wight (1993a) that it is a convenient label the tourism industry is using in an opportunist manner to harness the greening of the marketplace for tourism products as discussed in Chapter 1. In fact given the debate on ecotourism and nature tourism as separate and yet related concepts, Table 3.1 offers a good summary of the main definitions analysed by Fennell (1999). This is useful as it contains the many principles embodied in the definitions of ecotourism and nature tourism. By using Fennell's (1999) attempt to isolate the different principles embodied in each definition, it is possible for students and researchers to focus on key variables or elements which are helpful to structure the ecotourism/nature tourism dichotomy. As Fennell (1999: 40) rightly pointed out, 'The fact of the matter is that, either implicitly or explicitly, such variables or principles need to be more effectively used to observe, measure and evaluate what is and what is not ecotourism.' This led Fennell (1999: 43) to establish that

> Ecotourism is a sustainable form of natural resource-based tourism that focuses primarily on experiencing and learning about nature, and which is ethically managed to be low-impact, non-consumptive, and locally-oriented (control, benefits and profits and scale). It typically occurs in natural areas, and should contribute to the conservation or preservation of such areas.

Even so, Fennell (1999) recognised that there is still scope for a clearer distinction between the term nature-based tourism and ecotourism, since the latter is often too passive as a form of tourism leading it to be subsumed under the umbrella of mass tourism. In fact Sirakaya *et al.* (1999) argued for a redefinition of ecotourism from a supply-side (i.e., from the tourism industry) perspective. Through a content analysis of ecotourism definitions, Sirakaya *et al.* (1999) found that ecotourism could be defined as a new form of non-consumptive, educational and romantic tourism to undisturbed and undervisited areas of immense beauty. This raised what Acott and La Trobe (1998) distinguished as deep and shallow ecotourism, with the distinction between positive and negative aspects of ecotourism dependent upon the involvement of the tourism industry in such activities. What is evident is that ecotourism is still evolving in the twenty-first century, as are the conceptual frameworks some six years after Hvengaard's (1994) influential synthesis which noted the need to understand the parameters of ecotourism. This was endorsed by Fennell's (1999) review which concluded that there was a relationship between ecotourism and natural areas and the use of nature for tourism purposes. Fennell and Eagles (1990) also recognised that potential incompatibility between the ecotourism product and the environment and resource base required a series of management principles with the resource tour being the central component (Figure 3.4). Fennell and Eagles's (1990) framework for the ecotourism experience recognised that a number of elements need careful management from both the environmental perspective (e.g. see Hvengaard 1994) and the visitor's perspective. However, one of the most useful ways of establishing the nature

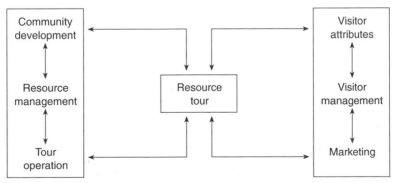

**Figure 3.4**  Ecotourism framework
*Source*: Modified from Fennell and Eagles (1990).

of ecotourism if definitions are problematic is to consider some of the characteristics which are accepted as key features of this phenomenon.

## The nature of ecotourism: establishing characteristics and principles of ecotourism

Kutay (1993) argued that real ecotourism is more than travel to enjoy or appreciate nature. It also includes minimisation of environmental and cultural consequences, contributions to conservation and communities, and environmental education, such as by the establishment of codes of conduct for travellers as well as the various components of the travel industry. In this sense it may be defined as an ethic as Jaakson (1997) recognised. According to Wallace and Pierce (1996), ecotourism may exist if it addresses the following six principles:

- It entails a type of use that minimises negative impacts to the environment and to local people.
- It increases the awareness and understanding of an area's natural and cultural systems and the subsequent involvement of visitors in issues affecting those systems.
- It contributes to the conservation and management of legally protected and other natural areas.
- It maximises the early and long-term participation of local people in the decision-making process that determines the kind and amount of tourism that should occur.
- It directs economic and other benefits to local people that complement rather than overwhelm or replace traditional practices (farming, fishing, social systems).

In contrast, Honey (1999: 22–4) suggested that real ecotourism had seven characteristics. It involves travel to natural destinations, minimises impact, builds environmental awareness, provides direct financial benefits for conservation, provides financial benefits and empowerment for local people, respects local culture, and supports human rights and democratic movements. Honey (1999: 25) defined ecotourism as 'travel to fragile, pristine, and usually protected areas that strive to be low impact and (usually) small scale'. Honey (1999) also added that it helps to educate the traveller, provides funds for conservation, directly benefits the economic development and political empowerment of local communities, and fosters respect for different cultures and for human rights. Fennell (1999: 44) suggested that important variables to be considered in establishing the nature of ecotourism include environmental awareness, employment skills or actions in the pursuit of the primary activity; the degree to which one subscribes to the conservation ethic (the emotional tie that one has with plants, animals or nature as a whole); and finally the degree of impact (consumptive to non-consumptive) caused by the type of tourism. Thus, ecotourism comprises a number of interrelated components all of which should be present for authentic ecotourism to occur.

As a result there are five core principles that are fundamental to ecotourism. They are that ecotourism is nature-based, ecologically sustainable, environmentally educative, locally beneficial and generates tourist satisfaction. The first three characteristics are considered to be essential for a product to be considered 'ecotourism' while the last two are viewed as being desirable for all forms of tourism (Dowling 1996a).

## Nature-based

Ecotourism is based on the natural environment with a focus on its biological, physical and cultural features. Ecotourism occurs in, and depends on, a natural

Plate 3.1   Blyde River Canyon Nature Reserve, Mpumalanga Province, South Africa. The 30km long canyon is one of the country's natural scenic highlights. Such features are the 'attractions' of ecotourism and emphasise its dependence on the natural environment.

setting and may include cultural elements where they occur in a natural setting. The conservation of the natural resource is essential to the planning, development and management of ecotourism.

## Ecologically sustainable

All tourism should be sustainable – economically, socially and environmentally. The sustainability of natural resources has been recognised by the national and state governments in Australia as a key guiding principle in the management of human activity. Ecotourism is ecologically sustainable tourism undertaken in a natural setting. Yet even this is fraught with philosophical and operational problems. For example, Acott and La Trobe (1998) noted that there is a continuum in terms of the forms of ecotourism and their compatibility with the ecological context. On the one hand there are small-scale forms of ecotourism which are environmentally and ecologically sensitive (i.e. deep forms of ecotourism). In contrast, and at the other end of the spectrum, are shallow forms of ecotourism which are less sensitive to the ecological resource base and verge on the mass forms of green tourism. This dilemma is also embodied in the work of Mowforth and Munt (1998) which recognised a similar continuum ranging from resource preservation through to resource conservation. The very incorporation of 'eco' in its title suggests that ecotourism should be an ecologically responsible form of tourism. The scale of such ecotourism activities implies that relatively few tourists will be allowed to visit the site and consequently supporting facilities can be kept to a minimum and will be less intrusive. Cater (1994) argued that ecotourism, with its connotations of sound environmental management and consequent maintenance of environmental capital, should, in theory, provide a viable economic alternative to exploitation of the environment.

Ecotourism may bring considerable attention to how tourism as a whole may be made more ecologically sustainable. Certainly, converting all forms of tourism to ecotourism is neither realistic nor consistent with principles of sustainability. Ecotourism is perhaps best thought of as involving an achievable ideal for one segment of the nature-based tourism market, and setting an example in environmental management for much of the rest (Australian Department of Tourism 1994: 6). This broadly defined travel oriented towards the natural environment is generally expected to respect and protect the environment and culture of the host country or region. However, according to Lawrence et al. (1997: 308) it is this larger goal of protecting or enhancing the environment that represents both its strength and weakness. Its strength is that ecotourism differentiates itself from the more traditional consumptive forms of tourism, while its weakness is inherent in the tension that often prevails between achieving economic goals at the expense of ecological aims. They added that the ecotourism industry faces the paradoxical situation that the more popular the product becomes, the more difficult it becomes to provide.

## Environmentally educative

The educative characteristic of ecotourism is a key element that distinguishes it from other forms of nature-based tourism. Environmental education and interpretation are important tools in creating an enjoyable and meaningful ecotourism experience. Interpretation is the art of helping people to learn and it is a central tenet of ecotourism (Weiler and Davis 1993). It is a complex activity that goes beyond making the communication of information enjoyable. 'Best practice interpretation requires a thorough understanding and integration of audience, message and technique' (McArthur 1998: 83). Ecotourism attracts people who wish to interact with the environment in order to develop their knowledge, awareness and appreciation of it. By extension, ecotourism should ideally lead to positive action for the environment by fostering enhanced conservation awareness. Ecotourism education can influence tourist, community and industry behaviour and assist in the longer-term sustainability of tourist activity in natural areas. Education can also be useful as a management tool for natural areas. Interpretation helps tourists see the big picture regarding the environment. It acknowledges the natural and cultural values of the area visited as well as other issues such as resource management. Crabtree (2000: 1) states that 'interpretation provided by ecotourism has a critical role in contributing to the world's environmental awareness', indicating that there are five key elements to make ecotourism educative in relation to the environment: make it personal, fun, relevant, unique and effective.

Ecotourists expect high levels of ecological information. The quality of the environment and the visibility of its flora and fauna are essential features of their experience. They demand conservation (Chalker 1994: 91). Clear statements of the nature and aims of ecotourism need to be incorporated into literature and publicity material to educate and encourage active participation by stakeholders as well as the tourists themselves (Hall and Kinnaird 1994). Lawrence *et al.* (1997) note that a dominant part of ecotourism is for tourists to learn about and appreciate the natural environment in order to advance the cause of conservation.

## Locally beneficial

The involvement of local communities not only benefits the community and the environment but also improves the quality of the tourist experience. Local communities can become involved in ecotourism operations, and in the provision of knowledge, services, facilities and products. These benefits should outweigh the cost of ecotourism to the host community and environment. Ecotourism can also generate income for resource conservation management in addition to social and cultural benefits. The contribution may be financial with a part of the cost of the tour helping to subsidise a conservation project. Alternatively it could consist of practical help in the field with the tourists being involved in environmental data collection and/or analysis.

Drumm (1998) argued that local communities view ecotourism as an accessible development alternative which can enable them to improve their living standards without having to sell off their natural resources or compromise their culture. In the absence of other sustainable alternatives, their participation in ecotourism is often perceived as the best option for achieving their aspiration of sustainable development. Ecotourism can provide a context for local incentives for conservation and protection. Norris (1992) has argued that ecotourism should integrate both the protection of resources with the provision of local economic benefits. For example, in the Annapurna Conservation Area Project of Nepal, local people are actively encouraged to take a leading role in conservation and development activities, expressing their needs and concerns in open forums (Gurung and de Coursey 1994). Gurung and de Coursey (1994) suggested that conservation and development are complementary rather than opposing forces, and that for either to be sustainable both must be carried out in a coordinated manner with the same main objective, the long-term welfare of the people and the environment. Ceballos-Lascurain (1998) noted that ecotourism is now beginning to produce positive benefits in the fields of conservation and sustainable development. There are many advocates of the need to integrate environmental conservation with tourism development in natural areas (e.g. Romeril 1985b; McNeely and Thorsell 1989).

According to Wight (1993a), partnerships between tourism and conservation take many forms including:

1. donation of a portion of tour fees to local groups for resource conservation or local development initiatives;
2. education about the value of the resource;
3. opportunities to observe or participate in a scientific activity;
4. involvement of locals in the provision of support services or products;
5. involvement of locals in explanation of cultural activities or their relationship with natural resources;
6. promotion of a tourist and/or operator code of ethics for responsible travel.

The implementation of ecotourism as an exemplar for sustainable development, stems largely from its potential to generate economic benefits (Lindberg 1998). These include generating revenue for management of natural areas and the creation of employment opportunities for the local population.

Wearing and Neil (1999: xv) noted that the current focus of the debate on tourism in protected areas is the extension of a long controversy, which has existed since the conception of protected areas. Their argument concluded that the imperative for conversation advocates becomes *how* to conserve rather than whether or not to conserve. In this way ecotourism, as a sustainable development strategy, is increasingly being adopted by protected area managers and conservation agencies as part of a political philosophy as a means of providing practical outcomes in the struggle to ensure a basis for continued protection for these areas.

## Tourist satisfaction

Satisfaction of visitors with the ecotourism experience is essential to the long-term viability of the ecotourism industry (Dowling 1997a). Indeed this incorporates elements of the concept of the visitor experience (Page *et al.* 2001) and the need to recognise the complexity of what constitutes the ecotourism experience in a marketing, experiential and satisfaction context. It is also necessary to recognise the importance of visitor safety in regard to political stability. Information provided about ecotourism opportunities should accurately represent the opportunities offered at particular ecotourism destinations.

## The global growth of ecotourism: scale and magnitude

Ecotourism is one of the fastest growing segments of the tourism industry globally and some commentators argue that it is rapidly growing out of control. It really constitutes a niche market for environmentally aware tourists who are interested in observing nature. It is especially popular among government and conservation organisations because it can provide simultaneous environmental and economic benefits. In theory it should be less likely than other forms of tourism to damage its own resource base but this is only true if such tourism is managed with great care (Fennell 1999). Estimates on the magnitude of ecotourism vary dramatically. The American-based Speciality Travel Index suggested that ecotourism accounted for between 1.5 and 2.5 per cent of all tourism in the late 1980s (Whelan 1991). In contrast, Hawkins (cited in Giannecchini 1993) proffered a figure of 20–25 per cent of all leisure travel, while The Ecotourism Society (1998) cited sources that suggest 20–40 per cent of all international tourists travel for wildlife-related purposes. Clearly, the first estimate adheres to a stricter interpretation of ecotourism, while the second and third embrace a generous interpretation of the entire hard-to-soft spectrum, and one that extends ecotourism into the mass tourism realm (Weaver and Oppermann 2000: 370).

Hvenegaard (1994) noted that ecotourism activities generate considerable economic impacts on a global, national and local scale. Ecotourism and wildlife-related tourism may account for up to US$1 trillion per year. In 1987 an estimated US$12–25 billion was spent on ecotourism in developing countries by international visitors. Khan and Hawkins (1997) reported that with the consumers' increased ecological awareness and the need for sustainable tourism development, it is not surprising that ecotourism is on the rise. Reports show that 8 million adult US travellers have taken an ecotour, and 35 million were likely to take an ecotour in the next three years. The potential ecotourism market, according to a study conducted by the United States Travel Data Center (1991), was 43 million, which estimated arrivals would grow by 10–15 per cent annually.

Honey (1999) suggested that many countries around the globe have now joined the ecotourism bandwagon. They include countries such as Bhutan and Myanmar (which once were wary of tourism), the former Soviet Union, eastern Europe, China and Vietnam (which once tightly controlled tourism) and South Africa and Cuba (previously international outcasts). Some entire countries, such as Costa Rica and Belize, are billed as ecotourism destinations. Elsewhere, pockets are promoted such as the Galápagos Islands in Ecuador; the habitat of the mountain gorillas in Uganda; and Fiordland in New Zealand. In 1998, the WTO predicted that developing countries would continue to gain from the tourism boom and that international travellers would remain 'interested in visiting and maintaining environmentally sound destinations' (Jaura 1998, cited in Honey 1999: 18).

## Growing international awareness of ecotourism

Reflecting the explosive growth in global ecotourism there has been a large number of conferences, symposia and workshops on the topic held in the past decade. Recent examples include World Ecotour 2000 held in Bahia, Salvador, Brazil in April 2000 and the 8th National Australian Ecotourism Conference held in Victoria, in October 2000.

Another recent development has been the establishment of ecotourism organisations and centres. Organisations include The Ecotourism Society (TES) (now The International Ecotourism Society – TIES), a surrogate global ecotourism association which is based in the United States of America, and the Ecotourism Association of Australia (EAA). Centres include the World Travel and Tourism Environment Research Centre (WRTTERC) in Oxford, England, the International Centre for Ecotourism Research (ICER) in the Gold Coast, Australia, and the Institute of Eco-Tourism in Bangkok, Thailand. In addition, a number of guidelines have been drawn up for ecotourism developers, operators and tourists. They include the Green Globe programme (WTTERC), the Blue Flag Scheme (WTO), the Green Leaf Award Scheme (PATA) and a set of Ecotourism Guidelines for Nature Tour Operators (TES 1993). Fennell (1999) noted in a review of the literature on the economic impact of the global ecotourism industry, that there is the feeling among some researchers that ecotourism is expanding even faster than the tourism industry as a whole (e.g. Lindberg 1991). A more recent estimate is that made at World Ecotour '97 in Rio de Janiero, Brazil, by Francesco Frangialli, Secretary-General of the WTO who stated that ecotourism now comprises upwards of 20 per cent of the world travel market (WTO 1998). But ecotourism is far from a homogeneous phenomenon and for this reason, it is useful to examine a number of types which can be discerned.

## Typologies of ecotourism: niches within a niche?

Early ecotourism is represented by a few, hardy individuals travelling alone or in small tour groups. These people use whatever accommodation, food and information that they can glean. Once visitor patterns are established, larger-scale operations evolve. Specialised accommodation, usually rustic and environmentally sensitive, and a well-trained guiding group that can identify and explain the features of the environment develop (Eagles *et al.* 1992). In planning for and managing ecotourism, it is also important to be aware of a number of different styles of ecotourism. They may vary considerably in regard to a range of factors including:

- the types of natural settings they require;
- the extent of direct contact and involvement with the natural environment;
- the group sizes involved;
- the use and extent of personal interaction with tour guides;
- the reliance on mechanised means of transport and supporting infrastructure;
- the types of visitor satisfaction and experience realised.

In Queensland, three broad styles of ecotourism have been identified (Queensland Department of Tourism 1997). They include self-reliant ecotourism, small group ecotourism and popular ecotourism and these forms are shown in Table 3.2. To summarise the significance of these styles of ecotourism they comprise the following.

## Self-reliant ecotourism

Self-reliant ecotourism involves individuals or small groups of generally 10 or less people who utilise non-motorised forms of transport (e.g. walking or canoeing) to visit relatively remote and lightly used natural areas. Visitors are generally very self-reliant and have few demands for supporting services and infrastructure. Theirs is a very special and unusual 'first-hand' experience that often requires a high degree of challenge and some knowledge of outdoor survival skills. Examples include trekking, rafting and kayaking.

## Small group ecotourism

This type of ecotourism involves individuals or relatively small groups (approximately 15 or less) who utilise motorised forms of transport (e.g. 4WD vehicle or small boat) to visit areas of special interest which are generally 'off the beaten track'. This type of ecotourism operation may involve moderately high levels of challenge and self-reliance but is generally suitable for participants from a wide variety of age groups who do not necessarily require any special outdoor skills.

## Popular ecotourism

This type of ecotourism involves the transport of larger numbers of visitors to, through or across a country's best known and most popular natural attractions. It relies on high-capacity mechanised forms of transport such as buses or large boats. There are low requirements for self-reliance and the degree of challenge is generally low. There may be substantial requirements for supporting infrastructure and services (e.g. visitor centres, food and drink outlets, boardwalks and toilets). This style of ecotourism is available to all visitors irrespective of

Table 3.2 Styles of ecotourism

| Criteria | Self-reliant ecotourism[a] | Small group ecotourism[a] | Popular ecotourism[a] |
|---|---|---|---|
| Main methods of travel during ecotourism activity | Non-motorised travel generally by foot, canoe, sea kayak or similar | Non-motorised or motorised low-capacity transport such as car, 4WD, minibus or small power boat or mountain bike | Motorised high-capacity transport such as larger bus or high-speed catamaran |
| Supporting infrastructure needs | Only those structures and facilities needed for public safety, environmental protection or interpretation | Roads, toilet facilities, campgrounds and interpretive displays. Possibly permanent accommodation facilities and some site hardening in popular areas | Full range of facilities generally expected of high-quality day-trip tourism |
| Group sizes | Generally 10 or fewer | Generally 30 or fewer | No maximum size |
| Degree of self-reliance required | High | Low/moderate | Low |
| Level of knowledge/skill required | Moderate/high knowledge and skills base required to make most of opportunity | Low/moderate knowledge and skills base required to make most of opportunity | Little knowledge and skills base required to make most of opportunity |
| Method of delivering educational and interpretive messages | Mainly through personal interaction with guide or through the use of self-guiding interpretive materials | Through guide commentaries or use of self-guiding interpretive materials. Interpretive signs and other information may be common in the field | A wide variety of techniques such as videos, cassettes, commentaries, information displays and photographs |

| | | | |
|---|---|---|---|
| Style of management | Primarily an off-site style of management through environmental education and information | A mixture of on-site and off-site management techniques. | A high degree of obvious on-site management |
| Likely nature of outcomes | Very much a 'hands on' experience where participants learn about the intricacies of biological and cultural systems | An increased understanding and knowledge of Queensland environments which are probably unfamiliar to the visitor | A general introduction to Queensland ecosystems and some of their special characteristics |
| Examples of activities/settings | Bushwalking with an environmental educational focus in remote areas or in remnant forest patches; camping on a coral cay; guided dive trips; interpreted river canoeing; rafting or sea kayaking; birdwatching study groups | Interpreted spotlighting tours in the rainforest at night; self-guided interpretive forest drives or walks; guided 4WD tours on Fraser Island; specialised dive trips to the Great Barrier Reef; interpretation of geological formations in western Queensland; tours of the Undara lava tubes; marine biologist guided snorkelling tour; Aboriginal guided tours of north-west Queensland which interprets Aboriginal heritage in the natural environment | High-capacity educational snorkelling and dive trips to the Great Barrier Reef; interpreted boat trips up the Brisbane River to bat colonies at Indooroopilly Island; some interpreted larger bus trips on Fraser Island; interpreted whale watching or marine education tours |

[a] Each of the three ecotourism styles is required to meet the principles of ecotourism, i.e. occur in a natural environment, include environmental education and interpretation elements, and contribute to conservation.

Source: *Queensland Ecotourism Plan* (1997), Tourism Queensland www.tq.com.au/ecotourism

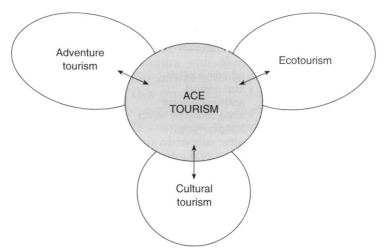

**Figure 3.7**   The changing face of ecotourism
*Source*: Modified from Fennell (1999: 53).

## CASE STUDY   Adventure tourism in New Zealand: issues of safety for the adventure tourism sector (Tim Bentley and Stephen Page)

Adventure tourism is also often taken to include more passive activities associated with ecotourism (e.g. safaris and trekking in difficult terrain). New Zealand is regarded as a major destination for overseas visitors wishing to participate in active adventure tourism activities, and the adventure tourism industry has expanded in recent years as a major niche sector within New Zealand's tourism industry (Berno and Moore 1996). The adventure tourism industry is chosen for the risk and challenge it poses to participants. The most popular of these activities include scenic flights, jet boating, white-water rafting, mountain recreation and bungy jumping. Recent research has examined the way these activities are marketed and promoted as an integral part of the New Zealand tourism industry (Cloke and Perkins 1998), with New Zealand being seen as synonymous with adventure tourism (Bentley *et al.* 2001).

While an important attraction of many of these activities is excitement and a high level of 'perceived' risk (Brannan and Condello 1992; Berno and Moore 1996), there is evidence that certain adventure tourism activities present a serious actual risk to the health and safety of participants. Hall and McArthur (1991) reported that 70 per cent of all adventure tourism injuries and 50 per cent of all adventure tourism fatalities in Australia were directly associated with white-water rafting. New Zealand Maritime Safety Council data revealed some 43 investigations with an adventure tourism component were undertaken in the four-year period to the end of 1998 (Bentley and Page 2001). This risk factor confirms what Fennell (1999) highlighted as a major differentiating factor for ecotourism and adventure tourism.

Research on outdoor recreation can help one to understand the factors which affect the decision-making of tourists to choose activities in the natural environment that involve physical risk such as adventure tourism. In health-related research which is informed by the discipline of psychology, it is possible to uncover the tourists' cognition of warnings and risk associated with adventure. Safety management research can also assist in assessing risk and in the investigation of accident causation to assess what chain of events contributed to specific tourist accidents.

According to Ryan (1997), white-water rafting has featured strongly in the promotion of New Zealand, as representing the images of fun, excitement and the outdoors. The number of overseas tourists who take a raft trip is estimated at over 80,000 a year, which represents two-thirds of the total number carried by rafting companies. The major part of the market is based around Queenstown, with major operators being based on the Shotover River. In 1994, the Adventure Tourism Council estimated the number of people carried by rafts was approximately 120,000, of whom about 45 per cent went rafting in the Shotover area. In New Zealand, rafting is worth possibly NZ$8.7 million although no real estimates exist. Mountain biking has also become a popular recreational activity in the past 10 years. The increase in the number of mountain bikers worldwide has raised a number of issues associated with conflict between different user groups and appropriate management strategies. Research was undertaken on the bikers in the Manawatu region of New Zealand during the summer of 1997/98 (Mason and Leberman 1998). This investigated the impacts of mountain biking and related management issues, noting that there were conflicts between user groups; access to mountain biking opportunities was a problem; information provision was poor and there was a lack of agreement on whether there should be dedicated or multi-use tracks. Young, active, professional males were the main mountain bikers in the area. They exhibited a preference for forest settings, and rides of 2–3 hours which provide a mixture of physical and mental challenge. The main areas of conflict are with motor cycles, horse riders and four-wheel drivers. Increased information and more tracks were desired, and to date, a mountain biking forum has been established. This has led to the selection of a dedicated site for mountain biking in Palmerston North, New Zealand, allowing easy access for both beginners and experienced riders. This research has shown that an alternate approach to conventional policymaking can provide opportunities for greater involvement of stakeholders when making decisions on recreation and tourism activities.

Recent research by Bentley et al. (2001) outlines the extent of adventure tourism activities within New Zealand. An accident experience questionnaire was posted to 300 adventure tourism businesses operating throughout the North and South Islands of New Zealand. A stratified sample, ensuring representation of operators from a wide range of adventure tourism businesses, was drawn from a sampling frame of about 400 businesses. The sampling frame was constructed from various sources, including the New Zealand Adventure Tourism Council's database of adventure tourism operators, tourist guides and brochures, flyers advertising adventure tourism operations, and a range of other publications. Operators representing 21 different activity sectors of the adventure tourism industry were surveyed. Some 142 (47 per cent) of New Zealand adventure tourism operators surveyed returned fully completed questionnaires; an encouraging result for a small business survey concerning a

Table 3.3   The distribution of adventure tourism activity sectors surveyed

| Environment | Activity sector | No. of operators | Percentage of sample (%) |
|---|---|---|---|
| Land-based | All terrain vehicles (ATV) | 5 | 3.5 |
| | Adventure education | 4 | 3 |
| | Bungy jumping | 5 | 3.5 |
| | Caving | 2 | 1 |
| | Cycle tours/mountain biking | 5 | 3.5 |
| | Ecotours | 9 | 6 |
| | Guided walk | 15 | 10 |
| | Horse riding | 10 | 7 |
| | Mountain recreation | 11 | 8 |
| | Quad biking | 3 | 2 |
| *Subtotal* | | *70* | *48* |
| Water-based | Black-water rafting | 3 | 2 |
| | Diving | 4 | 3 |
| | Fishing | 2 | 1 |
| | Jet boating | 5 | 3.5 |
| | Kayaking | 24 | 17 |
| | Marine encounter (dolphins/seals) | 7 | 5 |
| | Wind surfing | 3 | 2 |
| | White-water rafting | 10 | 7 |
| *Subtotal* | | *61* | *42* |
| Aviation | Ballooning | 3 | 2 |
| | Skydiving/parasailing | 3 | 2 |
| | Scenic flight | 9 | 6 |
| *Subtotal* | | *15* | *10* |
| Total | | 142 | 100 |

sensitive topic. The majority of the 142 adventure tourism businesses surveyed were either individually or jointly owned (95 per cent). Together, these operators catered for some 516,722 clients during the preceding year (1998), with client numbers for each operation ranging from 10 to 35,000 clients for the main activity provided by the business. Respondents' estimates suggest approximately one-half of clients of businesses surveyed were overseas visitors, although this varied widely between activities and locations. Table 3.3 shows the distribution of activities (the activity which the greatest number of clients of the business participate in) for adventure tourism businesses surveyed. Activities are organised under three main groupings, based on the type of environment in which they are undertaken: land-based, water-based and aviation.

Client injury-incidence rates per 1 million participation hours (IMPH) were determined for each of the businesses surveyed, and operators assigned to one of four injury-incidence groups: zero injuries; 1–99 IMPH ('low' incidence); 100–499 IMPH ('moderate' incidence); and 500+ IMPH ('high' incidence). It is noted that the majority

Table 3.4  Injuries per million participation hours grouped by activity sector

| Environment | Activity sector | Zero client injuries | | 1–99 client injuries | | 100–499 client injuries | | 500+ client injuries | |
|---|---|---|---|---|---|---|---|---|---|
| | | n | % | n | % | n | % | n | % |
| Land-based | All terrain vehicles | 2 | 40 | 2 | 40 | 1 | 20 | 0 | 0 |
| | Adventure education | 1 | 25 | 3 | 75 | 0 | 0 | 0 | 0 |
| | Bungy jumping | 1 | 20 | 2 | 40 | 2 | 40 | 0 | 0 |
| | Caving | 0 | 0 | 0 | 0 | 0 | 0 | 2 | 100 |
| | Cycle touring | 0 | 0 | 0 | 0 | 2 | 40 | 3 | 60 |
| | Ecotours | 8 | 89 | 1 | 11 | 0 | 0 | 0 | 0 |
| | Guided walking | 12 | 80 | 2 | 13 | 1 | 7 | 0 | 0 |
| | Horse riding | 3 | 30 | 3 | 30 | 2 | 20 | 2 | 20 |
| | Mountain recreation | 4 | 37 | 3 | 27 | 2 | 18 | 2 | 18 |
| | Quad biking | 0 | 0 | 0 | 0 | 0 | 0 | 3 | 100 |
| Water-based | Black-water rafting | 1 | 33 | 0 | 0 | 0 | 0 | 2 | 67 |
| | Diving | 1 | 25 | 2 | 50 | 1 | 25 | 0 | 0 |
| | Fishing | 0 | 0 | 0 | 0 | 1 | 50 | 0 | 50 |
| | Jet boating | 3 | 60 | 1 | 20 | 1 | 20 | 0 | 0 |
| | Kayaking | 20 | 83 | 3 | 13 | 1 | 4 | 0 | 0 |
| | Marine encounter | 4 | 36 | 3 | 27 | 1 | 14 | 0 | 0 |
| | Wind surfing | 2 | 67 | 0 | 0 | 1 | 0 | 0 | 0 |
| | White-water rafting | 3 | 30 | 0 | 0 | 4 | 40 | 3 | 30 |
| Aviation | Ballooning | 3 | 100 | 0 | 0 | 0 | 0 | 0 | 0 |
| | Skydiving/parasailing | 3 | 100 | 0 | 0 | 0 | 0 | 0 | 0 |
| | Scenic flight | 8 | 89 | 1 | 11 | 0 | 0 | 0 | 0 |
| Total | | 78 | 55 | 26 | 18 | 20 | 14 | 18 | 13 |

of operators in the 'high' incidence group had IMPH rates of over 3,000. Table 3.4 shows the distribution of adventure tourism operators by activity sector and injury-incidence group. Some 18 (13 per cent) businesses had client injury-incidence rates of 500+ IMPH. It is notable that three of the five cycle tour operators had client injury-incidence rates of 500+ IMPH. Further analysis showed cycle tour operators to have the highest mean injury-incidence rate of all activity sectors surveyed (7,401 IMPH). Other activity sectors with a high proportion of operators in the 'moderate' and 'high' injury-incidence groups were caving (6,626 IMPH), fishing (3,164), quad biking (3,096), horse riding (718) and black- (483) and white-water rafting (537). Lowest injury-incidence rates were found for ballooning, ecotours, guided walking, scenic flights, kayaking, jet boating and all-terrain vehicles, all of which had the majority of operators in the zero and 'low' client injury-incidence groups. Highest accident-incidence rates were observed for activities that involved the risk of falling from a height while in motion. Analysis of accident events and injuries sustained by clients of adventure tourism activities suggests injury prevention measures should specifically focus on reducing the risk of falls from heights and strip, trip and fall accidents on the level. These risks appear to be common across most sectors of the adventure tourism industry. Operators may also find the model presented in Figure 3.6 to be a useful tool in the identification and control of risks for their activity.

It is also notable that adventure activities having relatively high incidences of client injuries (with the exception of white-water rafting) represent the less well-regulated activity sectors of the adventure tourism industry. It is argued that the issue of regulation versus self-regulation for the adventure tourism industry should be revisited in the light of these findings, and recent well-publicised adventure tourism-related fatalities both in New Zealand and elsewhere. Further research by Bentley *et al.* (2001) also examined the issue of tourist safety from the perspective of the health sector using hospital data, and more detail on the findings can be found in that study which also highlights the scope and nature of tourist safety in the adventure tourism sector.

## Wildlife tourism

The quality of the natural environment plays a primary role in attracting tourists to specific destinations. Wildlife tourists seek an experience that will enable them to explore, no matter for how short a time, a new ecosystem and all its inhabitants. Some tourists are lifelong wildlife enthusiasts and others merely take day trips to a wilderness area from a luxury hotel base. Reynolds and Braithwaite (2001) examined the issue of wildlife tourism, and noted that The Ecotourism Society (1998) considered the scale of this market, estimating (perhaps somewhat optimistically) that between 40 and 60 per cent of international tourists were nature tourists, of whom 20–40 per cent were wildlife-related tourists. The Ecotourism Society (1998) estimated that in 1994 there were between 106 and 211 million wildlife-related tourists worldwide, although this could have included tourists who took a wildlife or nature-based trip as part of their holiday experience. According to Reynolds and Braithwaite (2001: 32) wildlife tourism (WT) may be defined as 'an area of overlap between nature-based tourism, ecotourism, consumptive use of wildlife, rural tourism, and human relations with animals' which is shown in Figure 3.8. Duffus and Dearden (1990) developed a conceptual framework for the non-consumptive recreational use of wildlife which was based on three elements: ecology, the recreational user and the historical context of human–wildlife interactions. In contrast, Orams (1995) emphasised a spectrum of tourist–wildlife opportunities with a number of components: interaction opportunities (how tourists might come into contact with wildlife); management strategy options and outcome indicators for tourists and wildlife. What was evident from Reynolds and Braithwaite's (2001: 40) study was that

> A wide range of activities fall within the ambit of WT, apparently catering for a wide range of needs and in a variety of ways. Some WT is more attractive to the general public than others, however it is critically important that the environmental sustainability of WT operations be given the highest priority due to the inherent fragility of the resource.

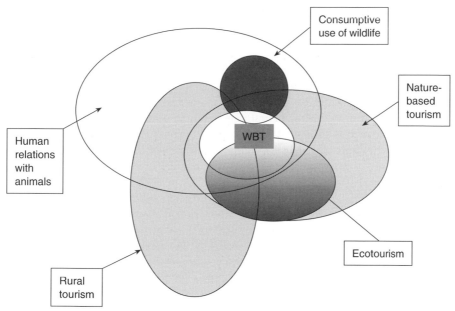

Figure 3.8    Wildlife-based tourism

Many such visitors seek to be informed and educated although others wish primarily to be entertained. There are many different kinds of wildlife-watching holidays – tourists can choose between a luxury hotel-based safari in Kenya, wilderness backpacking in the Rockies or an Antarctic cruise to watch penguins and killer whales (Shackley 1996). The growth in wildlife viewing in recent years has been phenomenal (Ceballos-Lascurain 1998). For example, in the United States over 75 million people watch wildlife each year and it is now the country's number one outdoor recreational activity. In response to this growth, a national group of governmental agencies and conservation organisations created the Watchable Wildlife Initiative in 1990. Its goals are to promote wildlife viewing, conserve biodiversity, foster environmental education and generate economic opportunities based on ecotourism. California's 'Watchable Wildlife Program' was established in 1994 and is now one of the largest and most successful programmes through its promotion of 'six steps to sustainable success' (Garrison 1997). They include selecting sites based on regional diversity, biological sustainability and quality viewing as well as ensuring that each site provides adequate visitor services and resource protection. Another key goal is to provide 'seamless' recreational and educational opportunities focusing on quality products and state-wide programmes of visibility shared between all agencies. Other goals include establishing partnerships, identification of market segments, and the development of cooperative market strategies. To illustrate the significance of growth in one segment of the wildlife tourism market, whale watching, the following case study examines the scale and significance of worldwide growth in this tourist activity.

## CASE STUDY   The global expansion of a wildlife tourism activity: whale watching

A recent report by Hoyt (2000) provides a detailed and exciting series of insights into the global growth and development of this wildlife tourism activity. According to Hoyt (2000), whale watching is not only a major commercial activity but also has important educational, environmental, scientific and other socio-economic benefits. The result is that it is estimated to be a US$1 billion business which attracts over 9 million participants a year in 87 countries. Whale watching expanded rapidly in the 1990s since a report by Hoyt in 1995. The number of countries now embracing whale watching has grown from 31 in 1991 to 65 in 1994 to 87 by the year 2000. A similar growth has occurred in the number of whale watchers that has expanded from 4 million in 1991 to 5.4 million in 1994 to 9 million in 1998. Growth in the expenditure by whale watchers has grown from an estimated US$504 million in 1994 to US$1,049 million in 1998 (Table 3.5). The economic impact of such an activity is reflected in the 492 communities now undertaking some form of whale-watching activity, where the direct expenditure on whale watch tours has grown from US$77 million in 1991 to US$299.5 million in 1998, an annual average rise of 21.4 per cent.

Globally, 22 new countries have started whale watch tours since 1994, and interestingly, 34 of the 40 member countries of the International Whaling Commission (IWC) now have at least some whale-watching activity. Some 7,731,885 people a year currently go whale watching in IWC countries and the majority of whale watching (86 per cent) occurs within these IWC countries. The only main country outside of the IWC, Canada, had just over a million whale watchers in 1998. The 'million whale watch club' has expanded from only one country in 1994 (the USA – see Table 3.6) which could claim a million whale watchers to three countries or areas (United States, Canada and the Canary Islands) which now have in excess of a million whale watchers a year. Two countries have over half a million which are expected to pass the million mark in due course (Australia and South Africa).

Table 3.5   World whale watch visitor expenditures

| Year | No. of whale watchers | Direct expenditures | Total expenditures |
|------|----------------------|---------------------|--------------------|
| 1991 | 4,046,957 | USD $77,034,000 or GBP £44,787,000 | $317,854,000 £184,799,000 |
| 1994 | 5,425,506 | $122,445,000 £75,583,000 | $504,278,000 £311,283,000 |
| 1998 | 9,020,196 | $299,509,000 £186,924,000 | $1,049,057,000 £654,716,000 |

Average annual % increase 1991–94: 10.3%.
Average annual % increase 1994–98: 13.6%.
Average annual % increase 1991–98: 12.1%.

*Source*: Hoyt (2000: 17).

Table 3.6   North America whale watch visitor expenditures

| Year | No. of whale watchers | Direct expenditures | Total expenditures (USD) |
|------|-----------------------|---------------------|--------------------------|
| 1991 | 3,430,225 | $46,230,000 | $225,275,000 |
| 1994 | 4,074,195 | $65,791,000 | $293,397,000 |
| 1998 | 5,500,654 | $194,575,000 | $594,267,000 |

*Source*: Hoyt (2000: 20).

There are many examples of communities which have been economically transformed by whale watching, including Kaikoura in New Zealand which won the British Airways Tourism for Tomorrow Award in 1994 and assisted in local economic regeneration for a declining small town on the east coast of the South Island of New Zealand. Most of the 83 known species of cetaceans are included in whale watch programmes, with the exception of the beaked whales. The most commonly watched species for whale-watching industries are humpback whales, grey whales, northern and southern right whales, blue whales, minke whales, sperm whales, short-finned pilot whales, orcas and bottlenose dolphins (Hoyt 2000), of which two species – the blue and northern right whales – are classified as endangered species. A further two species are considered vulnerable (humpback and southern right whales).

According to Hoyt (2000), the most common form of whale watching is boat-based (72 per cent of all whale watching), although more than 2.55 million people in 10 main countries (28 per cent) participated in land-based whale watching. In most contexts, whale watching is a major source of revenue from overseas tourists (with the exception of Japan), with some 4.3 million people participating in whale watching in the USA in 1998, which comprises 47.8 per cent of all whale-watching activity, having started there in 1955. While whale watching appeared to have begun to reach its peak in the USA, the most rapid growth was experienced by Taiwan which expanded from a zero base to 30,000 whale watchers between 1994 and 1998 (see Orams and Neil 1998 for a review).

## Summary

It is evident that a large literature exists on nature-based tourism (e.g. see Weiler and Hall 1992) and ecotourism and that there is a growing recognition that a new partnership has evolved in an integrated context in some localities, where the tourism industry and conservation community have recognised the sensitivity of the environment to responsible travel, which depends upon the appropriate use of natural areas set aside for conservation for ecotourism purposes (e.g. Giannecchini 1993). Clearly, ecotourism is a broad component of the nature-based tourism sector, and one of the most appropriate ways to attempt any definition is to examine the principles and underlying ethics associated with individual forms of tourism which are labelled as ecotourism to assess the extent to which they conform to either the five principles developed in this chapter or the multitude of checklists such as Honey's (1999). A reiteration of Honey's (1999: 22–4) seven characteristics – that true forms of ecotourism should involve travel to natural destinations, minimise impact, build environmental awareness, provide direct financial benefits for conservation, provide financial benefits and empowerment for local people, respect local culture and support human rights and democratic movements – outlines some of the underlying ethics of what ecotourism should be.

Ecotourism is more than a specific form of tourism – it is an ethic, a philosophy, an ideal and above all not a niche market for the mass tourist operator to play the green card. There is no simple solution to developing a working definition and Fennell's (1999) approach – to identify the principles and characteristics of specific ecotourism activities as a means of establishing if they fall within the criteria which many of the definitions embrace – is certainly a useful way forward for operationalising the concept. A number of useful studies have sought to develop this approach further (e.g. Bottrill and Pearce 1995) and this was useful in establishing that not all operations which describe themselves as ecotourism really deserve that label. There is certainly a growing demand for products and experiences which are labelled ecotourism, and increasing disquiet within the existing literature on the validity of using such labels and whether any type of tourism activity can really be ecologically sensitive. This is one of the major stumbling blocks for developing a workable definition, along with the worldview of the different groups contributing to the debate with the anthropogenic and ecocentric perspectives certainly causing conflict over what is possible. For this reason, it is perhaps useful to re-emphasise the criteria which Fennell (1999) advocated in an analysis of ecotourism definitions since any attempt to establish what characterises ecotourism as a phenomenon will need to consider whether the activity:

- has an interest in nature;
- contributes to conservation;
- is reliant upon parks and protected areas;
- benefits local people and has long-term benefits to them;
- advances education and study of the natural environment;
- is low impact and non-consumptive;
- has a commitment to ethical conduct and promotes responsible tourism;
- develops management principles to minimise visitor impact;
- is sustainable in principle and in the activities it undertakes;
- promotes enjoyment and appreciation of nature and the environment;
- is sensitive to local culture;
- has an element of adventure;
- is small scale.

The increasing growth of this form of tourism activity is certainly grounds to investigate its impacts and effects in the wider environment and to do this, one needs to understand the type of people who seek this type of experience. For this reason, the next chapter examines 'who is the ecotourist.'

## Questions

1. How did the term 'ecotourism' develop and what are its roots?
2. How easy is it to establish a working definition of ecotourism?
3. What are the basic tenets of ecotourism as a distinct form of tourism?
4. What criteria would you advocate in establishing whether a business is firmly embedded within an ecotourism ethic?

## Further reading

The following studies are a useful introduction to ecotourism:

Fennell, D. and Eagles, P. (1990) 'Ecotourism in Costa Rica: a conceptual framework', *Journal of Park and Recreation Administration*, **8** (1): 23–34. This is a good starting point for the conceptual issues associated with developing a working framework for ecotourism.

Honey, M. (1999) *Ecotourism and Sustainable Development: Who Owns Paradise?*, Washington, DC: Island Press. This is a good, although somewhat personalised view, of ecotourism and is useful for the critical insights it offers.

Liddle, M. (1997) *Recreation and the Environment: The Ecological Impact of Recreation and Ecotourism*, London: Chapman and Hall. This is a useful ecologically based book which addresses ecotourism and is a good introduction to the area.

Lindberg, K. and McKercher, B. (1997) 'Ecotourism: a critical overview', *Pacific Tourism Review*, **1** (1): 65–79. This journal article is a very useful concise overview of ecotourism and the literature.

The following references are useful overviews of ecotourism:

Blamey, R. (2001) 'Principles of ecotourism', in D. Weaver (ed.), *Encyclopedia of Ecotourism*, Wallingford: CAB International, 5–22.

Orams, M. (2001) 'Types of ecotourism', in D. Weaver (ed.), *Encyclopedia of Ecotourism*, Wallingford: CAB International, 23–36.

Hawkins, D. and Lamoureux, K. (2001) 'Global growth and magnitude of ecotourism', in D. Weaver (ed.), *Encyclopedia of Ecotourism*, Wallingford: CAB International, 63–72.

Weaver, D. (2001) 'Ecotourism in the context of other tourism types', in D. Weaver (ed.), *Encyclopedia of Ecotourism*, Wallingford: CAB International, 73–84.

# Chapter 4

# Ecotourists: consumers of nature and the environment

There has been a growing interest among tourism researchers in relation to what motivates tourists to travel, and while there is no universal agreement on why people take holidays (Page *et al.* 2001; Pearce 1993), there is a recognition that tourists are far from a homogeneous group: indeed they are increasingly sophisticated consumers who seek a diversity of experiences (see Ryan 1997) and outcomes from their travel-related activities which are encompassed by the term 'tourism'. The vast research literature that has now amassed on the motivation and activities of tourists and their tastes, attitudes and values has not necessarily filtered through to the operational areas of the tourism industry. This is exemplified by Marion and Farrell (1998: 155) who argued that 'managers are rarely able to differentiate among the many differing types of tourists (e.g. locals, domestic and international) so they are grouped together into the more general terms visitors, visitation and visitor impacts'. In the case of ecotourism, initial research during the early stages of its academic development argued that 'the term ecotourism describes a specific travel market. It has been characterised as being composed of those who select a certain travel experience and destination, that of nature-oriented experiences in pristine natural environments' (Eagles 1992: 3). The implication of Eagles' (1992) argument is that ecotourism by its very nature, generates 'ecotourists' as a distinct and identifiable group who consume ecotourism-related tourism products and experiences. As Ryan *et al.* (2000: 158) observed, 'The experience of ecotourism lies in the intensity of interaction with the site' (also see Ryan *et al.* 2000 for a more theoretical discussion of the tourist's experience of ecotourism). While this premise may appear logical and valid, identifying the 'ecotourist' is a far from straightforward process. Cater (1997) highlighted some of the inherent problems of identifying the 'ecotourist' as the following statement suggested:

> There is an inherent risk in assuming that the ecotourist is automatically an environmentally sensitive breed. Although small, specialist, guided groups of ecotourists may attempt to conform to this identity, the net has been cast sufficiently wide to include less responsible behaviour. Amongst those loosely defined as ecotourists will be those visiting a destination for a few days, unlikely to concern them. This can be referred to as 'this year the Galápagos, next year Antarctica' syndrome. It has been suggested that such tourists are unlikely to pay regard to the long-term repercussions of their activities, particularly as they may consider they have the

right to use the resources in the light of the significant outlay they will have made for the experience.

This highlights the diverse motivations and behavioural attributes of the diverse group often referred to as ecotourists. This also highlights a distinction between the deep forms of ecotourism identified in Chapter 3 and the more peripheral 'green', taste- and fashion-driven visitors who see ecotourism as a status experience. Mowforth and Munt (1998: 133) also argued that the term 'ecotourist has a double meaning, however, for not only does it signal an interest and focus on this type of tourist on the "environment" (ecology), it also indicates the ability to pay the high prices that such holidays command'. Even so, research by Woods and Moscardo (1998) and Ceballos-Lascurain (1998) recognised that the lack of clarity in existing definitions of ecotourism and absence of any consensus on how to operationalise the concept in a universal manner, have added to the problem of proceeding to define the ecotourist.

Therefore, in seeking to identify what an ecotourist is becomes a far from simple exercise in market segmentation which is frequently used in tourism marketing (Middleton 1988). Instead, it requires a more detailed analysis of a number of key issues. First, it is necessary to recognise the emergence of this form of demand for tourism experiences based on the 'eco' label, emphasising recent developments in the growth of tourism markets which have become more sophisticated in terms of tastes and requirements. Second, the characteristics of ecotourists can be examined from a range of existing studies of those visitors who choose 'eco' experiences to consider which characteristics from the tourism demand perspective can help define this market. Third, the types of experiences sought by the ecotourist can be examined to assess the ecotourist. However, what underlies much of this debate on what constitutes the ecotourist is the motivation for ecotourist activities, and for this reason attention now turns to the emergence of the 'new tourist'.

## The new tourist: a new market for eco-products?

There has a been a growing interest in the evolution of tourism and tourist typologies since the innovative research by Poon (1993), which suggested that there is a 'new' traveller or tourist which comprised a significant market segment in tourism activities worldwide, which was distinct from the existing or 'old' forms of tourism (see Figure 4.1). This segment was expected to increase rapidly in both absolute and relative terms in the decades following Poon's (1993) analysis. Weaver and Oppermann (2000: 356–7) suggested that if society was becoming more environmentally oriented, then it was possible that the new traveller could eventually emerge as the mainstream tourist market to replace the conventional mass tourists. If that was to prove the case, tourism businesses would have no choice but to become more sustainable in orientation if they wished to survive. The characteristics of this new breed of traveller are their environmental awareness and desire for environmental knowledge. Such travellers are supposedly sensitive to local cultures because of their social justice values and the wish to have a positive impact on

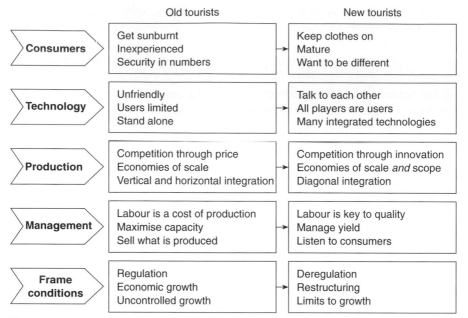

Figure 4.1    Poon's old and new tourists
*Source*: Poon (1993: 17)

the destination. The new traveller is supposed to carefully assess tourism products in advance, is in search of authentic and meaningful experiences, and prefers flexible and spontaneous itineraries. Finally they are motivated by a desire for self-fulfilment and learning and seek challenging experiences. These characteristics describe the nature of this new group of travellers who are far from homogeneous, but it does not account for their emergence in societal terms.

According to Mowforth and Munt (1998: 132) ecotourists are the new bourgeoisie, often employed in the service sector with high incomes (economic capital) and seeking authentic ecotourism experiences. This is complemented by the 'ego-tourists', who are drawn from the petite bourgeoisie who seek to differentiate themselves from the working classes (the mass tourist) and high-spending ecotourists. Typical experiences these groups seek are backpacking, overland trucking, experiences to build the curriculum vitae and bank of experiences. It reflects the pursuit of alternative forms of travel and pursuit of uniqueness. Ego-tourists believe their travel is beneficial and that they are certainly not part of the mass. What this debate highlights is the emergence of a new class of tourist and debate over what constitutes tourism. Indeed the use of the term 'traveller' has been seen as a de-differentiated form of activity which has only tenuous links with tourism as a process and phenomenon. The term 'traveller' emphasises the culture of individualism and a distinct distancing from the term 'tourist', particularly mass tourist (see Page *et al.* 2001 for more detail). In the context of ecotourism, Mowforth and Munt (1998: 142) recognised that

For tour-operators catering more for the young and adventurous ego-tourists where economic capital is clearly insufficient to confer taste, it is the individual distinction of participant travellers from tourists that has become critical. It advances the distinctions beyond a mere reference (or 'charge') to packaging and instead focuses on the qualities and practises of travel and contrast these to tourism.

What Mowforth and Munt's (1998) analysis indicates is that while Poon's (1993) 'new tourist' may underpin the development of ecotourism, they are not necessarily synonymous with ecotourism and are a diverse group as the eco–ego-tourist distinction indicates. In the context of ecotourism, Wight (1997a) argued that one could identify the changes which were evolving from traditional forms to new emerging forms and one therefore needs to emphasise the characteristics which define the ecotourist.

## The characteristics of ecotourists

Within any analysis of the demand for a tourism product or experience, it is apparent that motivation is a key element of the individual and group experience. As Hall and Page (1999) indicated, tourism demand is fundamental to the analysis of tourism activities, particularly why tourists do what they do, where and why. In the context of tourism, there is now a well-established conceptual and theoretical literature which debates why tourists go on holiday (see Hall and Page 1999; Pearce 1993) and in a specialist text such as this there is little need to reassess the nature of tourism demand and motivation to travel. What it is important to stress in the context of ecotourism, is the nature of the factors and issues which contribute towards the motivation for tourists to pursue the phenomenon identified as ecotourism. These then have to be evaluated within the existing tourism literature using the concepts of motivation to illustrate what is distinctive and what is common to the experiences of ecotourism as a form of tourism-related experience.

Eagles and Higgins (1998) is a useful starting point for the discussion of motivation, since they identified three factors which have been significant in generating the motivation for people to pursue ecotourism. These are:

- *changes in environmental attitudes*, which served as a basis for the development of ecotravel;
- *the development of environmental education*, which assisted in the creation of environmentally literate citizens;
- *the development of an environmental mass media*, which has utilised nature as a powerful force in the media.

What these three factors emphasised is the general trend towards environmentalism in the tourism experience, observed by numerous commentators in the 1980s and a range of other processes discussed in Chapters 1 and 2, the greater influence of the environment in consumerism and the rise of green marketing. This highlighted the significance of what Chapters 1 and 2 emphasised, that the values, attitudes and behaviour of people are fundamental when discussing genuine forms of environmental tourism or trying to identify potential ecotourists.

Ecotourists have often been distinguished from mass tourists on the basis of travel, planning and level of novelty. Mass tourists, both organised and individual, often travel within a familiar 'environmental bubble' of their own country and rarely get 'off the beaten track'. Depending on their motives, some ecotourists are often more tolerant of primitive conditions and unfamiliar territory (Laarman and Durst 1987).

In fact Luzar *et al.* (1998) supported this argument, with research conducted in Louisiana that indicated that environmental attitudes influence travel decisions. Yet it has been suggested that people are not necessarily ecotourists just because they visit an ecotourism location (Acott *et al.* 1998). Ecotourists who have a more ecocentric attitude towards nature have also been found to prefer businesses that are environmentally friendly (Khan 1997a). Such ecotourists also expected knowledgeable personnel who are willing to instil a feeling of trust and confidence.

Weiler and Richins' (1995) research observed that ecotourists sought enjoyment of relatively undisturbed natural phenomena but this in itself was not necessarily an identifiable characteristic of ecotourism, since early typologies of tourists (Plog 1973) found that different groups of tourists sought different attributes from the locations they holidayed in. In this respect, the undisturbed natural environment may well be an ideal sought by many visitors, but available to only a small proportion of the tourist market due to the constraints of price of ecotourism experiences. According to Wearing and Neil (1999), many different types of ecotourists exist in the same vein that within the wider tourism market, different market segments exist. While Wearing and Neil (1999: 129) suggested that mainstream tourists travel to satisfy leisure, pleasure and recreational needs, ecotourists travel to experience natural environments as well as to educate themselves about these areas. However, the large range of different environments combined with differing customer perceptions, needs, attitudes and levels of environmental stewardship, means that identifying the specific characteristics of ecotourists becomes all the more critical because natural area managers, ecotour operators and local communities must take into account the likely needs, form of demand and likely impacts to be caused by ecotourists.

As many commentators recognised, one of the distinguishing features of ecotourists is the emphasis on high-cost experiences within the natural environment, a feature discussed earlier and reiterated by Luzar *et al.* (1995) in a study within Louisiana which recognised that ecotourism tended to be pursued by those in the upper-income groups. This is often combined with the hobbies and nature interests, as Kretchmann and Eagles (1990) defined ecotourists as nature-oriented soft adventurers who wanted to hike or birdwatch. Backman *et al.* (1994) also suggested that ecotourists prefer to travel in order to experience natural phenomena, learn about nature, be physically active and meet people with similar interests. This expanded the range of characteristics which can be used to define the ecotourist, while Ballantine and Eagles (1994) suggested that ecotourists can be defined through their use of information and were usually viewed as being outdoor enthusiasts who are older, affluent, well-educated people who have reasonable amounts of discretionary free time in order to travel. There is also a growing body of evidence that indicates that gender is not a discriminating factor in relation to the type of people who choose ecotourism experiences, as females are a growing proportion of nature-oriented travellers (Keenan 1989; Ingram and Durst 1989; Payne and Graham 1993). Such features are informative, but do not lend themselves to an exclusionary definition.

According to Hvenegaard (1994), ecotourists represent a cross-section of society, but on average, are slightly older (40–50 years), are well educated (most having at least a bachelor degree), and have above-average incomes. Ecotourists had specific motivations and high expectations related to the natural environment and are also highly discerning. However, they are not homogeneous, and ecotourist subgroups require distinct management techniques. To understand their requirements and characteristics, researchers have classified ecotourists according to parameters such as group type, motivation/interest level, activity and physical rigour required. It is also important to emphasise the findings of Eagles and Cascagnette (1995) on Canadian ecotourists which found them to be older, more highly educated and with higher than average incomes than other tourists. What this indicated was that as more people gain post-secondary education, the ecotourism market was likely to grow as it became within the reach of more eco-motivated tourists. But Lumsden and Swift (1998) asserted that the distinction between 'soft' adventure and ecotourism was becoming less clear and suggested that both types of tourists are seeking similar experiences. Whereas the specialist ecotourist was concerned essentially with close observation of nature over a longer period of time, the ecoadventure tourist seeks to consume locations at a faster pace, generally in greater comfort (Schluter 1994). In this respect, the attempt to segment and divide the ecotourist market into a series of components is made more difficult if certain elements of the ecoparticipants are blurring.

Kusler (1991) identified three main groups of ecotourists. The largest is the 'do-it-yourself' ecotourists who have a high degree of flexibility, stay in a variety of accommodations and have the mobility to visit any number of settings. The second group is 'ecotourists on tours' who travel to exotic destinations and expect a high degree of safety, comfort and organisation on their tour. The third category comprises 'school or scientific groups'. This group is focused around environmental education or scientific research. They generally stay in the same region for long periods of time, and are willing to endure harsher site conditions than other ecotourists.

Other authors have distinguished between categories of ecotourists according to level of nature-related interest (dedicated versus casual, soft versus hard) (e.g. Ruschmann 1992), and amount of physical rigour involved (difficult versus easy). Indeed, Diamantis's (1999) study of British ecotourists identified two distinct groups: frequent ecotourists (more knowledgeable and driven by principles of sustainability) and casual ecotourists. Therefore, what emerges from the discussion of the characteristics of ecotourists is that to simplify the complexity of the ecotourist as a tourist group, one needs to develop a range of criteria by which groupings of ecotourism can be discerned.

## Towards a typology of ecotourists

Various attempts have been made by researchers to derive classifications of ecotourists, and this section briefly reviews some of the key elements of these studies to arrive at some degree of consensus on what the ecotourism market looks like based on the previous discussion of the characteristics of ecotourists. Fennell (1999) provided an excellent historical review of the early attempts by researchers to profile ecotourists and it is pertinent to examine some of the key issues which these studies raised. In an early study by Kusler (1991), ecotourists were allocated to three principal groups, namely:

- *do-it-yourself ecotourists*, which comprised the largest number of visitors. These visitors stayed in a variety of accommodation types with a high degree of flexibility to visit a variety of ecotourism environments and settings;
- *ecotourists on tours*, where a high degree of organisation characterised their visit, often involving visits to exotic locations such as Antarctica;
- *school groups or scientific groups*, where expeditions or scientific research accompanied the visit and meant visitors would endure harsher site conditions than other visitors.

In contrast, Lindberg (1991: 3) argued that dedication and time were important discriminating factors when distinguishing between different types of ecotourists, where four types could be discerned. Lindberg (1991) suggested that four types of nature tourists existed (although these are not necessarily ecotourists), based solely on the motivation and/or interest level of the participants:

- *hard core* – scientific researchers or members of educational or conservation tours;
- *dedicated* – people who visit protected areas to learn about local natural history;
- *mainstream* – people who visit unique natural area destinations just to take an unusual trip;
- *casual* – people who partake of nature incidentally as part of a broader trip.

Boo (1990) also classified nature tourists according to how important protected areas were in their decision to visit a site. Duffus and Dearden (1990) proposed a continuum between wildlife specialists and generalists, based partially on physical rigour and interest level. Specialists required little infrastructure, interpretive or management facilities, and their presence was absorbed by existing support systems. On the other hand, generalists were less ambitious, had little special interest in a site's attraction, relied heavily on infrastructure, and visited in larger numbers. Thus, in areas dominated by wildlife generalists, additional management was required to offset the impacts of increased pressure.

In a major survey of North American ecotourists, Wight (1997b) found that a shift in interest by general consumers was favouring the growth of ecotourists' preferences (Wight 1997b). Overall, the characteristics of current and potential ecotourists may be viewed as having a much wider impact on

Table 4.1   A threefold classification of ecotourists

| Feature | The rough ecotourist | The smooth ecotourist | The specialist ecotourist |
|---|---|---|---|
| Age | Young–middle-aged | Middle-aged–old | Young–old |
| Travelling | Individually or in small groups | In groups | Individually |
| Organisation | Independent | Tour-operated | Independent + specialist tours |
| Budget | Low: cheap hotel/ B&B; local/fast food; uses buses | High: 3*/5* hotels; luxury cafes; uses taxis | Mid–high: cheap-3* hotels; mid-lux. Cafes; as necessary |
| Type of tourism | Sport and adventure | Nature and safari | Scientific investigation/ hobby pursuit |

*Source*: Mowforth (1993).

tourism trends. In other words, the growing interest in ecotourism is spreading to many population segments, and the characteristics of the experienced ecotourist are becoming incorporated into mainstream markets. Despite this influence, it is useful to summarise the characteristics and typologies of ecotourism into a meaningful framework. One interesting classification of the ecotourist as a diverse and yet distinct series of tourist groups can be found in Mowforth (1993). Developing the earlier typology by Budowski (1976) which distinguished between two types of ecotourist: the scientific and nature tourists (which were also subdivided into the hard, soft and adventure tourists), Mowforth (1993) devised a threefold classification (see Table 4.1).

Mowforth's (1993) classification of ecotourists is useful in that it incorporates the different motivations of ecotourists in relation to the pursuits they engage in as well as the organisation and cost of the experience. The vital distinction between the traveller and packaged form of tourism, ranging from the individualised through to tour-operated form of ecotourism experience, was also implicit in Mowforth's (1993) classification together with the age profile of ecotourists. Although this classification may illustrate the scope of the criteria and characteristics of ecotourists, it is also important to recognise that ecotourism is also an attitude of mind – an experience and a perceived element which cannot always be readily classified. A study by Chirgwin and Hughes (1997) found that among visitors to Fogg Dam in Australia, an artificially created wetland, 90 per cent of those surveyed perceived it as an ecotourism destination. What this indicates is that the concept of an untouched, pristine natural environment is not necessarily the only defining characteristic of what defines ecotourism in the mind of the tourist. The fact that the experience was aesthetically pleasing and facilitated an opportunity to learn about wildlife and nature indicated that a degree of flexibility has to be incorporated into attempts to classify and allocate tourists to specific groupings that are labelled 'ecotourist'. Furthermore, Chirgwin and Hughes's (1997) study also raised one other vital element – the experience of ecotourism which is a complex amalgam of factors to which attention now turns.

## The ecotourism experience

The analysis of tourism and the characteristics of tourists has been a germane area of study, particularly since early studies by Cohen (1972) and Plog (1973) which identified types of tourists and their activities and preferences. Establishing the characteristics of tourists, classifying them and attempting to derive generalisations which can be applied to the wider study of tourism remains as valid now as it was nearly 30 years ago. Despite the growth of knowledge in the field of tourism studies, the pursuit of models which can be seen to characterise what motivates the tourist, in this case the ecotourist, to travel, experience and engage in activities labelled as 'ecotourism' has remained one of the goals of researchers with an interest in the social psychology of tourist behaviour (see Pearce 1982, 1993 for more detail). Since it is generally recognised what interests the ecotourist in broad terms as the discussion above shows in relation to the attempt to develop a typology of ecotourists, it is useful to consider the existing research which assists in explaining the nature and experiences which ecotourists receive. In conceptual terms, there is a growing literature on the tourist experience (e.g. Page *et al.* 2001) and what characterises the nature of the tourist encounter which in part helps to explain the type of visitors who seek out ecotourism experiences. It is the experience and the way in which it is developed for the ecotourist market that are fundamental to any discussion of who ecotourists are.

According to Graefe and Vaske (1987), the tourist experience is a culmination of a given experience which can be influenced by individual, environmental, situational and personality-related factors as well as the degree of communication with other people (Page *et al.* 2001). What this means is that the outcome is what the tourism industry and consumers constantly evaluate to assess whether the initial expectations of the experience have been met in reality. In other words, the tourist experience is a complex amalgam of factors which shape the tourists' feelings and attitude towards their visit (Page 1995). However, what has to be constantly emphasised in a tourism context is that it is impossible to predict tourist responses to individual situations where a range of interrelated factors may impact upon the tourist experience. For example, some tourists feel that overcrowding and high levels of usage of tourism resources diminish the visitor experience. This is likely to be the case for ecotourism, although in the wider tourism context, the evidence is inconclusive on this issue. What this indicates is that some people have a low tolerance for sites where the carrying capacity has been exceeded, where increased use of sites and resources may also raise the potential for conflict (Pigram and Jenkins 1999). Ryan's (2000: 369) analysis is useful since it highlighted a number of characteristics of holidays which impact upon the tourist experience which are relevant to the ecotourism experience, namely that a holiday has:

- a strong emotional attachment for the tourist;
- there is a strong motivation by the client (i.e. tourist) for successful outcomes from the holiday which has been purchased;
- a number of holiday services, so that visitors may select between alternatives;
- a structure whereby the tourist can perform a number of roles each of which can involve an element of satisfaction;
- a time dimension which resides in the memory of the tourist and is a resource for ego-sustainment during non-holiday periods.

In other words, the tourist experience is a complex combination of factors which shape the feelings and attitudes of the tourist towards their visit. Therefore, in an ecotourism context, recognising that the tourist interaction with nature, the environment and other sources of stimulation (e.g. wildlife viewing) is an element of the very product or service which the consumer wishes to experience, is necessary in attempts to classify the ecotourist into distinct types. But even attempting to investigate the ecotourist as a distinct type of tourist is problematic even if one can agree on a typology or classification of visitors, since Eagles and Higgins (1998: 12–13) recognised that

> a series of issues make it difficult to discuss the global patterns of ecotourism accurately. First, the various national agencies responsible for collecting information about tourist visits give little attention to questions or information concerning speciality travel. Second, many quantitative estimates of ecotourists occur in studies that do not utilise rigorous methodology. Third, international coverage of well-designed market studies is limited, although analysts suggest significant national differences in tourism behaviour . . . Fourth, although ecotour administered client surveys and commissioned market demand studies [exist], the results of these proprietary surveys are not publicly available. Many important questions about the character and profile of clients in this sub-sector of the travel industry remain unanswered. There is a conceptual distinction between independent ecotourists who arrange their own itineraries and ecotourists who utilize packaged tours.

What Eagles and Higgins's (1998) statement highlighted was the paucity of tailor-made tourism data available from global organisations such as the WTO which means that there is a reliance upon ad hoc studies on specific elements of ecotourism in different countries. It is important to consider both the similarities and differences among the profiles of ecotourists in and between countries and regions, as well as the early studies which attempted to develop classifications of ecotourists. One useful approach has been to investigate the nature of the ecotourist trip as a phenomenon.

## The ecotourist trip

Boyd and Butler (1996) related ecotourist specialists and generalists to trip duration, with specialists engaging in a recreational activity for more than 7 days and generalists for less than 48 hours. Boyd and Butler's (1996) market demand study pointed to a number of relevant trends, such as the growth of soft adventure, increased interest in environmental concerns, growth in the popularity of specific outdoor activities, and an increase in educational tourism. Even so Eagles and Higgins (1998: 13–14) argued that

> There is little systematic information on the origin and location of the demand for ecotourism. Relatively little is known about the global origin of ecotourists, the international destinations preferred by ecotourists, or comparisons between ecotourists from specific countries. It appears that the international market demand for ecotourism is centred in the western world, concentrated among those cultures in, or developed from, Northern European countries. The English-speaking countries of the world are particularly prominent as sources of . . . ecotourists . . . Japan is a developing market so much so that it may soon become a dominant player. However, the Japanese attitude appears to be an aesthetic understanding rather than ecological understanding.

The growing literature on the profile and characteristics of ecotourists indicates that party composition varies with the type of activity, but that families are not a large part of the adventure travel market. The majority of respondents prefer to travel as a couple (approximately 60 per cent for both consumers and ecotourists), while the experienced ecotourists had a larger percentage who preferred to travel alone. There is little available information on the trip duration of ecotourist visits. This varies considerably and is usually destination rather than market-specific. The average length of stay for all tourists in Nepal is 9.3 nights per visit. In the United States, nature-based travellers stayed an average of 5 nights at their destination, yet in Alaska conservation group trips averaged 12 days. Trip length may also vary by activity. In Canada, the average duration of packaged nature observation trips was 5.3 days, with wildlife-viewing trips ranging from 2.9 to 7 days and seal watching taking less than a day. The largest group of ecotourists (50 per cent) preferred trips lasting 8–14 days.

Destination appears to have a seasonality dimension embedded in it. According to Boyd and Butler (1996) ecotourists are more frequent travellers, with 41 per cent having travelled out of their state/province six or more times in the last three years versus 24 per cent of consumers. The majority of ecotourists preferred to travel in the summer months. However, there appeared to be enough interest in winter travel to justify four-season products. This was particularly true for the experienced ecotourist. Ecotourists were more prepared than general consumers to travel in winter and particularly in the shoulder seasons – over 25 per cent of ecotourists indicated April to October to be their preferred months of travel. In view of the paucity of data on ecotourists, the following review examines some of the principal studies and their findings spatially as a means of synthesising some of the main features of the ecotourist in a number of environments.

## Canadian ecotourists

A number of Canadian studies have been carried out on the characteristics of ecotourists. Ballantine (1991) surveyed a group of 120 Canadian tourists who had visited Kenya. Three criteria were chosen to assess whether the respondents of the survey could be defined as ecotourists: social motives, attraction motives and the commitment of time. The social motive comprised the desire to learn about nature as a motivation for travel, whereas the attraction motive focused on the desire to travel to wilderness or undisturbed areas. Time commitment was also measured, with the respondents spending at least one-third of their holiday in the natural environment. Ballantine (1991) found that Canadian ecotourists were older than the average Canadian traveller, with an average age of 49 and 72 per cent of the group being aged over 40. Canadian ecotourists had a distinct gender balance with more females (55 per cent) than males (45 per cent) who had travelled to Kenya. The group was highly educated, with 79 per cent having had some post-secondary education. The ecotourists had an average household income of $72,523 compared to the Canadian average of $42,686 in 1989. In terms of the ecotourism experience, the only dissatisfaction ecotourists had with their trip was the need for more information on conservation issues.

A similar survey of Canadian ecotourists to Costa Rica was carried out by Fennell (1990) and a combined summary of the findings of the two studies was published by Eagles *et al.* (1992). Kenya and Costa Rica have developed large-scale ecotourism industries over the previous three decades and the surveys of the Canadian ecotourists who had visited these destinations showed that they have high levels of education and income. Awareness and knowledge of ecotourism destinations emanated from a wide variety of sources, including personal references from friends, films, books and quality written materials. The ecotourists were also interested in visiting wilderness, national parks and tropical forests, as well as in viewing birds, mammals, trees and wild flowers. The ecotourists expressed a strong desire to learn about nature on their trip and photography of the landscapes and wildlife was important to them. The Canadian ecotourists also liked to experience new lifestyles, meet people with similar interests and visit historically important places.

In a study by Eagles (1992) of ecotourists, which examined the motivating factors that facilitated ecotourist trips, a range of factors emerged. As Table 4.2 shows, among the top 15 ranked factors which encouraged ecotourists to take a trip, a broad range of environmental factors existed. The importance of wilderness factors and an undisturbed environment in which to undertake these activities emerged as dominant considerations. In Table 4.3, Eagles (1992) conducted a *t*-test of the general tourist population and the ecotourists to discern the significantly different factors which motivated Canadian ecotourists to pursue such activities. Table 4.3 shows that two distinct themes emerged. There was a strongly held attraction factor and a social motivation factor which meant that the appeal of nature and the importance of personal development through such experiences were major motivations underlying the trips. Such findings fit within the social psychology of tourism literature (e.g. see Pearce 1993; Argyle 1996) in terms of some of the underlying psychological determinants of tourism demand (see Hall and Page 1999 for more discussion of this theme).

Table 4.2    Motivations of Canadian ecotourists

| Motivation | Mean | Rank |
|---|---|---|
| Tropical forests[a] | 3.95 | 1 |
| Wilderness and undisturbed nature | 3.94 | 2 |
| Learn about nature[a] | 3.87 | 3 |
| Birds[a] | 3.69 | 4 |
| Lakes and streams | 3.68 | 5 |
| Trees and wild flowers[a] | 3.66 | 6 |
| Photography of landscape/wildlife[a] | 3.58 | 7 |
| Mammals[a] | 3.52 | 8 |
| National and provincial parks | 3.41 | 9 |
| Be physically active | 3.39 | 10 |
| Meet people with similar interest | 3.33 | 11 |
| Mountains | 3.32 | 12 |
| Oceanside | 3.32 | 13 |
| See maximum in time available | 3.24 | 14 |
| Rural areas | 3.18 | 15 |

[a] Asked of the ecotourist populations only. These were not included as choices in the general Canadian travel study.

*Source*: Based on Eagles (1992: 5).

The existing studies of Canadian ecotourists (e.g. Fennell 1990; Eagles 1992; Eagles *et al.* 1992; Ballantine 1991) also indicated that ecotourists wanted to see and experience as much as possible in the time available and indicated their desire for quality guiding and interpretation services, seeking to spend their money on conservation as well as see their expenditures benefit the local economy. A survey by MacKay and McVetty (1996) of ecotourists to northern Canada found that ecotourists spent more money than the general travel market and visited in different seasons, the value of ecotourists being in their quality rather than quantity.

Wight (1996) undertook a comprehensive survey of North American ecotourists for the Alberta Economic Development and Tourism Department. Mail surveys were sent out to 1,200 experienced ecotourists who lived in the United States and Canada. Some 424 surveys were completed, representing a 42 per cent response rate. Wight (1996) found that ecotourists were generally older (56 per cent were 35–54 years old) than the general consumers (49 per cent were 25–44 years old). Older clients (aged 45 and over) were interested in polar bear watching, sailing, seal pup watching and winter activities such as heli-skiing. Younger clients (under 34 years) were interested in ice and rock climbing, trail riding, scuba diving, canoeing, cross-country skiing and rafting. One-third of all hikers were 19 years and under. Wight (1996) found that for experienced ecotourist participants, gender differentiation varied by activity. For example, females were under-represented in camping and cycling, over-represented in hiking, but equal to males in rafting. Males rated wilderness

Table 4.3   The motivations that are significantly more important to the ecotourists

| Motivation | Mean | t-value | Rank |
|---|---|---|---|
| Wilderness and undisturbed nature | 3.94 | −23.40 | 1 |
| Lakes and streams | 3.68 | −16.46 | 2 |
| Be physically active | 3.39 | −16.07 | 3 |
| Mountains | 3.32 | −14.56 | 4 |
| National or provincial parks | 3.41 | −14.33 | 5 |
| Experience new lifestyles | 2.89 | −13.22 | 6 |
| Rural areas | 3.18 | −12.59 | 7 |
| Oceanside | 3.32 | −12.34 | 8 |
| Meet people with similar interest | 3.33 | −12.17 | 9 |
| Simpler lifestyle | 2.79 | −12.01 | 10 |
| Visit historical places | 2.79 | −11.85 | 11 |
| Outdoor recreation | 3.12 | −11.00 | 12 |
| Be daring and adventurous | 2.51 | −10.61 | 13 |
| Cultural activities | 2.71 | −10.44 | 14 |
| See maximum in time available | 3.24 | −9.95 | 15 |
| Rediscover self | 2.47 | −7.95 | 16 |
| Change from a busy job | 3.06 | −8.81 | 17 |
| Local crafts | 2.66 | −8.53 | 18 |
| Historic sites and parks | 2.79 | −8.25 | 19 |
| Reduced fares | 2.47 | −7.95 | 20 |
| Thrills and excitement | 2.55 | −7.01 | 21 |
| Museums, art galleries | 2.42 | −6.59 | 22 |
| Budget accommodation | 2.62 | −5.68 | 23 |
| Escape from demands of life | 2.52 | −5.32 | 24 |
| Participate in sports | 1.91 | −5.30 | 25 |
| Try new foods | 2.18 | −5.27 | 26 |
| Have fun, be entertained | 2.92 | −5.09 | 27 |
| Smaller towns, villages | 2.56 | −4.53 | 28 |
| Local festivals and events | 2.28 | −4.23 | 29 |
| Go places friends have not been | 1.84 | −3.83 | 30 |
| Inexpensive meals | 2.63 | −3.77 | 31 |
| Talk about trip after return | 2.30 | −3.57 | 32 |
| Live theatres and musicals | 1.85 | −2.20 | 33 |

*Source*: Based on Eagles (1992: 6).

settings, participation in physically challenging activities, mountain climbing and rafting/canoeing/kayaking more important than females. Females rated casual walking, learning about other cultures, and interpretive education programmes as more important than males. Other activities, however, were of equal importance to males and females, such as visiting national parks or protected areas, wildlife viewing, cycling, ocean sailing/kayaking and cross-country skiing. Wight (1996) also noted that the literature consistently suggested that ecotourists tended to be much better educated than general tourists. Most of the experienced ecotourists surveyed were college graduates (82 per cent), while 14 per cent had some college education. For those consumers who indicated that they had a previous ecotourism experience, there was a tendency towards a somewhat higher education level. Expenditure by ecotourists clearly varied according to many factors, including length of trip, origin of ecotourist, economic ability to pay, destination for ecotourism, type of accommodation, vacation activities, and opportunities for expenditure. Eagles and Cascagnette (1995) reported that, on average, Canadian ecotourists spent considerably more per day than general Canadian travellers, since almost 75 per cent spent $2,000 or more during the year, with the mean being approximately $5,000 (see Eagles and Higgins 1998 for more detail on the profile of Canadian ecotourists).

## American ecotourists

A survey conducted in the states of Carolina and Georgia by Backman *et al.* (1994) revealed that nature-based travellers tended to be middle-aged to senior travellers, were married and had at least some university education. They resided equally in rural and urban areas and came from white-collar occupations or were retired, with incomes of US$50,000 or above. Some of these findings were confirmed in a survey of American ecotourists by Khan and Hawkins (1997) which also reiterated some of the findings from the studies of Canadian ecotourists. The survey comprised a self-administered questionnaire which was mailed to 1,051 ecotourists who had taken a tour in the previous 18 months. There were 324 usable returns, resulting in a response rate of 32 per cent. The mailing list was provided by seven tour operators specialising in ecotourism.

The majority of ecotourists were from the 45–54-year-old group (32.2 per cent), and respondents aged 35–64 comprised 76.8 per cent of the total population. The ecotourists were 43.7 per cent male and 55.4 per cent female and approximately 55.7 per cent had attended graduate school with 38.1 per cent having attended a four-year college programme. The majority of the travellers were married (54.2 per cent), and the majority of the households comprised married couples (55 per cent), from which 20.7 per cent were married couples without children. Income levels revealed that 24.5 per cent of the ecotourists had an income of over $100,000, approximately 66.3 per cent had incomes between $50,000 and $100,000, and only 1.2 per cent had income under $20,000. Respondents living in suburban areas comprised 33.4 per cent, followed by city dwellers (28.2 per cent). Many of the respondents were employed in professional or technical occupations (34.4 per cent) and the second highest group were retired people (17.6 per cent).

A higher proportion of ecotourists took overseas trips (59 per cent) compared to 41 per cent whose trips were domestic. The majority of ecotourists had visited Alaska in the USA and places in South America. Many ecotourists had travelled with organised groups (33.7 per cent) or with family members (32.5 per cent). There were four groups of ecotourists based on the length of their trip. They comprised those who stayed one week (20.4 per cent), two weeks (52.6 per cent), three weeks (18 per cent) and over three weeks (8 per cent). More than 50 per cent stayed two weeks and the average number of nights spent on their ecotour was 13. The majority of ecotourists stayed in hotels or motels (29.7 per cent), followed by cabins (26.3 per cent) and tents (13.8 per cent). Approximately 40 per cent stayed in cabins and tents combined. Three-quarters of the ecotourists used air travel as a primary mode of transportation to arrive at their destination. The total expenditure revealed three groups of ecotourists: those who spent under $2,000 (29.4 per cent), between $2,100 and $5,000 (51.8 per cent) and over $5,000 (18.8 per cent). The mean total expenditure was $3,714. From this survey Khan and Hawkins (1997) concluded that ecotourists appeared to be older, with higher education and income levels. A majority identified themselves as white, living in suburbs and large cities. The study also revealed that the majority of the trips taken by the ecotourists were overseas, and that they travelled with an organised or family group. Ecotourists had more leisure time and disposable income to stay away from home for an average of two weeks and on average they spent $3,700 per trip. Another interesting conclusion was that ecotourists spend a lot of time planning their tours, often over six months, and their trips are not planned on the spur of the moment.

## Australian ecotourists

A number of major studies have been carried out in Australia to examine the characteristics of the ecotourist and the most notable are those by Blamey (1995) and Blamey and Hatch (1998). Blamey (1995: 1) noted that 'although some consensus appears to have been reached in favour of restrictive definitions of ecotourism, an operational definition remains elusive. What is needed is a definition that is both valid and operational, permitting estimation of the size and growth of the ecotourism market, and an ecotourist profile.' Blamey (1995) indicated that there are a number of factors that make the identification of ecotourists difficult in market research studies, where questionnaires and focus groups are involved. First, difficulties arise largely due to the multi-dimensional nature of the definitions, and the fact that each dimension represents a continuum of possibilities. Second, problems stem from the fact that ecotourism, as defined in the Australian National Ecotourism Strategy, represented both a philosophy and a market segment. Third, ecotourism may be defined with reference to either consumer intentions or actual outcomes.

In the Australian survey carried out in 1994 (Blamey 1995), of 3.1 million inbound tourists aged 15 and over, key ecotourism activities were identified as being bushwalking (13 per cent), snorkelling (13 per cent), rainforest walks (12 per cent), coral viewing (12 per cent), scuba diving (6 per cent), wild flower viewing (3 per cent), rock climbing/mountaineering (3 per cent), horse riding (3 per cent) and outback safari tours (2 per cent). Approximately half of all Australian tourists visited protected areas such as national parks, state parks, reserves or caves and 8 per cent visited Aboriginal sites. The growth rate for bush walking was particularly high among visitors from Japan (32 per cent

**Plate 4.1**   The hosting of special events such as the America's Cup in Auckland can impact upon and conflict with wildlife-based tourism, particularly through pollution and boat strikes on mammals in the marine environment.

per year), Europe (28 per cent) and Asia (19 per cent). A high growth in participation in outback safari tours was also apparent among visitors from Germany (47 per cent a year) and Japan (37 per cent). With respect to scuba diving/snorkelling, outstanding growth was found among visitors from Japan (32 per cent a year), and Europe (27 per cent), specifically Germany (19 per cent). The average expenditure by inbound visitors to national or state parks was $2,132, which was 19 per cent higher than that of inbound tourists overall. The average per trip expenditure of international visitors undertaking bushwalks during their stay was $2,824 in 1993, 58 per cent more than the average expenditure of all inbound visitors. Scuba divers and snorkellers spent 42 per cent more on average than inbound visitors as a whole, and wild flower viewers spent 49 per cent more.

A more in-depth study was carried out by the Bureau of Tourism Research in 1997 to understand the Australian ecotourism market (Blamey and Hatch 1998). It was carried out as part of the International Visitors Survey (IVS) which provided a number of key indicators on the state of the ecotourism industry including the number of international visitors to nature-based places, participation in nature-based activities, demographics of visitors and travel patterns. A supplementary survey was also conducted in 1997 to determine the motivations and satisfaction of ecotourists. This survey determined the factors that influenced people to participate in ecotourism activities or tours, the length of tours taken, activities undertaken while on the tour, tour

**Plate 4.2**    Watching whales is a new $1 billion a year industry worldwide (Source: M. Orams).

**Plate 4.3**    Land-based whale watching is also growing in popularity (Source: M. Orams).

**Plate 4.4**  Orca or killer whales form the basis of a large ecotourism industry in the Pacific North-West of North America (Source: M. Orams).

expenditure, satisfaction determinants, information used to find out about the tour, and the transport used on tour. Nature-based visitors were defined as those visitors who went to a national park or participated in either snorkelling or scuba diving, whale watching, horse riding, rock climbing or mountaineering, bushwalking or outback safari or 4WD tours. Visitors aged 20–29 years accounted for the largest share of ecotourists (36.4 per cent). They were also most likely to participate in such activities with just under half (48.7 per cent) of all visitors undertaking at least one nature-based activity. Females accounted for the greatest share of ecotourists (54.7 per cent) and they also had the greatest propensity to undertake ecotourism activities. However, it seems that females prefer the less physically demanding activities. The study found that females preferred to undertake guided walks and non-guided walks of less than 2 hours, whereas males preferred to participate in most other activities, including overnight guided walks, non-guided walks of more than 2 hours, snorkelling, scuba diving and whale watching.

Asian visitors accounted for the majority of international participants in ecotourism activities, but this merely reflected the fact that Asian visitors account for the majority of all international visitors to Australia: in 2000, Asian visitors comprised 35 per cent of all international visitors to Australia. Scandinavian visitors accounted for less than 3 per cent of all ecotourists but they had the greatest participation rate with 72.1 per cent undertaking at least one nature-based activity during their stay in Australia. Participation rates for ecotourists from other countries included those from other Europe

(58.6 per cent), UK and Ireland (52 per cent) and the Americas (48.9 per cent). Professional people accounted for the highest percentage of all ecotourists and viewing the natural beauty of the sites visited was the most important factor for most visitors. However, the chance to see or experience something new, see wildlife in detail and be close to nature was also regarded as being important.

A majority of ecotourists ranked 'a different or unique way of experiencing nature' as a very important motivation for undertaking an ecotourist activity. The majority of visitors also stated that an educational or learning experience was important (69.5 per cent). They included observing animals, plants and landscapes, being provided with information about the biology or ecology of a species or region, learning about the cultural and/or historical aspects of the area, and being provided with information about the geology or landscapes of the area.

Ecotourists found out about their tours through word-of-mouth information which had a greater effect than advertisements in newspapers, magazines and radio or television. The activities undertaken by international ecotourists in Australia in 1995 included bushwalking, scuba diving and snorkelling, rock climbing and mountaineering, horse riding and trail riding, outback safari tours and wild flower viewing. The number of visitors to national parks had grown at an annual average growth rate of 17 per cent per annum. This growth was exceeded only by that for visitation to Aboriginal sites, which grew by 30 per cent per annum. Overall ecotourists to Australia were most satisfied by the quality of the sites visited, the number of the guides on tour, the measures taken to minimise the environmental impacts of the tour, as well as the information provided about the natural environment. However, they were least satisfied with the size of tours, time spent at sites and the food provided on tours. In a recent survey of ecotourists to Queensland, the research found that visitors were from professional and administrative occupations, with a tertiary or further degree and incomes in excess of A$60,000 per annum (http://www.tq.com.au/qep/snapshot).

## Ecotourism in the Northern Territory, Australia

An assessment of tourists' understanding of the term 'ecotourism' was carried out during a survey of tourist expectations and levels of satisfaction conducted for the Parks and Wildlife Commission of the Northern Territory (Chirgwin and Hughes 1997). Three hundred and fifty-eight visitors to Fogg Dam were surveyed in the first week of June, July and August. Some 78 per cent of the respondents to the survey were Australian, 18.2 per cent were from Europe, Asia (2.4 per cent) and the Americas (2.4 per cent). Some 94 per cent of those surveyed regarded their visit to Fogg Dam as ecotourism. Wildlife and birdlife were listed as highlights. The participants stated that an ecotourism experience was nature-based (natural area and wildlife abundant), it educated those involved and was sustainably managed. Those that responded with 'meaningless jargon' were scathing about the use of the term claiming that it was 'a marketing ploy', or just another example of the proliferation of terms that

cultural attractions, including the summit, birds and other wildlife, cool climate, and hill-tribe people. The number of birders in the park has doubled from 1989 to 1993. About 400 people live in the park, and a further 8,000 live within 5 km of it. Responses were obtained from a total of 857 individuals.

Members of the first cluster were labelled 'birding ecotourists' and were motivated primarily by their wish to see birds and wildlife (Hvenegaard and Dearden 1998). Almost all watched wildlife, hiked on trails and stayed more than one day at DINP. The average length of stay was longer for birding ecotourists (about 3.2 days) than other tourist types (about 1.1 days). This cluster visited the largest number of sites in the park, including information centres and trails known for their abundance of birds. Respondents in the second cluster were labelled 'general ecotourists'. They tended to call themselves eco/nature tourists and none called themselves general tourists. Motivations focused on the natural environment and scenery. Over half watched wildlife, and about a quarter hiked on trails and stayed more than one day at DINP. Common sites visited were waterfalls, hilltribe villages, chedis, information centres, Angka Luang Trail and the summit.

The third cluster all called themselves general tourists. They had diverse motivations, with a special interest in scenery. Less than a third watched wildlife, and only a few sites were visited. This cluster was labelled 'highlights general tourists'. The fourth cluster called themselves travellers and none called themselves general tourists. About a third of this cluster watched wildlife and hiked on trails. This cluster was labelled 'highlights travellers'. The last cluster considered themselves travellers or general tourists. This cluster only visited two sites in the park and few watched wildlife. They all participated in organised hilltribe treks and as a result were labelled 'trekkers'. This study provided a framework for segmenting ecotourists from other tourist types, and then comparing their conservation interest and involvement. The results allowed a five-part tourist typology to be developed based on researcher perceptions, and respondent perceptions, activities and motivations: these were travellers, tourists, trekkers, ecotourists and birding ecotourists (Hvenegaard and Dearden 1998). Ecotourists were more involved in conservation at their home than other tourist types, but financial donations to conservation in the destination country was low and did not vary among tourist types. Even though birding and general ecotourists were older and more educated than other tourist types, each type contains people from most sociodemographic groups. Ecotourists were more likely to watch wildlife, hike on trails, and stay longer at their destination than other tourist types. They are primarily motivated to see birds and other wildlife, and secondarily to experience the natural environment. Ecotourism growth in Thailand is constrained by the lack of qualified nature guides and limited infrastructure for ecotourism activities such as wildlife viewing.

## Africa

Ecotourism has emerged as a major element of the growing market for tourism in Africa, especially as destinations seek to develop niche products which appeal to high-spending visitors (Dieke 2000). A great deal of the existing research has been focused on beach tourism and strategies to develop Western forms of tourism, despite concerns over the appropriateness of this form of development (Dieke 1995, Brown 1998). While conventional forms of tourism may be more suitable for the developed world, ecotourism has led to a number of interesting experiments in Africa (see Honey 1999 for more detail of developments in Kenya, Zanzibar and South Africa). Despite this growing interest in ecotourism in African tourism development, there has been little research on the characteristics of ecotourists in Africa. For this reason, it is pertinent to focus on one useful study by Obua and Harding (1996) in Uganda.

Obua and Harding (1996) surveyed visitors in Kibale National Park, between October 1994 and June 1995. Their aim was to assess the characteristics of visitors and their attitudes towards the recreation site and facilities. The questionnaire was divided into three main parts, each covering different subjects. In part one, the questions sought information on visitors' travel and demographic characteristics. The first sequence asked visitors how they arrived at Kibale, the purpose of their visit, whether they were visiting for the first or second time, and how they came to learn about the park as a place to visit. Visitors were asked whether their visit was influenced by any publicity material about Kibale, whether their visit was planned beforehand, and the main reason for choosing to visit. To obtain their perception of forest/park conservation, the sequence ended with questions on the idea of protected areas/parks and whether this was important in their decision to visit. Part two concentrated on activity participation, as well as preferences and attitudes towards management of the site and facilities.

The survey found that 91.5 per cent of the visitors were from overseas, and 8.5 per cent were Ugandans. About half of the foreign visitors were from Europe, and the rest were from Australia, New Zealand, North America and other countries. The visitors were predominantly aged between 25 and 44, and more than half of them were females. The average group size was eight, comprising about three males and five females. Over four-fifths of the visitors said they were on vacation. Nearly all (96 per cent) were visiting for the first time, and only 3 per cent were visiting for the second time. The majority (85 per cent) of the visits were planned beforehand, and very few visitors (15 per cent) said they came on local advice. Visitors gave various reasons for choosing to visit the national park. About three-quarters stated their main reason for visiting was to view the wildlife, while over one-half gave the forest and its diversity as the second major reason. Almost half of the visitors visited the park for its tropical setting or to interact with the local people. Of the 10 major activities visitors participated in at Kibale, wildlife viewing, birdwatching, nature walks, hiking and relaxing were the most enjoyed.

The results show that visitors had low opinions about the facilities at Kibale and the common feeling was that most of the facilities were generally poor. However, the visitors were impressed by the trails which the majority felt were good. Others felt that the car park, map and area information service, and the resting huts were satisfactory. These findings are not unusual for two reasons. First, forest ecotourism is still fairly new in Uganda, so it can be argued that the managers of Kibale lacked the experience required for maintaining good standards of recreational facilities. Second, it appeared the management had concentrated more attention on the conservation than on recreation management. Asked whether they would return at a future date, 87 per cent of visitors stated that they would if it were possible. The survey found that more than four-fifths of the visitors stayed less than one day at the park; 35 per cent stayed from two to five days, and a very small proportion (1 per cent) stayed more than five days. The visitors shared two major views. The first was that no additional facilities should be provided at the park and the second was that the number of visitors should be kept low. This illustrated how visitors are concerned about preserving the park in a natural state and such suggestions need to be taken seriously, especially when they come from visitors.

Most visitors (52 per cent) were university graduates and about one-third were graduates from colleges. A smaller proportion (10 per cent) were secondary-school leavers. About 70 per cent of visitors were employed either in government or the private sector, and about 10 per cent were self-employed. Compared with the local visitors, the monthly earnings of foreign visitors were about 20 times higher and this could be the major reason why very few Ugandans visited the park. Nearly all the people visiting Kibale National Park were overseas tourists. The majority were young to middle-aged adults with far fewer older people. Many were on vacation and were visiting for the first time. The majority of trips are planned beforehand and visitors come mainly to view wildlife, to camp and relax in the forest. This study has shown that many people visit Kibale because of the need for direct contact with nature. One suggestion raised by visitors was the provision of extra access into the park for unguided walks. This suggestion could have been prompted by the desire for quiet and solitary moments in the forest.

## Summary

By investigating the profiles of ecotourists from several parts of the world, it is evident that different destinations have different ecotourism profiles. Therefore, an 'ecotourist' cannot be exactly defined, but they can be assumed to be a certain type of visitor based on a set of broad characteristics. From the preceding studies which have been undertaken on ecotourists, it is evident that ecotourists tend to be older than other tourists, with higher education and income levels. They have more leisure time and disposable income, and are serious travellers who know what they are looking for from their trips and experiences, taking a great deal of time to pre-plan and organise their travel and trip. There also appear to be slightly more female than male ecotourists although there may be some exceptions to this as a number of studies pointed out. Therefore while one can make assumptions about who 'ecotourists' are, there are no universal models or guidelines on who is an ecotourist. Different ecotourism destinations may attract different profiles of ecotourists, and this may also vary according to the type of definitions different destinations use. Rather than establish a rigid definition of the ecotourist, a set of broad characteristics may instead be established or at the least a range of parameters within which 'ecotourist' as a term may fit, until more research is undertaken on the similarities and differences among the ecotourists in different destinations globally. Fennell (1999) stated that as more studies of this nature surface in the future it will be interesting to see how the profile of the ecotourist changes (or stays the same) as a function of different variables, including the types of experiences and products offered to ecotourists, and the maturity of the industry. As Eagles and Higgins (1998: 36) poignantly observed,

> The number of people desiring to experience nature through travel is increasing. Ecotourists are primarily interested in learning about nature firsthand. They want to see, feel and experience wildness. While it is the job of the ecotourist industry to provide the services, programs and sites to fulfill this need, it is also important to understand the social, environmental and business implications of this growing sub-sector.

For this reason, the next chapter focuses on the ecotourism industry and the different facets of a business which has developed to service the needs of ecotourists.

## Questions

1. What explanations have been advanced by tourism researchers to explain the growth of the tourist typology broadly defined as 'ecotourism'?
2. What criteria would you use to establish a working definition of the term 'ecotourist'?
3. What are the principal characteristics of an ecotourist?
4. How useful are profile studies of ecotourists in explaining what motivates them to undertake such as experience?

## Further reading

One of the best sources available to review market studies is:

Eagles, P. and Higgins, B. (1998) 'Ecotourism market and industry structure', in K. Linberg *et al.* (eds), *Ecotourism: A Guide for Planners and Managers*, vol. 2, North Bennington: Ecotourism Society, 11–43.

A number of market studies are reviewed in:

Honey, M. (1999) *Ecotourism and Sustainable Development: Who Owns Paradise?* Washington, DC: Island Press.

Also see a recent overview of the ecotourism market:

Wight, P. (2001) 'Ecotourists: not a homogenous market segment', in D. Weaver (ed.), *Encyclopedia of Ecotourism*, Wallingford: CAB International, 37–62.

# Chapter 5

# The ecotourism industry

The development of a green awareness within the global tourism industry, as discussed in Chapters 2 and 3, has created a growth in commercial enterprises which have sought to develop products and experiences to match the demand for eco-experiences. Critics of the international tourism industry's development of green products as a means of capitalising upon the ecotourism boom led Honey (1999: 51) to comment that

> Much of what is marketed as ecotourism is simply conventional mass tourism· wrapped in a thin veneer of green. Ecotourism lite is propelled by travel agents, tour operators, airlines and cruise lines, large hotel chains, and international tourism organisations, which promote quick, superficially 'green' visits within conventional packages.

What this critique suggests is that the tourism industry is a purveyor of experiences and highlights the need to understand a number of issues before one can assess the extent to which Honey's (1999) comments are valid or simply rhetoric. In particular, one needs to consider the extent to which the resultant ecotourism operations that have developed globally are merely green labelled businesses, and to recognise market trends or operations which can be classified as bona fide ecotourism businesses, based on a range of criteria used to define such activities.

Yet prior to reviewing such issues, a number of questions need to be considered which are fundamental to any understanding of ecotourism as a business activity – What is the tourism industry as an economic phenomenon? How does it operate as a business? What is the nature of its activities? How is it regulated and what are the characteristics of the ecotourism industry? – if one accepts the premise that ecotourism is a subset of the tourism sector. These may seem simplistic issues and yet there is comparatively little research which examines the tourism industry as a phenomenon (see Page *et al.* 2001 for more detail), and a lack of conceptual analysis of the tourism industry. As a consequence, this chapter commences with a discussion of frameworks and issues which are helpful in understanding the complexity and interrelationships which exist within the tourism industry as a phenomenon known as supply-side analysis and how the tourism industry is regulated. This is followed by a discussion of the structure and organisation of the ecotourism industry and its different components since 'ecotourism suppliers (government or industry) seem particularly interested in developing supply in response to market demand' (Wight 1993b: 56). Therefore, 'Rather than trying to define ecotourism by specific products, it is more valuable to recognise that there is a spectrum of experiences (products) which may be supplied' (Wight 1993b: 57) which develops the theme of the tourist experience examined in Chapter 4. This also highlights the need to recognise how the ecotourism experience is delivered in its constituent parts and assembled for the tourist.

## Supply issues in tourism: conceptual issues

To meet the demand for ecotourism, businesses and operators can employ a range of concepts to analyse what they need to do to match supply to demand. What needs to be emphasised in any discussion of supply issues is that the supply of itself is not sufficient to stimulate ecotourism development but can be a catalyst if it is integrated as part of a wider strategy to develop attractions, accommodation and an ecotourism experience. There is a relative paucity of research on supply issues in tourism (Eadington and Redman 1991).

The absence of any synthesis of supply-related research which integrates tourism supply overlooks a fundamental assumption that the efficient management and operation of tourism systems for tourists requires that demand issues are analysed in relation to supply, since the two issues coexist and they determine the future pattern of use and activities which occur in time and space. Ecotourism is no exception to this. In fact, with the likely impacts that can occur in sensitive environments, the analysis of demand issues in relation to supply, particularly the products and experiences which operators are offering in spatial terms, is critical to the long-term sustainability of the resource base. Tourism supply is a complex phenomenon because of both the nature of the product and the process of delivery. Principally, it cannot be stored, cannot be examined prior to purchase, it is necessary to travel to consume it, heavy reliance is placed on both natural and man-made resources and a number of components are required, which may be separately or jointly purchased and which are consumed in sequence. It is a composite product involving transport, accommodation, catering, natural resources, entertainment and other facilities and services, such as shops and banks, travel agents and tour operators (Sinclair and Stabler 1997: 58).

Many businesses supply components which are combined to form the tourism product, and because they operate in different markets, this makes it difficult to analyse supply issues. In fact, it proves even more complex when seeking to separate out one element of the tourism product (i.e. transport) to identify the range of supply issues affecting an individual element. Sinclair and Stabler (1997) inferred that one can explain how firms operate under different economic conditions and therefore it may be possible to identify factors which affect supply issues in relation to tourism in general, and ecotourism in particular. While it is not possible to present a detailed analysis here, the main principles outlined by Sinclair and Stabler (1997) are discussed as they focus on four market situations in which tourism enterprises operate:

- perfect competition;
- contestable markets;
- monopoly;
- oligopoly.

This has an important bearing on both the tourism industry in general and the ecotourism industry in particular, since many of the enterprises can operate in a range of market conditions. In any analysis of supply issues, a range of criteria also need to be investigated in relation to different market conditions including (after Sinclair and Stabler 1997: 83):

- the number and size of firms;
- the extent of market concentration;
- entry and exit barriers;
- economies/diseconomies of scale and economics of scope;
- costs of capital, fixed capital and costs of operation;
- price discrimination and product differentiation;
- pricing policies (e.g. price leadership, price wars and market-share strategies).

Supply research in tourism is sometimes perceived as descriptive, lacking intellectual rigour and sophisticated methods of study, since 'generally there is little research on the tourism industry and its operation which is analytical in emphasis' (Sinclair and Stabler 1997: 2). However, by considering a range of theoretical perspectives and conceptual issues it may be possible to understand the tourism industry in a more holistic manner by applying concepts from other fields of study such as economics.

In the context of tourism supply, P.J. Buckley (1987) noted that the analysis of a firm or company is characterised by certain relationships within the organisation and with its purchasers or consumers. The external process of selling a product or service involves a transaction between two parties following an agreement to purchase often, though not exclusively, involving a monetary transaction. Commercial transactions are based on agreed conditions and enforced within a framework of contractual obligations between each party. Therefore, transaction chains develop to link the tourist with the suppliers of services in tourism, and the 'tourism product or service' is defined as the sum of these transactions (Witt *et al.* 1991: 81). Such research highlights the significance of the 'chain of distribution' for tourism services, which is the method of distribution of the service from production through to the eventual consumption by tourists.

## Transaction analysis to understand supply issues in tourism

P.J. Buckley (1987) described some typical transaction chains for tourism which identify the integral role of transport services in linking origin and destination areas (see Figure 5.1). The nature of the specific supply chain depends upon a wide range of factors which are internal and external to individual firms in the tourism sector. For example, what is the primary force driving the supply system? Is it driven by pull factors, where a tourist destination may market ecotourism to stimulate demand for tourism? Or, is it driven by

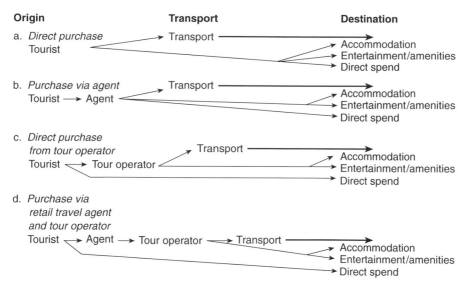

The broken line indicates opportunity for brokerage. Food may be included with accommodation or be in 'direct spend'.
———→ Transaction chain
———→ Tourist travel (to a domestic or international destination)
**Figure 5.1**   Four types of tourism transaction chain (redrawn from Page 1999, based on Witt *et al.* 1991)

push factors, where the tourist generates the demand for ecotourism experiences, and the tour operator and accommodation sectors respond to this as a commercial opportunity? The overall business environment, government predisposition to tourism and planning constraints (i.e. tourism policy issues) may also have a moderating influence on the supply system. In addition, transaction analysis illustrates the significance of 'agents' in the system, corporate policy in transport provision and contractual arrangements in the supply chain.

One of the critical issues in the distribution system for the seller is access to superior information on available services, so that these can be sold to the consumer. There are various studies which document tourism retailing (e.g. Holloway and Robinson 1995), where the agent or broker is normally paid a commission on their sales. The travel agent comprises a convenient one-stop location for tourists to buy tourism services as an inclusive package, which includes transport and accommodation, usually marketed through the medium of a brochure. The packaging of these products or services (much of the literature interchanges these terms) by wholesalers (e.g. tour operators) reduces the tourists' transaction costs of purchasing each element independently. Thus a travel agent normally receives around 10 per cent for a sale of a holiday marketed by a tour operator, but the overall cost to the consumer is markedly lower than arranging the same components independently. However, in the case of air tickets, commissions to agents are declining as airlines seek to reduce this expense in competitive market conditions. The tour operator is able to reduce the number of transactions involved by packaging a holiday, thereby making economies in the supply through wholesale purchasing and by entering into long-term contracts with the suppliers of accommodation and transport services. Not only does this have benefits for the price charged to the purchaser, but it has more beneficial effects for the supplier as the number of intermediaries or brokers in the chain are eliminated by large tour operators and airlines who control a significant part of the distribution system. In the case of ecotourism, one has to assess the extent to which this situation with regard to the control of the supply chain is replicated within the industry structure.

## Policy issues in the supply of tourism services

To achieve the government's objectives for the tourism sector, policies are formulated to guide the organisation, management and development of tourist and non-tourist sectors. This is normally followed by specific measures which seek to implement the policies through planning measures. For example, in the case of tourism development, this will often require national governments to invest in, or encourage private sector organisations to invest in, new infrastructure which may be dedicated to tourist travel such as airports. Conversely it may, more typically, require governments to develop policies and planning measures which expand and develop national, regional and local infrastructure to accommodate tourist and recreational travel alongside the use for commuting and non-tourist travel, and other forms of tourism infrastructure such as accommodation. Public sector involvement in tourism at national government level is designed to facilitate, control and in some cases regulate or deregulate the activities of private sector operators with a view to 'looking after the public's interests and providing goods whose costs cannot readily be attributed to groups or individuals' (Pearce 1990: 32).

Since the private sector's primary role is revenue generation and profit maximisation from tourism, the government's role is to promote and protect the interests of the consumer against unfair business practices, and to ensure safety standards are maintained to protect the interests of employees in large- and small-scale tourism operations. This normally requires the development of policies. The term 'policy' is frequently used to denote the direction and objectives an organisation wishes to pursue over a set period of time. According to Turner (1997), the policy process is a function of three interrelated issues:

- the intentions of political and other key actors;
- the way in which decisions and non-decisions are made;
- the implications of these decisions.

The policymaking process is a continuous process and Figure 5.2 outlines a simplified model of the policy process which is applicable to the way tourism issues are considered by government bodies. In a tourism context, Hall and Jenkins (1995) examine the issue of policymaking in more detail and it is a useful source to consult. What Hall and Jenkins (1995) also highlighted, as did Page et al. (2001), is that the public sector is also responsible for the coordination of many organisations and agencies which are involved in the production of tourism services as well as the management of this large body

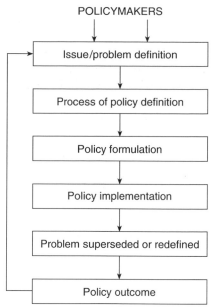

POLICYMAKERS

Issue/problem definition

Process of policy definition

Policy formulation

Policy implementation

Problem superseded or redefined

Policy outcome

**Figure 5.2**    The policymaking process

known as the tourism industry. Policy informs this management process. In the case of ecotourism, this policy process also has a significance for the environment, which is the underlying resource base upon which much of the ecotourism industry depends.

Hjalager (1996) argued that innovation is one way in which future tourism policies could limit tourism impacts on the environment which has a synergy with the needs of ecotourism. This required policy to regulate tourism by directing tourists, local people and the tourism industry through legislation, and through the provision of infrastructure. In the case of the regulation of the ecotourism industry, much of this has been conducted by industry groups and it is examined in more detail in relation to the management issues which ecotourism businesses face in Chapter 8. Therefore, the analysis of tourism supply issues identified those which are important to focus on when considering ecotourism as a specific sector of the tourism industry. The following section examines some of the characteristics of the different sectors which comprise the ecotourism industry.

## The ecotourism industry: structure and characteristics

Lindberg and McKercher (1997) suggested that several changes have occurred in the development of ecotourism in the last decade. As emphasised in Chapter 3, these changes include first, the desire for more educative and challenging vacations, combined with an increased environmental awareness, which has led to a growth in visitation at many natural areas, particularly in developing countries. Secondly, many economic development professionals view ecotourism as an opportunity for employment generation in regions that have experienced

**Plate 5.1** Small groups and the use of a local tour guide is a hallmark of ecotourism in its purist form, where local knowledge and expertise are accompanied by education of visitors in their impact on the environment they are visiting. This group is on a forest ecotour in South Western Australia.

decline, or lack of development, in other industries. Third, many conservation and resource management professionals view ecotourism as an avenue for providing conservation-supporting benefits. Finally, ecotourism is regarded as being a sustainable tourism activity, and an exemplar for all other aspects of the tourism industry. Therefore, against this context of underlying change, it is not surprising to find that a distinct industry form – the ecotourism industry – has emerged to capitalise upon the commercial opportunities afforded by the growth in ecotourism activity.

Epler Wood (1998a: 46) provided a basic overview of the structure of the ecotourism industry and this is expanded and revised as outlined in Figure 5.3. What Epler Wood (1998a) identified was a transaction chain which started with the purchase of the travel in the area of origin through to utilising the product in the destination region. Within this transaction chain, a range of bodies were involved in mediating the experience of ecotourism between the consumer and the destination, which typically involved travel agents (retailers), outbound tour operators (wholesalers), inbound and ground operators, accommodation providers (often in ecolodges) through to local vendors. In common with the supply of products and services in the tourism industry, the ecotourism industry has a range of travel agents which operate as retail operations selling both land and air travel products for commission. Outbound tour operators act as the principal sales and marketing organisations in the industry, but many of them also work at the retail level via direct mail advertising

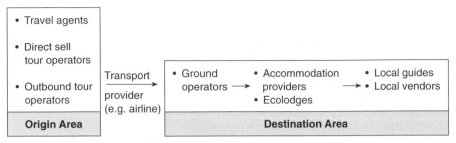

Figure 5.3   The structure of the ecotourism industry

(and increasingly through the world wide web and through e-commerce – see Page *et al.* 2001 for more detail on the use of this form of technology in the tourism industry). It is the outbound tour operators which create the brand names that sell ecotourism. Their inbound counterparts in the destination areas are responsible for the tour operations in destination countries consisting of travel, tours, accommodation and sightseeing. It is also apparent that there is a weakly developed interface between the tourism industry and the public sector in many destinations, as ecotourism is a fledgling industry that is only beginning to emerge as a sector of interest. For example, Carter and Davie (1996) suggested ecotourism in the Pacific was in a developing phase, yet in contrast with Australia, tourism development in the Pacific is viewed as embracing culture, benefiting local communities, and fostering environmental protection and management. In contrast, Australian ecotourism was a markedly different product focused on natural icons and largely ignoring the cultural elements of the landscape, which highlights the differentiation that was developing among ecotourism destinations in the 1990s.

In common with the wider development of the tourism industry, small businesses characterise the ecotourism industry (although other larger operators exist in the subsidiary activities such as transportation – see Page 1999). Epler Wood (1998: 58–9) stated that

> ecotourism is a creative, entrepreneur-driven industry in its first generation of development. There are no publicly owned ecotourism companies to date. Even the largest ecotourism lodge development chains are still launched with no more than $25 million, and most lodges are built for well under $1 million . . . efforts to create franchises and brand names for ecotourism are still in the early phases of development. And, so, for the time being, it remains a very personal business of individual owners, not large corporations.

Indeed, Eagles and Higgins (1998: 15) argued that 'As the size and complexity of ecotourism businesses has grown [*sic*], so has the variety of ecotourism consulting and supporting businesses . . . [and] . . . The diversity in size, location and orientation of ecotourism businesses pose a challenge for the understanding of the business structure supporting ecotourism.' This is reflected in The Ecotourism Society (1997) international membership directory which has the following categories of businesses listed: inbound tour operator, outbound tour operator, retail travel agency, hotel/lodging facility or campground, protected area, architect/landscape architect, green product supplies, developer, banking/ finance, consultant, guide/interpreter, public relations/marketing, engineer-renewable energy, cruise line and marketing research (cited in Eagles and Higgins 1998: 15). For this reason, it is pertinent to examine these different elements of the ecotourism industry in more detail as outlined in Figure 5.3 to consider the organisation, scale and scope of the industry.

## Travel agents in the ecotourism industry

According to Epler Wood (1998a: 47)

> Travel agencies have never played a big role in the nature travel or adventure industry, and are not having much luck in moving into the ecotourism market either. The main explanation for this is that travel agents do not have the time to educate themselves about ecotours at a time when many travel agencies are struggling to cope with reduced commissions.

However, as Honey (1999: 41) argued

> Although the functions of tour operators and travel agents often blur and overlap, generally travel agents are retailers who sell airline tickets and off-the-shelf packages put together by overseas tour operators. These packages are featured in brochures and distributed through the national network of travel agencies. The bulk of the retail trade consists of package tours. A package usually includes airfare, ground and internal air transportation, accommodation, some or all meals, transfers from airports to hotels, visa and other fees and taxes, often park entrance fees, and excursions, such as white-water rafting, mountain climbing, and balloon rides – in short, all but incidentals, souvenirs, and tips. A package has a fixed departure date, length of stay, itinerary, cost, and minimum (and often maximum) number of tourists.

In the USA, Honey (1999) estimated that 75–80 per cent of travellers book their products through travel agents. In terms of ecotourism, some travel agents have begun to sell eco-experiences, but this is normally an offshoot of a main holiday product as only a few are selling packages from ecotourism wholesalers. As Honey (1999) found, the American Association of Travel Agents (ASTA) in 1991 listed 500 companies selling environmental themes. Yet The Ecotourism Society disputed such claims and argued that travel agents had not played a major role in selling ecotourism products. What this debate highlights is the need to focus on the tour operator sector where the products are assembled and sold, often directly to consumers.

## Ecotourism tour operators

According to Eagles and Higgins (1998: 15)

> A key component of this industry is the outbound operator who arranges itineraries and market tours directly to clients. Though many operators are privately owned, a substantial number are non-profit, environmental organisations providing ecotravel for their members. Some outbound operators act as wholesalers and other outbound operators.

Table 5.1  Ziffer's Spectrum

| Ziffer's spectrum | Added subdivisions |
|---|---|
| NATURE-BASED TOURISM | |
| 1)(a) Tour operators that sell nature, and who are unaware or uncaring about its impact | (b) Operators that are aware of impacts, do the minimum to abide by any management rules, who do not seek to educate or change tourists' attitudes, but may provide information |
| 2) Sensitive tour operators | (a) Aware of impacts, actively seek to educate tourists by providing information |
| | (b) Actively seek to influence tourists' attitudes and behaviour. Support conservation, e.g. members of conservation groups |
| | (c) Practise minimum impact tourism (over and above management requirements), e.g. pack out rubbish, rotate sites |
| 3) Donors (in that they give something back to the environment) | (a) Act positively to improve the environment they use and restore damage |
| 4) Doers (those who initiate conservation projects or research) | Those involved actively in influencing policy and management towards sustainable practices |
| ECOTOURISM | |

Source: Ziffer (1989).

In a study by Ziffer (1989) representing the diversity of the tour operator sector in the field of ecotourism, a spectrum was devised (see Table 5.1) which developed an important argument that has subsequently characterised much of the debate within the academic literature. This argument posited that a continuum existed along which one could locate tour operators, dependent upon their ability to meet the criteria one established to define ecotourism operators. As Table 5.1 shows, at one end of the continuum was a range of nature-based tour operators who sell nature-related tours but who do not qualify as ecotour operators. At the other extreme were the 'donors' and 'doers' who fit within the definition of ecotourism which Ziffer (1989) used. This argument requires one to engage in the development of guidelines of what constitutes an ecotourism tour operator. According to Toplis (1994: 18) guidelines from The Ecotourism Society and the Ecotourism Association of Australia advocated that operators should:

- have pre-departure programmes to prepare travellers to minimise their negative impacts when visiting environments with a fragile culture or natural elements;
- have guiding programmes to prepare travellers for their encounters with nature and cultures through briefings and literature;

- have monitoring programmes so that group sizes are small enough to minimise impacts;
- have management programmes where managers and staff can help avoid unnecessary impacts and ongoing staff development programmes to maintain knowledge on good practice. The programmes should also contribute to the conservation of regions visited and local employment wherever possible;
- ensure that the local community benefits from the ecotourism activities and local accommodation should be available that is appropriate to the local context which also facilitates local understanding of the environment being observed.

This debate on what constitutes ecotourism has led many of the purist researchers to focus almost entirely on nature-based tour operators, particularly the small-scale operators, as a basis for maintaining a clear focus on ecotourism, what Ziffer (1989) described as the 'doers' and 'donors'. As a result a number of studies have been undertaken, particularly in the Americas on ecotourism operators.

However, Higgins (1996) found that there were 83 outbound operators in the USA which reflected the youthful state of the market in the mid-1990s. As Eagles and Higgins (1998) found, the number of studies of outbound operators are limited as reflected in the findings of Ingram and Durst (1989), Sorensen (1991), Rymer (1992), Higgins (1996) and Yee (1992). In the USA, Honey (1999) found that there was no licensing procedure for tour operators, since a US$250,000 bond is required to join the United States Tour Operator Association. The outbound operators usually subcontract with an inbound operator to meet tourists at the airport or point of entry and handle the tourists in the destination area.

Within the USA the baseline study of ecotourism operators was undertaken by Ingram and Durst (1989) which examined the Speciality Travel Index to derive 78 firms within the tour operator sector. The businesses had clients ranging from 20 to 3,000, and only 3 firms dealt with more than 1,000 clients a year. The most frequent destinations the operators visited were: Kenya, Nepal, Tanzania, Puerto Rico, Mexico, Brazil, Paraguay and Ecuador. A later study by Rymer (1992) also using the Speciality Travel Index in the USA calculated that approximately 75,727 ecotours a year were undertaken. In Australia, Weiler (1993) examined 59 tour operators who undertook ecotours while Eagles and Wind (1994) surveyed 347 operators in Canada. Comparatively few studies have been undertaken of inbound operators, and the most notable was Wilson's (1987) study of five Ecuadorian tour agencies and Place's (1988, 1991) case studies of Tortuguero in Costa Rica. What has emerged from the existing research has been a useful review by Higgins (1996) which summarised many of the findings from the published (and a number of unpublished) studies. This was an attempt to update, expand and develop the earlier study by Ingram and Durst (1989) to gauge changes in the ecotourism operator sector in the USA.

Higgins (1996) undertook a survey of 82 of the US nature-based tour operators in 1994. Of these 82, only 9 had been in operation in 1970. What was important in this study was the growth in the scale of tourists which the operators had handled during the period since Ingram and Durst's (1989) study. Some 73 of the 82 operators dealt with a range of clients from 25 to

15,000, and an average per operator of 1,674. In 1994, the number handling in excess of 1,000 clients a year rose to 35 while the number of firms beginning to consolidate on this growth was reflected in the five tour operators who handled 49,012 clients and some 40 per cent of the market. This degree of market concentration replicates much of what has happened globally in the tour operator sector (see Page *et al.* 2001 for more detail) as a growing market leads to competition, market development strategies and a greater degree of concentration (see Sinclair and Stabler 1997 for a fuller discussion of the economic theory behind such behaviour from tourism firms). What was also notable from Higgins's (1996) study was that the Speciality Travel Index in the USA was only listing 30 per cent of the nature-based tour operators. In fact Eagles and Higgins (1998: 16) rightly acknowledged the importance of the USA as an outbound market and major driver of the global ecotourism industry since 'these U.S. operators collectively guide over 100,000 ecotourists annually, [and] the particular destinations, countries and world regions they utilise have a profound impact on the global structure of ecotourism'. In the case of the USA much of the interest is focused on Central America. It is also important as Eagles and Higgins (1998) argued, to acknowledge the growing role of independent travellers and who do not use tour operators and who make their own arrangements and deal directly with inbound operators in the destination area, although there is a paucity of research on this area.

In the UK, Holden and Kealy (1996) undertook a survey of UK outbound tour operators in relation to those which claimed to offer green or environmentally friendly images. This was used as a basis for examining the ecotour market, using a list of operators from the Green Holidays section of the *Directory of Real Holidays* compiled by the Association of Independent Tour Operators (AITO), members of Green Flag International, the *Travel Trade Gazette Directory*, the *Green Magazine – Guide to Holidays* and holiday supplements in national newspapers. What their research focused on was 45 operators, a 39 per cent sample of the known population of possible operators. Table 5.2 shows the range of activities which the operators undertook in Europe, South East Asia, the Americas and Australasia. Among the themes described by the operators, the most popular adjectives used were 'not mass', 'adventure' and 'wildlife', while the marketing terminologies used typically involved 'special-interest tourism' (30 operators), 'adventure tourism' (18), 'responsible tourism' (17), 'green tourism' (12), 'wildlife tourism' (10), 'ecotourism' (10) among a number of other terms including 'alternative tourism', 'sustainable tourism', 'nature-tourism', 'soft tourism', 'ethical tourism' and 'appropriate tourism'. Educating the tourist emerged as a strong theme in the study and also limits to the number of tourists and tour guides, as well as being sensitive to the cultures and environments being visited. In fact 20 of the operators undertook regular monitoring of their environmental impacts and were committed to minimise impacts. Some 14 operators also contributed to charitable organisations as well as attempting to inform their clients about the local environment and culture. What the study found was that many of the operators could be classified as special-interest operations, but a

Table 5.3  Victorian Mallee: classification of tour operators

| Operator continuum | Ecotourism tour operators | | | Nature-based operators | |
|---|---|---|---|---|---|
| | (i) | (iii) | (ii) | (iv) | (v) |
| *Nature-based tourism*<br>Selling nature, unaware/uncaring of impact | | | | | |
| Aware of impact. Abide by rules, do not seek to educate | | | | * | * |
| *Shallow green sensitive*<br>Aware of impact | | | | | |
| Educate | * | * | | | |
| Educate to alter attitude and influence behaviour | * | * | * | | |
| Member of conservation group | | | | | |
| *Sensitive positive action*<br>Minimum impact tourism, rotate sites | * | | * | | |
| *Donors*<br>Constructive action to improve environment, e.g. pack out others' rubbish, plant trees, donate % trip costs to conservation, support local initiatives | * | * | | | |
| *Doers*<br>Initiate conservation projects, involved in policymaking | | | | | |
| *(Deep green) ecotourism* | | | | | |

\* Positive response.

*Source*: Burton (1998: 130).

can be classified as ecotourism operators. For this reason, discussion now turns to this issue in the Australian context.

### Ecotourism operators in Australia

Burton's (1998) study of ecotourism operators in Australia critically examined the issue of where individual operators lay on the continuum developed by Ziffer (1989), using three regions with a concentration of ecotourism operators: Victorian Mallee, the Top End in the Northern Territory (NT) and the Wet Tropics (WT) of northern Queensland (see Figure 5.4 for the location of the areas). What was notable in Burton's (1998) critique was the attempt to select three diverse and climatically different

Table 5.4  Top End: classification of tour operators

| Operator continuum | Ecotourism tour operators | | | | | | | | | Nature-based tour operators | | | | | | | |
|---|---|---|---|---|---|---|---|---|---|---|---|---|---|---|---|---|---|
| | K | I | G | N | P | Q | E | F | J | A | B | C | D | H | L | M | O |
| *Nature-based tourism* Selling nature, unaware/uncaring of impact | | | | | | | | | | | * | * | | | | | |
| Aware of impact. Abide by rules, do not seek to educate | | | | | | | | | | | * | | * | * | * | | * |
| *Shallow green sensitive* Aware of impact | | | | | | | | | | | | | | | | | |
| Educate | | | | * | | | * | | | | | | | | | | |
| Educate to alter attitude and influence behaviour. Member of conservation group | * | * | * | * | * | * | * | * | * | | | | | | | | |
| *Sensitive positive action* Minimum impact tourism, rotate sites | * | * | * | | | * | | | | | | | | * | | | |
| *Donors* Constructive action to improve environment, e.g. pack out others' rubbish, plant trees, donate % trip costs to conservation, support local initiatives | * | | | | | | * | | | | | | | | | | |
| *Doers* Initiate conservation projects, involved in policymaking | * | * | | * | | | | | | | * | | | | | | |
| *(Deep green) ecotourism* | | | | | | | | | | | | | | | | | |

\* Positive response.

*Source*: Burton (1998: 131).

regions in Australia as well as destinations with different volumes and intensity of tourist use. For example, the Victorian Mallee is a flat semi-arid desert region with national park and wilderness areas. The Top End in NT has a monsoon climate and an abundance of freshwater crocodiles and wildlife attractions and the wetland eco-systems of the Kakadu National Park. The WT area of Queensland had the greatest

Table 5.5  Queensland wet tropics: classification of tour operators

| Operator continuum | Ecotourism tour operators | | | | | Nature-based tour operators | | | |
|---|---|---|---|---|---|---|---|---|---|
| | 3 | 5 | 6 | 1 | 2 | 4 | 7 | 8 | 9 |
| Nature-based tourism Selling nature, unaware/uncaring of impact | | | | | | | | * | * |
| Aware of impact. Abide by rules, do not seek to educate | | | | | | * | | | |
| Shallow green sensitive Aware of impact | | | | | | | | | |
| Educate | | | | * | * | | * | | |
| Educate to alter attitude and influence behaviour. Member of conservation group | * | * | * | | | | | | |
| Sensitive positive action Minimum impact tourism, rotate sites | * | * | * | | | | | | |
| Donors Constructive action to improve environment, e.g. pack out others' rubbish, plant trees, donate % trip costs to conservation, support local initiatives | | * | * | | | | | | |
| Doers Initiate conservation projects, involved in policymaking | * | | * | | | | | | |
| (Deep green) ecotourism | | | | | | | | | |

* Positive response.

Source: Burton (1998: 132).

diversity of tourism environments and resources and the most highly developed tourism industry (see Burton 1998 for more detail).

Burton (1998) surveyed those nature-oriented tour operators who were required to have a licence to operate in the three regions and this was supplemented by operator details from regional tourism organisations. The operators were stratified according to the characteristics of their tour operations (i.e. cost of tour, size of groups, visiting one or more sites and length of trip). Interviews were conducted in a structured and unstructured manner over a five-year period which also added a longitudinal element to the survey. What resulted was five interviews in the Mallee

Table 5.6   Victorian Mallee: tour operator characteristics

| | Ecotourism tour operators | | Nature-based tour operators | | |
|---|---|---|---|---|---|
| Size of business (number of full-time guides employed) | 0 + 2 PT | 1 | 0 + 5 PT | 2 + 2 PT | 2 |
| Number of tours offered | 2 | 4 | 8 + C | 10 + C | 1 + C |
| Tour operator's background | IND/P | P | IND | T | IND |
| Tour group size (maximum number) | 12 | 18 | V | 50 | 20–40 |
| Cost per person per day (A$) at date of interview | V | 45–100 | 45–120 | 30–50 | V |

*Key*: PT = part-time; P = professional; B = bushman; IND = Exploitative or other industry (excluding tourism); T = tourism industry; V = variable; C = charter.

*Source*: Burton (1998: 133).

region (a 62 per cent sample), 17 interviews in the Top End region (a 45 per cent sample) and 9 interviews in the WT area of Queensland (a 20 per cent sample). Within the research, Burton (1998) utilised Ziffer's (1989) continuum to classify operators and a definition of ecotourism derived from Valentine (1993: 108) where it was based on undisturbed natural areas, non-damaging and non-degrading tourism, should contribute to the continued protection and management of the region and is subject to an adequate management regime. The results from Burton's (1998) detailed survey are summarised in Tables 5.3–5.8 and provide operator detail which is notable by its absence in many studies of ecotourism supply issues. What these findings showed was that only one operator in the NT area and one in the WT area of Queensland met the criteria according to Valentine (1993) for an ecotourism operation. Approximately 40 per cent of the operators met the criteria for sustainable ecotourism. These findings are consistent with other studies such as Bottrill and Pearce's (1995) analysis of 22 ecotourism companies in Canada where the majority met 'reasonable standards of environmental management' but only 5 qualified as ecotourism ventures. Burton's (1998) research indicated that a gradation existed in the types of operators working within the environmental field and Tables 5.3–5.5 illustrate that those companies most likely to meet the criteria for ecotourism operations were:

● small companies employing up to three guides;
● those offering small group tours of 4–25 per tour, where small group experiences were accompanied by uncrowded environments;
● offering relatively expensive tours, in excess of A$98 at 1998 prices;
● those where the operations were run by professionals or those with a background in the Australian bush.

However, one of major issues for the businesses operating in each environment was the viability of their operations due to the scale of the experience as the

Table 5.7  Top End: tour operator characteristics

| | Ecotourism tour operators | | | | | | | | | | | | | Nature-based tour operators | | |
|---|---|---|---|---|---|---|---|---|---|---|---|---|---|---|---|---|
| Size of business (number of full-time guides employed) | 1 + 8 PT | 2 | 1 | 2 | 1 | 1 | 1 | 5 | 1 | 1 | 6 | 12 | 8 | 8 | 4 | 3 |
| Numbers of tours offered (in the case study area) | 2 (+) | 1 | 1 (+) | V | 1 | 1 | 2 | 8 | 2 | 1 | 9 | 12 | 9 | 15 | 4 | 2 |
| Tour operator's background | P | B | B | P | T | P | T | IND | B | IND | IND | T | T | IND | IND | T |
| Tour group size (max. no) | 12 | 7 | 24 | 9 | 22 | 9 | 18 | 22 | 7 | 20 | 48 | 48 | 38 | 3+ | 20 | 22 |
| Cost per person per day (A$) at date of interview | 51–95 | 105 | 182 | 60 | 95–112 | 97–247 | 45–75 | 108 | 85–210 | 62–188 | 85–260 | 114–249 | | 175–306 | 142–231 | 79–90 |

(+) also offers tours outside the case study area.

*Key:* PT = part-time; P = professional; B = bushman; IND = exploitative or other industry (excluding tourism); V = variable; C = charter.

*Source:* Burton (1998: 134).

Table 5.8  Queensland wet tropics: tour operator characteristics

| | Ecotourism tour operators | | | | | | Nature-based tour operators | | |
|---|---|---|---|---|---|---|---|---|---|
| Size of business (number of full-time guides employed) | 3 | 3 | 1 | 4 | 3 | 1 | 6 | 4 | 10 |
| Numbers of tours offered | 4 | 2 | 1 | 2 | 3 | 1 | 4 | 5 | 11 |
| Tour operator's background | P | P | P | IND | T | IND | T | T | T |
| Tour group size (max. no) | 4 | 8 | 22 | 12 | 22 | 14 | 22 | 14 | 22 |
| Cost per person per day (A$) at date of interview | 115–160 | 98 | 66 | 150 | 89–99 | 45–75 | 50–140 | 45–87 | 49–185 |

Key:  P = professional; IND = exploitative or other industry (excluding tourism); T = tourism industry.

Source: Burton (1998: 134).

non-ecotours were having less financial problems. This is an issue to which the discussion will return in Chapter 8 on the management issues for ecotourism operations. While the perceived success of ecotourism in Australia has been showcased by many organisations, there are major issues in developing, enhancing and ensuring the viability and commercial success of the high-quality ecotourism experiences which Burton's (1998) survey encountered.

## Non-governmental organisations

According to Honey (1999: 71)

> A number of environmental, educational, and scientific organisations also offer nature, adventure, study, and service tours to their members. Usually these travel programmes contract with international or inbound tour operators in the host countries. In the US the best known of these organisations include the Smithsonian Institution, The Nature Conservancy, the Audubon Society, the World Wildlife Fund, the Earthwatch Institute . . . and the Sierra Club . . . Increasingly these programmes are incorporating ecotourism principles. Although they tend to use the larger, best-advertised U.S. nature tour operators and overseas ground operators, which are not always the most innovative and responsible ecotourism outfits. The main purposes of these trips are to promote the education and professional development of members, showcase the organisations projects in other countries.

In fact Epler Wood (1998a: 54) suggested that the ecotourism industry has seen the influence of non-governmental organisations (NGOs) as purveyors of standards within the ecotourism field, marketers of non-profit, outbound travel programmes, specialists in the field of sustainable development and developers of ecotourism projects in destination countries. Indeed,

> NGOs and academic institutions which had supported the development of the tourism industry have found in ecotourism a mechanism with which to practise sustainability. In this context, they were able to have a clarified role in the industry, such as acting as intermediaries between the private sector and local interests in ecotourism development (Wearing and Neil 1999: 136).

Drumm (1998: 200) stated that conservation NGOs have become involved in the development of community-based ecotourism projects as a means of stimulating sustainable development in ecologically important areas. In such cases, the NGO often replaces the tour operator as intermediary with the market, providing funds to communities for infrastructure, promotion and training programmes. One useful example in this context is Conservation Corporation Africa.

## Conservation Corporation Africa

Conservation Corporation Africa (CCAfrica) is one of the world's largest nature-based ecotourism companies (Christ 1998). CCAfrica set out to develop the large-scale potential of the ecotourism industry – beginning on the African continent – by building a commercially successful portfolio of upmarket lodges and camps in remote wilderness areas. The company believed that by embracing the principles of ecotourism it would ensure that the wilderness areas in which it operates remain both economically viable as conversation sites and ecologically sustainable in the long term.

The corporation does not seek to own wilderness land; rather, it endeavours to create partnerships with national and regional governments and, most importantly, with the local communities intimately associated with that land. It also strives to adhere to the principles of environmentally sustainable design in the building of its lodges and camps, and environmentally friendly management in its operations. The company's motto is 'Care of the land. Care of the wildlife. Care of the people'.

CCAfrica has assets and revenues exceeding $60 million and a corporate goal of establishing 60–100 of the world's finest luxury lodges and camps (Christ 1998). In 1990, Conservation Corporation had one ecolodge, Londolozi Camp, on the western border of Kruger National Park in South Africa. By 1998 the company had within its ecotourism portfolio, four private sanctuaries (two owned, two leased) and more than 20 lodges and camps located across the African continent.

In the early stages, CCAfrica created its own Rural Investment Fund (RIF) as a direct programme and department within the company (Christ 1998). The aims of the RIF were to ensure that ecotourism activities were discussed and endorsed by the local communities, to raise funds and support local economic benefits through community development projects, and to illustrate how the private sector can address sustainable development in rural economies.

Between 1991 and 1997, CCAfrica leveraged more than $1 million through the RIF to fund development projects within communities existing next to its lodges, camps and private reserves, primarily in South Africa. These projects have included everything from building classrooms in village areas to constructing a residential health clinic serving 30,000 people in an area where only limited medical facilities previously existed (Christ 1998).

CCAfrica's Phinda Private Game Reserve (established in 1992), is a successful model of community involvement, and laid the foundation for community planning and involvement efforts at other Corporation properties (Christ 1998). Phinda was heralded as an unprecedented conservation victory and private initiative that at the time hosted the largest private game relocation programme undertaken, while painstakingly restoring in excess of 17,000 ha of degraded and bankrupt farm land, creating opportunities for rural communities and stimulating the regional economy. The reserve has four lodges, and covers an area of land with seven diverse ecosystems. Phinda is actively involved in a number of community projects including the Rural Investment Fund, training and production centres, small business development and cultural development. Phinda also conducts conservation lessons for surrounding schoolchildren with an environmental education centre planned for the near future. Phinda is an example of a successful ecotourism operation at work. In 1997, Phinda was awarded the coveted British Airways Tourism for Tomorrow Award for achieving an outstanding example of ecotourism principles put into action. It was the second time in five years that the award has gone to a CCAfrica project (Christ 1998).

Honey (1999) also observed that NGOs have also worked with government aid agencies in the USA, notably USAid which is the US Agency for International Development, and similar examples can be found in other parts of the world as ecotourism becomes a more acceptable area for investment in the development potential of less developed or developing countries seeking to harness their tourism potential. As Honey (1999) suggested it is also a means to give value to nature and a vehicle for sustainable development as well as a mechanism to promote small-scale enterprises to develop around this area of tourism without the multinational and transnational corporations taking control of the local context. One of the unsuccessful examples cited from USAid by Honey (1999) was the assistance to the Annupurna Conservation Area Project in Nepal in 1985 through the auspices of the WWF's Wildlife and Human Needs Programme. This project sought to address the adverse environmental impacts of trekkers in the region. A more recent article is examined by Mason et al. (2000) which is the involvement of the World Wide Fund for Nature in a nature Arctic project which integrated conservation ideals into tourism in Arctic locations to enable communities, tourists and operators to work towards more sustainable forms of tourism.

## Ecotourism attractions

One of the vital elements of the ecotourism industry is the very resource base upon which it depends – the areas and nature which are observed and form part of the ecotourism experience. This forms the attraction sector of the ecotourism industry and has to be recognised as the key asset to be managed and protected. A number of illustrations of this have been given within the nature tourism context, notably Ryan (1999) and saltwater crocodiles in Kakadu National Park, Australia, as tourist attractions and Shackley's (1998a) analysis of stingrays as attractions in the Cayman Islands. More psychologically grounded research by Schänzel and McIntosh (2000) considered some of the emotional and emotive aspects of wildlife tourism, while Tyler and Dangerfield (1999) explored the issue of the resource base as a vital element and the need for a resource-based philosophy for ecotourism. The role of attractions in ecotourism can be illustrated by the example of the Danube Delta in Romania.

## The Danube Delta, Romania

The 564,000 ha Danube Delta is arguably the most important wildlife area in the whole of Europe (Hall and Kinnaird 1994). As a major wetland area, it contains a diversity of species and habitats. It is located at the crossroads of several

**Plate 5.2**  The kea bird, a New Zealand parrot, at Mount Cook National Park. This bird congregates in tourist areas on the South Island in the alpine environment and is an opportunist feeder which adds a wildlife attraction for the casual visitor.

**Plate 5.3**  The Mount Cook National Park, New Zealand is an alpine environment which is rich in bird life and wildlife and a major area for adventure activities.

major bird migration routes and acting as a natural biofilter for Danubian waters, the importance of the delta extends far beyond its own borders. Four-fifths of the delta's area lies in Romania. Agriculture, fishing, tourism, reed cultivation and gravel extraction were all being considerably stepped up during the 1980s, resulting in large-scale reclamation and destruction of important habitats. The Danube Delta was declared a biosphere reserve and given international recognition as a RAMSAR site (wetland of international importance). The Danube Delta Biosphere Reserve Administration (DDBRA) was set up in September 1990.

Two clear priorities existed for the DDBRA to render 'ecotourism' an ecologically meaningful and economically profitable reality for the delta (Hall and Kinnaird 1994). First, detailed information on both the delta's human and natural resources was urgently required. Secondly, given the depressed nature of European tourism in the Balkans in general and in Romania in particular, markets for ecotourism would need to be very carefully defined and targeted. Romanian resources and expertise available for this task appeared to be minimal. Zones of protection established in the delta entailed the designation of 16 'core zones' (totalling over 50,000 ha, 10.7 per cent of the total DDBRA area), surrounded by 'buffer zones' and 'transition areas', reflecting the relative ecological importance of the delta's habitats (Hall and Kinnaird 1994: 132). A nucleus of trained and often very experienced personnel, a corp of wardens, was established, largely recruited from the local population, to serve a three-fold function:

- most obviously, to protect the area's resources from human predators – the wardens carry firearms but have no resources from human predators;
- to provide a means of skill transfer to the indigenous population;
- to assist the local population in understanding that protection of the delta is in their own economic and cultural interests.

Plans to recruit local people for employment in information centres (at 'honeypots' and 'gateways') have added a further educational dimension (Hall and Kinnaird 1994). Encouragement and assistance in the establishment of farm tourism have additionally emphasised the economic benefits of conservation and ecotourism for local people and reduce the pressures on them to intensify their agricultural practices.

What has taken place in the Danube Delta is the establishment of a model and likely precedent for reversing environmentally detrimental processes. At the same time positive, ecologically enlightened conservation policies have been instigated which are appropriate both for an important yet vulnerable natural environment and for the human population continuing to live in, and gain its livelihood from, that environment. 'Properly managed, the delta will be able to confirm that sustainable forms of tourism can have key conservation, education and economic roles in the integrated management of protected areas' (Hall and Kinnaird 1994: 128–32).

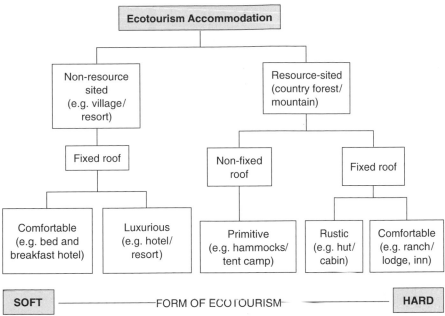

Figure 5.5  Wight's ecotourism accommodation spectrum
*Source*: Modified from Wight (1993a).

## Accommodation

As part of the accommodation sector ecolodges are emerging as a separate niche in this fast-growing segment of the tourism industry. Accommodation plays a major role in the ecotourism experience, and research by Wight (1993a, 1996) has examined the spectrum of accommodation types used by ecotourists. Wight (1993b: 57) explained that 'The accommodation offered in ecotourism operations ranges along a spectrum, from no fixed roof accommodation, through basic shelter in the form of cabins or lodges, to luxurious accommodation.' As Figure 5.5 shows, accommodation providers can be situated along a continuum meeting the needs of hard to soft types of ecotourists with different types of accommodation available (see Figure 5.5). In the case of Brazil, Wight (1993b) described the difference between on-site accommodation and off-site through to the more luxurious ecolodges. Such lodges offer accommodation, meals, local guides and nature interpretation facilities. The local vendors provide a variety of services including ground transportation services, specialised tours and interpretive guides.

One area which Fennell and Weaver (1997) examined was the vacation farm sector in Canada and its utilisation for ecotourism activities (see Table 5.9 for a list of visitor activities). As a form of rural accommodation, Fennell and Weaver (1997) examined its use in the Saskatchewan region of Canada

Table 5.9   Vacation farm visitor activities

| Activity | *n* | Mean* | SD |
| --- | --- | --- | --- |
| Wildlife viewing | 34 | 3.82 | 1.51 |
| Hunting | 36 | 3.47 | 1.73 |
| Casual photography | 35 | 3.46 | 1.22 |
| Touring | 36 | 3.31 | 1.49 |
| Hiking | 35 | 3.29 | 1.43 |
| Camping | 35 | 2.83 | 1.48 |
| Professional photography | 31 | 2.68 | 1.51 |
| Horseback riding | 34 | 2.53 | 1.69 |
| Petting zoo | 36 | 2.53 | 1.75 |
| Cultural tourism | 31 | 2.42 | 1.46 |
| Speciality meals | 37 | 2.35 | 1.57 |
| Cross-country skiing | 32 | 2.34 | 1.36 |
| Conference/retreats | 32 | 2.16 | 1.50 |
| Study/research | 32 | 2.09 | 1.30 |
| Cycling | 34 | 2.03 | 1.29 |
| Fishing | 31 | 1.90 | 1.16 |
| Snowmobiling | 30 | 1.87 | 1.20 |
| Purchasing souvenirs | 32 | 1.78 | 1.21 |
| Assist in farm work | 34 | 1.62 | 0.92 |
| Canoeing | 30 | 1.50 | 1.25 |
| Ice fishing | 30 | 1.43 | 1.86 |
| Boating | 30 | 1.33 | 0.88 |
| Barn dancing | 32 | 1.25 | 1.80 |

* Based on five-point scale: 1 = 'not at all important', 5 = 'very important'.

*Source*: Fennell and Weaver (1997: 470).

for wildlife viewing (see Table 5.10 for wildlife viewing activities) and the issues surrounding such accommodation and the development issues for operators. The majority of operators had no training or experience in ecotourism and Fennell and Weaver (1997) recognised the potential for further growth in this area. Two additional examples which illustrate the role of ecotourism and accommodation are the Coco Beach Hotel in Mauritius and Couran Cove Resort, Australia.

## Coco Beach Hotel, Mauritius

The Coco Beach Hotel has become environmentally friendly. This family-type hotel, which has always sought to integrate harmoniously with its environment, now offers to its clients ecological itineraries spread around the grounds of its vast estate of 37 ha (*New Wave Magazine* 1998a). Three paths of several hundred metres each, give the opportunity to nature lovers to discover most of the endemic plant species growing in Mauritius. The management has invested money in a nursery in which 26,000 plants patiently wait to be

Table 5.10 Wildlife viewing characteristics

| Group | | Importance | | | Mode of Viewing | | | | Season | | | | Time of day | | | |
|---|---|---|---|---|---|---|---|---|---|---|---|---|---|---|---|---|
| | | Major | Common | Minor | Foot | Boat | Vehicle | Horse | Winter | Spring | Summer | Fall | Dawn | Afternoon | Dusk | Night |
| Mammal viewing | (%) | 24.0 | 48.0 | 24.0 | 42.3 | 5.8 | 28.8 | 23.1 | 10.8 | 27.7 | 32.3 | 29.2 | 39.2 | 11.8 | 43.1 | 5.9 |
| | (n) | 6 | 12 | 6 | 22 | 3 | 15 | 12 | 7 | 18 | 21 | 19 | 20 | 6 | 22 | 3 |
| Bird viewing | (%) | 26.7 | 56.7 | 13.3 | 50.0 | 5.4 | 23.2 | 21.4 | 7.9 | 31.6 | 34.2 | 26.3 | 37.7 | 13.2 | 45.3 | 3.8 |
| | (n) | 8 | 17 | 4 | 28 | 3 | 13 | 12 | 6 | 24 | 26 | 20 | 20 | 7 | 24 | 2 |
| Reptile/ amphibian viewing | (%) | 16.7 | 25.0 | 58.3 | 50.0 | 8.3 | 25.0 | 16.7 | 0.0 | 25.0 | 41.7 | 33.3 | 30.8 | 30.8 | 30.8 | 7.7 |
| | (n) | 2 | 3 | 7 | 6 | 1 | 3 | 2 | 0 | 3 | 5 | 4 | 4 | 4 | 4 | 1 |
| Fish viewing | (%) | 9.1 | 0.0 | 90.9 | 66.7 | 16.7 | 16.7 | 0.0 | 0.0 | 30.0 | 50.0 | 20.0 | 30.0 | 10.0 | 50.0 | 10.0 |
| | (n) | 1 | 0 | 10 | 4 | 1 | 1 | 0 | 0 | 3 | 5 | 2 | 3 | 1 | 5 | 1 |
| Insect viewing | (%) | 0.0 | 46.2 | 53.8 | 62.5 | 12.5 | 12.5 | 12.5 | 0.0 | 35.7 | 42.9 | 21.4 | 22.2 | 44.4 | 33.3 | 0.0 |
| | (n) | 0 | 6 | 7 | 5 | 1 | 1 | 1 | 0 | 5 | 6 | 3 | 2 | 4 | 3 | 0 |
| Plant viewing | (%) | 26.1 | 43.5 | 26.1 | 55.9 | 0.0 | 23.6 | 20.6 | 4.4 | 33.3 | 37.8 | 24.4 | 23.5 | 35.3 | 35.3 | 5.9 |
| | (n) | 6 | 10 | 3 | 19 | 0 | 8 | 7 | 2 | 15 | 17 | 11 | 8 | 12 | 12 | 2 |

*Source:* Fennell and Weaver (1997: 471).

transferred to their new place in the grounds. It is hoped that one day all vegetation adorning the gardens may consist of endemic plants.

## Couran Cove Resort, Australia

The 567-unit Couran Cove Resort is the world's first five-star resort designed from the ground up according to sustainable engineering practice (EAA 1999). It has won numerous awards for its across the board commitment to best practice environmental management. The resort manages its own water, wastewater, gas and electricity systems and features superefficient water and energy technologies throughout, including a gas-fired power station, a wind generator and a state of the art energy management control system which controls all of the resort's major energy loads.

Gas is the sole fuel source and is reticulated across the resort for a variety of uses including gas boosting of solar hot water systems, commercial dishwashers and even cappuccino machines. There are many other innovative environmental management practices in place at the resort including electric vehicles, a native plant nursery, a worm farm that recycles all of the resort's organic wastes and even natural control of the mosquitoes. This approach has resulted in significant savings – both in terms of costs and environmental impacts. Efficient use of energy has saved over $1.5 million in upfront capital costs. And each year it saves over $1 million in operational costs (the resort uses a third of the energy of similar-sized resorts). More importantly, greenhouse gas emissions have been reduced by 70 per cent. But what is also significant is that these savings have been achieved without compromising client services in any way. The resort offers all the usual luxuries associated with a five-star hotel.

## Ecotourism associations

Many countries have established national ecotourism associations to promote the appropriate development of ecotourism (Ceballos-Lascurain 1998). These include Australia, Bolivia, Brazil, Ecuador, Estonia, Indonesia, Kenya, USA and Venezuela. Drumm (1998: 204) suggested that ecotourism associations should assist each of the sectors involved in ecotourism development to develop and implement guidelines to ensure sustainability. One of the most notable examples is The Ecotourism Society (TES) (K. Murphy 1997). It was founded in 1990, and has nearly 1,100 members from over 75 countries and 35 professions and while it now has a new name – the International Ecotourism Society – it continues a range of research, information, lobbying and educational functions through offering leadership in this growing area of tourism activity (see K. Murphy 1997 for more detail and the excellent web site on http://www.ecotourism.org.). Such organisations at the international and national and regional levels within countries are a growing area of activity which interfaces with the ecotourism industry, often as the intermediary with the public sector such as national and regional tourism organisations.

## Summary

At its best, ecotourism offers a set of principles and practices that have the potential to fundamentally transform the way the tourism industry operates (Honey 1999: 5), but it has certainly expanded in many countries worldwide as a new area of commercial and not-for-profit activity, with an antecedent demand for interpreters and guides (Shephard and Royston-Airey 2000). Christ (1998: 193) argued that final conclusions on whether ecotourism is commercially viable at the large corporate level cannot yet be drawn and the limited evidence which exists on the ecotourism industry in each country highlights a major shortcoming in the research area. The sector would appear to be dominated by small-scale operators in contrast to the tourism industry generally, and although the evidence which exists is fragmented, this small-scale activity does mean that community planning and involvement are possible which may be vital to the sustainability of the ecotourism industry itself.

McKercher (1998: 2) suggested that ecotourism plays an important role in the delivery of a world-class tourism product and the consequence of firms operating in this field is that it may:

1. help broaden a region's product base by providing ancillary services or experiences to complement mainstream accommodation and attractions;
2. provide special interest tourism experiences for niche markets;
3. provide low-cost business opportunities for people in regional centres;
4. be able to reduce adverse social and environmental impacts by providing a means of controlling tourists' activities;
5. provide a source of management funds for protected areas through licensing fees;
6. be able to spread better the message of environmental protection.

McKercher (1998: 2), using some of the evidence discussed in this chapter and more detailed international research findings, reached similar conclusions from the data since ecotourism businesses tend to be small operations lying outside the mainstream of the travel industry. The businesses are usually run by owner-operators with limited staff, are often marginally economically viable and many of them need assistance with business issues as will be examined in Chapter 8. In the Australian context McKercher (1998) suggested that ecotourism requires the adoption of a number of business skills. These include undertaking research, business planning, marketing skills, operating systems, ethical matters, environmental integrity and personal issues.

The evidence from Burton (1998) in Australia would tend to suggest that whilst ecotourism is still in its infancy in some countries, even established businesses need to undertake appropriate research in order to distinguish between opportunities and ideas and work with a realistic and dynamic business plan. In any growth sector of the tourism industry, a period of consolidation and reassessment of the viability and necessity of ecotourism operations will occur and this highlights the need for ecotourism operators to develop a business plan which can act as an internal management tool or as a map to help guide a venture to an improved competitive position. While McKercher

(1998) argued that this does not necessarily guarantee business success, it helps in the identity of uncertainties and reduces the risk to acceptable levels, particularly in what has become a competitive market and has seen some degree of integration and consolidation in the USA.

The ecotourism industry is an embryonic sector compared to the mass package market which has come to characterise the excesses and vagaries of the international tourist. While the growth of ecotourism businesses has sought to recognise changing tastes and demands from consumers, it is also apparent that the crowding of the marketplace in some instances has led to a continuum of operators which do not necessarily meet the benchmark standard for a pure ecotourism operator. These environmental tours and activities should not be confused with ecotourism, although in conceptual terms, Ziffer's (1989) spectrum is a helpful start in screening out the pure ecotourism operators. One might also argue that what the marketplace is seeing is not just a greening of the tourism product, and ecotourism lite, to reiterate Honey's (1999) critique. What is being seen is a market diversification and emergence of repositioned ecotourism products and a growth in environmentalism in the wider tourism industry and their product offerings. In philosophical terms, there is no difference here from what has happened to the tourism industry in the greening era. However, the real concerns emerge at an operational level for the ecotourism industry for one simple reason: more tourists seeking to consume nature and wilderness will raise additional impacts, particularly on sensitive environments. This leads into the concerns of the next chapter – which are the ways in which the activities of the ecotourist and ecotourism industry impact upon the resource base, communities and the economy. Without pre-empting the discussion in Chapter 6, the implications of Ziffer's (1989) spectrum of operators may highlight the need for a more tightly defined range of management tools (i.e. pricing) to limit access to the most sensitive and fragile environments. Although this raises ethical and moral issues, it may mean that the natural environment may have to be increasingly classified and managed according to principles of carrying capacity, resource capability and a continuum where tourism is screened and managed more tightly.

## Questions

1. How would you go about defining the 'ecotourism industry'?
2. How does the supply chain operate in relation to the production and retailing of ecotourism products?
3. Why should consumers be concerned about the types of ecotourism products they select from outbound tour operators? What types of questions should they ask about operators and the impact on the environment?
4. What is the value of a locally based inbound ecotourism operation?

## Further reading

For further information on the nature of the ecotourism industry see:

Eagles, P. and Higgins, B. (1998) 'Ecotourism market and industry structure', in K. Lindberg, M. Epler Wood and D. Engeldrum (eds), *Ecotourism: A Guide for Planners and Managers*, vol. 2, North Bennington: Ecotourism Society, 11–43.

Higgins, B. (1996) 'The global structure of the nature tourism industry: ecotourists, tour operators, and local businesses', *Journal of Travel Research*, **35** (2): 11–18.

For a very detailed synthesis of the situation in Australia, see the following report:

Higginbottom, K., Rann, K., Moscardo, G., Davis, D. and Muloin, S. (2001) *Status of Wildlife Tourism in Australia: An Overview*, Wildlife Tourism Report Series: Report No. 1, Status Assessment of Wildlife Tourism Series, CRC for Sustainable Tourism Research Report Series, Gold Coast University, Brisbane, Australia.

For a review of the supply issues in ecotourism see:

Sirakaya, E., Sasidharan, V. and Sonmez, S. (1999) 'Redefining ecotourism: the need for a supply-side view', *Journal of Travel Research*, **38** (2): 168–72.

For different overviews of the industry segments associated with the ecotourism industry see:

Gardner, J. (2001) 'Accommodations', in D. Weaver (ed.), *Encyclopedia of Ecotourism*, Wallingford: CAB International, 525–34.

Higgins, B. (2001) 'Tour operators', in D. Weaver (ed.), *Encyclopedia of Ecotourism*, Wallingford: CAB International, 535–48.

Weiler, B. and Ham, S. (2001) 'Tour guides and interpretation', in D. Weaver (ed.), *Encyclopedia of Ecotourism*, Wallingford: CAB International, 549–64.

McKercher, B. (2001) 'The business of ecotourism', in D. Weaver (ed.), *Encyclopedia of Ecotourism*, Wallingford: CAB International, 565–78.

# Chapter 6

# The impact of ecotourism

With the worldwide growth in ecotourism activity over the last 20 years, there is a growing concern about the cumulative impacts of tourism on the ecological resource base and environments which ecotourism utilises. As Nicholson-Lord (1997: 18) poignantly argued,

> The world, clearly, is not going to stop taking holidays – but equally clearly we can no longer afford to ignore the consequences. And if one of the major culprits has been the industrialisation of travel, a genuine post-industrial tourism, with the emphasis on people and places rather than products and profits, could turn out to be significantly more planet-friendly.

Honey (1999: 83) questioned whether ecotourism was a form of post-industrial tourism which might turn out to be the saviour of the tourism industry since 'ecotourism is not a panacea. At present it is a set of interconnected principles whose full implementation presents multi-layered problems and challenges. There are, in fact, pressing issues surrounding ecotourism that are crying out for deeper investigation', not the least of which is the impact of tourism. This chapter examines the existing literature on how to analyse the impact of tourism activity, thereby developing a framework within which to analyse the impact of ecotourism. This necessitates a discussion of impact methodologies and the economic, sociocultural and environmental impacts of ecotourism. An understanding of these issues is fundamental to any debate which seeks to attribute the costs and benefits of ecotourism in specific locations, and make overall assessments on the role of ecotourism in tourism development in specific locations. The principles of ecotourism activity, as small scale and locally based, are often used to justify its development and beneficial effects for communities through their empowerment in the development process and in relation to resource conservation. This chapter critically evaluates the validity of such assumptions and examines the evidence to support or refute such assessments as well as the methodologies used to monitor ecotourism activity.

## Tourism impact analysis

The concern for the impact of tourism is not confined to developed countries: it is part of a growing concern for the impact and long-term sustainability of tourism across the world (Hall and Lew 1998), as Chapters 1 and 2

148

confirmed. As Pearce (1989) argued, research on the impact of tourism has led to varying degrees of emphasis on the economic, cultural, social and environmental impacts induced by tourism, and in the context of competition for visitors, destinations aggressively market their unique attributes in spite of the impacts. One of the main criticisms of many studies of the impact of tourism is that they do not pay adequate attention to the various types of tourism which induce the impacts. All too often the studies are unable to identify and understand the processes creating the impacts.

In any attempt to assess the impact of ecotourism, the immediate problem facing researchers and planners is the establishment of an appropriate baseline, on which to measure the existing and future changes induced by tourism. This is a problem that affects all aspects of impact assessment, although it is frequently cited in environmental assessment (EA) (see Weston 1997). Numerous studies of EA acknowledge the practical problems of establishing baseline studies and in disaggregating the impact of tourism from other economic activities, and their different contribution to environmental impacts. Mathieson and Wall (1982) highlighted the precise nature of the problem, since in many tourist destinations public use has existed for long periods of time so that it is now almost impossible to reconstruct the environment minus the effects induced by tourism. However, failure to establish baseline data will mean that it will be impossible to fully assess the magnitude of changes brought by tourism (Mathieson and Wall 1982: 5).

Even when it is possible to establish a baseline of data for a specific destination or area, the problem which Pearce (1989) identified was the extent to which pre-existing processes and changes in the physical and built environment were induced by tourism. While it is widely acknowledged that tourism is a major agent affecting the natural and built environment at a general level, isolating the precise causes or processes leading to specific impacts is difficult: is tourism the principal agent of change or is it part of a wider process of economic development in a particular destination? Mathieson and Wall (1982: 5) highlighted the common problem that 'tourism may also be a highly visible scapegoat for problems which existed prior to the advent of modern tourism. It certainly is easier to blame tourism than it is to address the conditions of society and the environment.' This is compounded by the reality of impact assessment – that the complex interactions of tourism and the built and physical environment make it virtually impossible to model or measure with any degree of precision. Even if it is possible to precisely gauge these impacts, they may not manifest themselves in a tangible form that is easily measured or gauged by survey methods. Impacts may be large scale and tangible (e.g. where a locality is saturated by visitors) and/or small scale and intangible: but how does this affect the interaction between the resident and visitor, and when should one measure these impacts?

The real difficulty is in attributing cause and effect in relation to tourism which is not necessarily continuous in time (due to seasonality) and space (as tourism activity tends to concentrate in certain locations). The precise indicators chosen to represent the complex interaction of tourism and the destination

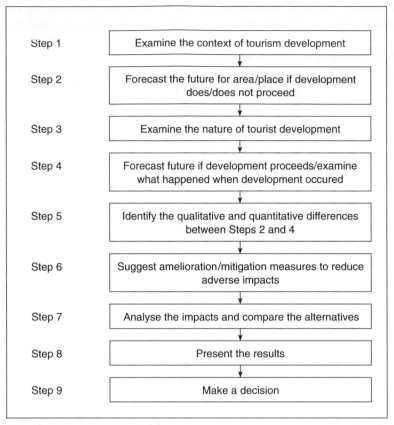

**Figure 6.1**  Impact assessment model

require the establishment of a methodological framework by which to guide the impact assessment. It is not surprising, therefore, to find many general texts in tourism studies reducing the impact of tourism to costs and benefits for specific destinations, rather than entering into the complex relationships that exist for specific tourism environments.

Pearce (1989) presented an interesting framework for impact assessment, pointing to the stimulus from EA in North America to consider impacts, especially in relation to proposed developments. Potter (1978) provided a general methodology for impact assessment. As Figure 6.1 shows, the assessment of the impact incorporates environmental, social and economic issues, all of which can be applied to tourism. As Pearce (1989: 185) argued, the real value is in its ability to assess both the existing and proposed developments. Potter's (1978) methodology comprises a number of steps, beginning with the context of the development and proceeding through to making a decision on a particular development. Pearce (1989) moved a stage further, arguing that impact studies should also consider the wider context of development rather than just the destination. In this respect, both the origin of visitors, the processes and linkages between origin and destination area and factors influencing the outcome – the impact – need to be considered. Pearce (1989) argued that a systems model may help to provide a more holistic framework for understanding the impact of tourism.

## The economic impact of tourism

Tourism is increasingly being viewed by many national and local governments as a mechanism to aid the regeneration of the ailing economies and in less developed countries (LDCs), to stimulate economic development. There is a prevailing perception among national and local governments that economic benefits accrue to tourism destinations, which then create employment opportunities and stimulate the development process in resorts and localities. For the local population, it is often argued by proponents of tourism development that investment in tourist and recreational facilities provides a positive contribution to the local economy. Assumptions about the economic effects of tourism as a stable source of income for communities is not without problems, since tourists are not noted for their high levels of customer loyalty to tourism destinations and a number of features support this argument:

- tourism is a fickle industry, being highly seasonal, and this has implications for investment and the type of employment created. Tourism employment is often characterised as being low skill, poorly paid, low status and lacking long-term stability;
- the demand for tourism can easily be influenced by external factors (e.g. political unrest or unusual climatic and environmental conditions) which are beyond the control of destination areas;
- the motivation for tourist travel to urban destinations is complex and variable and constantly changing in the competitive marketplace;
- in economic terms, tourism is price and income elastic (see Bull 1995), which means that it is easily influenced by small changes to the price of the product and the disposable income of consumers.

Despite these underlying concerns, the need to promote tourism is also underpinned by political pressure where politicians need to strategically consider the economic structure of regions with limited economic potential, particularly remoter rural areas that often have immense potential for tourism in natural areas. For example, Akama's (1996) analysis of nature-based tourism in Kenya indicated that approximately 10 per cent of the country had been set aside for nature-based tourism in a country where tourism accounted for 12 per cent of GDP and was the leading source of foreign exchange earnings (see Akama 1996 for an excellent case study tracing the evolution of nature-based tourism in Kenya and the influence of Western environmental values). Pearce (1989: 192) argued that 'the objective and detailed evaluation of the economic impact of tourism can be a long and complicated task'. One immediate problem is that there is little agreement within the literature on what constitutes the tourism industry. As Chapter 5 indicated, the sectors which are usually included under the heading of the tourism industry are:

- accommodation;
- transport;
- attractions;
- the travel organisers sector (e.g. travel agents);
- destination organisation sector.

Hospitality and ancillary services also have a major role to perform.

After such a working definition has been agreed, isolating the flow of income in the local tourism economy is notoriously difficult. This is because it is difficult to attribute the proportion of tourist expenditure on goods and services in relation to the total pattern of expenditure by all users of the region or area (e.g. residents, workers and visitors). There are a range of factors which influence the scale of the economic impact of tourism which include:

- the volume and scale of tourist expenditure in the locality;
- the state of the economic development and economy in the individual city;
- the size and nature of the local economy (i.e. is it dependent on services, manu-facturing or is it a mixed economy?);
- the extent to which tourist expenditure circulates around the local economy;
- the degree to which the local economy has addressed the problem of seasonality (after Page 1995).

On the basis of these factors, it is possible to assess whether the economic impact will be beneficial or if it will have a detrimental effect. In this respect, it is possible to identify some of the commonly cited economic *benefits* of tourism:

- the generation of income for the local economy;
- the creation of new employment opportunities;
- improvements to the structure and balance of economic activities within the locality;
- encouraging entrepreneurial activity.

In contrast, there are also a range of *costs* and these include:

- the potential for economic overdependence on one particular form of activity;
- inflationary costs in the local economy as new consumers enter the area and potential increases in land prices as the tourism development cycle commences;
- a growing dependence on imported rather than locally produced goods, services and labour as the development of facilities and infrastructure proceeds;
- seasonality in the consumption and production of tourism services leading to limited returns on investment;
- leakages of tourism expenditure from the local economy.

## Techniques to analyse the economic impact of tourism

Cooper *et al.* (1998: 115) argued that 'the measurement of the economic impact of tourism is far more complicated than simply calculating the level of tourist expenditure'. It is important to distinguish between the economic impact derived from tourist expenditure and that due to the development of tourism (e.g. the construction of facilities). Murphy (1985) pointed to the necessity of understanding the tourism economy of localities and the concept of economic cycles, since tourism experiences:

- *short-term economic cycles*, which commonly occur within a one-year time span and reflect the seasonality in demand which destinations and their economies have to accommodate;
- *medium-term economic cycles*, where changes in the circumstances of the tourism market may lead a destination to readjust to conditions occurring over a couple of years. For example, changes in the exchange rate and costs of producing tourism services make specific destinations expensive for overseas visitors;
- *long-term economic cycles*, where long-term business cycles become important and the destination is viewed in relation to the product life-cycle concept used in marketing and subsequently applied to resort development (Butler 1980). What is suggested is that the long-term economic viability of a destination may follow the growth curve of a new product where it is produced and seeks to establish an identity. If the product is a success with consumers, it gains growing acceptance leading to increased sales and peak production. However, as the number of suppliers increases, the demand for the product, patronage and sales decline and a state of low sales emerges and the product may be replaced or relaunched in a new form to stimulate sales. This principle has also been applied to resort areas to explain their evolution. It is also useful to understand the stage of development of specific tourism economies since it will condition the scale, volume and extent of tourist expenditure.

Butler's (1980: 6) concept of the resort cycle is extensively documented and reviewed in the tourism literature thus:

> Visitors will come to an area in small numbers initially, restricted by a lack of access, facilities, and local knowledge. As facilities are provided and awareness grows, visitor numbers will increase. With marketing, information dissemination, and further facility provision, the area's popularity will grow rapidly. Eventually, however, the rate of increase in visitor numbers will decline as levels of carrying capacity are reached . . . As the attractiveness of the area declines relative to other areas, because of overuse and the impacts of visitors, the actual number of visitors may also eventually decline.

Butler's (1980) model is divided into six stages:

1. the exploration stage (e.g. only small numbers of tourists visit the destination);
2. the involvement stage (e.g. the local community provides limited facilities for tourism);
3. the development stage (e.g. rapid tourism growth occurs which corresponds with the same process in the product life cycle);
4. the consolidation stage (e.g. a slower rate of growth and visitor numbers continues to expand and marketing activity is undertaken to maintain market share and to extend the season);
5. the stagnation stage (e.g. peak numbers are reached and economic, environmental and social problems occur due to pressure on the locality by visitors);
6. future options (e.g. how should the area respond to the future once stagnation has set in?).

In the analysis of tourism expenditure, primary and secondary data is normally required to establish:

- *direct expenditure* by tourists on goods and services consumed (e.g. hotels, restaurants and tourist transport services), although this is not a definitive account of expenditure due to leakage of tourist spending to areas and corporations outside the local economy;
- *indirect expenditure* by visitors which is often estimated by identifying how many tourism enterprises use the income derived from tourists' spending. This spending is then used by enterprises to pay for services, taxes and employees which then recirculates in the local economy. In other words, tourist expenditure stimulates an economic process which passes through a series of stages (or rounds). Specific forms of economic analysis, such as input–output analysis may be used to identify the types of transactions which occur between tourism businesses to assess how indirect expenditure influences the tourism economy;
- *the induced impact* by calculating the impact of expenditure from those employed in tourism and the effect of the spending in the local economy.

On the basis of the direct, indirect and induced impacts, one can produce an estimate of the total impact of tourist spending. These different impacts are indicated in Figure 6.2 where the tourism economy is viewed as an open system which varies according to the degree of penetration by outside interests and amount of goods imported.

Figure 6.2 is useful as it highlights the interrelationships which exist within the tourism economy of an area and the flow of income within the economic system. It also introduces the concept of *leakage*, which occurs due to the taxation of income derived from tourist spending, and loss of expenditure to other areas and economies. Clearly, 'visitor expenditures represent only the first stage of economic impact on a destination community, for like other generators of basic income, tourism's contribution can multiply as the extra income passes throughout an economy' (Murphy 1985: 90).

## Tourism multiplier analysis

There is a vast literature which reviews the concept of multiplier analysis (e.g. Archer 1982, 1987; Tribe 1995), which Mathieson and Wall (1982: 64) define as 'the number, by which initial tourist expenditure must be multiplied in order to obtain the total cumulative income effect for a specified period'. The multiplier concept is 'based on the recognition that the various sectors which make up the economy are interdependent . . . Therefore, any autonomous change in the level of final demand will not only affect the industry which produces that final good or service, but also that industry's suppliers and the suppliers' suppliers'. The multiplier is expressed as a ratio which measures those changes, the final demand resulting from the effect of changes in variables such as economic output, income, employment, government revenue and foreign exchange flows (if appropriate). The multiplier ratio (see Cooper *et al.* 1998 for more detail on the formulae used to calculate different types of multipliers), measures the changes to the final demand resulting from the aforementioned changes and expresses the estimate of the total change in output (the output multiplier). A similar value can also be derived to estimate

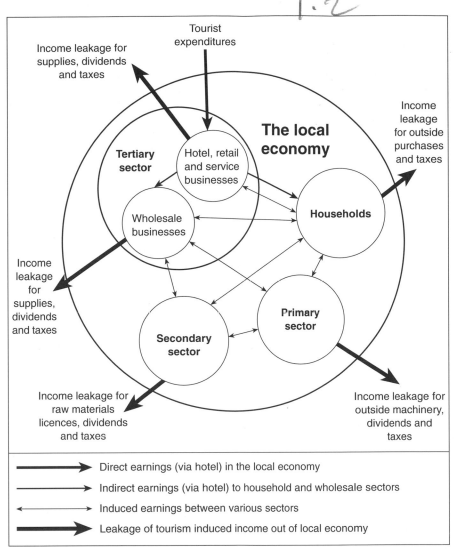

Figure 6.2   The tourism economy
*Source*: Page (1995)

the total change in income (the income multiplier) to illustrate the effect of changes in demand on tourism income. These concepts help to establish the estimated changes in the direct, indirect and induced effects on the tourism economy, resulting from changes in demand.

The actual size of the multiplier reflects the expected economic benefit of tourism to the economy: the more self-sufficient a given economy, the greater degree of tourist revenue that is retained in the economy. It is widely acknowledged by tourism economists that the national multipliers are larger due to the greater propensity of the national economy to be self-sufficient compared to

Table 6.1   Tourism income multipliers for selected urban destinations

| | |
|---|---|
| Metropolitan Victoria | 0.65 |
| Edinburgh | 0.35 |
| City of Carlisle | 0.40 |
| Great Yarmouth | 0.33 |
| Kendal/Keswick | 0.28 |
| Towns and villages in Wales | 0.18–0.47 |
| UK | 1.73 |

*Source*: Based on Archer (1982), Murphy (1985) and Pearce (1989).

lower-order economic systems (e.g. isolated rural areas). A range of tourism income multipliers reported in the literature are listed in Table 6.1. Pearce (1989: 208) argued that while values vary from place to place, there is a certain amount of consistency in similar areas in multiplier values.

In contrast, employment multipliers are more difficult to operationalise due to problems in establishing the relationship between employment and its role in tourist expenditure. Employment does not necessarily expand as tourist expenditure increases because it depends on the state of the local economy, the nature of the tourism activity and degree of change in demand. Thus, employment multipliers are only an indication of possible full-time employment which may result. Yet it is not just the number of jobs created, but the type and quality resulting from tourism which are important (Mathieson and Wall 1982). Although there are a range of useful studies which examine the technical aspects associated with different types of multipliers (e.g. Archer 1987) and their role in economic theory, one can summarise the significance of multipliers in the analysis of the economic impact of tourism thus:

- multiplier analysis helps researchers to measure the present economic performance of the tourism industry and the effect of short-term changes in demand on the urban tourism economy;
- multipliers may be used to assess the effects of public and private sector investment in urban tourism projects, and who are likely to be the main beneficiaries;
- multipliers are frequently used to estimate the impact of tourist expenditure on tourism enterprises within cities together with the effect on direct, indirect and induced forms of employment and income.

## Analysing the economic impact of ecotourism

According to Lindberg and McKercher (1997) there are various stakeholders within the ecotourism industry from operators to protected area managers and local communities that have to be considered in the economic analysis of this business activity. What Lindberg and McKercher (1997) highlighted was the growing problems which accrued from protected areas in relation to economic benefits as the number of competing sites and opportunities have expanded within and between countries for ecotourism. Ecotourism has been seen as a source of revenue to offset declining public sector subsidies to manage conservation and in some cases to replace declining economic activities such as forestry. For example, the Tortuguero area, located on the Caribbean coast, consists of a village of 211 residents and Tortuguero National Park (Lee and Snepenger 1992). Historically, Tortuguero's economy thrived on sea turtle harvesting, logging and small-scale agriculture, but tourism is now its major source of revenue. Recreation activities in Tortuguero reflected ecotourism values. A large portion (90 per cent) of the respondents to Lee and Snepenger's (1992) study participated in nature-oriented activities, such as guided canoe tours and sea turtle walks. These activities generated revenues consistent with ecotourism objectives. Visitor groups stayed 2–4 nights and spent somewhere between $70 and $150 per person per night on lodging, meals, transportation and other expenses. The significance of tourism to the household economies of residents was evident from over half of the households (57 per cent) who had at least one person employed directly in host services. The tourism business survey revealed that 70 per cent of the owners lived in the village, and most businesses were staffed by local residents. While this example is not necessarily typical of the economic impact of ecotourism in most localities, it does give a graphic illustration of the scope, extent and nature of the impacts in a local context.

However, a number of critics of ecotourism indicate that while ecotourism has the potential to generate considerable economic benefits, often a large proportion of this money is spent at the place of origin, primarily to pay for travel, with usually relatively little being spent at the destination (Wall 1994: 7). Thus, the local economic impact of ecotourism is not always large and sometimes it may not be a benefit at all, a feature emphasised by Honey (1999) in relation to the impact of American ecotourists where many of the economic benefits accrued to the USA and the nature-based tour operators. In addition, one also has to acknowledge that tourism may increase local reliance upon a global economy, leaking many economic profits outside of the community back to the companies and countries that control most of the travel infrastructure. At the same time, tourism decreases dependence on local resources, as technologies, food and health services are imported. Local people may also be pushed out or sell out, and local prices for commodities and services rise, as do taxes (McLaren 1998: 17).

One useful way to summarise the scope of the economic impacts of ecotourism a stage further than the Tortuguero example is to focus on one country. This is useful to evaluate the scope and magnitude of impacts from a range of studies, to synthesise the findings and generate a baseline by which other countries and regions can compare and contrast the impacts. For example, Master (1998) examined marine wildlife tourism in the Highlands and Islands of Scotland and reviewed a range of economic impact results which are now discussed since this highlighted the diverse range of findings and examples that exist for one locality.

Plate 6.1    Adult osprey at perch, Scotland (courtesy of RSPB Images).

## The scope and extent of the economic impact of ecotourism in Scotland

In a study by Mackay Consultants (1989), tourists interested in wildlife were estimated to have created 152 full-time equivalent (FTE) jobs and £4.4 million of visitor spending on Islay and Jura in Scotland in 1989. According to the Surrey Research Group (1993, cited in Mason 1998), tourism multipliers in Scotland ranged from one FTE per £19,000 of visitor spending through to one FTE per £28,000 of visitor spending depending on the local context. In contrast, Crabtree *et al.* (1994) in a study of Wester Ross, Orkney and Highland Perthshire

Plate 6.2   White-tailed eagle, Scotland (courtesy of RSPB Images).

Plate 6.3   A puffin with sandeels, Scotland (courtesy of RSPB Images).

Plate 6.4    Sea otter, Scotland (courtesy of RSPB Images).

Plate 6.5    Red kite in Scotland: these are an endangered species and the RSPB is leading their preservation and conservation (courtesy of RSPB Images).

estimated site-based wildlife tourism revenue to be £5.15 million in 1993, which supported 351 FTE jobs. Morrison (1995) extended this work to assess marine tourism, concluding that The Minch whale-watching trips generated £445,000 in 1994 and supported 29 full-time and 17 part-time jobs. A study for the Royal Society for the Protection of Birds (RSPB) found that 26 per cent of tourism expenditure in the Shetland Isles in 1994 was derived from birdwatchers which amounted to £1.07 million and supported 43 FTE jobs. In Scotland, visits to RSPB reserves were estimated to have created 1,200 jobs. In a further study by Mackay Consultants (1997, cited in Master 1998), total wildlife and environmental tourism-related spending generated £105 million in Scotland and supported 12,730 jobs. Arnold (1997), however, examined the Moray Firth and revenue from dolphin-adoptee holidaymakers and found that initial revenue was £1.4 million which had risen to £7.4 million. A & M Training (1997) calculated that wildlife tourism in Scotland created 1,973 jobs in 1996. What these initial ranges of studies show is that the economic impact studies have great variations in their findings according to what is measured, the methodologies used and the scope of the tourism sector. Crabtree *et al.* (1994) provided an interesting regional perspective, in that wildlife tourism in Wester Ross generated £0.67 million a year in expenditure, while Orkney generated £1.78 million and Highland Perthshire generated £2.79 million.

What all these studies also indicate is that the impacts in employment creation may be small but vital given the nature of the rural economies in each area, many of which have highly seasonal employment opportunities and suffer from many problems associated with declining rural areas. Master (1998) concluded that for the Highlands and Islands of Scotland, direct annual expenditure from marine wildlife tourism as a specific market segment of ecotourism amounted to £9.3 million a year while associated subsistence expenditure (e.g. accommodation, food and drink not on site) generated £35.5 million. Using these figures, and estimated expenditure multipliers of between 1.25 and 1.3, downstream expenditure was estimated to be £12.4 million. As a result, the total expenditure on marine wildlife tourism in the Highlands and Islands of Scotland amounted to an estimated £57.2 million a year. On the basis of these calculations, Master (1998) calculated that one full-time equivalent job was created for every £21,500 of visitor expenditure and this translated into 432 directly employed jobs in marine wildlife tourism, associated employment of 1,652 in the hospitality sector, with a further 577 downstream jobs as a result of the multiplier factor. As a result this created a total of 2,661 jobs associated with marine wildlife tourism. More detailed calculations are shown in Table 6.2 which is derived from Master's (1998) report.

Increasingly, tourism is often used to provide an economic rationale to preserve natural areas rather than developing them for alternative uses such as agriculture or forestry when the results from studies by Master (1998) are considered in a public policy context. Such evidence is certainly playing a major role in a Scottish context with the proposed formation of the country's

**Table 6.2**  Estimated annual expenditure and associated employment arising from marine wildlife tourism in the Highlands and Islands of Scotland

This table shows our financial calculations, using data from the preceding tables, of the total expenditure on marine wildlife tourism, and the total number of jobs this supports

| | Number | Days visited | Fee | Related food | Incidental spend | Total direct expenditure | Subtotal | Accommodation & food | Entertainment | Total indirect expenditure | Subtotal | Multiplier | Total revenue | Subtotal |
|---|---|---|---|---|---|---|---|---|---|---|---|---|---|---|
| **Focused trips of a week or more** | | | | | | | | | | | | | | |
| Bird watching | 10,937 | 6 | £8 | £0 | £1 | £590,571 | | £25 | £5 | £1,965,289 | | 1.25 | £3,194,825 | |
| Sailing | 2,544 | 6 | £24 | £0 | £2 | £396,864 | | £10 | £2 | £183,168 | | 1.25 | £725,040 | |
| Walking | 802 | 6 | £8 | £0 | £2 | £48,090 | | £28 | £5 | £157,735 | | 1.25 | £257,282 | |
| Field trip | 5,000 | 6 | £8 | £0 | £0 | £240,000 | | £19 | £2 | £634,500 | | 1.25 | £1,093,125 | |
| Survey | 75 | 6 | £5 | £0 | £0 | £2,250 | | £22 | £2 | £10,868 | | 1.25 | £16,397 | |
| Working holiday | 275 | 6 | £6 | £0 | £0 | £9,900 | | £20 | £3 | £38,610 | | 1.25 | £60,638 | |
| Painting, etc. | 3,129 | 6 | £15 | £0 | £1 | £300,384 | | £31 | £5 | £678,680 | | 1.25 | £1,223,830 | |
| | | | | | | | £1,588,059 | | | | £3,668,850 | | | £6,571,136 |
| **Several or day outings** | | | | | | | | | | | | | | |
| Bird watching | 72,910 | 3 | £0 | £3 | £1 | £874,920 | | £25 | £5 | £6,550,964 | | 1.25 | £9,282,354 | |
| Aquarium | 40,673 | 1 | £4 | £3 | £2 | £366,053 | | £26 | £2 | £1,138,830 | | 1.25 | £1,881,103 | |
| Other visitor centre | 27,115 | 1 | £4 | £3 | £1 | £216,920 | | £26 | £2 | £759,220 | | 1.25 | £1,220,175 | |
| Boat trip | 38,160 | 1 | £10 | £3 | £0 | £496,080 | | £38 | £5 | £1,646,604 | | 1.25 | £2,678,355 | |
| Guided walk | 4,008 | 1 | £4 | £3 | £0 | £28,053 | | £22 | £3 | £100,789 | | 1.25 | £161,051 | |
| Nature reserve | 36,455 | 1 | £0 | £3 | £1 | £145,820 | | £22 | £3 | £916,843 | | 1.25 | £1,328,329 | |
| | | | | | | | £2,127,845 | | | | £11,113,249 | | | £16,551,368 |

**Day trip, booked in advance**

| | Number | Days visited | Fee | Related food | Incidental spend | Total direct expenditure | Subtotal | Accommodation & food | Entertainment | Total indirect expenditure | Subtotal | Multiplier | Total revenue | Subtotal |
|---|---|---|---|---|---|---|---|---|---|---|---|---|---|---|
| Aquarium | 8,135 | 1 | £4 | £3 | £2 | £73,211 | | £26 | £2 | £227,766 | | 1.27 | £382,240 | |
| Other visitor centre | 2,712 | 1 | £4 | £3 | £1 | £21,692 | | £26 | £2 | £75,922 | | 1.27 | £123,970 | |
| Boat trip | 50,880 | 1 | £8 | £3 | £0 | £559,680 | | £38 | £5 | £2,195,472 | | 1.27 | £3,499,043 | |
| Guided walk | 6,412 | 1 | £6 | £3 | £0 | £57,708 | | £25 | £3 | £179,536 | | 1.27 | £301,300 | |
| Nature reserve | 18,228 | 1 | £0 | £3 | £1 | £72,910 | £785,201 | £25 | £3 | £510,370 | £3,189,066 | 1.27 | £740,766 | £5,047,318 |

**Day trip made on impulse – no prior booking**

| | Number | Days visited | Fee | Related food | Incidental spend | Total direct expenditure | Subtotal | Accommodation & food | Entertainment | Total indirect expenditure | Subtotal | Multiplier | Total revenue | Subtotal |
|---|---|---|---|---|---|---|---|---|---|---|---|---|---|---|
| Aquarium | 81,345 | 1 | £4 | £3 | £2 | £732,105 | | £29 | £2 | £2,489,157 | | 1.3 | £4,187,641 | |
| Other visitor centre | 111,172 | 1 | £5 | £3 | £1 | £1,000,544 | | £29 | £2 | £3,401,848 | | 1.3 | £5,723,109 | |
| Boat trip | 162,816 | 1 | £10 | £3 | £0 | £2,116,608 | | £29 | £5 | £5,470,618 | | 1.3 | £9,863,393 | |
| Guided walk | 4,809 | 1 | £6 | £3 | £0 | £43,281 | | £27 | £3 | £143,068 | | 1.3 | £242,253 | |
| Nature reserve | 226,021 | 1 | £0 | £3 | £1 | £904,084 | £4,796,622 | £24 | £3 | £6,046,062 | £17,550,752 | 1.3 | £9,035,189 | £29,051,568 |

| | | | | | | | | | | | | | | |
|---|---|---|---|---|---|---|---|---|---|---|---|---|---|---|
| **Total annual expenditure** | | | | | | | **£9,297,726** | | | | **£35,521,917** | | **£12,401,765** | **£57,221,408** |
| Associated employment (FTE) £21,500 FTE equivalent | | | | | | | 432 | | | | 1,652 | | 577 | **2,661** |

*Source*: Master (1998: 12).

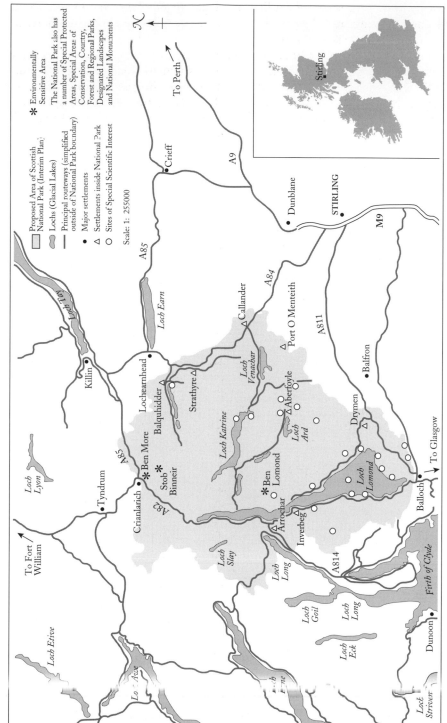

**Figure E3**   The first Scottish National Park: Loch Lomond and Trossachs National Park

first national park north of Stirling (see Figure 6.3) where ecotourism activities currently exist and their further development is likely due to the potential for employment creation and the expansion of the rural economic base.

The economic benefits of ecotourism occur in several ways and may generate higher economic returns than other resource activities (Hvenegaard and Dearden 1998). It may also benefit local economies by providing an incentive to ensure regional biodiversity is used sustainably. Such economic benefits may serve as a stimulus for the establishment of protected areas such as national parks. In addition, ecotourists may contribute to the conservation and management of ecotourism sites, through mechanisms such as entry fees and donations (Wallace and Pierce 1996). In current analyses of natural or protected areas it is this element that has become central, pushing debate on to the question of maintaining an area in its natural state as opposed to exploiting the resources it contains. This economic valuation is increasingly being used to justify the existence of protected areas through the demonstrable 'value' of both the wildlife and ecosystem features. 'Tourism is becoming increasingly central to these strategies given that tourists are willing to pay to experience these natural areas' (Wearing and Neil 1999: 43). Much of the debate has been focused on the issue of user fees to which attention now turns.

## User fees and revenue generation from ecotourism

The issue of user fees has been controversial in many countries and has generated a substantial literature. Many members of the public and the tourism industry oppose fees for entry to public natural areas. In addition, there is concern that fees will change the nature of the visitor experience by making it more structured and commercialised. Lindberg (1998) noted that fee supporters argue that visitation imposes environmental (adverse impacts), social (experiential) and economic (financial) costs on natural areas. Such costs should be paid by those who impose them, that is, the developers, operators and visitors. Various management objectives may also exist, including creating profits; cost recovery; the generation of business opportunities, foreign exchange and tax revenues; education and interpretation; and visitor management.

According to Lindberg (1998) the effective achievement of cost recovery and other objectives requires information regarding ecotourism demand and costs. The demand for an ecotourism site depends on a variety of factors including the cost of travel (time and money) to the destination country as well as from the destination gateway to the attraction; the destination image; the quality of the icon and complementary attractions; the political and economic stability of the destination visited; visitor income, tastes and trends; availability and prices of competing attractions; quality of general trip experience.

In an innovative paper by Laarman and Gregersen (1996) on pricing policy in nature-based tourism, they developed the willingness to pay concept based on the economists' contingent valuation methodologies. What they reviewed was the guiding principles which should be used for fee policies in natural

Table 6.3   Guiding principles for fee policy in nature-based tourism

| Principle | Rationale |
| --- | --- |
| Fees supplement but do not replace general sources of revenue | Even for heavily visited sites, fee revenue rarely covers total costs, especially capital costs. Heavy dependence on fee revenue reduces visitor diversity and the scope of attractions that can be offered. Yearly fluctuations in fee revenue make fees an unstable income source |
| At least a proportion of fee revenues should be set aside ('earmarked') for sites that generate them | Earmarking increases management's incentives to set and collect fees efficiently. Visitors may be more willing to pay fees if they know that fees are used on site |
| Fees should be set on site-specific basis | National guidelines specify fee objectives and policies, yet management goals and visitor patterns vary across NBT sites, requiring local flexibility in assessing the type and amount of fee |
| Fee collection is not justified at all sites | Fees are not cost-effective at places with low visitation demand and high collection costs |
| Fee systems work best when supported by reliable accounting and management | Administrative decisions about fees require acceptable data on costs and revenues of providing NBT for different sites and activities |

*Source*: Laarman and Gregersen (1996: 249).

areas (see Table 6.3) dependent upon the pricing objectives which the agency or policymakers have for specific resources. This needs to evolve through time as Table 6.4 suggests in relation to the resource, and a range of categories of fees may be levied as shown in Table 6.5. What is important for the next section on the social benefits of these initiatives is the role of revenue sharing with local communities. Yet research by Wells and Brandon (1992) found only three examples in Kenya, Mexico and Nepal of revenue sharing. Maile and Medelsohn (1993) found that open access may in fact lead to economic and environmental inefficiencies and policy instruments were necessary for public, private and community-owned land to limit access and improve efficiency. Yet Steele (1995) recognised that there were definite limitations to the application of a user pay system.

Lindberg (1998: 97) continued this debate in that 'once overall fee policies have been determined, managers must determine the goods and services for which fees should be charged, as well as how they should be collected'. Some of the common fee categories include area entrance fees, admissions to specific facilities, use fees charged for use of specific objects (such as rented equipment), or opportunities (such as camping sites); licence and permit fees, which are similar to a use fee; sales and concessions which includes profit from direct sales of souvenirs, lodging and other goods or services; fees from concessions

**Table 6.4**   An approximate evolution of pricing strategies in nature-based tourism

| Objectives | Experience |
| --- | --- |
| Introduction of token charges | Nominal fees become accepted as a way to impute value to visitation |
| Fees for revenue | 'Reasonable' fees become accepted as a necessary budget supplement |
| Fees to offset costs | Fees are set to recover some or all of operating costs |
| Fees as management tools | There are many discussions but few test cases of using differential pricing to affect use patterns (e.g. fees varying by season, day of the week, and site) |
| Fees for profit | Profit can be appropriate even in public agencies, e.g. to build capital reserves and replace facilities. Yet there is little evidence to date of profit-making behaviour in most parks agencies |

*Source*: Laarman and Gregersen (1996: 250).

**Table 6.5**   Categories of fees and charges in nature-based tourism

| Fee type | Observation |
| --- | --- |
| General entrance fee | 'Gate fees' allow free or priced access to facilities beyond the entry point |
| Fees for use | Examples: fees for visitor centres, parking, campsites, guide services, boat use, trail shelters, emergency rescue, etc. |
| Concession fees | Charges (or revenue shares) are assessed on individuals and businesses which sell food, accommodation, transportation, guide services, souvenirs and other goods and services to NBT visitors |
| Royalties and profit shares | Can be charged on sale of guidebooks, postcards, tee-shirts, souvenirs, books, films, photos, etc. |
| Licences and permits | For tour operators, guides, researchers, wildlife collectors, mountain climbers, river rafters, etc. The concept can be extended to individual campers, bikers, etc. |
| Taxes | Examples: room taxes, airport taxes, vehicle taxes, excise taxes on sports and outdoor equipment, etc. |
| Voluntary donations | Include cash and in-kind gifts, often through 'friends of the park' organisations |

*Source*: Laarman and Gregersen (1996: 250).

to private businesses for selling these goods and services; and revenues from licensing natural-area logos and trademarks which is a broader conceptualisation than Laarman and Gregersen (1996).

Lindberg (1996) undertook a case study of sites in Belize, to evaluate the extent to which selected ecotourism objectives have been achieved. The revenues and expenditures associated with ecotourism were identified through a review of protected area budget records and interviews with staff. The direct revenues from tourism included the tourism-related user fees, donations and souvenir sales that are channelled into the protected area budget. The indirect revenues from tourism included the portion of governmental and donor agency funding that results from ecotourism at the protected area. The expenditures from tourism were calculated using cost accounting principles. Expenditures were grouped into three categories: solely tourism products, rival products and non-rival products. The solely tourism category includes expenditures made for goods and services solely related to tourism. The rival product category included expenditures for goods and services that can be used for either tourism or traditional management functions but not both at any one time. The non-rival category includes expenditures for goods and services that can be used for both tourism and traditional management functions at the same time.

Three expenditure scenarios were developed using different expenditure assumptions. The low scenario was based on the actual budget and reflected an assumption that tourism is insignificant as a motivation for establishment and maintenance of the sanctuary. The medium expenditure scenario was based on the actual budget and the high scenario was based on a proposed budget. The tourism-related revenues and expenditures were BZ$42,213 and BZ$4,681 from providing tourism opportunities during the period of evaluation.

Using visitation rates from the period of evaluation, a modest entrance fee of BZ$3.00 charged to foreign visitors would have generated BZ$19,575 during this period. This revenue would more than cover the current net loss. An alternative was to seek a reduction in expenditures. However, expenditures are currently very modest, and reductions would adversely impact the visitor experience. Employment generation by ecotourism also provided a strong rationale for interest in this phenomenon by protected area managers and environmentalists as tangible outcomes of such tourism development (Lindberg *et al.* 1996) as well as the local economic benefits (Shackley 1996). What existing studies show is that benefits vary by locality, in line with the economic literature, dependent upon the nature of the attraction, access and economy. Yet even in remote areas small numbers of jobs can be beneficial to the local employment base. To increase visitor spending in ecotourism areas, the promotion of local handicrafts (Healy 1994) and the fostering of backward economic linkages (e.g. the use of local agricultural produce, see Lindberg and Enriquez 1994; Telfer and Wall 1996) can also be useful. Fennell (1999: 169) asserted that the use of variable tariffs or tiered pricing is an efficient way to increase revenue where foreigners are charged a higher entrance fee than locals. One well-known example is the Galápagos Islands, where foreign tourists are charged the equivalent of $40 and local tourists $6. Among the

key issues in the existing economic impact literature, Lindberg and McKercher (1997) argued that the impact of fees on the local economy needs to be more carefully researched, particularly the geographical impact on the distribution of visitors, and asked whether increased fees would increase or decrease visitor numbers.

## Ecotourism and economic development

Lindberg (1998) argued that ecotourism has been embraced by many countries and entrepreneurs as an opportunity to generate income and employment in areas relatively untouched by traditional development efforts and to generate tangible economic benefits from natural areas. There are three reasons for generating such local benefits. First, it is equitable in so far as conservation of the area designated for ecotourism may reduce or eliminate traditional resource use. Second, the ecotourists, as consumers, may support the importance of tourism benefiting local residents. Third, when residents receive benefits they are more likely to support tourism and conservation, even to the point of protecting the site against poaching or other encroachment. Lindberg (1998) noted that several studies of ecotourism's national, regional and local economic impacts have been conducted. For example, Aylward et al. (1996) estimated that nature tourism in Costa Rica generated over $600 million in foreign exchange in 1994, and that visitors to Australia's Great Barrier Reef World Heritage Area spent A$776 million ($543 million) in 1991/1992.

Ecotourism's economic contribution depended not only on how much money flows into the region of interest (the country, state, province or local community), but also on how much of what comes into the region stays in the region, thereby producing multiplier effects (Lindberg 1998). A consistent finding of economic impact studies, particularly in developing countries, is the high level of leakage. More than 90 per cent of tourism spending is thought to leak away from communities near most nature tourism sites. For example, it has been estimated that less than 6 per cent of the income generated by tourism at Tortuguero National Park, in Costa Rica, accrued to the local communities.

Lindberg (1998) suggested that a common priority in ecotourism is to increase local economic benefits, and the traditional approach is to increase the number of visitors. This is short-sighted: it is preferable to generate more ecotourism benefits by increased spending per visitor; local participation in the tourism industry; backward linkages with related local industries (reducing leakages); revenue sharing and direct payment programmes; and/or local control and ownership. There are also opportunities for increasing visitor spending on infrastructure and services at ecotourism destination areas including accommodation, food outlets, souvenir shops and visitor centres. In summary, ecotourism has the potential to generate economic benefits for people living near these areas, but there is considerable debate regarding the extent to which this potential has been realised (Lindberg 1998) and the social and cultural consequences of such development, to which attention now turns.

## The social and cultural impact of tourism

In recent years there has been a recognition by academics and community groups that the development of tourism not only leads to economic impacts, but also results in less visible and more intangible effects (Murphy 1985). While economic impacts may be measured and quantified to identify financial and employment effects, social and cultural impacts on visitors and host communities are often only considered when tourism development leads to local opposition. Therefore, it is important to understand the types of social and cultural impacts which result from tourism to try and avoid negative effects and conflicts in areas, between the host community and visitors. Otherwise the *tourist experience* may be tainted by underlying conflicts and an unwelcoming attitude towards tourists which will ultimately erode the destination's popularity and competitive position. The attitudes of residents are a key component in identifying, measuring and analysing the impact of tourism (Ryan and Montgomery 1994). Such attitudes are also important in determining local policy, planning and management responses to the development of tourism and in establishing the extent of public support for tourism. Getz (1994) argued that resident perceptions of tourism may be one factor in shaping the attractiveness of a destination, and negative attitudes may be one indicator of an area's ability to absorb tourism. Although Getz suggests that 'identification of causal mechanisms is a major theoretical challenge, and residents can provide the local knowledge necessary to link developments with their consequences' (Getz 1994: 247), this assumes that residents are sufficiently aware, willing, perceptive and able enough to articulate their views to decision-makers and planners. But what is meant by the social and cultural impact of tourism?

According to Fox (1977), cited in Mathieson and Wall (1982: 133), 'The social and cultural impacts of tourism are the ways in which tourism is contributing to changes in value systems, individual behaviour, family relationships, collective lifestyles, safety levels, moral conduct, creative expressions, traditional ceremonies and community organisations,' which they identify as 'people impacts', due to the effect of tourists on host communities and the interaction between these two groups. In other words, the analysis of social and cultural impacts of tourism involves the analysis of the:

- *tourist*, especially their demand for services, their attitudes, expectations and activity patterns;
- *host*, particularly their role and attitude towards the provision of services for tourists and their concerns for the impact of visitors on the traditional way of life in the locality;
- *relationship between tourists and hosts*, and the type of contact which occurs between these two groups and the outcome for each group.

The most notable study to analyse these relationships is Smith's (1989) *Hosts and Guests: The Anthropology of Tourism* which contains an interesting range of studies of the effect of imported tourist culture on host communities. For example, Smith (1989) notes that the type of tourist visiting a destination is an important precondition for their ability to adapt to local norms. Table 6.6 indicates that while certain cultural, linguistic and educational barriers inhibit

Table 6.6  Types of tourists and their adaptation to local norms

| Type of tourist | Numbers of tourists | Adaptation to local norms |
|---|---|---|
| Explorer | Very limited | Accepts fully |
| Elite | Rarely seen | Adapts fully |
| Off-beat | Uncommon but seen | Adapts well |
| Unusual | Occasional | Adapts somewhat |
| Incipient mass | Steady flow | Seeks Western amenities |
| Mass | Continuous influx | Expects Western amenities |
| Charter | Massive arrivals | Demands Western amenities |

*Source*: Based on V. Smith (1989).

the interaction and integration of tourists into a local community, this varies according to the volume of visitors and their expectations.

UNESCO (1976) recognised that the host:guest relationship is:

- *transitory in nature*, since most tourist visits are short in duration which are also artificial if spent in a hotel where non-local staff are employed who are usually expected to speak the language of visitors;
- *limited in time and space*, especially when the visitor is on a short break to an urban area which often leads to distinctive forms of visitor behaviour. For example, visitors may seek to maximise the time available by high spending on activities and tourist services;
- *often lacking in spontaneity*. Where package and organised itineraries are used by tourists, these lead to formal, commercialised and contractual relationships between the tourist and service providers, removing the opportunity for spontaneous interaction between visitors and the tourist service worker;
- *unequal and unbalanced*. For the tourist, the experience of a destination is one based on an image of the place as a novel and exciting opportunity. Yet for the tourist worker, it is often a routine, mundane and regulated experience. There are often material differences between the affluence of visitors and the spending patterns and the relatively low levels of remuneration of workers undertaking tourism service tasks. Such relationships may lead to resentment among workers and residents in extreme cases.

## Analysing the social and cultural impact of tourism

As research on the impact of tourism has developed, different methodologies have been proposed to analyse social and cultural impacts (Smith 1989). One of the most widely cited is Doxey's irridex.

### Doxey's index of tourist irritation (irridex)

Doxey (1975) developed his 'irridex' to illustrate how the interaction of tourists and residents may be converted into different degrees of irritation. Using observations from the West Indies and Canada, Doxey (1975) argued that residents' responses will change in a predictable manner, passing through four

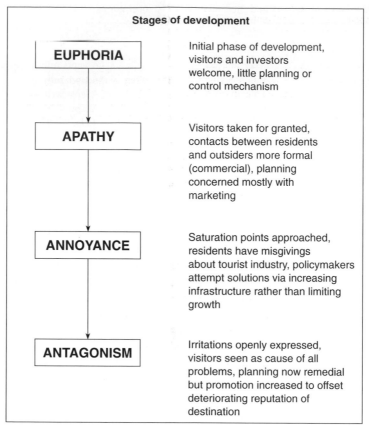

**Stages of development**

| EUPHORIA | Initial phase of development, visitors and investors welcome, little planning or control mechanism |

| APATHY | Visitors taken for granted, contacts between residents and outsiders more formal (commercial), planning concerned mostly with marketing |

| ANNOYANCE | Saturation points approached, residents have misgivings about tourist industry, policymakers attempt solutions via increasing infrastructure rather than limiting growth |

| ANTAGONISM | Irritations openly expressed, visitors seen as cause of all problems, planning now remedial but promotion increased to offset deteriorating reputation of destination |

Figure 6.4   Doxey's irridex model

stages – euphoria, apathy, annoyance and antagonism (Figure 6.4). Doxey's (1975) index assumes that large numbers of visitors cause tensions and ultimately lead to antagonism. Yet it overlooks situations where such numbers of visitors do not ultimately lead to this situation (e.g. Garland and West 1985). It is also a unidirectional model that does not permit destinations to pass back to a situation where annoyance may be reduced by sensitive visitor management schemes. Garland and West (1985: 35) place resident irritation with tourists in context as 'host irritation with the presence of tourists in Rotorua is just that – irritation, and then only among small proportions of residents'. Ap and Crompton (1993) proposed an alternative model (Figure 6.5) to assess resident attitudes to tourism. What Ap and Crompton (1993) illustrate is that in any community affected by tourism, a variety of stakeholder interests and attitudes will exist, as opposed to the simplified model proposed by Doxey (1975). At any one point in time, a community will be characterised by a range of views and that grouping them into a simplified model such as Doxey's does not recognise the diversity in the locality.

Assessing attitudes to tourism requires a fundamental understanding of 'attitude' as a 'state of mind of the individual towards a value' (Allport 1966,

| Embracement | Residents eagerly welcome tourists |
|---|---|
| Tolerance | Residents show a degree of ambivalence towards tourism (there were elements of tourism they liked or disliked) |
| Adjustment | Residents adjusted to tourism, often by rescheduling activities to avoid crowds |
| Withdrawal | In this context, residents withdrew temporarily from the community |

NB: All four strategies are likely to be adopted concurrently, since in any community there are going to be different reactions to tourism. The strategies and behaviour adopted by individuals and groups of residents need to be viewed in relation to thresholds and tourism impacts.

Figure 6.5 Ap and Crompton's model

cited in Getz 1994: 247) and the way in which individuals view and analyse their environment. Getz (1994) rightly recognised that attitudes are reinforced by the way individuals and groups perceive reality. However, such perceptions do not change quickly. Although research in social psychology has debated the other factors which affect attitudes, including the role of human behaviour and beliefs, McDougall and Munroe (1994) recognised that attitudes may be analysed along three dimensions:

- cognitive (perceptions and beliefs);
- affective (likes and dislikes);
- behavioural (actions or expressed intent).

Attitudes will also be determined by the way in which individuals and groups view the 'real world' and synthesise the complex dimensions of reality into a mental image of a place. Therefore, attitudes can be shaped by various situational factors, though predicting behaviour based on attitudes is notoriously difficult. One additional complexity in analysing attitude is the tendency for some researchers to substitute the term 'perception', which Ap (1990) acknowledged is the meaning attributed to an object. This suggests that some people may attribute a meaning to the impact of tourism without understanding it. Consequently, it is a 'perceived view' rather than an 'attitude'. Thus, various studies of resident attitudes towards tourism are probably only looking at a perceived view of tourism. The implication here is that research projects which analyse attitudes to tourism need either to explain the concept of tourism or test the respondents' understanding of tourism.

The main research on attitudes to tourism has been exploratory and descriptive in most cases (Ap 1990), with the exception of a limited number of longitudinal studies (e.g. Getz 1994). The outcome, as Ap (1990: 666) argued, is that 'there is limited understanding of why residents respond to the impacts of tourism as they do, and under what conditions they react to those impacts'. Rothman (1978) acknowledged that communities with a history of exposure to tourism adapt to accommodate its effects, so that their attitudes may change through time. This is supported by arguments that communities can simultaneously hold both positive and negative attitudes towards tourism. Likewise active or passive support for tourism or opposition to it may exist at any given time, as small interest groups take political action to achieve specific aims in relation to tourism.

## The social impact of ecotourism operations

According to Lindberg and McKercher (1997: 73), 'As with the natural environment, the sociocultural environment serves as both an attraction and a recipient of ecotourism's impacts . . . If these impacts become, on the whole, too negative, the local sustainability of ecotourism can be jeopardised.' For the tourism industry, the main concerns are to ensure the local population are not alienated or adversely impacted to the point that they may want to affect the local resource base or deny future access to the resource, where they are the custodians. What is notable in the existing literature, is the absence of longitudinal studies of communities affected by ecotourism to assess changes in attitudes and cultural changes towards tourists, within the context of existing models of social impacts. According to McKercher (1996) this is one of the most pressing areas for research, because if access is denied to the resource base, then ecotourism will not be able to proceed. In addition, 'Many ecotourism activities involve interaction between greatly differing cultures, and these differences may exacerbate the negative sociocultural impacts of ecotourism' (Lindberg and Mckercher 1997: 74).

In some research contexts such as Labuan Bajo in Indonesia, external operators derived greater benefits from ecotourism than local residents (Walpole and Goodwin 2000), although Wunder (2000) found that in Cuyabeno Wildlife Reserve in Ecuador, ecotourism did provide additional income for local people. In the case of butterfly tourism, Slinger (2000) noted that ecotourism was a useful supplement to agroforestry, as was the case in Canada's west Arctic (Notzke 1999). Within the existing research literereature on the impact of ecotourism, community economic benefits derived from such activity dominate the discussion, as Schluze (1998) examined in Sabah, Malaysia in the Lower Kinabatangan area. However, Kangas et al. (1995) concluded that in a study of one ecotourism operation in Belize, local communities benefited, particularly as 80 per cent of the economic benefits filtered through to residents at the Possum Point project. As Victurine (2000) outlined in the context of Uganda, building community-based skills to enable entrepreneurs to ensure a viable community-based tourism sector such as this is vital in the case of ecotourism. Walker's (1998) study of residents' perceptions of ecotourism in Mexico found different communities benefited in different ways, with between 70 and 75 per cent of the local population considering they benefited even though only 3.2 per cent of the local population were employed in ecotourism activities. Similarly, Campbell (1999) observed that while residents in Ostional, Costa Rica had positive attitudes towards tourism, they had limited awareness of employment or investment opportunities and this restricted their own opportunities to benefit from ecotourism-related development.

One of the key elements of ecotourism is that it should be locally beneficial, which also raises issues related to the degree of control local people have over ecotourism ventures, highlighting the need to consider the empowerment of local communities (Ashley and Roe 1998). In a seminal study by Scheyvens (1999), the key element of ecotourism is that it should contribute to improved cultural appreciation and understanding both for host communities and for tourists; cultural heritage and local pride (Ross and Wall 1999a) were highlighted. Khan (1997b: 990) also suggested that by emphasising local lifestyles, values and economic well-being, ecotourism may promote local identity, pride and self-accomplishment. By empowering the community through local participation, ecotourism can create an opportunity for self-generating tourism as opposed to capitalist control of mass tourism. Ecotourism with its small-scale development, provides opportunities for local empowerment, encourages the use of local knowledge and labour, promotes local ownership, perpetuates local identity and strengthens economic equity. As mentioned above, the empowerment thesis posits that if positive attitudes to ecotourism are to be fostered, residents living in or adjacent to a protected area should be receiving economic and social benefits or compensations which will support or complement their livelihoods (Lindberg and Enriquez 1994).

Lindberg *et al.* (1998a) also suggested that local residents should decide what level of tourism they want (i.e. self-determination), what cultural practices they wish to share, and where tourists will be allowed to go. Several different levels of community involvement are possible, from full local development of facilities to partnerships or joint ventures with industry, to the delegation of rights in exchange for fees (Brandon 1996). The process should include raising the awareness of probable tourism impacts so that residents can make informed decisions regarding the desirability of tourism.

A number of surveys of residents and visitors have been carried out to determine the attitude of visitors to tourism and the environment in the Shark Bay World Heritage Region of Western Australia (Dowling 1991, 1993a, 1996d, 2000d). This has led to a longitudinal study which is now in its second decade of operation and indicates that the majority of visitors are from Western Australia (70 per cent), Australia (17 per cent) or overseas (13 per cent). The popular activities were dolphin viewing, swimming, photography and fishing. Residents also undertake four-wheel driving and power boating. Visitors indicate a desire to return and see more of the region as well as the unspoiled environment and the region's wildlife. A number of management issues have also been examined to increase the region's use as well as more stringent environmental protection measures (Dowling and Alder 1996; Dowling 2000d).

Zeiger (1997: 88) suggested that ecotourism, by its very nature, builds up expectations and raises the risk of hit-and-run tourism. This is described as an influx of nature lovers and culture addicts to the latest wild spot, followed by its abandonment once discovered and degraded. Moreover, ecotourism attractions can be located in the most remote and rural areas. Therefore, ancient cultures and economies may be harmed or disrupted. He added that sustainable development not only ensures that consumption of tourism does not exceed

**Table 6.7** Framework for determining the impacts of ecotourism initiatives on local communities

| | Signs of empowerment | Signs of disempowerment |
|---|---|---|
| Economic empowerment | Ecotourism brings lasting economic gains to a local community. Cash earned is shared between many households in the community. There are visible signs of improvements from the cash that is earned (e.g. improved water systems, houses made of more permanent materials) | Ecotourism merely results in small, spasmodic cash gains for a local community. Most profits go to local elites, outside operators, government agencies, etc. Only a few individuals or families gain direct financial benefits from ecotourism, while others cannot find a way to share in these economic benefits because they lack capital and/or appropriate skills |
| Psychological empowerment | Self-esteem of many community members is enhanced because of outside recognition of the uniqueness and value of their culture, their natural resources and their traditional knowledge. Increasing confidence of community members leads them to seek out further education and training opportunities. Access to employment and cash leads to an increase in status for traditionally low-status sectors of society, e.g. women, youths | Many people have not shared in the benefits of ecotourism, yet they may face hardships because of reduced access to the resources of a protected area. They are thus confused, frustrated, uninterested or disillusioned with the initiative |
| Social empowerment | Ecotourism maintains or enhances the local community's equilibrium. Community cohesion is improved as individuals and families work together to build a successful ecotourism venture. Some funds raised are used for community development purposes, e.g. to build schools or improve roads | Disharmony and social decay. Many in the community take on outside values and lose respect for traditional culture and for elders. Disadvantaged groups (e.g. women) bear the brunt of problems associated with the ecotourism initiative and fail to share equitably in its benefits. Rather than cooperating, individuals, families, ethnic or socio-economic groups compete with each other for the perceived benefits of ecotourism. Resentment and jealousy are commonplace |
| Political empowerment | The community's political structure, which fairly represents the needs and interests of all community groups, provides a forum through which people can raise questions relating to the ecotourism venture and have their concerns dealt with. Agencies initiating or implementing the ecotourism venture seek out the opinions of community groups (including special interest groups of women, youths and other socially disadvantaged groups) and provide opportunities for them to be represented on decision-making bodies, e.g. the Wildlife Park Board | The community has an autocratic and/or self-interested leadership. Agencies initiating or implementing the ecotourism venture treat communities as passive beneficiaries, failing to involve them in decision-making. Thus the majority of community members feel they have little or no say over *whether* the ecotourism initiative operates or *the way* in which it operates |

*Source*: Scheyvens (1999: 247).

the ability of the host destination to prosper, but also provides for the freedom, education and welfare of the host community. One example of a tour operator which has helped to contribute in this way is Overseas Adventure Travel.

Overseas Adventure Travel (OAT), based in Cambridge, Massachusetts, and founded in 1979, is one of the largest nature tourism outbound operators in the United States with a sophisticated marketing programme for its exclusive, well-guided packaged tours. During its early years, it concentrated on camping safaris in East Africa (Honey 1999: 69). It has set up a non-profit foundation that provides material and financial assistance for a number of local projects, including the International University for Peace in Costa Rica, the Himalayan Trust in Nepal, and the Eastern Africa Environmental Network. It is also moving towards offering 'home stays' with local families in order to increase the cross-cultural experience and bring more money into local communities (Honey 1999: 70).

As Scheyvens (1999: 245) noted, from a development perspective ecotourism ventures should only be considered successful if 'local communities have some measure of control over them and if they share equitably in the benefits emerging from ecotourism activities'. As Table 6.7 shows, Scheyvens (1999) developed a useful framework for determining the impacts of ecotourism on local communities in relation to signs of empowerment and disempowerment, and its value lies in its application in both the developed and developing world, emphasising that 'the rationale behind the framework is that ecotourism should promote both conservation and development at the local level' (Schyvens 1999: 249).

## The environmental impact of ecotourism

Since much of Chapter 2 discusses the tourism–environment relationship and the nature of tourism impacts on the environment, it is useful in this section to examine a number of themes: first, how ecotourism impacts on the natural environment, given the close relationship between nature-based tourism, nature and the natural world; second, what methodologies have been developed by ecotourism researchers to draw together environmental impacts of ecotourism in a more holistic manner so that impacts are set within the context of the site, locale and area.

Hvenegaard (1994) described a litany of adverse environmental impacts caused by tourism in protected areas. They include overcrowding, overdevelopment, unregulated recreation, pollution, wildlife disturbance and vehicle use. These effects are more serious for ecotourism than general tourism because the former is more dependent on relatively pristine natural environments than the latter, in terms of attracting new travellers. In addition, since ecotourism impacts are often concentrated in ecologically sensitive areas, he argued that they must be controlled. Thus, ecotourism is reliant on natural phenomena in relatively undisturbed sites such as protected areas (Hvenegaard and Dearden 1998). As Lindberg and McKercher (1997: 71) argued, ecotourists often go to environmentally fragile areas; visit during sensitive seasons; may be the first stage of mass tourism; may cause off-site as well as on-site impacts. What is beyond doubt is that 'there is relatively little accumulated knowledge regarding ecotourism's impacts on the environment and the effects on the ecotourist's experience'. For example, Deming (1996) described the adverse impacts of tourists on birds at Point Peele National Park in Ontario, Canada during the spring migration. The birders still continued to venture off the designated paths to view and photograph species despite being advised not to do this. In some cases visitor impacts on water birds in wildlife refuges have caused the refuges to close during certain times of the year and to limit access so that migratory bird habits are not intruded upon by birdwatchers and their behaviour.

McLaren (1998: 89) suggested that tourism development, even in ecotourism destinations, was often at odds with both ecological preservation and local use. The large numbers of tourists going to these places often greatly exceed the carrying capacities. Most tourism destinations are energy intensive and highly pollutive and tend to be built in 'cluster sites' or development nodes, such as a row of hotels along a beach. Thus, McLaren (1998) argued that this pattern of development diverts resources (energy, land and water) away from the local population to accommodate the tourist sector. It also puts heavy stress on the environment, since tourist sites require reconstruction of the landscape and increased use of petroleum products and toxins such as chemicals, fertilisers and pesticides. These cluster sites greatly disturb natural human patterns of living and are at odds with wildlife and the natural world. Most ecotourism definitions include a stipulation that the visitation be environmentally and culturally sensitive, adhering to a low-impact ethic. However, ecotourists still hike, camp and have measurable impacts on protected areas, impacts that are often confounded with those of tourists, recreationists and even local residents (Marion and Farrell 1998: 155).

Much of the existing impact research on ecotourism, particularly in the environmental context, has been notable for its absence of systematic, ecologically informed assessments of tourism impacts. The failure to monitor the ecological change induced or affected by ecotourism activities means that many studies remain ad hoc case studies which do not utilise many of the tools and techniques that exist within environmental science to monitor the impacts of tourism on the environment discussed in Chapter 2. Rather than review each impact study of ecotourism and its contribution to an understanding of environmental impacts, it is helpful to consider a case study of the scope and extent of environmental impacts of ecotourism in one location – Borneo – to illustrate the issues, then to consider two methodologies used by ecotourism researchers to gauge environmental change associated with ecotourism.

## CASE STUDY – Bako National Park, Borneo

Tourism has long played an important role in the economy of Malaysia, representing the second most important industry sector and generating at least RM9.6 billion of

Table 6.8    Importance of activities undertaken by visitors in Bako National Park

| Activity | Very important | Important | Not important |
|----------|----------------|-----------|---------------|
| | | (Percentage of respondents*) | |
| Close to nature | 78 | 15 | 4 |
| Observe/encounter wildlife | 72 | 21 | 6 |
| Learn about nature | 70 | 20 | 6 |
| Scenery | 70 | 24 | 5 |
| Break from routine | 54 | 28 | 15 |
| Solitude | 30 | 34 | 33 |

* Percentages have been rounded to the nearest whole number, and therefore do not necessarily sum to a total of 100 in all cases.

the country's GDP (Razak 1995). The dual aims of a recent study were to identify problem conditions or unacceptable visitor impacts, and to identify indicators for the management of these impacts in Bako National Park in Sarawak, on the island of Borneo. The study represented one of the first efforts to identify problems in the condition of a national park in Sarawak from an ecotourism perspective.

Bako National Park is an established ecotourist destination, and existing management objectives for the park are compatible with ecotourism. The primary management objective for Bako is conservation, while secondary objectives include recreation, research and education (Good 1988). Bako was the first gazetted national park in Sarawak, constituted in 1957. Recreational access within the park is facilitated by a 30 km trail system that incorporates 16 trails, and offers a number of trekking options. The proximity of Bako National Park to the capital city of Kuching (37 km) means that it is easily accessible to both local and international visitors, and has attracted increasing numbers of overseas visitors (Nor 1992). However, despite the growth of ecotourism activity in Bako National Park, very little information existed regarding the environmental (biophysical and social) impacts of visitor activity, or the acceptability of these impacts to visitors.

A questionnaire was designed to gain information from people who have visited Bako National Park and 236 individuals were sampled between December 1996 and January 1997. The questionnaire had three parts: to ascertain visitor and visit characteristics; activities undertaken; and visitor perceptions of impacts and management strategies. A total of 210 responses were obtained from the 284 questionnaires distributed by on-site researchers, representing a 74 per cent response rate. Of the 46 questionnaires distributed by park staff, 26 were returned, representing a 56 per cent response rate. More than half of the visitors surveyed (58 per cent) stayed at least one night in the park, while the remaining proportion stayed less than 24 hours. The activities participated in related to the enjoyment of nature and included hiking (76 per cent), sightseeing (72 per cent), observing wildlife (66 per cent), relaxing (61 per cent) and photography (61 per cent) (Table 6.8).

The impacts most frequently observed by visitors included soil erosion along walk trails, litter along the beach/shore, wildlife attracted to garbage bins, and

Table 6.9  Visitor perceptions of observed and potential impacts in Bako National Park

| Impact | Observed | Potential | Comparison: observed and potential |
|---|---|---|---|
| | (Percentage of respondents) | | (Significance (P)) |
| Soil erosion at walk trails | 50 | 40 | NS* |
| Litter along beach/shore | 42 | 58 | < 0.01 |
| Wildlife attracted to rubbish bins | 38 | 45 | < 0.05 |
| Smelly/discoloured water | 36 | 31 | NS* |
| Vegetation damage – walk trails | 29 | 39 | < 0.05 |
| Litter around accommodation area | 27 | 41 | < 0.01 |
| Feeding monkeys | 26 | 47 | < 0.01 |
| Hiking away from walk trails | 22 | 45 | < 0.01 |
| Soil erosion at accommodation area | 19 | 35 | < 0.01 |
| Too many people | 5 | 28 | < 0.01 |

* NS = no significance.

smelly/discoloured water (see Table 6.9). Vegetation damage along walk trails and hiking away from walk trails was also noted. A number of respondents also commented on impacts such as litter on the forest floor, waterlogging along some trails and at the accommodation area, provocation of wildlife, and a lack of enforcement of park regulations. The significance of litter as one of the most basic concerns of Bako visitors is supported by the results of similar studies in Western Australia (Dowling 1993b; Morin *et al.* 1997), Canada (BC Forest Service 1995) and the USA (Lucas 1990). The intolerance of visitors to litter may be explained by the view that littering violates deeply held societal norms, which means it is seen as abuse rather than normal use of natural areas (Lucas 1990).

The greater proportion of respondents expressed concern about potential impacts compared with observed impacts (Table 6.10). In particular, almost five times as many respondents indicated that too many people represented a potential impact compared with the observed impact. Further, hiking away from trails, feeding monkeys and soil erosion at the accommodation area were identified as potential impacts by about double the proportion of visitors that had observed the impact. All of these impacts are explicitly caused by the presence of people. Therefore, these results imply a recognition by visitors that impacts and degradation are an integral part of human use of the environment. The results also indicated a belief that park management is not able to prevent such impacts from becoming more significant in the future.

The results suggested that litter, erosion along walk trails and vegetation damage represent potential indicators for monitoring visitor impacts, based on the premise that the best indicators are conditions of importance to visitors. Thirty per cent of respondents provided comments and suggestions to aid management. All management strategies gained substantial support (see Table 6.11), including regulatory actions often deemed to be 'unpopular', such as limiting forest use and limiting the number of people overall and in a group.

Table 6.10   Visitors' perceptions regarding the conditions in Bako National Park

| Concern | Significant problem | Slight problem | No problem | No response |
|---|---|---|---|---|
| | | | (Percentage of respondents*) | |
| Litter around park | 34 | 35 | 26 | 4 |
| Damage to natural vegetation | 19 | 38 | 35 | 9 |
| Erosion along walk trails | 17 | 45 | 32 | 7 |
| Health/condition of wildlife | 15 | 26 | 44 | 15 |
| No. of people encountered | 11 | 20 | 65 | 4 |
| Size of groups encountered | 8 | 25 | 62 | 5 |
| No. of human-made structures | 4 | 24 | 66 | 6 |

* Percentages have been rounded to the nearest whole number, and therefore do not necessarily sum to a total of 100 in all cases.

Table 6.11   Visitor responses to potential management actions for Bako National Park

| Management action | Support | Oppose | Do not care |
|---|---|---|---|
| | | (Percentage of respondents*) | |
| Educate visitors on conservation | 79 | 3 | 18 |
| Provide more maps and signs | 61 | 12 | 26 |
| Limit overall number of people | 60 | 14 | 26 |
| Limit use of forest area | 58 | 17 | 25 |
| Limit number of people per group | 56 | 16 | 28 |
| Provide more staff | 49 | 8 | 43 |
| Limit length of stay at peak times | 48 | 22 | 30 |
| Provide more facilities | 40 | 36 | 23 |

* Percentages have been rounded to the nearest whole number, and therefore do not necessarily sum to a total of 100 in all cases.

Visitor support for education in the Bako study replicates that found in Western Australian (Morin *et al.* 1997) and British Columbian (BC Forest Service 1995) studies. Bako users also supported the provision of maps and signs in the park. Bako respondents provided less support – and increased opposition – for more facilities and limiting the length of stay, which indicates that visitors perceive the potential for these actions to reduce the wilderness experience. The main impacts as perceived by respondents were biophysical, including litter, erosion along walk trails and vegetation damage, which are also very visual impacts with the potential to reduce the natural experience ecotourism offers. Further, greater visitor concern for potential impacts, as compared with observed impacts, indicates a perception that social and biophysical conditions in the park are likely to worsen in the future. Management concerns identified by a larger proportion of respondents – litter, erosion and vegetation damage along walk trails – correspond to the impacts identified as of greater concern to visitors. Therefore, the findings of this study suggest that litter, erosion and vegetation damage represent potential indicators for monitoring visitor impacts in Bako National Park. Respondents indicated strong support for management actions in general, including both educational and regulatory strategies such as controlling visitor numbers and limiting forest use, indicating a belief that human influence (including numbers and behaviour) is a major cause of existing impacts. This broad support for management provides managers with a choice of strategies to address environmental concerns. The study identified the effects of ecotourists, both on the natural environment and on the recreation experience, considered to be of most concern to visitors themselves. This work is an essential first step towards establishing a comprehensive wilderness planning framework for sustaining ecotourism in Bako National Park.

Source: Chin et al. (2000)

## Assessing environmental impacts from ecotourism: the multiple parameter rating system

In a study of one of Uganda's forest national parks, Kibale, ecotourism was only introduced in 1992. The number of tourists visiting the park rose from 1,300 in 1992 to 5,000 in 1996. Given park managers' concerns related to environmental problems stemming from ecotourism, Obua and Harding (1997) employed the multiple parameter rating system (MPRS) developed by Parsons and MacLeod (1980) to assess impacts. In essence, the technique collates information on a range of environmental parameters and a series of scores and weightings are used to quantify the observations. This is a highly subjective tool, but does consider the visible impacts of visitors. In Kibale Park, nine camp sites in the wet and dry season were examined as shown in Table 6.12, and the impact indices are shown in Table 6.13. As Table 6.13 shows, the impacts were greater in the dry season, since the wet season allowed grass cover to regenerate. This is a useful, if not rudimentary, method to assess visitor impact at key sites. Obua and Harding (1997) also examined environmental degradation on nature trails, thereby developing the holistic assessment of ecotourism's impact on-site and off-site discussed by Lindberg and Hawkins (1993).

Obua and Harding (1997) examined a series of cross-sections along nature trails as snapshots of trail degradation at specific points in time and space. Two types of trails were examined – grid trails and road and loop (winding) trails. Only 9 people were allowed on trails at any one time to reduce visitor pressure. A series of 90 sampling points were examined on the trails and a range of environmental parameters were considered (see Table 6.14). Approximately 10 per cent of trails had experienced some form of erosion, with 30 per cent of grid trails with a moderate form of erosion, which are more heavily used than the loop trails. Therefore, in spite of low visitor numbers, substantial elements of environmental damage had occurred in four years of use at

Table 6.12  The criteria, rating and weight used for the evaluation of recreational impact on the camping sites at Kibale National Park

| Criteria/parameter | Rating | Weight |
|---|---|---|
| *Vegetation loss* | | 2 |
| Both $S_0$ and $S_1$ belong to the same vegetation class | 1 | |
| Vegetation coverage on $S_0$ is one class lower than on $S_1$ | 2 | |
| The difference in vegetation coverage on $S_0$ and $S_1$ is two or more classes | 3 | |
| *Mineral soil increase* | | 3 |
| Both $S_0$ and $S_1$ have the same mineral soil exposure | 1 | |
| Mineral soil exposure on $S_0$ is one class lower than on $S_1$ | 2 | |
| The difference in mineral soil exposure on $S_0$ and $S_1$ is two or more classes | 3 | |
| *Tree damage* | | 2 |
| No trees damaged | 1 | |
| 1–8 trees damaged or 1–3 trees felled | 2 | |
| More than 8 trees damaged or more than 3 trees felled | 3 | |
| *Root exposure* | | 3 |
| No tree with exposed root | 1 | |
| 1–6 trees with exposed roots | 2 | |
| More than 6 trees with exposed roots | 3 | |
| *Development* | | 2 |
| No fire site | 1 | |
| One fire ring, log seats or both | 2 | |
| Two or more fire rings | 3 | |
| *Cleanliness* | | 1 |
| One fire scar, no scattered charcoal, no human waste | 1 | |
| Two or more fire scars, some evidence of human waste | 2 | |
| Scattered litter and greater occurrence of human waste | 3 | |
| *Social trails* | | 1 |
| One discernible trail | 1 | |
| Two or more discernible trails or one well-worn trail | 2 | |
| More than three discernible trails or well-worn trail | 3 | |
| *Camp area* | | 3 |
| Less than 50 $m^2$ disturbed | 1 | |
| About 50–200 $m^2$ disturbed | 2 | |
| More than 200 $m^2$ disturbed | 3 | |
| *Barren core area* | | 2 |
| Bare area less than 5 $m^2$ | 1 | |
| Bare area is about 5–50 $m^2$ | 2 | |
| Bare area is more than 50 $m^2$ | 3 | |

*Source*: Obua and Harding (1997: 217).

**Table 6.13** The impact indices derived for the nine camping sites at Kibale National Park in the wet and dry seasons. The indices for the dry season are in parentheses

| Parameter | Sites | | | | | | | | | Σ | Mean |
|---|---|---|---|---|---|---|---|---|---|---|---|
| | 1 | 2 | 3 | 4 | 5 | 6 | 7 | 8 | 9 | | |
| Area (m²) | 150 | 110 | 150 | 150 | 150 | 120 | 200 | 400 | 500 | | |
| Vegetation loss | 4 | 4 | 4 | 4 | 4 | 4 | 4 | 4 | 4 | 36 | 4.0 |
| | (4) | (4) | (6) | (4) | (4) | (4) | (4) | (8) | (4) | (42) | (4.6) |
| Mineral soil increase | 3 | 3 | 3 | 3 | 3 | 3 | 3 | 3 | 3 | 27 | 3.0 |
| | (6) | (3) | (9) | (3) | (6) | (3) | (6) | (6) | (3) | (45) | (5.0) |
| Tree damage | 2 | 2 | 2 | 2 | 2 | 2 | 4 | 4 | 4 | 24 | 2.7 |
| | (2) | (4) | (4) | (4) | (4) | (4) | (4) | (4) | (2) | (32) | (3.6) |
| Root exposure | 3 | 3 | 3 | 3 | 3 | 3 | 3 | 3 | 3 | 27 | 3.0 |
| | (3) | (3) | (3) | (3) | (3) | (3) | (3) | (3) | (3) | (27) | (3.0) |
| Development | 4 | 4 | 4 | 4 | 4 | 4 | 4 | 6 | 4 | 38 | 4.2 |
| | (4) | (4) | (4) | (4) | (4) | (4) | (4) | (4) | (6) | (38) | (4.2) |
| Cleanliness | 1 | 1 | 1 | 1 | 1 | 1 | 1 | 2 | 1 | 10 | 1.1 |
| | (1) | (2) | (2) | (1) | (1) | (2) | (2) | (1) | (2) | (14) | (1.6) |
| Social trails | 2 | 2 | 2 | 2 | 2 | 2 | 2 | 4 | 2 | 20 | 2.2 |
| | (2) | (2) | (2) | (2) | (2) | (2) | (4) | (6) | (2) | (24) | (2.7) |
| Camp area | 3 | 3 | 3 | 3 | 3 | 3 | 6 | 9 | 6 | 39 | 4.3 |
| | (6) | (3) | (6) | (6) | (6) | (6) | (9) | (9) | (9) | (60) | (6.7) |
| Barren core area | 2 | 2 | 2 | 2 | 2 | 2 | 2 | 2 | 2 | 18 | 2.0 |
| | (2) | (2) | (2) | (2) | (2) | (2) | (2) | (4) | (2) | (20) | (2.2) |
| Cumulative impact index (I) | 24 | 24 | 24 | 24 | 24 | 24 | 29 | 37 | 29 | 239 | 26.5 |
| | (30) | (27) | (38) | (38) | (32) | (30) | (38) | (45) | (33) | (302) | (33.6) |
| Impact class | L | L | L | L | L | L | M | H | M | | L |

*Source*: Obua and Harding (1997: 218).

Table 6.14  Description of the parameters considered in the appraisal of impacts on the trails at Kibale National Park

| Parameter | Description |
|---|---|
| *Erosion* | *Mean incision (cm) x mean width (cm)* |
| Negligible | < 2 × < 25 |
| Low | 2–6 × 25–50 |
| Moderate | 6–8 × 50–100 |
| High | > 8 × > 100 |
| *Root exposure* | Number of trees |
| Negligible | 0 |
| Low | 1–3 |
| High | 4–8 |
| Severe | > 8 |
| *Vegetation* | Proportion (%) of dominant plant type |
| Grassland | > 50 grass |
| Shrub | > 50 shrubs |
| Forest | > 50 trees |
| *Slope* | Degrees (°) |
| Gentle | 0–20 |
| Moderate | 21–30 |
| Steep | > 30 |

*Source*: Obua and Harding (1997: 219).

camp sites and trails. This is consistent with other research where trail erosion followed a rise in visitor numbers in national parks in Costa Rica.

Obua and Harding (1997) argued that Kibale Park needed to establish the carrying capacity of the area so that ecotourism principles do not conflict with conservation goals. This reaffirms the need for sound environmental management for ecotourism to avoid degradation of the resource to the point where ecotourism activities have to cease. What this example illustrates is the need to conduct impact research that can recognise the extent of environmental conflicts, to recommend appropriate action to address the problem. One further approach recently used in ecotourism is the Sorensen Network to determine the potential effects of ecotourism on the marine environment.

## The Sorensen Network to assess the potential effects of ecotourism

Mason and Moore (1998) examined the scope of environmental impact methodologies available to identify effects in terms of ad hoc methods, checklists, matrices and networks. Networks allow one to link causes and effects in the ecosystem, such as a marine environment. Whereas the example of Kibale Park used visual observation to derive data on existing impacts, the Sorensen Network approach considers impacts in a diagrammatic form (Bisset 1987) to establish causal chains which link activities, impacts and their outcome.

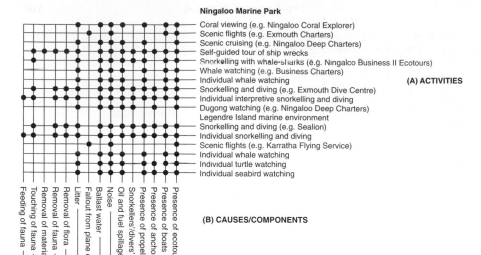

**Ningaloo Marine Park**

Coral viewing (e.g. Ningaloo Coral Explorer)
Scenic flights (e.g. Exmouth Charters)
Scenic cruising (e.g. Ningaloo Deep Charters)
Self-guided tour of ship wrecks
Snorkelling with whale-sharks (e.g. Ningalco Business II Ecotours)
Whale watching (e.g. Business Charters)
Individual whale watching
Snorkelling and diving (e.g. Exmouth Dive Centre)
Individual interpretive snorkelling and diving
Dugong watching (e.g. Ningaloo Deep Charters)
Legendre Island marine environment
Snorkelling and diving (e.g. Sealion)
Individual snorkelling and diving
Scenic flights (e.g. Karratha Flying Service)
Individual whale watching
Individual turtle watching
Individual seabird watching

**(A) ACTIVITIES**

Feeding of fauna
Touching of fauna
Removal of material
Removal of fauna
Removal of fauna
Removal of flora
Litter
Fallout from plane engines
Ballast water
Noise
Oil and fuel spillage
Snorkellers'/divers' flippers
Presence of propellers
Presence of anchors
Presence of boats
Presence of ecotourists

**(B) CAUSES/COMPONENTS**

| (C) PRIMARY EFFECTS | (D) CONSEQUENT CONDITIONS |
|---|---|
| **Biophysical** | |
| *Negative* | |
| Decrease in abundance and diversity of flora | Change in structure/compostion of flora |
| Decrease in abundance and diversity of fauna | Change in structure/composition of fauna |
| Displacement of fauna | Fauna occupying less desirable habitats |
| Change in fauna behaviour | Fauna become stressed |
| Decrease in the aesthetics of the area | Impairment of natural scene |
| Decrease in water quality | Increase in contamination |
| Decrease in air quality | Aesthetics of the area decrease |
| *Positive* | |
| Conservation awareness | Reduction in environmental effects |
| **Sociocultural** | |
| *Negative* | |
| Overcrowding of site | Host community and ecotourists are in conflict causing dissatisfaction |
| Demonstration effect (alien ideas, behaviour and lifestyle) | Alteration of the host community |
| Effect on social pathology | Increase in crime and associated activities |
| Change in the pace of life | Change from a slow to a fast pace of life |
| Lack of sufficient infrastructure (e.g. electricity, water, roads) | Increased pressure on existing infrastructure and demand for new facilities |
| Commodification of local culture | Loss of traditional knowledge |
| Degradation of archaeological sites (e.g. shipwrecks) | Loss of cultural value and heritage |
| Diversion of resources | Resources diverted from ecotourist and into other activities |
| Conflict of marine uses | Alter or maintain current uses |
| *Positive* | |
| Improvement in infrastructure | Diversification of facilities and services |
| Better services | Increase in diversification of services |
| Cultural appreciation | Encourages host community and ecotourists to value cultural assets |
| Improved environmental education | A more environmentally informed community |

**Figure 6.6** The Sorensen Network

*Sources:* Australian Conservation Foundation (1994); Boo (1990); Buckley and Pannell (1990); Burns and Associates (1989); Commonwealth Department of Tourism (1993); Dowling and Alder (1996); Hall (1995); United States Congress Office of Technology Assessment (1993); Westman (1985)

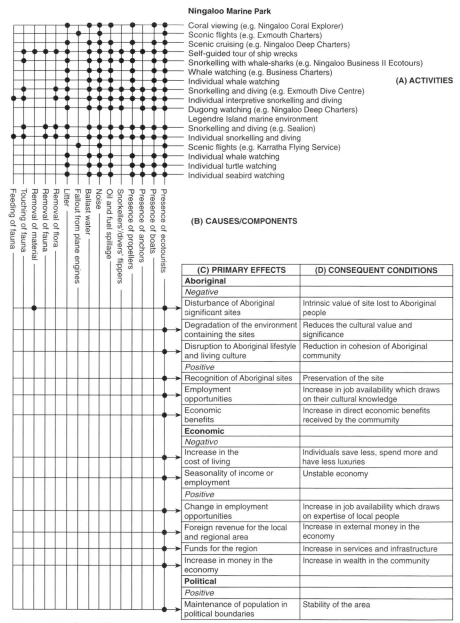

**Ningaloo Marine Park**

Coral viewing (e.g. Ningaloo Coral Explorer)
Scenic flights (e.g. Exmouth Charters)
Scenic cruising (e.g. Ningaloo Deep Charters)
Self-guided tour of ship wrecks
Snorkelling with whale-sharks (e.g. Ningaloo Business II Ecotours)
Whale watching (e.g. Business Charters)
Individual whale watching                              **(A) ACTIVITIES**
Snorkelling and diving (e.g. Exmouth Dive Centre)
Individual interpretive snorkelling and diving
Dugong watching (e.g. Ningaloo Deep Charters)
Legendre Island marine environment
Snorkelling and diving (e.g. Sealion)
Individual snorkelling and diving
Scenic flights (e.g. Karratha Flying Service)
Individual whale watching
Individual turtle watching
Individual seabird watching

Column labels (B) CAUSES/COMPONENTS:
Feeding of fauna
Touching of fauna
Removal of fauna
Removal of material
Removal of fauna
Removal of flora
Litter
Fallout from plane engines
Ballast water
Noise
Oil and fuel spillage
Snorkellers'/divers' flippers
Presence of propellers
Presence of anchors
Presence of boats
Presence of ecotourists

**(B) CAUSES/COMPONENTS**

| (C) PRIMARY EFFECTS | (D) CONSEQUENT CONDITIONS |
|---|---|
| **Aboriginal** | |
| *Negative* | |
| Disturbance of Aboriginal significant sites | Intrinsic value of site lost to Aboriginal people |
| Degradation of the environment containing the sites | Reduces the cultural value and significance |
| Disruption to Aboriginal lifestyle and living culture | Reduction in cohesion of Aboriginal community |
| *Positive* | |
| Recognition of Aboriginal sites | Preservation of the site |
| Employment opportunities | Increase in job availability which draws on their cultural knowledge |
| Economic benefits | Increase in direct economic benefits received by the community |
| **Economic** | |
| *Negative* | |
| Increase in the cost of living | Individuals save less, spend more and have less luxuries |
| Seasonality of income or employment | Unstable economy |
| *Positive* | |
| Change in employment opportunities | Increase in job availability which draws on expertise of local people |
| Foreign revenue for the local and regional area | Increase in external money in the economy |
| Funds for the region | Increase in services and infrastructure |
| Increase in money in the economy | Increase in wealth in the community |
| **Political** | |
| *Positive* | |
| Maintenance of population in political boundaries | Stability of the area |

**Figure 6.6**   (*cont'd*)

However, one major drawback is their visual complexity. To operationalise this approach in Western Australia, Mason and Moore (1998) collected data on the potential effects of ecotourism operations in two marine environments (Ningaloo and Legendre) from existing research studies and a review of ecotourism company operations in each area. Figure 6.6, which is Part A of the Sorensen Network, outlined the scope of activities and effects. In Part B, the causal element was examined, which could be potential effects of something foreign in the environment (i.e. the ecotourist), pollution effects, removal of part of the marine environment and human interaction (i.e. feeding or touching mammals). This can result in primary effects (Part C) in the Sorensen Network and conditions associated with the effects are included as consequent conditions in Part D. The technique gives a holistic view of the impacts of ecotourism activities. In the case of Ningaloo and Legendre, 28 of the 32 possible effects were identified for ecotourism activities. The positive effects were sociocultural and economic (i.e. improvements in infrastructure and additional visitor spending). Most of the negative effects were biophysical (i.e. reduction in the diversity and extent of flora and water quality). The benefit of such an approach is a more integrated impact methodology which not only groups potential effects together but combines economic, sociocultural and environmental impacts. It also provides a balanced assessment of the costs and benefits of ecotourism development. It also allows one to consider which forms of ecotourism are the least detrimental to the marine environment. As Mason and Moore (1998: 152) concluded,

> The Ecotourism Sorensen Network, as an impact assessment tool, allows the integration of qualitative data from the biophysical and sociophysical and socioeconomic environments, for both potential and existing impacts. The Network then provides a basis for further analysis . . . It also provides a mechanism for managers to identify the causes of environmental effects and the links between activities, causes and effects.

## Summary

The impact of ecotourism on the economic, sociocultural and environmental context of development has emerged as an important area for analysis to answer a simple question: should areas and their communities develop ecotourism? To date, most of the existing evidence has been focused on the economic returns to the locality and research is far from conclusive about the benefits. While residents frequently perceive the benefits, this may not be matched in reality due to the impact of external agencies such as tour operators. Where ecotourism has been developed, it is worth recognising that 'Locally based ecotourism can be less susceptible to the whims of the outside world if the communities maintain other forms of economic activity. Some of the most successful ecotourism projects are tied to scientific research stations, working farms, or fishing communities where there are several sources of income' (Honey 1999: 91).

In a sociocultural context, Honey (1999: 90) also warned of the potential impacts since

> By definition, ecotourism often involves seeking out the most pristine, uncharted and unspoiled environments. Often these are home to isolated and fragile civilizations. In some areas, ecotourism is the front line of foreign encroachment and can accelerate the pace of social and environmental degradation and lead to a new form of Western penetration and domination of the last remaining 'untouched' parts of the world.

Ensuring the visitor not only respects nature and the host population is vital to the long-term viability of ecotourism. Otherwise, local opposition and resource degradation will ensure it is a short-lived economic activity. Issues of sustainability emerged very clearly in the example of Kibale Park, Uganda, and ensuring that environmental impact methodologies are used to assess potential impacts and to monitor ongoing impacts is vital. This highlights the need for appropriate forms of planning for ecotourism activities to which attention now turns in Chapter 7.

## Questions

1. What techniques exist to examine the economic impact of ecotourism?
2. How would you set about assessing the economic impact of an ecotourism operation?
3. What are the scope of sociocultural impacts of ecotourism developments?
4. What is the Sorensen Network?

## Further reading

For the community impact of ecotourism and the innovative models proposed see:

Drumm, A. (1988) 'New approaches to community-based ecotourism management. Learning from Ecuador', in K. Lindberg, M. Epler Wood and D. Engeldrum (eds), *Ecotourism: A Guide for Planners and Managers*, Vol. 2. North Bennington: Ecotourism Society, 197–213.

Johnston, A. (2000) 'Indigenous peoples and ecotourism: bringing indigenous knowledge and rights into the sustainability equation', *Tourism Recreation Research*, **25** (2): 89–96.

On the economic impact of ecotourism see:

Lindberg, K. and McKercher, B. (1997) 'Ecotourism: a critical overview', *Pacific Tourism Review*, **1** (1): 65–79,

which also offers a good overview of other impacts associated with ecotourism and on the impacts of ecotourism, the following offer a recent overview of each theme:

Lindberg, K. (2001) 'Economic impacts', in D. Weaver (ed.), *Encyclopedia of Ecotourism*, Wallingford: CAB International, 363–78.

Buckley, R. (2001) 'Environmental impacts', in D. Weaver (ed.), *Encyclopedia of Ecotourism*, Wallingford: CAB International, 379–94.

Wearing, S. (2001) 'Exploring socio-cultural impacts on local communities', in D. Weaver (ed.), *Encyclopedia of Ecotourism*, Wallingford: CAB International, 395–410.

## Appendix 6.1  Wildlife tourism in Scotland

### Public viewing of birds of prey

There are now a number of viewing sites both via live CCTV and live viewing for birds of prey in Scotland. These are as follows:

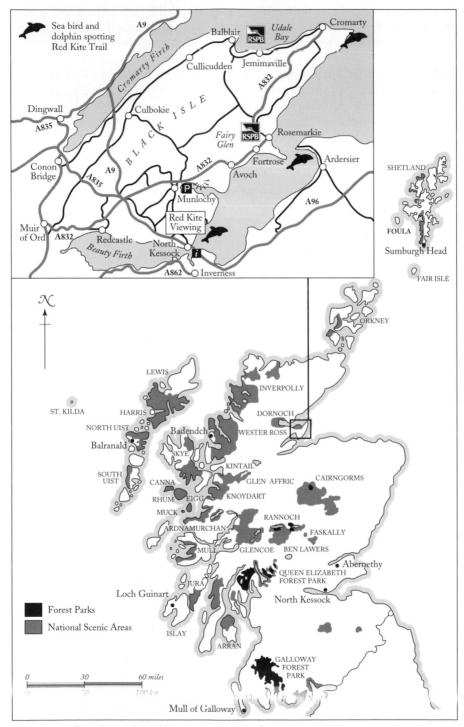

Figure 6.7   Sea bird and dolphin spotting sites in Scotland

- peregrine, Aberfoyle – CCTV;
- osprey, RSPB Loch Garten Osprey Centre – viewing centre + CCTV;
- red kite, North Kessock Tourist Information Centre, near Inverness – CCTV;
- sea eagles – Aros Centre Isle of Skye – CCTV, Isle of Mull – hide;
- hen harrier and merlin – RSPB Forsinard Nature Reserve – CCTV.

Note that in all cases viewing is subject to a nest being available and where CCTV is being used, technology operating. Further details are given below.

### Sea eagle public viewing facility
A local partnership of Aros (Isle of Skye) Ltd, RSPB Scotland, Scottish Natural Heritage, The Highland Council, and Skye & Lochalsh Enterprise has been formed to establish a public viewing facility for sea eagles on the island of Skye. The project is also supported by Forest Enterprise, a local landowner and a Crofting Township. The public viewing facility involves 'live' CCTV being transmitted from a sea eagle nest in Skye to the Aros Centre. RSPB Scotland will be the licence holder authorised to visit and photograph sea eagles at their nest.

The overall cost of setting up the project is around £30,000. The project includes the appointment of a new seasonal information warden to be based at the Aros Centre. The viewing facilities will be free. This initiative is seen as an integral part of a wider wildlife visitor management plan for Skye which will promote the wildlife and natural heritage of the island including existing facilities. Opportunities to deliver live pictures of other species such as herons are also being developed.

### Live viewing on sea eagles on Mull – pilot project
Viewing facilities were also set up on Mull, where RSPB Scotland, Forest Enterprise and Scottish Natural Heritage established a small hide from which a sea eagle nest could be viewed directly. Numbers had to be limited to 20 per visit, and a booking system was required (through the Forest Enterprise Oban Office), but guided by local naturalist Joyce Henderson over 1,000 people saw the Mull birds during the 2000 season. The pair successfully reared two chicks, and profits went to the Mull and Iona Community Trust for use in community environmental projects on the island. These are the first close-up viewing facilities for eagles in Britain, so if you are planning a trip north next year, do consider them for your itinerary.

### Red kites
In 1998 the RSPB joined up with the HOSTB to establish a red kite viewing facility in the Tourist Information Centre at North Kessock. The TIC now has TV equipment which lets visitors see close-up pictures of red kites on their nest. The facility is designed to provide a visitor attraction which not only raises awareness of the species, but also minimises any disturbance. This project has been supported by the RSPB, Highlands of Scotland Tourist Board, a grant of £10,000 from LEADER 11 and similar assistance from Ross and

Cromarty Enterprise and the Highland Council. The RSPB also appointed an information warden. Approximately 30,000 people visit this facility between May and September.

### Osprey

Operation Osprey has been run at Loch Garten since 1958 when ospreys first returned to nest in Scotland after an absence of 40 years. On 3 May a new Visitor Centre at Loch Garten was opened. The centre has been carefully designed so as to blend into the forest landscape and the extremely sensitive environment. Much of the timber used to build the centre has been sourced from Abernethy Forest. It is hoped that this will provide a strong policy message that Scots pine forests are valuable for both nature conservation and local economies. For the first time the visitor centre will also have toilets – composting toilets – a first for Scotland! In previous years approximately 50,000 visitors visited the ospreys at Loch Garten in the period May to August. Where possible local contractors were used to construct the £250,000 development. The Osprey Centre was formally opened on Monday 19 July 1999 by Jim Wallace QC, MSP, MP, Deputy First Minister of Scotland.

### Hen harrier and merlin

In 1997, 1998 and 1999, live pictures of a breeding hen harrier were relayed from a nest on the reserve to a large screen in the visitor centre. The CCTV has helped to boost visitor numbers in June, a notoriously poor month for visitors in north Scotland. The cost of installing the CCTV at Forsinard is being borne by the EU-funded LIFE Peatlands Project with additional support from Caithness and Sutherland Enterprise. This year merlin have been filmed and we are currently showing live pictures. For further information contact Norrie Russell, RSPB Forsinard Manager, Tel/Fax (01641) 571225.

## Background

We are lucky that Scotland still supports many rare and attractive species, which draw visitors from the rest of the UK as well as abroad to see them: corncrakes, red kites, sea eagles, golden eagles, black-throated divers, Scottish primrose, dolphins and otters to name but a few. This heritage should play a central role in promoting high quality tourism – this has not yet been fully realised. There is of course a balance to be struck between developing the potential, adding value to the visitor experience while at the same time not destroying the product, i.e. the wildlife.

RSPB Scotland continues to play an active part with innovative CCTV and interpretation from the seabird cliffs of Sumburgh Head, the puffins at the Mull of Galloway, red kites at North Kessock on the Black Isle, hen harriers at our Forsinard Reserve in Sutherland and sea eagles on the island of Skye. The natural heritage can make for good business but it requires investment and wise management to be sustainable.

## Wildlife assets

The Highlands and Western Isles support some 50 internationally important bird areas, making this one of the most significant regions in Europe for bird conservation. For example, the region approximately supports 93 per cent of the UK's breeding black-throated divers, 92 per cent of Slavonian grebe; 80 per cent of goldeneye, 66 per cent of golden eagles, 60 per cent of the corncrakes, 59 per cent of osprey; 55 per cent of the dotterel, 33 per cent of capercaillie and 21 per cent of black grouse. Red kite and white-tailed eagle are also two species that people come to the Highlands specifically to see. It is also the key area for rare habitats such as Caledonian pinewood, bog woodland, montane, peatland and machair and the Moray Firth holds internationally important numbers of wildfowl and waders. Dolphins, otters and seals are also huge attractions for visitors to the Highlands, as is the Scottish primrose.

The role of green or wildlife tourism is growing and its contribution to rural economies is considerable. The RSPB in north Scotland is actively involved in promoting the wildlife of the Highlands both through collaboration with the Tourist Board and through promotion of our own sites, particularly Forsinard (Sutherland), Abernethy (Strathspey) and Balranald (North Uist).

## RSPB Scotland nature reserves

We have over 50 reserves in Scotland. A majority of the sites are managed in conjunction with local landowners, crofters and farmers. In north Scotland we are involved with the management of 18 nature reserves. We encourage responsible access and each year we welcome around half a million people to our reserves in Scotland. Some specific examples from throughout Scotland are as follows.

### Abernethy, Badenoch and Strathspey

Six full-time staff are employed on this reserve, with up to 16 additional seasonal staff. The reserve, and particularly the Osprey Centre, also attracts large numbers of visitors (c.50, 000) who contribute to the local economy. A report in 1997 estimated that in total over 87 FTE jobs in Badenoch and Strathspey were supported by the reserve.
*Source*: Rayment, M. (1997) In *Working with Nature in Britain: Case Studies of Nature Conservation, Employment and Local Economies*, Sandy: RSPB.

### RSPB Forsinard Nature Reserve, Sutherland

This reserve supports two full-time staff and several seasonal staff. A recent survey by an independent consultant estimated that visitors to the reserve contributed some £630,000 to the Caithness and Sutherland economy in 1997. Deer management and trout fishing on the reserve are leased locally, providing further jobs and income. Around 1,600 ha of the reserve are also managed by a local farmer/crofter.
*Source*: MacPherson Research (1998) *RSPB Forsinard Reserve Visitor Survey 1997: A Report for the LIFE Peatlands Project*, Inverness: MacPherson Research.

### RSPB Loch Gruinart Reserve, Islay

A survey carried out in 1998 estimated that visitors to the RSPB reserve at Loch Gruinart spend almost £1 million per annum on Islay, of which £311,000 is spent during the winter months when geese are present. Annually the reserve receives about 6,500 visitors.
*Source*: Andrew Marston (1998) *A Survey of Tourism Businesses on Islay*, Aberdeen University.

## Shetland

A visitor survey in 1995 estimated that holidaymakers visiting Shetland that year spent a total of £4.1 million, of which just over £1 million was by those giving birdlife as their main reason for visiting. This supported an estimated 43 full-time equivalent jobs.
*Source*: TMS (1996) *Shetland Islands Visitor Survey 1995*.

## Geese and local economies

Recent estimates by RSPB Scotland and the British Association for Shooting and Conservation show that between them birdwatchers and goose shooters spend a total of £5.4 million in local economies around Scottish goose sites, much of it in the autumn and winter 'off seasons'. This expenditure supports over 100 FTE jobs.

## Wildlife tourism in Caithness

In a new initiative to promote wildlife tourism in north-east Caithness, RSPB Scotland is working with the Tourism and Environment Forum, Scottish Natural Heritage and Caithness and Sutherland Enterprise to set up a pilot project. The project aims to ensure that wildlife tourism develops in a sustainable way, to improve the wildlife experience for visitors to Caithness and to generate additional business through tourism. The project will focus on improving facilities and promoting and packaging wildlife holidays in Caithness.

Reproduced courtesy of Maimie Thompson
Public Affairs and Community Liaison Officer
©RSPB North Scotland

# Chapter 7

# Planning and developing ecotourism

In Chapter 6 the impacts associated with ecotourism were examined. In order to maximise the benefits and minimise the adverse impacts of tourism development in general and ecotourism in particular, there is a definite need for planning to be instigated at all levels of tourism development. Such planning should embrace environmental concerns, especially in the development of ecotourism, which is dependent upon the environmental resource base. Fennell (1999: 273) advocated that 'both planning and management are critical to the delivery of ecotourism, and must occur through the institutional arrangements that have been put in place to allow for it to occur'. In the case of Panama, Lieberknecht et al. (1999) argued that if the country was to harness ecotourism in its tropical forest areas, a range of planning steps were necessary. Even in the development of nature-oriented trails, planning is required as Hugo (1999) explained in terms of hiking trails for ecotourism. In fact, Fagence (1997) argued that many Pacific Islands were adopting tourism strategies with ecotourism as a central component even though it was not well understood but required planning measures to implement it. These examples illustrate the central role of planning and managing the long-term development of ecotourism. There are a number of principles that are common to tourism planning approaches which impact upon ecotourism. Prominent among them is the need to incorporate environmental and social values. This chapter examines the rationale behind planning, its role in tourism, the tourism planning process and the development of environmental planning in relation to the needs of ecotourism.

## Planning: what is it and why have it?

Within the wider management literature, planning is normally one task which is subsumed under the heading of management. Although there are many divergent views on what constitutes management, McLennan et al. (1987) describe the principal activities in management as:

- *planning*, so that goals are set out and the means of achieving the goals are recognised;
- *organising*, whereby the work functions are broken down into a series of tasks and linked to some form of structure. These tasks then have to be assigned to individuals;
- *leading*, which is the method of motivating and influencing staff so that they perform their tasks effectively. This is essential if organisational goals are to be achieved;

- *controlling*, which is the method by which information is gathered about what has to be done.

These four tasks are common in most forms of management and are important for tourism destinations in coordinating the private and public sector interests (i.e. the stakeholders which include the residents) in relation to the tourist experience. This is where a managing agency with a view of the 'tourist experience' of ecotourism can be important in ensuring that some of the potential interactions are managed. Yet there are also examples of the private sector taking the lead when the public sector is not effective. There are a number of stakeholders in any given destination which can impact upon the ecotourism industry, ranging from the different businesses producing the supply of services and goods, the ecotourist (i.e. demand) and the residents who also impact upon the environment and experience of ecotourism. Achieving a balance between each of their needs and the viable development of the local ecotourism industry is a challenge. Therefore, managing the ecotourist is a complex task and there are good reasons why the public sector is normally charged with this activity in most destinations. There are two reasons for this: first, the public sector is charged with statutory tasks that are normally in the wider public good, and designed to consider the sustainability of the resource base; second, in theory, these bodies should be able to take a holistic perspective which assesses both the wider issues for a destination. This is a strategic perspective which has a 5–10-year time frame to consider the consequences of continued tourist development. Therefore, it is important to distinguish between the management roles of National Tourism Organisations (NTOs), Regional Tourism Organisations (RTOs) and local tourism agencies and the specific management responsibilities which public sector agencies such as local government perform. In this respect, it is useful to consider what is meant by planning and who performs it and what it comprises in a tourism context.

## What is tourism planning?

According to Chadwick (1971: 24), 'planning is a process, a process of human thought and action based upon that thought – in point of fact for the future – nothing more or less than this is planning, which is a general human activity'. What this means is that change and the need to accommodate change in the future requires a process whereby a set of decisions are prepared for future action. Hall (2000: 10) argued that

> Demands for tourism planning and government intervention in the development process are typically a response to the unwanted effects of tourism development at the local level. The rapid pace of tourism growth and development, the nature of tourism itself and the corresponding absence of single agency responsibility for tourism related development has often meant that public sector responses to the impacts of tourism on destinations has often been ad hoc, rather than predetermined strategies oriented towards development objectives.

Planning is therefore a process which aims to anticipate, regulate and monitor change so as to contribute to the wider sustainability of the destination, and thereby enhance the tourist experience of the destination or place. What Hall (1999) and other commentators recognised, is that while tourism planning has followed trends in regional planning, tourism is not always seen as a core focus of the planning process.

Getz (1987) observed that there are four traditions to tourism planning: boosterism, an economic–industry approach, a physical–spatial approach and a community-oriented approach, while Hall (2000) has recognised that a fifth approach now exists – sustainable tourism planning, which is 'a concern for the long-term future of resources, the effects of economic development on the environment, and its ability to meet present and future needs' (Page and Thorn 1997: 60). As Page and Thorn (1997: 61) suggested, 'In most countries, tourism planning exists as a component of public sector planning, and its evolution as a specialist activity has been well documented (Gunn 1988; Inskeep 1991)'. As a component of public sector planning, tourism planning (where it exists as a discrete activity or is subsumed within wider economic planning processes), aims to optimise the balance of private sector interests which are profit-driven and a position where the public sector contributes to managing the growth without being directly involved in tourism development, as this rarely achieves optimal economic benefits.

## Tourism planning

Pearce (1989) argued that unplanned, uncontrolled tourism growth when taken to the extreme can destroy the very resource on which it is built. By extension, Hall (1991) asserted that demands for tourism planning are a response to the effects of unplanned tourism development. Tourism planning is usually considered to be planning for tourism. This traditional view focuses on planning for tourist developments. It lays great emphasis on providing destination attractions and facilities in order to attract tourists and increase economic development. During the late 1980s a sustainable development approach to tourism planning was advanced by a number of authors (Inskeep 1987, 1988; Gunn 1987, 1988; Pearce 1989; Romeril 1989a, b). It has also been suggested that tourism planning cannot be carried out in isolation but must be integrated into the total resource analysis and development of the area with possible land and water conflicts resolved at any early stage (Inskeep 1988). Inskeep (1988) also noted that recently prepared tourism plans gave much emphasis to socio-economic and environmental factors and to the concept of controlled development. This was supported by Goodwin (1996) who suggested that policy-related actions are increasingly required to ensure that tourism development is consistent with the needs of both local communities and their surrounding environment.

The underlying concept of sustainable tourism development is equating tourism development with ecological and social responsibility. As Chapters 1 and 2 indicated, its aim is to meet the needs of present tourists and host regions while protecting and enhancing environmental, social and economic values for the future. Sustainable tourism development is envisaged as leading to management of all resources in such a way that it can fulfil economic, social and aesthetic needs while maintaining cultural integrity, essential ecological processes, biological diversity and life support systems. Such approaches assert that there must be social and environmental planning components which lay additional emphasis on the potential contribution to human welfare and environmental quality (Gunn 1979a, 1988, 1994; Braddon 1982; Murphy 1985; Getz 1987; Inskeep 1988, 1991). These approaches advocate tourism planning as embracing the following goals: tourist satisfaction, rewards for owners, the conservation of resources and community integration.

Another important concept in contrast to traditional tourism planning is that it is not just solely planning of the destination zone. Rather it requires the planning of a number of elements including attraction clusters, the service community, circulation corridors and travel linkages between the service area and attractions. Inskeep (1991) identified a number of planning concepts which are an integral part of any tourism planning process: tourism planning should be a continuous process, systems oriented, integrated within the overall planning of an area, include environmental and community considerations, and be pragmatic in application. Inskeep (1991) advances a systems approach because tourism is viewed as an interrelated system and should be planned as such, utilising systems analysis techniques. The third concept was that tourism should be integrated within the overall planning of an area. A fourth concept was that tourism should be planned, developed and managed in such a manner that its natural and cultural resources are not depleted or degraded but are maintained as viable resources on a permanent basis for continuous future use. Inskeep (1991) argued that any tourist development policy, plan or recommendation should include an action programme or strategy which clearly identifies how it will be achieved.

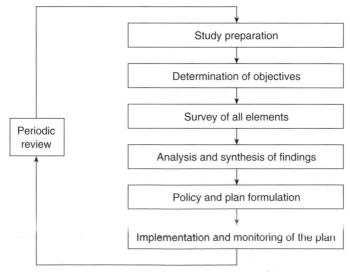

**Figure 7.1**  The tourism planning process (after Page 1995: 171)

According to Inskeep (1994: 6), the effective management of tourism requires certain 'organisational elements'. The most important of these in a
planning context are organisational structures, which include government agencies and private sector interest groups as well as the involvement of local and
regional government bodies to plan for tourism activity as well as tourism-
related legislation and regulations. One also has to have appropriate marketing
and promotional programmes together with sources of capital and finance.
When a government agency engages in tourism planning, a set process is
usually followed which involves a series of steps (Figure 7.1).

## The tourism planning process

The tourism planning process typically comprises:

- *Study preparation*, which is where the planning authority within the local or regional government (it may be one national agency on small islands that do not
  have a complex planning structure) decides to proceed with the development of a
  tourism plan. Heeley (1981) observed that while a number of agencies may be
  actively involved in tourism, it is normally a statutory body which undertakes the
  plan although quite often where a local and regional agency both develop a tourism
  plan, it is important that they dovetail and are integrated to ensure a unified
  structure to tourism.
- *Determination of objectives* is where the main purpose of the plan is identified (i.e.
  is it pursuing a sustainable strategy to development? Is it being undertaken in
  response to a crisis such as saturation tourism to identify managerial measures to
  reduce the social, cultural and environmental impacts?).
- *Survey of all elements* is where an inventory of all the existing tourism resources and
  facilities are surveyed together with the state of development. This will require the
  collection of data on the supply and demand for tourism, the structure of the local
  tourism economy, investment and finance available for future development. It will
  also involve identifying the range of other private and public sector interests in
  tourism within the destination or locality.
- *Analysis and synthesis of findings* is where the information and data collected in the
  previous stage are analysed and incorporated as data when formulating the plan. As
  Cooper *et al.* (1998) argued, four principal techniques are frequently used here:
  asset evaluation, market analysis, development planning and impact analysis (especially economic impact analysis such as input:output analysis, multiplier analysis
  and tourism forecasting).
- *Policy and plan formulation* is where the data gathered in the previous stage is used
  to establish the various options or development scenarios available for tourism.
  This frequently involves the drafting of a development plan with tourism policy
  options, with certain goals identified. Acernaza (1985) argued that there are three
  main elements evident in most tourism policies that are germane to the tourist
  experience: visitor satisfaction, environmental protection and ensuring adequate
  rewards exist for developers and investors. By developing a range of policy options
  at this stage of the planning process, the future direction can be considered.
- *Consideration of recommendations* is where the full tourism plan is then prepared
  and forwarded to the planning committee of the public agency responsible for the
  process. A period of public consultation is normally undertaken in most Western

industrialised countries. The draft plan is then available for public consultation so that both the general public and tourism interests can read and comment on it. A number of public hearings may also be provided to gauge the strength of local feeling towards the plan. Once this procedure is completed, the plan will then be approved by the planning authority and the final plan is then produced.

- *The implementation and monitoring of the tourism plan* is when the plan is put into action which is normally seen as an ongoing process by the planning team. In some instances, legislation may be required to control certain aspects of development (e.g. the height of buildings and developments) which will need to be implemented as part of the plan. The political complexity of implementing the plan should not be underestimated (see Hall and Jenkins 1995 for more detail). Often, the political complexion of the elected representatives on the statutory planning authority may change and cause the priorities to change although if an action plan is produced alongside the plan, then it will allow for some degree of choice in what is implemented and actioned in a set period of time. At the same time as the plan is implemented, it will also need to be monitored. This is an ongoing process where the planning agency assesses if the objectives of the plan are being met. The operational time frame for a tourism plan is normally five years after which time it is reviewed.

- *The periodic review* refers to the process of reporting back on the progress once the plan has run its course and been implemented. Some of the reasons for the failure of the plan to achieve its stated objectives may relate to a change of political complexion among the elected members of the planning authority (e.g. where an anti-tourism lobby dominates the local authority when the plan was commissioned by a pro-tourism council), a failure to achieve a degree of consensus between the private and public sector on how to address 'bottlenecks' in the supply of services and facilities for tourists; inadequate transport and infrastructure provision; and public opposition to tourism from a misunderstanding of residents' attitudes.

Yet as Page and Thorn (1997) show in relation to the development of sustainable tourism planning in New Zealand, while some local authorities may have plans for tourism, an absence of a regional or national plan for tourism to spread and distribute the benefits of tourism, highlights the need for integration of planning between the three levels at which it commonly occurs: the national (i.e. the country level), regional (the county or state level in the USA) and local level (i.e. the specific city, district or locality). Even within cities with a multitude of planning organisations and different city councils, achieving some degree of consensus on managing the tourist experience is necessary given the significance of tourism to the wider regional economy. However, often parochialism and vested interests and a certain degree of tunnel vision mean that destinations fail to adopt a strategic perspective with a vision of the future shape and form which tourism will assume in a city-region context. This is often a failure at management level where leadership skills are required to adopt a vision of how tourism should develop over the next five years which cannot be embodied in proper plans. When planners are holistically advising in the context of tourism, is that destinations require more than simple notions of land-use planning which has remained a permanent feature of urban and regional planning where local and global processes of tourism development are recognised. Yet in the real world, *planning for tourism* is a more apt description of the way tourism is treated by the public sector, since it is frequently incorporated in wider planning considerations which influence tourism development. Ultimately, the public sector needs to recognise that 'Tourism, like any other industry, has problems which stem from market failures and imperfections and from subsequent government responses' (Hall 2000: 19), but it is often hard to monitor the impacts of tourism because of the structural and service characteristics of the tourism sector. Nevertheless, in the new millennium, any destination which is not planning for its tourism sector will not be systematically evaluating its market position and future for a growing global economic activity which has consequences (i.e. impacts for its resident population and local economy). Whatever form of management or planning which is developed for tourism in a given locality must take a strategic view to identifying and developing a range of tourism resources and environment(s). This strategic vision will need to satisfy the long-term provision of tourist experiences that are compatible with the locality, environment and resources available to planners and managers of the tourism.

## Environmental planning

The most commonly adopted approach to the planning of natural resources which is the focus of ecotourism is land-use planning. This involves identifying resources, expressing an appraisal about their use and implementing development or use strategies. The major aim of land-use planning is to assist in making responsible decisions about the use of land. Land-use planning incorporates environmental planning. The former views the biosphere as resources that are to be used wisely, whereas the latter type of planning focuses specifically on either environmental preservation or conservation. Therefore, in the context of ecotourism, tourism planning is not sufficiently sensitive to the environmental context. The environmental ethics embraced in environmental planning encompass the broad themes of protection and stewardship, as outlined in Chapter 1. Therefore, environmental planning incorporates the concepts of environmental preservation and resource conservation. The environmental preservation comprises the protection of parts of the natural environment for their own sake, that is, looking after the environment for intrinsic purposes. This includes the protection of species and setting aside environmentally significant or sensitive areas. Resource conservation is the protection of the usefulness of the environment, that is, looking after the environment for humankind. Conservation planning approaches include land-use planning and Environmental Assessment. In this respect, ecotourism does not fit within tourism planning easily, since environmental planning approaches have arisen from conservation planning for outdoor recreation in natural areas, including a wilderness planning approach (Pigram 1983), carrying capacity approaches such as the recreation opportunity spectrum (Clark and Stankey 1979) and the limits of acceptable change (Stankey *et al.* 1984), as well as threshold analysis (Kozlowski 1986).

There are several approaches to conservation planning in natural areas for recreation and tourism that do not have their origins in either traditional tourism or environmental methods. One approach is to separate out land use by placing a protective buffer around a wilderness core (Pigram 1983). It has parallels in the zoning approach used on a smaller scale within parks in order to separate use and reduce environmental conflicts (Walther 1986). Two other approaches lie within the general concepts of 'carrying capacity' and 'threshold analysis'. The former has its origins in recreation planning for natural areas and itself originates from rangeland management techniques. The latter has its origins in regional planning and initially stemmed from research on the economic effects of urban planning. Both approaches have been used primarily in relation to the planning of recreational use in wilderness areas and national parks.

Two approaches to recreation planning in wilderness areas which have their origins in the carrying capacity concept discussed in Chapter 2 are the recreation opportunity spectrum (ROS) (Clark and Stankey 1979) and its successor the limits of acceptable change (LAC) (Stankey et al. 1984). Both have been applied in wilderness and other environmentally sensitive areas and have utility as a starting point for examining environment–recreation planning frameworks. The ROS is a largely resource-based approach to providing recreational diversity. The concept of a spectrum of recreation opportunities was reflected in most of the systems developed for inventorying outdoor recreation resources over the 1960s and 1970s (Brown et al. 1978). Those systems attempted to ensure that inventories of outdoor recreation resources would identify the potential of land areas to provide diverse types of recreation opportunities. Progress was made in identifying and measuring the relative importance of different types of satisfying outdoor recreation experiences to different types of uses (Clark et al. 1971; Driver 1975) as well as the features of recreation settings on which different types of experiences might depend (Shafer et al. 1969; Peterson 1974). Many of these research efforts employed a behavioural definition of recreation opportunity that moved beyond the conventional activity–opportunity definition (Driver and Tocher 1970).

The ROS planning framework was developed to assist in the match of recreation demand and supply. It involves specifying recreational goals in terms of broad classes of recreational opportunity, identifying specific indicators of these opportunities that permit their operational definition and defining specific standards for each indicator that make distinctions among the opportunities possible. The result is a clear definition of recreation opportunities as both the products of management and the services desired by recreationists. These opportunities, with their explicit specification of appropriate conditions for each indicator, can be incorporated into a land-use planning process and used to provide guidance for on-site recreation management. The framework is one in which acceptable levels and types of environmental and social impacts of recreation are defined. The three dimensions of an ROS reflect recreation preference related to behaviour, setting and experience. The activity could be bushwalking, in a preferred setting such as a wilderness area, in order to realise the desired experiences of nature appreciation, isolation and exercise. The ROS is not accepted universally and is based on a number of assumptions which have yet to be validated. These include the relationships among users' preference and revealed choices for experiences, settings and attributes as well as the management of these (Driver *et al.* 1987), the links between behaviour and physical setting (Schreyer and Roggenbuck 1978) and between the environment and its use (Stankey 1988). In addition it has also been argued that the application of the framework in areas set aside primarily for conservation is inappropriate and contrary to the central goal in these areas of environmental protection (van Oosterzee 1984).

A planning tool which has emerged from the ROS, and which also appears to have its antecedents in the natural resource–tourist opportunities link espoused by Nolan (1980), is the tourism opportunity spectrum (TOS). The approach presents a framework for tourism development incorporating factors of accessibility, infrastructure, social interaction, other uses and the acceptability of regimentation or control (Butler and Waldbrook 1991). However, in a similar manner to the ROS, a problem lies with attempts to control tourism development and identifying responsibility for this control. In wilderness areas the control is more likely to rest with a single management agency but many tourist destinations lie outside these areas. In an effort to find an appropriate answer to the question of 'how much is too much?' in relation to environmental capacity, research has now shifted focus on to 'what kinds of conditions are desired?' (Stankey *et al.* 1984). The shift in focus from 'how much use' to 'how much change' directs attention from use level as the key management concern to the environmental and social conditions desired in wilderness and natural areas. This orientation has led to the formation of a new planning framework called the LAC approach which focuses on managing for desired conditions rather than on how recreation use *per se* should be managed. Thus it addresses the matter of what constitutes acceptable change and it establishes limits on the extent to which human-induced change is considered acceptable in a given setting. The process involves nine steps which can be summarised in the following five points:

- description of the desired conditions in terms of resource, social and managerial attributes;
- establishment of the current conditions through a baseline inventory;
- comparison of existing and desired conditions;
- initiation of management actions to maintain or achieve desired conditions;
- monitoring of the results and modification of management actions as appropriate.

Despite the call of others for its application the framework has some limitations. First, it accepted the notion that some change in nature is the norm, and that a decision to allow recreational use is a de facto decision to allow some level of impact to occur (Stankey 1989). Second, Hammitt and Cole (1987) argued that it is a decision for management as to what constitutes an acceptable level of human-induced change and Pigram (1990) argued that this decision is not determined entirely by ecological criteria.

A conservation planning model which encompasses tourism is the ultimate environmental threshold (UET). It originated from threshold analysis which itself has its origins in analysing the economic effects of urban planning (Malisz 1963; Scottish Development Department 1973; United Nations 1977). This method spawned the UET method with its intrinsic environmental criteria and analysis of the relationship between activities and resources (Kozlowski 1986, 1990). Applications of the method have been in Tantry National Park, Poland (Kozlowski 1984) and on the Great Barrier Reef, Australia: North West Island (Kozlowski *et al.* 1988), Heron Island (Rosier *et al.* 1986) and the Capricornia Marine Section (Kozlowski *et al.* 1988). Underlying the wilderness and national park planning approaches of the ROS, LAC and UET methods is the concept of carrying capacity. This is now reviewed in regard to its utility for ecotourism planning.

## Carrying capacity and its use as a planning tool

Having outlined the key elements of carrying capacity in Chapter 2, the discussion here focuses on environmental–resource planning and use issues and how the carrying capacity concept is central to the debate (Lime and Stankey 1972; Bouchard 1973; Lindsay 1980). Carrying capacity is the level of use beyond which impacts exceed acceptable levels specified by evaluative standards (Shelby and Heberlein 1984). It focuses on one management parameter – use level. It assumes a fixed and known relationship between use level and impact parameters, and the capacity will change if other management parameters alter that relationship. The carrying capacity approach used in tourism planning stems from its application in determining wilderness use (Stankey 1978) which in turn has been drawn from range and wildlife management (Dasmann 1945). It is a markedly simple approach to the issue as it equates use to environmental degradation. If this is accepted, then the higher the use of an area the more damage to the natural resource will occur. By extension then it should be easy to analyse the resource base and tourist use and deduce a maximum number of people who can use a site without an unacceptable alteration in the physical environment. Wearing and Neil (1999: 48) advocated that carrying capacity is fundamental to environmental protection and sustainable development, arguing that it refers to 'the maximum use of any site without causing negative effects on the resources, reducing visitor satisfaction, or exerting adverse impact upon the society, economy and culture of the area'.

In ecotourism planning, the major components of the process are to identify both environmental and tourism opportunities and constraints. Once these factors have been identified, analysed and reviewed, the next phase is to systematically determine the upper limits of development and visitor use as well as the optimum utilisation of tourism resources (Inskeep 1991). In the past carrying capacities have often been applied to site-specific developments, but a wider view embraces regional aspects, cumulative effects, the spectrum of uses and activities, as well as the concept of development clustering versus dispersal, though Lindberg and McKercher (1997) question the validity of such an approach to ecotourism. Ethical guidelines for these situations include the size and scale of a tourism development being planned carefully from the outset with the environment as a critical, limiting component. It is also essential to view the environmental implications and consequences of large developments both in a regional sense as well as in the light of their cumulative effects. In its purest form, Ayala (1995) advocated resort ecotourism to embody such a planning concept to an entire resort area.

However, carrying capacity approaches to recreation and tourism planning are not universally accepted. After completing a detailed study of the recreational carrying capacity of an area in Birmingham, England, Burton (1974) concluded that the nature of the problem makes it highly unlikely that any set of universal capacity values, applicable to a wide variety of sites, environments and circumstances can ever be produced. A decade later researchers still agreed with this view; for example, Murphy (1985: 64) stated 'that (while) the carrying capacity concept is simple, its application is complex, due to the difficulty of measuring changes and establishing causal relationships'. Other researchers have identified a number of capacity problems, the main one being the difficulty of putting it into practice (Stankey and Lime 1973; Godschalk and Parker 1975; Mitchell 1979; Wall 1982; Romeril 1989a; Witt and Moutinho 1989; Mitchell and Murphy 1991; Farrell and Runyan 1991). The main problems can be grouped into three categories (Stynes 1977, 1979). First, there is no clear and predictable relationship between use and impact. Second, the scope of carrying capacity as used above does not take into account social aspects. A third problem with carrying capacity stems from the fact that in any given situation there are limits to the volume of visitors that management can handle. Although efforts have been made to limit visitor numbers in many locations, including the Galápagos Islands and in several parks in Costa Rica, in recent years environmental scientists have realised that the very concept of setting fixed visitor numbers is flawed (Honey 1999). Thus, while carrying capacity studies obviously have a role to play in helping shape sustainable ecotourism, it will require a perspicacious approach to ensure that it is not used as a panacea by developers keen to reduce environmental concerns to an oversimplified numbers game. Wearing and Neil (1999) recognised that carrying capacity limits can sometimes be difficult to quantify, but they argue that it is still an essential tool in environmental planning for tourism and recreation. Therefore, how does ecotourism planning and environmental planning translate to ecotourism?

## Ecotourism planning

Although there are many environmental planning models as well as numerous tourism planning approaches, there are few planning frameworks designed specifically for ecotourism development (one of the best sources to consult is Lindberg *et al.* 1998a, *Ecotourism: A Guide for Planners and Managers*). The few planning processes for environment–tourism at the regional level that have already been proposed include the ecological approach of van Riet and Cooks

(1990) and the regional strategic tourism framework of Gunn (1988). Underlying these frameworks for tourism and the environment was the intrinsic belief that tourism developments must not only maintain the natural and cultural resources but must also sustain them. To achieve this goal strategic regional land-use planning should include such components as resource protection, agriculture, pastoral use, urban areas and mining to be established in a carefully planned and controlled manner which sets conditions on growth and maintains or enhances environmental quality. Outstanding natural features can continue to be significant tourist attractions only if they are conserved. If there is any doubt that the natural environment cannot be protected or enhanced then tourism development should not be allowed to proceed.

Ecotourism planning involves aspects of both environmental and tourism planning. Components of the former include environmental protection, resource conservation and Environmental Assessment while tourism planning provides aspects of area development and social assessment. One aspect of tourism planning which is often fostered is the need for the integration of tourism in area development. However, there are fewer approaches which advocate the need for the integration of environmental protection and tourism. Yet a real need exists for this to take place if the symbiotic link between the two is to be transferred from concept to reality. Inskeep (1987: 128) argues that tourism planning of natural attractions 'should be closely coordinated and integrated with park and conservation planning at the national, regional and local levels with respect to both geographic distribution and intensity of the tourism development'. Achieving environmental–tourism compatibility in natural areas is best undertaken at the regional level where it is suggested that tourism planning can provide one of the best opportunities for attaining environmental goals (UNDP and WTO 1986).

Many similarities can be drawn between environmental and tourism planning goals and approaches. First, the goals of environmental preservation and tourism development are able to meet in the crucible of conservation and sustainable development. Second, models in both approaches include the same general planning steps, namely goal setting, followed by data collection and analysis, synthesis, recommendations and implementation. A third is the heterogeneous nature of the two planning approaches. Geographic heterogeneity is both an environmental and tourism planning postulate. In the different planning approaches there is the recognition that not every place has the same environmental attributes nor tourism potential. Despite their different goals, both environmental planning and tourism planning share a common spatial framework. Within their approach to environmental planning, Smith et al. (1986) identified cultural activity nodes, hinterlands and corridors whereas in the tourism destination zone approach Gunn (1988) identified attraction clusters, the service community and linkage corridors. A final similarity concerns the integration of social values in each of the two planning approaches. The role of people as part of the ecosystem is central to emerging ecological approaches just as the incorporation of social values forms part of recent tourism planning processes.

From the review of literature the following summary and conclusions are proposed on planning for tourism developments in natural environments where ecotourism is located.

- Traditional environmental planning incorporates environmental protection measures in land-use planning.
- The goals of environmental planning are to: maintain ecological processes, preserve biological diversity and ensure that use of resources is sustainable.
- Within environmental and ecological planning approaches an emerging trend is the incorporation of the values of society.
- There exists a wide range of criteria to evaluate the significance of natural areas.
- Environmental and ecological planning methods offer ways of evaluating environmental attributes for protection and conservation within a tourism planning framework.
- The concept of carrying capacity has inherent difficulties with quantification. ROS/LAC approaches to environment–tourism use are better suited to discrete areas under the authority of one control such as national parks and reserves. Threshold analysis is limited by its partial analysis of key elements solely of the natural environment.
- An environment–tourism planning approach needs to encompass social values by seeking out and incorporating community and tourist views.
- Tourism planning in natural areas should be part of a continuous process based on an iterative, strategic planning approach.
- Regional planning offers the best method for achieving environmental protection and tourism development strategies.
- There is a need for the establishment of a tourism planning framework for natural areas which is grounded in the sustainable development concept, is based on environmental protection and conservation, and incorporates community and tourist values.

Nelson (1994) noted the conditions and procedures for ecotourism planning consistent with these guidelines, which were: setting of goals and procedures; research to provide a good understanding of relevant ecological and socio-economic systems; concern for efficiency; environmental education; employee involvement; codes of ethics; monitoring and assessment procedures. Involvement of stakeholders in ecotourism participation was viewed as another vital component.

Ceballos-Lascurain (1996) outlined an ecotourism planning process based on a general approach to tourism planning which included the following seven factors:

1. *Study preparation* – which includes an assessment of the type of planning required and the preparation of terms of reference.
2. *Determination of objectives* – which should reflect the government's general ecotourism policy/strategy, and include development priorities, temporal considerations, heritage, marketing and annual growth.
3. *Survey and analysis* – this is an inventory of existing environmental attributes which are then evaluated in regard to their resource potential.
4. *Synthesis* – this step brings the preceding ones together in an attempt to place the study in context of the overall tourism development in the area. It includes an

analysis of the opportunities and constraints to development as well as the examination of other economic-related variables.

5. *Policy and plan formulation* – includes the preparation of relevant ecotourism policies which reflect the economic, social and environmental aspirations of the area. Such policies are then incorporated in an ecotourism plan or strategy.

6. *Recommendations* – are made based on the resultant policies in regards to development nodes, attractions, facilities and transport links. It is at this time that recommendations are also made in relation to spatial and temporal aspects such as land-use zoning and the staging or phasing in of implementation.

7. *Implementation and monitoring* – this is an essential part of the ecotourism planning process but it is often the one that is least carried out. Without implementation the whole planning process becomes redundant so careful attention should be paid to ensuring that any ecotourism plan is actually put into practice.

This process is consistent with the tourism planning process developed earlier in this chapter, with a greater focus on the natural area concept. Thus the future of ecotourism planning is couched in the recognition of the link between environmental conservation and tourism development. The major conclusions drawn in this analysis are that some of the goals, principles and approaches of environmental planning and tourism planning are similar and therefore it should be possible to integrate into a unified planning framework.

## Levels of ecotourism planning

Ecotourism planning can occur at a variety of levels including intranational – involving two or more countries from the same region (Pearce 1989) – national, regional, local and site scale (WTO 1980). An example of an intranational tourism development plan is the large-scale plan the United Nations Development Programme (UNDP) has applied to the Adriatic coast (Mlinaric 1985). National ecotourism planning incorporates economic, social and environmental aspects and details policies, strategies and phases commensurate with overall national tourism planning goals. An ecotourism plan includes identification of the major ecotourism attractions, designation of ecotourism regions, transportation access to and within a country, as well as ecotouring patterns. National plans also recommend development, design and facility standards and the institutional elements to effectively implement and operate ecotourism. Such plans are usually based on projections of demand and represent 5 or 10-year policies that are subject to periodic review. Fennell (1999: 140) suggested that one of the finest examples of policy development involving stakeholders in ecotourism can be found in the Australian National Ecotourism Strategy (Commonwealth Department of Tourism 1994). This was an integrated approach to the development of ecotourism, adopted with the belief that development and management of ecotourism are fundamental to optimising the benefits it offers. This strategy was truly a national document in that it integrated the collective opinions of Australians through the implementation of a series of public consultation workshops involving government, industry, conservation groups, educational institutions and community groups.

The regional level of ecotourism planning identifies appropriate regional policies and strategies, the major tourist access points, and the internal transportation network, primary and secondary ecotourism attraction features, specific ecoresorts and other ecotourism sites, and regional ecotour pattern. It also usually incorporates economic, social and environmental factors. For example, a tourism development plan has been completed for the environmentally sensitive international resort region of Whistler, British Columbia, Canada (Careless 1990).

Ecotourism development must fit into the overall regional and tourism development planning frameworks so that it is integrated within the regional planning process. One method is to follow a hierarchical approach with a large town forming the major gateway to the region. The regional centre is developed for tourism as the major one providing higher-order services and functions. It should be close to the bulk of the region's ecotourism attractions and should project a strong promotional image. The centre should also be the hub of the transport network (Page 1999). Social factors include the need for public participation in the preparation of a regional ecotourism plan. These factors form part of the community approach advocated by Murphy (1985). Environmental concerns at the regional level include the need for adequate zoning to encourage the concentration or dispersal of ecotourist activity. Areas of concentration should be those with highly resistant environments or should have been hardened to protect the environment. Dispersal allows for the distribution of small-scale ecotourism developments throughout the region so as to reduce environmental pressures in any particular spot. Of all the levels of ecotourism planning it is the regional level that appears to offer the best opportunity for achieving both tourism and environmental protection goals.

Based on the ecotourism development areas designated in the national or regional plan, planners formulate land-use plans for specific sites. Ecotourism must comply with the land-use regulations as set down by the local council. Consideration must be given to the overall elements of supply, that is, attractions, transport, accommodation and services. There is a need to develop the area harmoniously with an adequate balance between and among different sectors in terms of capacity, quality and style as well as compatibility of different functions (Pearce 1989).

## Environmentally sensitive design

At the site scale the planning of tourist resorts, hotels and associated facilities includes locational analysis, financial feasibility, environmental assessment and site planning. This last factor incorporates environmentally sensitive architectural and engineering designs as well as landscaping (Gunn 1987). Ecoethics which encourage the environmentally sensitive design of tourist developments in natural areas should be included for every ecotourism development. Thus, ecolodges which rely on natural environmental features should be designed so as to emphasise, as far as practicable, the highest degree of positive, creative interaction with those natural features and the highest degree of respect for natural forces. In the planning, development and operation of a tourism project, rapport and empathy with the site should be developed, and its ambience maintained and enhanced harmoniously. Ecotourism developers should view the environment not as an undesirable constraint but as a positive challenge to their professional ability to work ingeniously and constructively in harmony with the millennia of work that preceded them. In its final form an ecotourism development shall not reduce the environmental attractiveness of the vicinity, and during construction any adverse environmental effects should be minimal and short term. Sustainable ecotourism design was advocated in the early 1990s by two initiatives in the USA. The first was the National Park Service Vail Symposium in October 1991 which discussed, among other things, the severity of environmental stresses within parks; while the second was the Virgin Islands National Park initiative in November 1991, which specifically dealt with issues related to sustainable design in parks and protected areas (US Department of the Interior 1993). Russell, *et al.* (1995) have surveyed international ecolodges in nine regions around the world (Belize, Costa Rica, Peru, Brazil, Ecuador, the state of Alaska, Australia, New Zealand and Africa) and methods for environmental audits of these facilities have been developed (Carter and O'Reilly 1999).

There has also been a trend towards building ecotourist facilities which embrace low impact design, construction and management. Andersen (1993, 1994) advocated that ecolodges should act as 'a window to the natural world'. A significant potential exists for the indirect environmental impacts of tourism to be reduced through the utilisation of alternative energy sources and the implementation of recycling programmes (Lindberg *et al.* 1998). The substitution of kerosene for firewood in Nepal is a widely cited example of reducing such indirect impacts.

## Ongoing responsibility

An environmental assessment of a proposed site should be a routine part of an ecotourism development feasibility study. However, such a process is increasingly being extended to include ongoing environmental monitoring. This ensures that environmental responsibility is continuous and does not cease upon project operation. Thus, any ecotourism development should bear an ongoing responsibility for environmental protection, including assessments and management as well as for the local community, particularly indigenous people (The Ecotourism Society 2000). Around the world there are many guides for ecotourism operators. They are often based on the general principles of the need to preserve land values, environment–recreation compatibility, equity of use and adequacy of management.

## Ecotourism planning in practice

Both the environment and tourism are extremely heterogeneous and each particular destination has its own unique tourism and environmental phenomena.

Part of this uniqueness is due to the perceptions of the environment and its preservation or use among the tourists, residents and resource managers. There are a growing number of case studies of tourism planning encompassing major environmental components at both the national and regional levels. Some have been identified and others described by Gunn (1994) and Pearce (1989). National plans with strong environmental elements include those for Germany (Klopper 1976; Romsa 1981), Thailand (TDC-SGV 1976; Hiranyakit 1984), Mexico (Reyes Rodriquez 1980), Canada (Gunn 1982) and Malaysia (Din 1982). A large number of regional development tourism plans have been outlined by Lawson and Baud Bovy (1977). Specific regional plans include Michigan, USA (Blank and Gunn 1965), Penang, Malaysia (Georgulas 1970), Brittas Bay, Ireland (An Foras Forbatha 1973), Ottawa, Canada (Balmer Crapo and Associates 1977), Texas, USA (Gunn 1979b), Tamil Nadu, India (Hyma and Wall 1979), Kwazulu and Natal, South Africa (Ferrario 1981), Lesotho, South Africa (Wellings and Crush 1983) and California, USA (Smith *et al.* 1986). Specific environments such as coasts, islands and mountains are also well covered (Farrell and McLellan 1987; Saenger 1990). It has been noted that of all the types of ecosystems which people use for outdoor recreation, certain preferences emerge and overriding them all is the attraction of water (Simmons 1981). General coastal environment–tourism studies have been carried out (e.g. Miller and Ditton 1986; Pearce 1988) as well as on specific coastlines, such as Washington, USA (Miller 1987); British Columbia, Canada (Murphy 1988); the UK Heritage Coasts (Edwards 1977; Romeril 1988) and Scotland (Turnbull 1990). In addition there are many general coastal management strategies which include tourism such as the ones for Western Australia (Chape and Chalmers 1984) and the Caribbean (Williams 1988). Others have been undertaken for coral reefs (for example, in Indonesia, Salm 1985; and Australia, Kozlowski *et al.* 1988; Kelleher 1990). Considerable work has been completed on islands including: the Canary Islands (Baud Bovy 1964), Patmos Island, Greece (Spanoudis 1982), Hawaii, USA (Farrell 1982), the Channel Islands, UK (Romeril 1983, 1985b), the Caribbean – Antigua and St Lucia (Jackson 1986) and Dominica (Burnett and Uysal 1991; Weaver 1991), Heron Island, Australia (Rosier *et al.* 1986), Easter Island, Chile (Marsh 1986a, b, c) and the Galápagos Islands, Ecuador (Marsh 1986a, b, c; Kenchington 1989). Mountains and alpine areas have also been the focus of many general studies (Hamill 1975; Brugger and Messerli 1984; Singh and Kaur 1985a). Specific studies have been carried out in the Swiss Alps (Krippendorf 1984), Bavarian Alps (Groetzbach 1985), Southern Alps, NZ (Pearce 1985) and the Himalayas, India (Singh and Kaur 1985b, 1988).

Case studies of the coastal islands and mountains are disproportionately higher than for other areas because these form the major tourist destination zones. However, tourism is not just confined to these regions, and environment–tourism planning studies have been undertaken for wetlands (Caribbean, Bacon 1987), lakes (South Island, New Zealand, Pearce 1978) as well as a host of recreational studies within parks (both generally, e.g. Hawkins *et al.* 1980, and specifically, e.g. Paul and Rimmawi 1992). Relatively little environment–tourism planning research has been carried out in the arctic and alpine tundra, savannah regions, or the tropical rainforests. In some of these regions are located the greatest tourism destination zones of the world, for example, the Mediterranean coast and the southern part of the USA. In the arid and semi-arid zones few planning studies have been made although environment–tourism research has been carried out on some aspects of the relationship including the impacts of motorcycles (Kay 1980) and using tourism as a tool for conservation (Brake 1988).

## An ecotourism planning model

A regional ecotourism planning approach has been devised which essentially seeks to foster environmental protection and tourism development through a sustainable resource and development planning framework (Dowling 1993c). Initially named the environmentally based tourism development planning model, but now renamed as the regional ecotourism development planning approach (REDPA), its major thrust is not towards the determination of land-use sustainability or capability, carrying capacity, threshold analysis or pattern analysis. Instead it determines opportunities for ecotourism development through the identification of significant features, critical areas and compatible activities. Significant features are either environmental attributes which are valued according to their level of diversity, uniqueness or representativeness, or tourism features valued for their resource value. Critical areas are those in which environmental and tourism features are in competition and possible conflict. Compatible activities are outdoor tourism recreational activities which are considered to be both environmentally and socially compatible. The essential elements of the model include its grounding in the sustainable development approach, that is, being based on environmental protection, community well-being, tourist satisfaction and economic integration in order to achieve environment–tourism compatibility. Other essential elements include its being strategic and iterative, regionally based, incorporating land-use zoning, and environmentally educative, that is, fostering the environmental ethic.

REDPA is a strategic planning approach to environment–tourism planning in five stages. It includes: stage (A) a statement of objectives, (B) survey and assessment, (C) evaluation, (D) synthesis and (E) proposals. The 5 stages can be expanded into 10 processes (Figure 7.2). The first stage consists of one process (1) the statement of objectives. It begins with a background analysis of the environment–tourism relationship in order to produce the basic direction for the succeeding stages. The direction is determined by the objectives or planning goals which have emerged from the environment–tourism relationship review. The objectives are imported into the framework from the survey of the study area and its ecotourism issues and they are not arbitrarily fixed for all applications. However, as a general guide, a number of planning zones are defined which are designed to protect conservation values while fostering tourism developments and activities. These zones are identified and described based on an approach where the land and water areas of a region

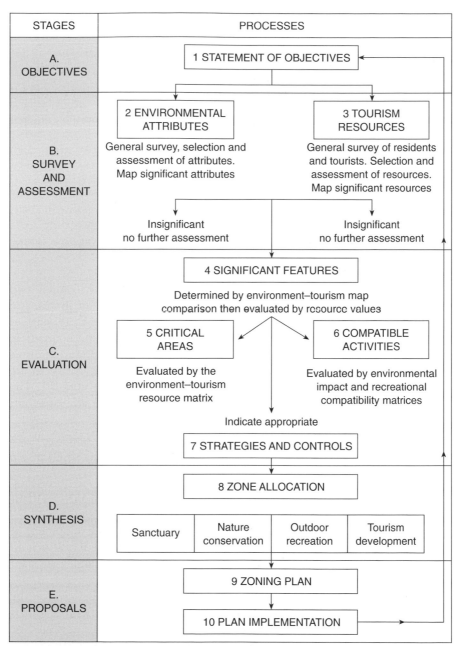

**Figure 7.2** The environmentally based tourism planning framework
*Source*: Dowling (1993c)

are classified according to their need for protection and compatibility with tourism. The following general zones and their primary functions are proposed. These include:

- sanctuary zones – areas requiring special preservation;
- nature conservation zones – areas sustaining a combination of protection and use but with emphasis on the former;
- outdoor recreation zones – natural areas that can accommodate compatible outdoor recreation activities;
- tourism development zones – small areas of concentrated attractions.

All other areas in a region are designated as areas with other uses.

This provides a guide for future environmental planning, tourism planning and regional development planning (Figure 7.3). Zoning also assists in managing the tension between preservation and use and more importantly seeks ways of fostering tourism in natural areas. The main argument against zoning is possibly rigid and inflexible prescriptions for use; however, the zones are used as general guides rather than rigid prescriptions.

The second stage consists of survey and assessment. This includes two processes, (2) the description and assessment of environmental attributes, and (3) the description and assessment of tourism resources. The third stage is one of evaluation of significant features (4), critical areas (5) and compatible activities (6) together with suggestions of appropriate strategies and controls (7). Following the evaluation the resultant information is amalgamated in the fourth stage of synthesis in which the planning zones are allocated (8). The final stage outlines the proposals and includes the preparation and presentation of the final zoning plan (9) as well as its implementation (10).

The strategies devised to implement REDPA's planning objectives in the Gascoyne region, an Australian region used to test the model, included strategies for environmental protection, tourism development and tourist management. Environmental protection and the conservation of environmental values underpin the approach in any regional application not only for their intrinsic values, but also because the natural and social environment forms the basis for the sustainable development, including tourism development of the region. The principal aim of tourism development within REDPA is to promote environmentally compatible tourism developments and associated recreational activities.

Tourism management in natural areas serves two main objectives – the reduction of adverse environmental impacts and the enhancement of tourist experiences. To be acceptable to tourists, management intervention should be low-key and persuasive. Explanation and education through interpretation are the key to affecting tourist behaviour in ways considered to be environmentally and socially acceptable. Tourist management measures have been described as involving a spectrum of approaches from soft to intermediate and hard (Jim 1989). Soft techniques are aimed at influencing user behaviour, intermediate techniques focus on redistributing use and hard techniques are those which are regimented and aim at rationing use (Table 7.1). Such a

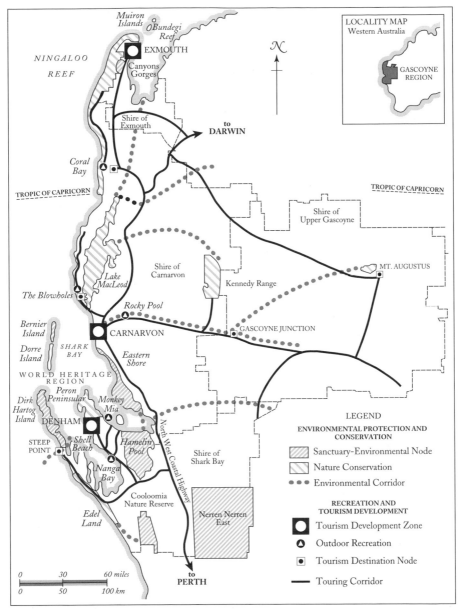

**Figure 7.3** The Gascoyne region ecotourism development plan
*Source*: Dowling (1997a)

spectrum of tourist management approaches is offered for consideration and possible application at individual sites within a region.

Following the development of REDPA in the early 1990s, it was implemented in many different environments. Through an ongoing evolutionary sequence the original three major elements have been expanded and incorporated

Table 7.1   The tourism management spectrum

| Measure | Management objectives | Techniques |
|---|---|---|
| SOFT<br>Influencing use<br>behaviour | To change user attitudes and behaviour<br>Determination of tourist preference by market research<br>Determination of tourist use by observation, visitor books, etc. | Using environmental information and education<br>Establishment of a code of ethics |
| INTERMEDIATE<br>Redistributing use | To reduce the contrast between heavily used and lightly used areas over time<br>To raise lower use levels to match carrying capacity levels<br>To redistribute uses so that their desired preference is matched by more appropriate settings | Concentration versus dispersion<br>Information dissemination |
| HARD<br>Rationing use | Controlling tourist numbers relative to type, place and time | Information dissemination<br>Advanced reservation by permit<br>Differential pricing, fees and queueing |

*Source*: After Jim (1989).

in regional ecotourism strategies in Australia for the state of Queensland and the southern region of Western Australia. The elements of the ecotourism strategies comprise environmental protection, product development, marketing and promotion, infrastructure development and industry assistance, each of which are now examined.

## Environmental protection

The underlying platform of any region's ecotourism strategy is the maintenance and enhancement of its environmental, social and economic assets. Maintenance or improvement of lifestyle and protection of a region's natural and cultural attributes are fundamental to and underpin any form of development. In this regard ecotourism development is no exception (see Table 7.2). The unique natural environment and lifestyle of the region are what attracts visitors and these need to be protected for the benefit of both the local communities (tourism's hosts) as well as the visitors (tourists). Key areas which are identified as being important for environmental protection are called significant areas and are not included in the areas identified as having potential for ecotourism development.

The development of tourism in natural settings brings with it an inherent responsibility to ensure that the resource is not degraded. One form of tourism development policy in natural areas is to contain facilities and activities in

Table 7.2  Key elements of an ecotourism strategy

| Environmental protection | Product development | Infrastructure development | Marketing and promotion | Industry involvement |
|---|---|---|---|---|
| Protection of natural assets | Identification of resource settings | Development of appropriate accommodation facilities | Identification of target markets | Assist tourism industry with knowledge of ecotourism niche |
| Conservation of resources | Identification of existing and potential products | Development of new and existing access points such as airports, railways and roads | Promotion of products to key market segments | Establish industry networks and information and develop a strong partnership between government and industry |
| Maintenance of cultural assets | Development of new products | Development of related facilities such as signage and visitor centres | Development of an efficient and effective delivery system | Develop and implement appropriate industry standards and accreditation |
| Protection of lifestyle | Identification and establishment of gateways, destination zones and touring circuits | Develop infrastructure which will also provide benefits to the host community | Position the region as a major area of ecotourism opportunities | Involvement in international promotion through known channels, including databases |
| Monitoring of impacts | Development of appropriate product packages | Consider alternative technologies in infrastructure development | Develop a coordinating body for marketing and promotion | Develop effective training programmes for people involved in the ecotourism industry |
| Setting of limits to change | Establishment of links with other industries | Ensure infrastructure developments are of a high standard | Evaluate marketing and promotion efforts | Encourage industry to be involved in research |

*Source*: After ERM Mitchell McCotter (1995a, b).

specified areas in contrast to allowing dispersion of development and/or activities throughout a region. These ecotourism development zones should be located where they do not pre-empt areas more suitable for other types of development or environmental preservation. The tourists either remain within the cluster or take day tours to attractions outside the area. Clustering is superior to dispersal in terms of benefits to visitors and reduction of unacceptable impacts to the host community and environment. The environmental argument for clustering is two-edged. The argument in favour is that it can leave much of the environment (between clusters or nodes) in a relatively natural state and thus, by implication, enjoyable, renewable and cheap to maintain. The alternative, that of continuous strip development, is usually regarded as unsatisfactory for both environmental and practical reasons. Another strategy used to reduce the negative environmental impacts of nature-based tourism is to separate out land-use zones according to REDPA. The monitoring of impacts is important with the need to adapt and fine-tune management strategies in response to feedback on progress and performance. It is particularly important as part of the process of determining appropriate levels of use.

## Product development

The main aspects of this strand of the strategy are the need to identify resource settings, identify and fill product gaps, establish regional gateways, touring circuits and destination zones, and establish links with other industries. The key to the development of the ecotourism product in a region is to establish products which are unique, authentic and manageable. All three aspects are required to meet the increasing discernment of tourists who are seeking these elements. A key challenge for a region is to ensure that ecotourism demand does not exceed the resources available for its development. This demand–resource match is crucial to the future well-being of the whole regional ecotourism industry as it clearly separates key areas which should be set aside for protection from those which may be developed for ecotourism. A number of key issues exist in regard to supply. They include providing a diversity of ecotourism opportunities throughout a region, determining appropriate types and levels of ecotourism activities and services, and managing natural areas effectively for ecotourism.

Where there is a desire to develop an ecotourism product it is essential that this product comprises activities that are both environmentally and socially acceptable. One approach to identifying such activities is by the 'compatible activities matrix'. First the region's entire range of ecotourism activities is identified, inventoried and categorised according to whether they are based on land, water, land and water, or in the air. Next they are evaluated in terms of their environmental and social compatibility. An environmentally compatible tourism activity is one whose impacts on the biophysical environment are either minor, negligible, nil or positive. A socially compatible ecotourism activity is one which is generally accepted as being able to coexist both spatially and temporally with another ecotourism activity, for example, canoeing and rafting. Such activities can be described as being either compatible, compatible under management, incompatible or not applicable, i.e. unlikely to compete for the same areas or resources.

The development of ecotourism in the region will also comprise the identification of development of existing and potential touring routes which link gateway areas with destination zones. The touring system includes the attractions, transport, services and information functions for those who utilise a tour of several locations. Attractions are most closely associated with the touring route and they are usually visited only once on a tour. Activities are slightly more passive and time constraints become very important because of a fixed touring schedule. The development of an ecotourism product also needs to embrace existing industries in a region. Ecotourism is not only the tourism industry in the natural environment but also, through its educative character-istic, it attracts consumers who want to learn about the destination they are visiting. Therefore, the development of ecotourism should include examination of links with other industries in a region, for example, horticulture, forestry and mining, and establish multi-purpose tours.

## Marketing and promotion

This element of the strategy fosters the identification of target markets and the development of an efficient and effective distribution system for the delivery of the product. It aims to raise a region's profile in this target market so it can compete effectively with other ecotourism markets within a country and/or surrounding region. Difficulties exist in marketing a sector that currently comprises many small operators with a diverse range of products and a lack of uniformity or agreed standards for operation or products. However, with proper management and marketing, the potential could exist for a region to become a leading ecotourism destination.

## Infrastructure development

Key infrastructure requirements must be attained for the effective delivery of an ecotourism product. Essential components of this arm of an ecotourism strategy include the stimulation of appropriate accommodation suitable for the ecotourism market. Other important factors are the increase in access through the provision of the development of airports, railways and roads, as well as other infrastructure development such as an increase and/or upgrade of information including signage. The provision of infrastructure should support but not determine or dictate the development of ecotourism opportunities. Where possible, ecotourism should make use of established infrastructure. The provision of infrastructure should be the minimum that is necessary to be consistent with the desired style of an ecosystem and facilitate the delivery of quality ecotourism products. Ecotourism also has a role to play in the applica-tion of environmentally sensitive or 'alternative' technologies to real world situations. It offers potential for the development and trialling of specialised waste minimisation and energy-efficient technologies which may have potential for wider application within and outside the tourism industry.

## Industry involvement

A region must strive to ensure that their ecotourism product stands up to the requirements of this discerning market, for without visitor satisfaction there is no tourism industry. Major aspects of this element of a strategy are the need to implement industry standards and accreditation, the establishment of industry networks and information, and the establishment of links with existing industry wholesalers and entrepreneurs. The tourism industry must have a clearly identifiable vision for its future if it is to achieve a high degree of integrity in the marketplace. To achieve this it is essential that there is a clearly identifiable and consistent standard of quality that is accessible to the consumer. The tourism industry has a prime responsibility for maintaining high levels of quality in service and content, particularly through the provision of training, accreditation and literature. The tourism industry has become increasingly aware of the need for environmental guidelines to protect its long-term interests. This has often led to the adoption of guidelines on environmental issues. This recognition of environmental responsibilities needs to continue to be emphasised and implemented on a practical level. Industry should therefore provide the development initiatives and the venture capital to meet the primary infrastructure needs of ecotourism developments. It could also develop and adopt an ecotourism code of ethics to provide self-regulation of the industry and meet recognised standards of the tourism industry (see Chapter 8 for more detail on codes of ethics). REDPA has, on balance, been successfully applied in a number of regions in Western Australia including the Gascoyne region (Dowling 1993c), the South-West region (Dowling and James 1996) and in North-West Cape region (Dowling 1999b). In addition it has been profiled by the European Union (ENVIREG 1994) and has formed the basis of the Queensland Ecotourism Plan (Queensland Government 1997).

**Plate 7.1**  Whale excursion centre, Vava'u, Tonga, has provided an impetus for tourism growth (Source: M. Orams).

**Plate 7.2**   There she blows! Watching a humpback whale and the newborn calf, Vava'u, Tonga (Source: M. Orams).

## Ecotourism development

Probably the most prominent benefit of ecotourism planning is to foster development that provides benefits for local communities and their natural and cultural environments. As Chapter 6 indicated, such benefits might include:

- new jobs and businesses;
- additional income;
- new markets for local products;
- improved infrastructure and community facilities and services;
- new skills and technologies;

- greater environmental and cultural awareness and protection;
- improved land-use patterns.

Ecotourism at the community level must be developed within the context of sustainable regional, national and even international tourism development. At the regional and national levels, development policies, plans and programmes, laws and regulations, and marketing, all influence tourism development. The three main principles of sustainable development that can also be applied to regional ecotourism development are as follows.

- Ecological sustainability ensures that development is compatible with the maintenance of essential ecological processes, biological diversity and biological resources.
- Social and cultural sustainability ensures that development increases people's control over their lives, is compatible with the culture and values of people affected by it, and maintains and strengthens community identity (see Epler Wood 1998b).
- Economic sustainability ensures that development is economically efficient and that resources are managed so that they can support future generations.

It can also be argued that the growth in ecotourism, or the ecological perspective for tourist visits, appears to be related to the general increase in community environmental awareness, media exposure of natural areas, and the desire for experiences other than urban tourism as well as the degree of satisfaction gained from non-urban recreation activities. However, ecotourism growth in particular areas appears to be governed by a different, though often related, group of factors including the degree of promotion, the controversy associated

**Plate 7.3**  Indigenous people in South Africa explaining to a group of visitors the principles of ecological sustainability in the African bush and ways to enjoy wildlife without impacting upon their natural habits and activities.

with an area, and the range of accommodation and other service opportunities available. These trends suggest that, despite the quality of the natural attraction, growth of visitation will be slow unless a range of facilities is provided (i.e. it is supply driven). It can be interpreted that without a range of facilities and services, only the adventurous tourist will be attracted. With facilities, the market is broadened considerably and visitor rates grow rapidly with associated economic benefits to the community, indicating that infrastructure provision may control the ecotourism spectrum one seeks to develop in any locality.

## Spectrum of uses and activities

Use of the land is becoming increasingly competitive. Therefore, the concept of 'multiple use' is gaining favour with government and commercial land users. Traditionally, tourism and nature conservation have gained acceptance as compatible activities in national and marine parks. The preservation of wilderness areas incorporates the intrinsic value of its ultimate ethical worth and therefore, tourism in these areas should not be encouraged. On the other hand though, indigenous reserves, pastoral lands and forested areas often offer opportunities for compatible ecotourism activities. Such activities cover a wide range of environmental, educational and recreational opportunities and all may be analysed to assess their optimal environmental and social carrying capacities. Thus, an ecotourism development should recognise that there was a valid spectrum of land-use values and allocations before its involvement. Any extension of recreational opportunities should not distort the range of fundamental land-use values, particularly towards the wilderness end of the spectrum.

There are a number of aspects to ecotourism development including the temporal strategy of staging, the application of controlled development, and the alternative tourism market segment. Appropriate staging of development is one temporal strategy that has been used effectively for ecotourism planning at the regional level. Its use provides the opportunity to phase in growth over a long period of time so that when one area starts reaching the saturation level, a new area can be opened up to absorb the increased flow of tourists. Inskeep (1987) claimed that even within one area additional attractions such as parks can be developed so that user demand is more widely distributed and environmental impact lessened on existing parks. Another temporal strategy often employed is that of limiting use during peak demand periods, which has been used in Yosemite National Park in California, USA.

An integral element of sustainable management is the notion of 'controlled development', that is, promotion of the balance of development and conservation rather than one at the expense of the other. This was recognised by Cohen (1978) who suggested that in the long run, the present widespread policy aimed to achieve the greatest possible number of tourists will have to be superseded by a policy aimed to achieve an optimal yearly number of tourists, optimally distributed throughout the country, so as to take off pressure from the most delicate, special environments and presently overexploited tourist regions. This was later expounded by Mathieson and Wall (1982) who also suggested that planners should be asking such questions as how many, and what type of tourists, does an area want to welcome and how can tourists contribute to the enhancement of the lifestyles of residents of destination areas. A decade after Cohen there were still calls for tourism controls. Inskeep (1988) noted the abuse of the environment by tourist activities such as the collection of live seashells and coral, removal of scarce plant and animal species, and littering, must be carefully controlled. He advocated setting limits on ecotourism development by establishing regional planning policies for opening up new areas and manipulating admission and pricing policies to help minimise overuse of important attraction features. Some of these approaches are being employed in the Tatra Mountains of Poland in order to protect the glacial and karst landscapes from adverse tourist impacts (Wiszka and Hindson 1991). Control of tourism has also been implemented for a small French Polynesian Island near Tahiti (Gunn 1991). The island has outstanding scenery which is being ruined by insensitive development and pollution of the lagoon. Gunn (1991) described many of the island's other tourism–environment problems and states that such problems occur in many other places as well. Controlled development is important for ecotourism management as the pressure for introducing such controls comes from both within planning, with its emphasis on environmental conservation (Romeril 1989a), as well as from groups concerned with global ethics (Millman 1989).

## Community consultation

Involvement of the public in planning has been more of a feature of environmental planning than tourism planning, especially through the Environmental Assessment process. In the past inadequate attention to qualitative socioeconomic impacts has been a major reason why many tourism development plans were not implemented (Baud Bovy 1982). There has now been a move away from the narrow concern with physical or promotional planning facilitating the growth of tourism, to a broader more balanced approach recognising the needs and views of not only tourists and developers but also the wider community (Dowling 1991, 1997a). Participation by residents in ecotourism planning is also fundamental to the process as Chapter 6 indicated, so stakeholders have a buy-in and a degree of empowerment in the process of ecotourism development. The public now demand that their concerns be incorporated into the decision-making process. Appropriate ecoethics for resident and tourist participation in the planning process include the need for developers to take account of local community attitudes and feelings, including the way that a local unaltered environment contributes to a community's sense of place (WATC 1989). Any ecotourism development should not lessen enjoyment of the local environment by the local community and where practicable, should enhance it. Nature-based ecotourism development at the regional level must be developed within the context of sustainable local, national and even international tourism development. At both the regional and national levels, development policies, plans and programmes, laws and regulations,

Table 7.3    Regional ecotourism development planning strategies

| Theory | Practice | |
|---|---|---|
| Regional | The Gascoyne region, WA | Queensland and south-west Western Australia |
| Development plan | (Dowling 1993c) | (ERM Mitchell McCotter 1995a, b) |
| | 1. Environment protection<br>2. Tourism development<br>3. Tourist management | 1. Environment protection<br>2. Product development<br>3. Infrastructure development<br>4. Marketing and promotion<br>5. Industry involvement |

Source: Dowling (1997a: 117).

and marketing, all influence tourism development. The three main principles of sustainable development which can also be applied to regional ecotourism development planning are its concentration on ecological, social and economic issues and Table 7.3 provides two examples from Western Australia.

## Summary

Ecotourism can provide the opportunity to present a region's natural areas, promoting an identity that is unique. It can create new and exciting tourism experiences, promote excellence in tourism, present and protect natural areas, benefit local communities and encourage commercially successful and environmentally sound tourism operations. The vision for regional ecotourism development is for a vibrant and ecologically, commercially and socially sustainable ecotourism industry that leads the way in tourism development (Dowling and James 1996). Ecotourism should be an exemplar for other forms of environmentally responsible tourism, promoting best practice in planning, design, management and operation. The vision for regional ecotourism development planning is to identify, encourage and promote a range of unique tourist and recreational experiences which can be sustained environmentally, socially and economically to meet the needs of visitors and the local community. This vision reflects the desire to have managed growth which maintains the lifestyle and environment for people who live in the region.

The key to capitalising on the potential benefits offered through regional ecotourism development is to maximise the opportunities and minimise the adverse impacts through environmentally sustainable development planning as outlined in the REDPA framework. If this is carried out then a sound base will have been established for regional ecotourism to develop and flourish in harmony with the natural and cultural environments on which it depends. However, ecotourism should not be viewed as an economic panacea for the problems of underdevelopment and there are a number of issues facing the future of ecotourism. These include changing consumption patterns, industry education, achieving sustainable development, making ecotourism profitable, protecting indigenous cultures, and effectively and ethically marketing and promoting ecotourism.

One also needs to be conscious of concerns related to tourism generally and ecotourism specifically. It is well acknowledged that not all places have tourism potential and not all communities want to go down the tourism development track. Therefore, there needs to be some thorough investigative studies carried out before assuming that ecotourism will indeed provide economic, social and environmental benefits for a business, community or region. When this occurs the potential of ecotourism will have been realised and then both the natural environment as well as the communities which live in them will be enhanced.

## Questions

1. Why do we need to plan for ecotourism development?
2. How does the planning process operate?
3. What are the specific requirements for ecotourism planning?
4. How useful is the REDPA approach to ecotourism planning?

## Further reading

On the planning for ecotourism see the following sources as a good starting point for further research:

Dowling, R.K. (1993) 'Tourism planning, people and the environment in Western Australia', *Journal of Travel Research*, **31** (4): 52–8.

Dowling, R.K. (1997) 'Plans for the development of regional ecotourism: theory and practice', in C.M. Hall, J. Jenkins and G. Kearsley (eds), *Tourism Planning and Policy in Australia and New Zealand: Cases, Issues and Practice*, Sydney: Irwin Publishers, 110–26.

Fennell, D., Buckley, R. and Weaver, D. (2001) 'Policy and planning', in D. Weaver (ed.), *Encyclopedia of Ecotourism*, Wallingford: CAB International, 463–78.

Parker, S. (2001) 'The place of ecotourism in public policy and planning', in D. Weaver (ed.), *Encyclopedia of Ecotourism*, Wallingford: CAB International, 509–20.

# Chapter 8

# Managing ecotourism: principles to practice

In Chapter 7, the framework for planning ecotourism activities, to minimise environmental and other detrimental impacts, was introduced. What was evident from the discussion of planning was that it formed one element of the overall management of ecotourism. If planning and policy issues germane to ecotourism were concerned with strategic issues related to how, where, when and at what scale ecotourism was to develop, then management issues are about how ecotourism can be integrated as a sustainable, resource-dependent activity. If the very essence of management is about how things are done and the process of organising other people to undertake tasks towards common goals, then the ecotourism industry (see Chapter 4) has to be managed at a number of levels to achieve a number of outcomes. As Figure 8.1 shows, management policies and organisations are critical to achieving successful outcomes in ecotourism which is discussed by Ross and Wall (1999b: 130) in terms of policies, management strategies and the responsibilities of different agencies in the ecotourism industry (Table 8.1).

At a macro level, planning agencies need to be able to manage ecotourism in both time and space, and for that reason vital planning tools used to

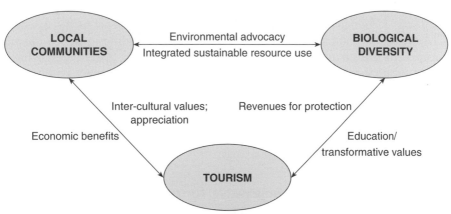

**Figure 8.1** The ecotourism paradigm: in successful ecotourism, the dynamics between people, resources and tourism are such that each makes positive contributions to the others
*Source*: Redrawn from Ross and Wall (1999b: 126).

227

**Table 8.1**  Examples of indicators which may be used to assess the status of relationships between people and protected areas

| Community characteristics | Characteristics of natural area ecosystems and their inhabitants | Examples of relationship indicators |
| --- | --- | --- |
| Population sizes (e.g. per sq km) | Size of protected area | Degree of independence of natural resources |
| Livelihood strategies | Ecosystem health (including extent of external impacts) | Local attitudes towards conservation |
| Social welfare of residents (including health, safety and education) | Number of endangered species/ habitats | Extent of local participation in conservation (number and types) |
| Social structure/values *Religion* *Culture* *Traditional values* *Familial cohesion* *Exposure/flexibility to change* | Population dynamics/statistics and composition of flora and fauna (minimum viable populations) | Integrated use zones? (frequency of use) |
| Local uses of protected area | Inherent ecosystem sensitivities Disturbance/succession regimes Soil qualities Predatory–prey relationships Interdependent links among species | |

*Source*: Ross and Wall (1999b: 127).

manage ecotourism activity are discussed, namely visitor management zoning. This is followed by a discussion of management issues among ecotourism businesses and organisations which interact to create and distribute ecotourism products. Although the underlying premise of management, as discussed in Chapter 6, was planning, controlling, organising and leading in an ecotourism context, in this chapter it is also about how ecotourism operators and businesses create experiences using management principles to meet commercial and resource conservation objectives. This also raises the issue of how public sector agencies and private sector tourism interests control the inherent tension between commercial objectives for profit from ecotourism and resource conservation. In this context, the chapter considers issues of regulation (i.e. self-regulation and voluntary guidelines).

## Visitor management: an imperative for ecotourism

One important measure of both the success and sustainability of ecotourism is the management of visitor impacts to ensure the long-term protection of natural and cultural resources, as well as continued visitor enjoyment and use

**Plate 8.1** Chicf ranger in Nambung National Park, Western Australia, addressing a group on the principles of environmental management of the area and tourist use of the park.

(Marion and Farrell 1998: 173). Allowing visitor use makes impacts unavoidable, so ecotourism management seeks to redress this situation through the protection of natural and cultural resources, the provision of tourist activities and experiences, and generation of social and economic benefits for host communities. Without effective visitor management (see Shackley 1998b for more detail), ecotourism can lead to adverse impacts on the natural, cultural and heritage environments to the extent that they may also negatively affect visitor satisfaction (Marion and Farrell 1998: 156). From a management perspective, visitor impacts are significant because they directly reflect management success in meeting two primary mandates: resource protection and recreation provision (Marion and Farrell 1998: 161). In this respect, Marion and Farrell (1998: 173) recognise that visitor impacts need to be managed, since:

1. Visitor use can negatively affect vegetation, soil, water and wildlife resources, as well as the quality of visitor experiences.
2. Visitor crowding and conflict can reduce the quality of visitor experiences.
3. Environmental attributes such as vegetation and soil resistance and resiliency, influence the type and severity of visitor resource impacts.
4. The use/impact relationship limits the effectiveness of visitor use reduction and dispersal strategies.
5. Decision-making frameworks can provide an explicit and flexible means of managing visitor impacts.
6. Indirect management strategies are often less costly to implement and are preferred by visitors.

According to Hall and McArther (1998: 108–10), the visitor management techniques available to managers of natural resources include:

- regulating access by area (i.e. zoning);
- regulating access by transport (i.e. only pedestrian/foot access);
- regulating visitor numbers by group and size (i.e. Antarctica);
- regulating visitation by visitor type (i.e. through pricing);
- regulating visitor behaviour (i.e. codes of conduct);
- regulating equipment (banning certain types of vehicles);
- implementing entry or user fees;
- modifying the site;
- undertaking market research;
- undertaking visitor monitoring and research;
- undertaking promotional marketing (i.e. to advertise alternative destinations not under pressure);
- providing interpretation programmes and facilities;
- encouraging operators to seek alternative resources;
- concentrating on allowing accredited organisations to bring visitors to the site.

The incorporation of monitoring programmes is also critical in evaluating the success of management strategies and determining whether resource impacts have increased, decreased or remained the same (Marion and Farrell 1998: 174). In an ideal world, Marion and Farrell (1998) argued that a panel of experts could be convened periodically to:

1. review monitoring data and evaluate management success in achieving stated objectives;
2. describe problems and their underlying causes;
3. identify and evaluate alternative strategies;
4. make recommendations for addressing existing and future problems.

One important way in which planning agencies manage visitors, as already mentioned, is through zoning, to which attention now turns.

## Zoning as a spatial management tool for ecotourism

As Chapter 6 has shown, ecotourism is an area- and resource-based activity which requires management. Spatial differentiation underlies the strategies of clustering and zoning. Pearce (1989: 263) has stated that 'environmental considerations become important at the regional level where a range of spatial strategies may be implemented'. These strategies which include zoning, concentration and dispersion will now be investigated in relation to their relevance for environment–tourism planning. The Western Australian government has divided the state into a number of 'zones of opportunity' for potential tourism development (WATC 1997). This strategy has chosen to focus on a geographic approach to the development of the zones (Dowling 1999a). Identifying the endemic tourist resources of a specific area is fundamental to this approach. These features form the core around which other nature-based tourism products can be developed.

## Clustering

A tourism development policy often recommended for environmental and other reasons is containment of tourist facilities as integrated resorts in contrast to allowing dispersion of development throughout a region. Inskeep (1988: 366–7) states that the 'concentration of tourist attractions and facilities in specified areas allows for efficient provision of infrastructure, offers a variety of easily accessible activities and facilities for tourists, encourages integrated planning and application of development controls, and contains any negative impacts in certain areas'.

The spatial location of tourism developments in a regional setting has long been the subject of debate. The options commonly favoured are either clustering – where tourism developments are located in selected development zones (nodes), or dispersal – in which numerous but smaller developments are dispersed throughout the region. Clustering in nodal developments is superior to dispersal because it favours more efficient management (Gunn 1994). Economically it is more efficient to provide service facilities such as access, electricity, water supply and sewerage and it also leaves more of the environment between nodes in a relatively natural state. Examples of national and regional tourism plans which have incorporated the nodal concept of tourism development concentration include Bali, Fiji, Hawaii, Jamaica and Taiwan (Inskeep 1987).

These tourism destination zones should be located where they do not preempt areas more suitable for other types of development or environmental preservation. The tourists either remain within the cluster or take day tours to attractions outside the area. Gunn (1988) suggested that clustering is superior to dispersal in terms of benefits to visitors and reduction of unacceptable impacts to the host community and environment. This approach is particularly relevant where large-scale tourism is being developed and substantial impacts are anticipated. Clustering generally allows for a more efficient infrastructure such as water supply and sewage disposal systems, thus mitigating pollution. This provides the opportunity for better controls and a higher level of environmental quality. The environmental argument for clustering is two-edged. The argument in favour is that it can leave much of the environment (between clusters or nodes) in a relatively natural state and thus by implication, enjoyable, renewable and cheap to maintain. The alternative, that of continuous strip development, is usually regarded as unsatisfactory for both environmental and practical reasons (WATC/EPA 1989).

Another strategy used to reduce the negative environmental impacts of tourism is to separate out land-use zones (Walther 1986). This can be applied on a variety of scales from small (within local parks) to large (at the regional level). The first process involves specific internal classification or zoning and the second centres on land classification. The environmental protection and conservation of resources have generally been approached through the separation of functions in park classification. One of the most common approaches is that proposed by the IUCN (1975). In many regions the protection of natural environments has been achieved by the establishment of wilderness areas. These are special areas in which the influence of humans is reduced to a minimum and in which the expression of nature can be readily seen. Other areas which have an environmental protection orientation include marine and nature reserves. With increasing use lands managed for conservation and recreation include international parks (such as World Heritage Areas and Biosphere Reserves), national and marine parks, conservation parks and state forests. Areas in which the primary use is for more intensive recreation are usually designated as recreation parks. These and the more accessible national parks have often been viewed as 'honeypots' which attract tourists and recreationalists and are managed for a variety of often intensive uses.

Land-use classification has achieved a measured degree of environmental protection and utilisation but within each park where it has been applied there are still conflicts over protection and use. To deal with this problem, park managers use the strategy of land-use classification and zoning which, as Hoole and Downie (1978: 10) stated, 'classifies park areas for certain kinds and groupings of use or non-use and, in so doing, defines spatial limits of future use allocations'. It provides a broad framework for land management that attempts to balance a park's dual goals of environmental preservation and public use by setting aside some areas primarily for protection and others for recreation and visitor facilities.

Forster (1973) advocated that in the national park context, zoning is one of the most important tools for planning, development and management. A five-class zoning system that allocates land-use priorities to different areas of a park was developed by Parks Canada (1983). This zoning system was a resource-based approach by which land and water areas of a national park were classified according to their need for protection and their capability to accommodate visitors. It provided a guide for the activities of both visitors and managers within a national park and assists in managing the tension between use and preservation.

At the preservation end of the continuum are special preservation zones based on specific and sometimes small areas within the park which possess unique, rare or endangered species. The second zone is classified as wilderness and represents areas with specific natural history themes and environments. These areas provide outdoor recreation opportunities for hiking and primitive camping, with the activities widely dispersed so as to be consistent with the primary preservation role. The third zone is classified as natural environment and is intended to permit those intermediate levels of outdoor recreation that are compatible with natural settings. Motorised access is allowed for the first time, but on a limited basis to the periphery of this zone. In this way, visitors have easier access to the zone, but to enter it they must use strategically located and well-maintained trails. The natural environment zone represents a balance between preservation and visitor access goals, and as such is the crucial buffer between the park's two differing functions. The fourth zone is an outdoor recreation zone that is a limited area accommodating a broad range of education, outdoor recreation opportunities and related facilities. Recreation opportunities are provided in locations that can maintain the activities with minimal impairment to the environment, and interpretative services are used to explain the local ecosystem and the human place within it. The fifth and final zone is park services. These areas provide centralised visitor support services as well as park administration functions. Even in these highly developed, some-times urbanised, areas the preservation of natural values and environmental qualities is attempted, with the location, design and size of the infrastructure and buildings being made as compatible as possible with the national park setting (Dowling 1996c).

Shackleford (1985) noted that implicit in the above policy directives was the concept of classification or zoning, whereby areas with a particularly sens-itive or fragile environment were not developed for tourism or at least had severe restrictions on tourism access. Zoning for environmental protection and tourism development has been carried out successfully in many locations and environments. Examples include Patmos Island, Greece (Spanoudis 1982), Les Mielles, Jersey (Romeril 1983), the Seribu Islands, Indonesia (Salm 1985) and the Great Barrier Reef, Australia (Kelleher 1987, 1990).

## Managing ecotourism businesses: operational issues

Within the literature on ecotourism, comparatively little research has been conducted on the business and management issues associated with ecotourism operations. McKercher's (1998) excellent synthesis of the area is among the most notable studies and it is certainly useful for further detail on this area. Lindberg et al. (1998) noted that there is a tendency for protected area staff to be trained in the natural sciences, particularly biology or ecology. However, it has become clear that the challenges natural area managers face often are more social and political than ecological and technical. A major part of natural resource management is managing people, with only a small focus required to manage the resource. Fennell (1999) suggested that this increased focus on social issues and corresponding staff skills inevitably enhanced the ability of natural area managers to respond effectively to ecotourism and broader con-servation challenges. A study by McKercher and Robbins (1998) examined many of the operational issues associated with running a new nature-based tourism operation in Australia. While the existing literature on tourism and small business development may be helpful as a starting point (see Page et al. 1999), since most operators are small businesses, there are certainly issues specific to the sector. A worrying observation by McKercher and Robbins (1998: 173) was that 'the failure rate of nature-based tourism ventures is high, and many that survive remain only marginally viable'. Meredith (1995) has characterised nature-tourism businesses as 'micro-businesses', being small, re-gional and outside the mainstream sectors of the travel industry. This has led to a sector, often run in an owner-operator mode, where the owner has little knowledge or training in tourism and marketing (Cotterill 1996).

McKercher and Robbins (1998) undertook a postal survey of 265 Austral-ian ecotourism operators, and some 52 operators responded, yielding a 20 per

Table 8.2   Major and minor theme areas identified

| Major theme | Sub theme |
|---|---|
| Business planning | Business planning<br>Financial management<br>Research<br>Conceptual issues |
| Marketing | Generic marketing issues<br>Strategic marketing issues<br>Project<br>Price<br>Place<br>Promotion |
| Operational skills | Business skills<br>Customer service skills<br>Operational skills |
| Personal attributes | Personal attributes<br>Ability to cope with bureaucracy<br>Affinity with natural areas |

*Source*: McKercher and Robbins (1998: 178).

cent response rate. As McKercher and Robbins (1998) noted, one reason for the low response rate is that this sector is 'surveyed out' in Australia, a feature also observed by Page *et al.* (1999) in relation to small tourism businesses in New Zealand. McKercher and Robbins (1998) sought information on three things they wished operators had known before entering the sector or three skills nature-tourism operators must have. The issues which emerged are illustrated in Table 8.2. Among the most frequently mentioned skills were business planning, financial management, marketing and advertising.

In relation to business planning, McKercher and Robbins (1998: 178) found that 'Existing operators feel that many new entrants fail to identify clear goals and objectives for the business or alternatively set unrealistic goals. In addition, many enter the marketplace with unrealistic sales and profit expectations, assuming naively that the business will perform strongly in its first year.' As with most other small tourism businesses, the initial business plan needs to be viewed as a dynamic document which the owner revisits annually to reassess progress and to reorientate to the business environment and performance. As would be expected in the small business sector, nature-based tourism operators failed to recognise how slow growth could lead to financial crises. Two constant problems which McKercher and Robbins (1998) observed among Australian operators, were that businesses underestimated the amount of time needed for a business to establish itself and many were substantially underfinanced. The underfinancing belies a problem among operators that banks would not be interested in such enterprises. Yet, conversely, some businesses were overcapitalised in terms of plant. In relation to financial analysis, cash-flow and break-even analysis were seen as vital skills, especially as many operators underestimated the true cost of doing business, with product pricing often too low to ensure profitability.

In research terms, McKercher and Robbins (1998) found that many businesses commented on insufficient knowledge of markets and how to use research to differentiate the product from the competition (see Chapter 9 for more detail on this issue in relation to marketing). In terms of bureaucracy, some businesses endured frustration with the agencies regulating ecotourism operations (e.g. national park agencies) which added to business costs. Marketing and advertising issues to generate business underlined the problem of the feasibility study businesses needed to undertake to assess if a viable venture could succeed and tap into tourism markets. Among the typical problems facing operators were acquiring a sound understanding of marketing skills and how to reach markets in a cost-effective manner. What emerged in the survey was a fundamental need to recognise strategic marketing issues, including defining the product, investment required for marketing, strategies to use (i.e. pricing policy) and the need to constantly fine-tune the product. Yet operators also recognised how small the 'pure ecotourism' market was and saw the need to offer more differentiated products. In pricing the product, a cost-plus approach had been adopted by many operators due to concerns about the markets willing to pay for the product offering. This may have led to consumers undervaluing the product and the experience. Even so, advertising was seen as expensive and ineffective, especially where new entrants adopted a shotgun approach to advertising.

The reality of dealing with the travel trade and commission rates of up to 35 per cent deterred many operators from using this distribution network in Australia, with large hotel commission rates acting as a deterrent to effective market penetration. Managing business operations on a day-to-day basis highlighted the diverse management skills which owners belatedly recognised as vital to business success, particularly the management of staff and visitors (i.e. risk assessment, legal issues and safety issues). For interpretive tours, effective communication skills and an entertaining personality were seen as a vital element of the visitor experience. At an individual level, patience, courage, knowledge, drive, determination and a desire for hard work as well as common sense were some of the personal attributes listed by operators in McKercher and Robbins's (1998) survey, as well as professionalism in the interaction with visitors. It was also paramount that operators had a good knowledge of and affinity with natural areas. Established operators also raised ethical issues for new operators in setting limits on the number of clients taken to visit fragile areas. The tension between profit and conservation also emerged.

What is vital for the new and existing nature-tourism operator to recognise was the 'multi-skilled' nature of juggling the demands of managing such a business. A weakness in one area may impact upon operational areas (i.e. poor staff retention) and strong financial acumen is vital to maintain a profitable business. Ensuring that operators have sufficient resources to maintain the business and running a service business which deals with experiences that are intangible, heterogeneous, perishable and simultaneously produced and consumed remains the perennial challenge for most tourism-related enterprises. While the nature-tourism sector has specific needs and idiosyncracies (i.e. a commitment to nature), many of the problems they faced are not dissimilar to those encountered by small tourism businesses globally (Page *et al.* 1999).

Other challenges for operators include ensuring they are equipped with the skills needed to provide high-quality ecotourism experiences and the minimisation of any potential adverse impacts of their operations (Dowling 1992b). This highlighted the need for a greater concern for human resource management issues so that operators have sufficient knowledge and training (Finucane and Dowling 1995). A number of possible approaches to meet the requirements of training include:

- developing training programmes for tourism operators to enable them to communicate messages appropriately, be aware of the means to minimise adverse impacts of tourism, and provide opportunities for active involvement in environmental protection and management;
- identifying and addressing training needs for ecotourism operators, guides and natural area managers;
- raising awareness of the value of and the need for interpretation;
- providing training for natural area managers jointly with tourism operators to promote a better understanding of each party's interests and concerns;
- including skills in communication in the training of operators and natural area managers;
- developing codes of practice for ecotourism operators, guides and tourists;
- requiring that appropriate training be a prerequisite for accreditation;
- using incentives to encourage training.

## Ecotourism training issues: accreditation, interpretation and guiding

Morrison *et al.* (1992) stated that accreditation is the means by which an association or agency evaluates and recognises a programme of study or an institution as meeting certain predetermined standards or qualifications. It applies only to institutions and their programmes of study or their services. Wearing (1995) suggested that accreditation provides an ecotour operator with an accepted operational practice as well as increased professional standing. It also ensured that the ecotourist is led by guides whose knowledge of the region is at an accepted industry standard and who operate at a high level of safety. However, Wearing (1995) also noted that accreditation implied the idea that one needs a service which is best provided by an expert. This can create a relationship of mutual dependency and hence social distance between the ecotourist, the operator, the host community and the natural environment. Fennell (1999) added that through accreditation some professionals may tend to rationalise and focus on facts, objective data and procedures, thus potentially losing the intrinsic, intuitive association so often formed through

**Plate 8.2** The newly opened National Seabird Centre, North Berwick, Scotland, funded by a Millennium Grant and opened in 2000. The centre has a vital role to play in ecotourism in relation to its educational and interpretative function of bird life in Scotland and the need for conservation and preservation, as well as providing viewing opportunities nearby.

ecotourism. In addition the rules and regulations imposed by the ecotour operator may imply a loss of perceived freedom by an ecotourist, and thus restrict their ecotourism experience.

Within the ecotourism experience, finding appropriate mechanisms to interpret and convey the essence of what is being consumed and delivered is vital to the quality of the experience. In this respect, interpretation is vital. McArthur (1998) noted that there is no single definition of interpretation that has been adopted by ecotourism practitioners. However, the most widely accepted definition is that of Tilden (1977) who stated that interpretation is an educational activity which aimed to reveal meaning and relationships through the use of original objects, by first-hand experience, and by illustrative media, rather than simply to communicate factual information. McArthur (1998) recognises that most ecotourism operators undertake interpretation in order to attract high-yield tourists, add value and better position their product, reflect personal or organisational ethics, and/or to comply with the rules of the property on which they operate.

McArthur (1998: 66) stressed the need for operators to plan for interpretation and argued that for many ecotourism operators their interpretative techniques are relatively ineffective because of poor planning as 'planning binds the three essential ingredients of ecotourism-based interpretation together – the audience, the message and the technique'. It is these three components that define the three essential planning stages necessary for successful interpretation. These are defining a target audience, determining content and its structure, and selecting a technique. Successful techniques include organised talks and discussions, guided tours and walks, theatrical performance, as well as building location, design, construction and operation.

Beckmann (1991) identified four key benefits of interpretation. They were promotional, recreational, educational and management/conservation benefits. Wearing and Neil (1999: 70) added as a fifth benefit the economy and noted that

> interpretation is not just the communication of information, regardless of how jazzed up and enjoyable it becomes. Interpretation seeks to reveal meaning and stimulate a cognitive and emotional response. This response should impel people into reconsidering their value base and behaviour. The way in which interpretation is delivered can be as varied as the individual imagination, and generally speaking, the more imaginative the approach, the more successful the interpretation. Interpretation is a core part of any ecotourism experience.

The participants and clients of the tourism industry are increasingly scrutinising and evaluating the quality of services being provided under the banner of 'ecotourism', particularly the quality of interpretation provided by tour guides. Tour guides operate across the spectrum of the natural and cultural environment, and activities include tours of national parks and outdoor activities, caves, heritage sites, observatories, mines, shopping centres, museums and art galleries, wineries and restaurants. The range of tour guide activities is as broad as the elements that make up the natural and cultural environment. The principal characteristics of guides often advanced are the 4 'E's:

- Education or knowledge both of the product and the surrounding region;
- Environmental awareness of the natural, cultural and heritage environments;
- an Ethical approach which fosters integrity and honesty;
- Enthusiasm, which was noted by all presenters as representing the essential difference between an 'average' and an 'excellent' tour guide (Dowling and Field 1999).

The key role of guides is to enhance the quality of visitor experience both through the information and understanding given, and by the way in which it is imparted. It is one way of adding value to the ecotourism experience. The highest standards of guiding are essential to ensure that the needs and aspirations of visitors are met. Thus, the role of interpretive activity design is central to enhance the quality of guided tours. The design of an activity is just as important as its presentation. A sound design with clear objectives and a definitive theme for a guided experience that goes beyond presentation to include demonstration and participation will assure the interpretive quality of the activity. The presentation skills of the guide will significantly enhance the quality of the experience. However, the converse of a skilled presenter with a poor design will more often relegate a guided activity into the realm of entertainment and not interpretation. There is much more to interpretation than 'gawk 'n' talk'. Ecotour guides need to familiarise themselves with the suite of

Interpretive design techniques that include concept building, problem solving, arts and crafts, sensory activities and wildlife observation skills. To illustrate the significance of interpretation and guiding, a case study of professional ecotour guide development in Australia is examined.

## CASE STUDY    Professional ecotour guide developments in Australia

One useful tool produced in Australia to help ecotourist guides design and deliver quality interpretive activities is outlined in the book *Best Recipes for Interpreting Our Heritage: Activities for Ecotour Guides and Others* (Field 1998). The guidebook, produced by the WA Department of Conservation's Visitor Interpretation Services section, evolved out of a 'Designing Interpretive Activities Workshop' which was nationally recognised by the Australian Travel and Tourism Review Panel as meeting tourism industry competency standards. Participants in this four-day workshop designed activities according to an interpretive activity planner or framework. Many of the activities demonstrated by the leaders of the workshop were provided according to this framework in the guidebook. Other activities of significance were designed by participants in the workshop. Some were specifically requested or revised for incorporation in the guidebook because of their success as interpretive activities.

The guidebook set a standard for interpretive activity design in presenting a comprehensive framework. This included the topic, theme or message, design techniques, the experience desired for participants, the character of the audience, the presenter's objectives, an outline of the steps in presenting the activity, the preferred site, the duration of the activity, the preferred time of day, the props required, a promotional paragraph and the script. However, the creative process is not linear. An idea can come from anywhere and the components of the framework may be approached in any order. As long as all of them are addressed the integrated interpretive experience will be sound.

Field (1998) provided a number of completed interpretive activity plans with full scripts to act as a stimulus. Activities were listed by topic, audience and design technique. The topics were landscape/seascape/natural processes; animals; plants; ecology; culture; history; heritage values and management issues. The activities primarily targeted ecotour guides working with adults. However, many activities were suitable for families where teenagers and children were accompanied by adults. There were six design techniques from which to choose – arts and craft, concept exploring, guided walks, problem solving, sensory activities and wildlife observations. Information was also provided on presenting activities and evaluating their success. Effective presenting involved creating a pleasant social environment before getting started by establishing the appropriate expectations and identifying the theme. This was followed by using one's voice, body and group dynamics before bringing the activity to a close with a strong motivating ending that reinforced the theme and message. Evaluating the success of the guided activity was about checking to see if the objectives had been achieved and how it could be improved next time. An ongoing evaluation should occur throughout the activity. Key tasks included

**Plate 8.3** Dr David Bellamy, launching the Australian EcoGuide Programme at the 8th Australian Ecotourism Conference, Lorne, Victoria, 2 November 2000.

observing client reactions, looking for eye contact, smiles, questions, participation, as well as other feedback. In addition a 'participant feedback form' should be distributed and collected.

Weiler (1999) has argued that tour guiding is at a crossroads, with it now being timely to work towards moving it from its early phase of growth to a more mature position in the industry, where it is respected as an integral part, and where the personnel involved are viewed as fully equipped professionals. To meet this challenge in Australia a national EcoGuide Programme was launched by Dr David Bellamy at the Australian Ecotourism Conference in November 2000. The programme is a voluntary, industry programme run by the Ecotourism Association of Australia that provides

**Plate 8.4**  Awards for achievements in ecotourism and good practice are vital to encourage this sector of the tourism industry to develop its full potential, as this ceremony in Western Australia at a FACET conference indicates.

recognition and reward for best-practice nature and ecotour guides. Certification is based on benchmarks provided by national competency standards. The programme provides tourists with an assurance that guides are committed to providing quality ecotourism experiences in a safe, culturally sensitive and environmentally sustainable manner.

At a regional level in Western Australia (WA), the professional tourism organisation Forum Advocating Cultural and Ecotourism (FACET) has established an award for excellence in guiding – the FACET Golden Guide Award (Dowling 1999a). The vision is for WA to have the best tourist guides in Australia, who facilitated excellence in tourist activities and the tourism experience. Presented annually as part of the state's annual tourism awards, FACET's Golden Guide Award helps to develop a level of excellence in tourism guiding. Nominees for the award have to be actively involved in the delivery of tourist guiding activities that are available to the public. The primary objectives of the award are to:

- increase the profile, awareness and importance of tour guiding;
- bring recognition of the importance of quality tour guiding as an integral part of the tourism industry;
- assist in improving the standard of natural and cultural interpretation in tour guiding;
- improve the quality of tourist experience for people participating in natural and cultural tourism;
- improve the understanding of the scope and nature of tourist guiding based on natural and cultural resources world;
- assist in developing networks and relationships within the WA tourism industry.

The award is also open to individual tour guides operating in WA who delivered an interpretive service to visitors at a facility or site/locality. It focuses on the interpersonal communication and interpretive skills of the individual, that is, on face-to-face guiding. Applicants are judged on the design, content and presentation of their interpretive activity. Guides can be in the tourist or recreational arena, publicly or privately employed, self-employed or volunteer. What the award system highlights is the need to showcase excellence in guiding so that other operators aspire to receiving this award as a sign of success and achievement in their activities.

## Ethics and the management of ecotourism

One of the areas of research which has seen a significant growth in relation to the management of ecotourism is the application of ethics to understand the extent to which ecotourism activity demonstrates ethical behaviour which is acceptable in specific contexts (Dowling 1992b). Some of the recent studies in the area include D'Amore (1993) which examined the code of ethics for socially and environmentally responsible tourism in Canada and globally post-Brundtland Commission (see Chapters 1 and 2 for more detail on the Brundtland Commission). More recently, Mason (1994), Malloy and Fennell (1998a) and others have begun to question the need for regulation in the ecotourism sector to address the conflict between business objectives and resource conservation. Much of the debate on ethics and ecotourism has its philosophical roots in the debate engaged in Chapters 1 and 2 on the continuum through which biocentric philosophies based on resource protection were juxtaposed with resource development principles in the anthropocentric paradigm.

Fennell (1999: 254) argued that 'Fundamentally, there is a very weak foundation of research in tourism ethics studies to date. There does however appear to be growing recognition within tourism's public, private and not-for-profit sectors that, from the perspective of sustainable development, ethical concerns have not fallen upon deaf ears.' In the case of ecotourism, a number of studies have examined ethical issues in general (i.e. Duenkel and Scott 1994; Kutay 1989), although more substantive reviews have been provided by Karwacki and Boyd (1995) and Wight (1993a) as well as marketing issues (Wight 1993b), which are discussed in Chapter 9.

Fennell and Malloy (1999), in a study of tourism operator types, used a multidimensional ethics scale (MES) to gauge their ethical nature. The MES technique provides respondents with ethical scenarios and asks for responses. Their study examined 167 operators, of whom 39 were ecotourism operators in North America, 49 specialised in adventure tourism, 45 in fishing and 43 in golfing and cruiselines. The results indicated that 'operators in the tourism industry cannot be considered homogeneous in terms of their ethical orientation. Specifically, the results demonstrate that ecotourism operators appear to have a more heightened sense of ethical conduct than do their peers in other ventures' (Fennell and Malloy 1999: 938). This was explained in terms of the operators' educational attainments and the greater use of codes of ethics. This was an important finding for a sector of the tourism industry which deals with the natural resource base and where decision-making related to ethical issues may be at the fore of their business activities.

One of the recurrent themes in the discussion of ethical issues is the need for codes of conduct in the absence of public sector regulation of ecotourism activities. The British Columbia Ministry of Development, Industry and Trade (BC Ministry of DIT 1991: 2–1, cited in Fennell and Malloy 1999) defined a code of ethics as 'a set of guiding principles which govern the behaviour of the target group in pursuing their activity of interest'. In an industry context, Stevens (1994: 64) argued that they act as 'messages through which corporations hope to share employee behaviour and effect through explicit statement of desired behaviour'. In a tourism context, such codes have also incorporated a wider range of people (i.e. local communities) and agencies (i.e. public sector bodies) as well as businesses and tourists in establishing guidelines for ethical codes of conduct (see Mason and Mowforth 1995).

In a wide-ranging review of the relationship between ethics and the tourism industry, Payne and Dimanche (1996) argued that codes of ethics should embody a number of values, including competence, integrity, justice and utility, which should be reflected in three principles.

- The tourism industry has a resource base which is limited and finite (i.e. the environment) and sustainable economic development requires limits to growth.
- The tourism industry is a community-based activity, so that sociocultural costs of tourism need to be considered.
- The tourism industry is a service activity, and employees and customers must be treated ethically.

Some critics have argued that this may just be another marketing ploy for the tourism industry, and that it needs to permeate business activities to be implemented successfully. Genot (1995) identified the following principles as the basis of any code of ethics: environmental commitment, responsibility, integrated planning, environmentally sound management, cooperation between decision-makers and public awareness. These principles have been considered in more detail by Dowling (1992a) and The Ecotourism Society (1993).

In an in-depth analysis of codes of conduct, Malloy and Fennell (1998b) examined 40 such codes (containing 414 individual guidelines) to assess their content, focus, orientation and the messages conveyed. What emerged was a range of variables which embodied two philosophies of ethics – *deontology* and *teleology*. Deontology is concerned with whether 'an act is right or wrong on the basis of rules and principles of action or duties or rights or virtues. This approach advocates behaviour that is means-based, or intentions-based, in its orientation. Deontology, or right behaviour, provides us with guidance through the provision of rules and regulations to follow' (Fennell 1999: 258). Here, what we ought to do is laid out to work within established cultural and environmental norms (i.e. this site is fragile and observe it but do not enter). In contrast, teleology, or good behaviour, is an ethical approach which suggests that an act is right or wrong solely on the basis of its performance. Because of its orientation towards the consequences of one's action, it is ends-based. In this sense, the stakeholder is released from following the tradition or dogma of the past and is able to choose in a manner which is consistent with the changing circumstances of societies and cultures. An example of a teleological code is as follows: Do not enter buildings at the research stations unless invited to do so. Remember that scientific research is going on, and *any intrusion could affect the scientists' data* (the consequences of the action is highlighted in italics) (Fennell 1999: 259).

From the 414 guidelines, some 77 per cent were found to be deontological. Malloy and Fennell (1998a) argued that these failed to provide the decision-maker (the tourist) with any rationale for abiding by a code. This assumed that an explanation, which is the premise of the teleological approach, was unnecessary to the tourist or stakeholder. Many of the codes were developed by NGOs for tourists, and many were ecologically based. What Malloy and Fennell (1998a) concluded was that codes needed a deeper philosophical meaning, with a greater emphasis on teleological perspectives in code development. This was vital if tourists were to understand how their activities and subsequent behaviour may need to change to achieve specific ecotourism objectives. Even so, critics such as Wheeller (1994) remain unconvinced of their utility and value in tourism, but what is clear is that their development highlights key management concerns about how to develop guidelines in this growing field of interest. One last area of interest which has also emerged, partly as a consequence of concerns raised in ethical codes of conduct, is the ability of local communities to manage ecotourism development.

## Community-based ecotourism: management and development issues

With the growing recognition among communities that ecotourism may offer opportunities for sustainable development, there has been an increased awareness among researchers that 'active local participation in the planning process and in operations management is essential in order to achieve the conservation and sustainable development goals of ecotourism' (Drumm 1998: 197). Yet there is a recognition that this is far from an easy process (Ashley and Roe 1998).

Integrating local community needs, lifestyle and activities is necessary to avoid conflicts and problems for ecotourism resources. As Drumm (1998: 198) argued, 'Community-based ecotourism management refers to ecotourism programs which take place under the control and active participation of the local people who inhabit a natural attraction.' This is part of a community tourism paradigm, where indigenous people and local communities are included and benefit from tourism. According to Tourism Concern, an NGO based in the UK (www.tourismconcern.org.uk), community tourism should:

1. be run with the involvement and consent of local communities;
2. give a fair share of profits back to the local community;
3. involve communities rather than individuals;

**Table 8.3**   *Community–tourism relationships in ecotourism*

Renting land to an operator to develop while simply monitoring impacts

Working as occasional, part- or full-time staff for outside operators

Providing selected services such as food preparation, guiding, transport or accommodations (or a combination of several or all these) to operators

Forming joint ventures with outside operators with a division of labour, which allows the community to provide most services, while the operator takes care of marketing

Operating fully independent community tourism programmes

*Source*: Drumm (1998: 201).

4.  be environmentally sustainable;
5.  respect traditional culture and social structures;
6.  have mechanisms to help communities cope with the impact of Western tourists;
7.  keep groups small to minimise cultural/environmental impact;
8.  brief tourists before the trip on appropriate behaviour;
9.  not make local people perform inappropriate ceremonies;
10. leave communities alone if they do not want tourism.

As a result, local communities have been encouraged to set up their own ecotourism projects, often initiated by NGOs and companies outside of the destination area (see also Mann 2000 for further discussion on community-based tours). In cases where communities choose to be involved in ecotourism projects, Drumm (1998: 201) argued that the following options existed as Table 8.3 shows.

The full involvement of the community is required at each stage of planning and management. Some of the management challenges for local communities are not dissimilar to those highlighted by McKercher and Robbins (1998), including:

- training;
- access to the market;
- participation in planning and management, particularly where ecotourism use zones are established;
- political and legal issues related to institutional bureaucracy.

One interesting example examined by Colvin (1994) was Capirona as a model of indigenous ecotourism using a community-based approach.

## Indigenous ecotourism in Capirona

Capirona, in Ecuador, was a community of 24 Quichua Indian families who committed to preserving the local rainforest and in sharing their culture and tradition with visitors. This was viewed as a way of deriving income while avoiding the destruction of a local resource. As an example, it has been widely cited as a mechanism which combined visits to a natural attraction with cultural exchange. As a result of the project, a further 12 communities developed

Table 8.4  The Capirona Guidelines

---

1. Donations or exchanges of clothing and other personal articles with the community members are prohibited
2. Help us maintain our community way of life by not giving individual tips
3. If you would like to make a donation to the whole community, please direct it to the community leaders or the programme directors
4. Place all garbage in its place and please take with you what you brought to the community, especially plastic products
5. Photographs are permitted providing permission is asked and granted. Nature is full of beautiful and diverse landscapes and curiosities for taking pictures
6. People enjoy the sounds of the jungle; if you decide to bring a radio please use headphones and keep the volume low
7. Collection of plants, insects or animals is prohibited without prior authorisation
8. Please do not enter a house without being invited
9. Do not make promises that are difficult or that you cannot keep, such as sending photos
10. The consumption of drugs and excessive use of alcohol is prohibited
11. Please wear clothing appropriate for your protection (from insects, the sun, etc.); this will also demonstrate your respect for others
12. Given that we desire to protect the integrity of our community and way of life, we do not allow visitors to stay in the tourist facilities or community for longer than the agreed period
13. Please maintain the appropriate distance that should exist between guides/community members and tourists. This will help to maintain the co-living arrangement of the programme. Please avoid intimate contact, which could disturb ethical and moral traditions of the community

---

*Source*:  Drumm (1998: 210).

similar projects with limited funding from an NGO – Ayuda en Acción. The resulting network of 12 projects (RICANCIE) has trained local guides, created packages and developed community-based tourism within a framework – the Capirona Guidelines (see Table 8.4). The success in managing the flow of visitors, reinvesting revenues in the local community which permits other sustainable economic activities to take place (i.e. handicrafts, agriculture and agroforestry), has ensured tourism is not just for sale as a commodity to visitors – but is a key element in community identity. One of the greatest issues according to Drumm (1998: 209, 211) was that RICANCIE's plans were challenged by local tourism law, which does not facilitate community-based tourism but requires communities to establish themselves as companies. In 1997, RICANCIE was forced to establish a corporation since the law would not recognise the basis of the organisation. Nevertheless, the tangible benefits of the projects are still heralded as a success and a model for other communities. What emerges from the Capirona example and other studies of community-based ecotourism (e.g. Sproule and Suhandi 1998) is that it raises a new organisational model of tourism activity which is appropriate for local communities. Internal politics within communities related to issues of participation, gender, decision-making and non-community partners may be problematic in relation to concessions, guiding and promotion. Yet community-based ecotourism does offer prospects for communities to be actively involved rather than be observers who only see the trickle-down effect of economic benefits while dealing with the costs to the community.

## Summary

This chapter has examined some of the management issues associated with ecotourism from the perspective of planning bodies through the use of zoning techniques in controlling ecotourism activities through to the issues for individual operators. What is clear is that intervention in the natural environment by operators in terms of regulations and planning is seen as adding to bureaucracy and costs of operation (McKercher and Robbins 1998). Yet with the natural environment as a fragile resource and demand from ecotourism operators and ecotourists, some degree of intervention is necessary to establish the ground rules for ecotourism operations. Planning agencies can take a strategic view of such issues and while this may cause tensions with operators, where controls and restraints are put in place, Chapter 7 emphasised the importance of planning. In this chapter, it is clear that zoning is one mechanism to manage visitor impacts and guide ecotourism development. At the operator level, it is evident that 'micro businesses' as exemplified by McKercher and Robbins's (1998) study in Australia, highlighted the all too familiar problems of establishing and developing small tourism businesses.

Since ecotourism is still characterised as a growth driving the tourist experience in many countries, it is not surprising to find new small ecotour operators developing in response to perceived opportunities. Yet as McKercher and Robbins's (1998) experiences of new firm formation show, enthusiasm and drive need to be tempered by a multi-skilled approach to managing an ecotourism operation. This was very much in evidence in relation to some of the case studies of businesses examined in Page and Getz (1997). Running a new venture requires a range of professional skills, such as marketing, financial acumen and communication which many entrepreneurs overlook. As a nascent sector of the tourism industry in some countries, ecotourism represents a challenge for the public sector in how to assist such businesses to remain viable and to achieve their goals. Critics argue that the market will ultimately determine which businesses fail, survive or prosper. Yet as McKercher and Robbins (1998) recognised, such a view overlooks the oft quoted statement that the sector is only as good as its weakest operators. Where intervention through training, accreditation and licensing does not occur, the impact on the tourist experience of ecotourism will be unpredictable and variable and could damage the industry's image. Such arguments have particular relevance to those sectors of the ecotourism industry which specialise in adventure activities which place clients in risk-taking situations (see Bentley and Page 2001; Bentley *et al.* 2000, 2001; Page 1997 for more detail).

Consequently, ensuring that ecotourism operators have access to advice, training and opportunities for professional development are important prerequisites for the future development of prosperity through ecotourism. Increasingly, codes of conduct and ethical concerns are also facing operators and this sector of the tourism industry as their activities are placed under greater public scrutiny as the industry matures. This is certainly one area which is attracting interest from researchers, NGOs and operators alike. Likewise, managing the ecotourism experience so that local communities benefit accordingly is also a growing area of concern (Finucane and Dowling 1995). For operators, ecotourism may be an opportunity to realise personal ambitions and feelings of success in owning and operating a business. Yet as many operators frequently mention, the idea, business plan and sources of finance are just the starting point of an unknown and often unchartered path. Acquiring the right skills in managing an ecotourism business are vital to ensure its success, and being able to successfully market it to the target audience is vital. It is this latter point – marketing ecotourism, to which attention now turns in Chapter 9.

## Questions

1. Why do planners employ zoning techniques to manage ecotourism?
2. Outline the range of management issues facing micro-level ecotourism operators.
3. Why are ethical issues important in ecotourism?
4. Why is community development important to ecotourism?

## Further reading

A good introduction to the issue of community-based ecotourism can be found in:

Drumm, A. (1998) 'New approaches to community-based ecotourism management. Learning from Ecuador', in K. Lindberg, M. Epler Wood and D. Engeldrum (eds), *Ecotourism: A Guide for Planners and Managers*, Vol. 2, North Bennington: The Ecotourism Society, 197–213.

For an overview of management issues in ecotourism see:

Halpenny, E. (2001) 'Ecotourism-related organizations', in D. Weaver (ed.), *Encyclopedia of Ecotourism*, Wallingford: CAB International, 479–508.
Backman, S., Petrick, J. and Wright, B. (2001) 'Management tools and techniques: an integrated approach to planning', in D. Weaver (ed.), *Encyclopedia of Ecotourism*, Wallingford: CAB International, 451–62.
Cohen, J. (2001) 'Ecotourism in the inter-sectoral context', in D. Weaver (ed.), *Encyclopedia of Ecotourism*, Wallingford: CAB International, 498–508.

# Chapter 9

# Marketing for ecotourism

Marketing is widely acknowledged as a vital prerequisite to communicating the product or service offering of businesses or suppliers to the market, which in the case of ecotourism is the ecotourist. Within the existing research published on ecotourism, there are a dearth of studies which address the marketing issues that are relevant to ecotourism. Probably the most significant landmark study in this area was Ingram and Durst's (1987) review of the marketing of nature-oriented travel in developing countries and the subsequent study of promoting nature tourism in developing countries (Durst and Ingram 1988). These seminal studies highlighted the need for public sector tourism officers in developing countries to improve their marketing efforts, as nature-based tourism was a missed opportunity for many countries from failing to market the natural attractions and attributes upon which ecotourism is based. These findings remain as valid today as they were on publication in the late 1980s, and highlight the need for both the public and private sector to market ecotourism products and experiences.

This chapter examines the notion of marketing to explain what it is, why it is used, what it seeks to achieve and its application to ecotourism. The discussion focuses on three elements of marketing, SWOT analysis, marketing research and the marketing mix as the fundamental elements of marketing. This is followed by a review of some of the basic marketing principles necessary for ecotourism operators. Attention then moves to the market segments which comprise ecotourism in relation to their marketing needs. The language and material used in ecotourism marketing are also reviewed together with some of the tools used to reach the ecotourist as a consumer. However, prior to discussing ecotourism marketing, it is necessary to briefly examine marketing as a concept.

## What is marketing?

According to Kotler and Armstrong (1991), marketing is a process whereby individuals and groups obtain the type of products or goods they value. These goods are created and exchanged through a social and managerial process which requires a detailed understanding of consumers and their wants and desires so that the product or service is effectively and efficiently delivered to the client or purchaser. Within tourism studies, there has been a growing interest in marketing (Middleton 1988; Jefferson and Lickorish 1988; Laws 1991; Lumsdon 1997; Horner and Swarbrooke 1996; Seaton and Bennett 1996) and the ways in which it can enhance the promotion of tourism services. More recently, new marketing for tourism texts have begun to incorporate material on sustainable tourism (e.g. Middleton and Hawkins 1998); and increased concerns for green consumers (e.g. Horner and Swarbrooke 1996). In ecotourism, marketing has assumed less importance than operational and organisational issues, but there is a growing awareness that ecotourists are a distinct market and that reaching them is a complex marketing proposition. Yet for ventures and organisations seeking to promote ecotourism activity, there are certain types of aspects of marketing one has to consider. Within marketing, three key areas exist:

- strategic planning;
- marketing research;
- the marketing mix.

## Strategic planning

Within any business or company, there is a need to provide some degree of order or structure to its activities and to think ahead. This is essential if companies are to be able to respond to the competitive business environment in which organisations operate. For this reason, a formal planning process is necessary which is known as *strategic planning*. According to Kotler and Armstrong (1991: 29), strategic planning can be defined as 'the process of developing and maintaining a strategic fit between the organisation's goals and capabilities and its changing marketing opportunities'. Businesses need to be aware of their position in the wider business environment and how they will respond to competition and new business opportunities within an organised framework. To illustrate how strategic planning operates and its significance to ecotourism, it is useful to focus on the structured approach devised by Kotler and Armstrong (1991). As Figure 9.1 shows, the first stage is the definition of an organisation's purpose which requires a company to consider:

- What business are they in?
- Who are their customers?
- What services do their customers require?

Following the definition of purpose, a company may incorporate these principles into a *mission statement* (see David 1989).

The next stage following the setting of objectives and goals is termed the *business portfolio*. Here the company analyses its own products or services in

Figure 9.1   Strategic planning for ecotourism (based on Kotler and Armstrong 1991)

terms of its own business expertise and how competitors' products and services may affect them. This is frequently undertaken as a SWOT analysis, which considers:

- the *S*trengths
- the *W*eaknesses
- the *O*pportunities
- the *T*hreats

of its products and services in the business environment.

For those tourism operators who may wish to develop a strategy which incorporates an element of organisational growth and expansion, a number of options exist. As Horner and Swarbrooke (1996: 325) show, these can be divided into:

- marketing consortia, where a group of operators cooperate to create and develop a product;
- strategic alliances where different businesses agree to cooperate in various ways. This has varied by sector in the tourism industry, such as marketing agreements or technical cooperation;
- acquisition, which is the purchase of equity in other operations;
- joint ventures, where operators seek to create new businesses;
- franchising, where major operators use their market presence and brand image to further extend their influence by licensing franchisees to operate businesses using their corporate logo and codes.

In the case of ecotourism operators, they may be vulnerable to such growth strategies from predatory competition, with the marketing consortia one of the most viable options for micro-scale enterprises.

## Marketing research

This process is one which is often seen as synonymous with market research but as the following definition by Seibert (1973) implies, in reality it is a much broader concept as 'marketing research is an organised process associated with the gathering, processing, analysis, storage and dissemination of information to facilitate and improve decision-making'. It incorporates various forms of research undertaken by organisations to understand its customers, markets and business efficiency. The actual research methods used to investigate different aspects of a company's business ultimately determine the type of research undertaken. The main types of research can be summarised into six categories (see Middleton 1988 for more details). A number of good introductions to marketing research are available and more recent books on tourism research are recommended as preliminary reading on this topic (e.g. Witt and Moutinho 1989; Veal 1992). Marketing research allows the company to keep in touch with its customers to monitor needs and tastes which are constantly changing in time and space. However, the actual implementation of marketing for tourist transport ultimately depends on the 'marketing mix'.

## The marketing mix

The marketing mix is 'the mixture of controllable marketing variables that the firm [or company] uses to pursue the sought level of sales in the target market' (Kotler cited in Holloway and Plant 1988: 48). This means that for a given ecotourism organisation, there are four main marketing variables which it needs to harness to achieve the goals identified in the marketing strategy formulated through the strategic planning process. These variables comprise the 4 Ps of product formulation, price, promotion and place:

- *Product formulation* – is the ability of a company to adapt to the needs of its customers in terms of the services it provides. These are constantly being adapted to changes in consumer markets.
- *Price* – is the economic concept used to adjust the supply of a service to meet the demand, taking account of sales targets and turnover.
- *Promotion* – is the manner in which a company seeks to improve customers' knowledge of the services it sells so that those people who are made aware may be turned into actual purchasers. To achieve promotional aims, advertising, public relations, sales and brochure production functions are undertaken within the remit as promotion. Not surprisingly promotion often consumes the largest proportion of marketing budgets. For transport operators, the timetable is widely used as a communication tool while brochures and information leaflets are produced to publicise products.
- *Place* – is the location at which prospective customers may be induced to purchase a service – the point of sale (e.g. a travel agent).

These are incorporated into the marketing process in relation to the known competition and the impact of market conditions. Thus, the marketing process involves the continuous evaluation of how a business operates internally and externally and it can be summarised as 'the management process which identifies, anticipates and supplies customers' requirements efficiently and profitably' (UK Institute of Marketing, cited in Cannon 1989).

## Marketing issues for ecotourism: challenges and opportunities

In a tourism context, marketing differs from other products because tourism is a service industry, where the intangibility, quality of delivery and evaluation of experiences are difficult to visualise and envision. The heterogeneity (i.e. diversity), perishability (i.e. a tour cannot be stored and resold at a different time) and intangibility of ecotourism services make marketing a challenge when combined with two other key problems: the customer must travel to the product/resource base to consume it; and the ecotourism activity (holiday) over which the operator has little influence. For the ecotourism industry, there must be a recognition that the market is divided into different segments and that targeting these consumers may occur geographically, demographically (i.e. by age, gender and race) or psychographically (i.e. by lifestyle, attitude or values).

Ecotourism, as a subset of tourism, also has particular requirements for marketing to be successful. Ryel and Grasse (1991) recognised that attracting ecotourists is dependent upon biodiversity, cultural history and unique geography of areas as well as the infrastructure available to support ecotourism development. In particular, Ryel and Grasse (1991) were concerned with attracting 'The right sort of ecotourist', including the 'born ecotourist' (with a predisposition to nature and nature travel) and 'made ecotourists', a form of latent demand waiting to be attracted. To harness the 'born' and 'made' ecotourist, Ryel and Grasse (1991) identified the following approach to marketing ecotourism:

- the identification of the characteristics of the desired target group;
- appropriate advertising;
- careful development of the advertising message;
- the development of a mailing list.

Through this approach it is possible to identify ecotourist types in relation to geographic, demographic and psychographic variables, which were examined by Silverberg *et al.* (1996) in relation to 336 nature-based travellers to the south-east USA. Fennell (1999) noted that this is one area which has begun to attract research interest given the importance of marketing to connect the ecotourist with the ecotourism industry. Yet marketing ecotourism is not a new phenomenon, given the history of adventure tourism, exploration and the naturalist-explorer. But what is important as Epler Wood (1998a: 45) observed is the simultaneous broadening and deepening of the ecotourism clientele, as the market has developed and become more sophisticated. The ongoing demand for ecotourism is likely to continue for at least 25 years, according to Epler Wood (1998a: 59), due to demographic changes. For the ecotourism industry, also recognising that 'consumers are switching allegiances, challenging traditional ethics, and actively seeking out products that are perceived to fulfil their needs, even if more costly' (Wight 1993a: 8) poses many challenges for the ecotourism industry. This means ensuring that the values inherent in ecotourism are incorporated into ecotourism products and activities is the challenge for marketers who wish to tap consumer interest in ecotourism (Wight 1993a).

The challenges involved in marketing an ecotourism product include identifying and promoting opportunities for diversity and the special attractions of a region's natural areas in a way which is ecologically sustainable (Middleton and Hawkins 1998). It also embraces redressing any lack of knowledge about ecotourism market demand and visitor motivations, expectations and needs, as well as assembling and delivering product information to meet the needs of potential visitors.

Some possible approaches to overcoming these challenges are to (Wearing and Neil 1999: 109–14):

- identify present and emerging domestic and international nature-based and ecotourist market segments;

- seek to promote a better understanding among all private and public sector stakeholders about market demand, visitor motivations and expectations, product diversity and service requirements;
- encourage operators to develop marketing plans;
- distribute marketing and pre-visit information which links visitor expectations with sustainable activities and opportunities in natural areas;
- increase the diversity of opportunities used in marketing a region's natural attractions to reduce pressure on current high visitation areas, i.e. alternative sites/locations to currently popular areas should be provided.

One of the major issues facing ecotourism operators is the misconception that many consumers, the market and industry have with the term 'ecotourism'. As stated by Wight (1993a: 4); 'there is no question that "green" sells. Almost any terms prefixed with "eco" will increase interest and sales. Thus, there has been a proliferation of advertisements in the travel field with references such as ecotour, ecotravel, ecoadventures, ecocruise, ecosafari, ecoexpedition and, of course, ecotourism.' This has caused confusion over exactly what 'ecotourism' is and in some cases has caused the term 'ecotourism' to lack credibility in the consumer's mind. As James Sanno, CEO of Inner Asia Expeditions (cited in Wight 1993a: 4) observed, 'ecotourism is a fashionable marketing ploy right now. It's often misunderstood, but more often it's exploited.' The term 'eco' is often just used for marketing purposes to attract tourists. Ecotourism is a buzzword which is not understood. As Wight (1993a) noted, operators have not changed their itineraries; they just use the word for marketing purposes. In recent years there has been a move to establish accreditation and certification within the ecotourism industry, and this can help to dispel any negative perceptions of the industry and enable consumers to know what operators are 'true' ecotourism businesses, as Chapter 8 recognised. This is also of use for operators wanting to market their products, as being certified or having accreditation is a guarantee that they are a legitimate ecotourism business, and this can be an extra marketing tool against competitors.

Gilbert (1997) suggested that there are a number of marketing guidelines for ecotourism, in that effective marketing requires the establishment of a realistic budget and the employment of individuals with tourism marketing experience. The key objective is to 'know your market' and establish the ecotour as a unique, niche market. Gilbert (1997) also noted that those in the business of ecotourism should be genuine in their 'green' commitment. Other key elements of a successful ecotourism business include the requirement to promise only what you can deliver as every aspect of an ecotour operation must withstand scrutiny. Eco-efficiency, including project design and energy use, should be given adequate attention by ecotourism operators. It should meet clients' expectations and be acceptable to host communities. In fact, Gilbert (1997) advocated the need to take note of comments from ecotour participants for they are the most discerning commentators. Another suggestion was to organise both formal and informal contact to maximise opportunities for feedback. It may also be necessary to cover language needs for the main groups that form the tourism markets. This can be achieved by providing interpretation as part of the tour, and supporting the information provided with basic facts printed in the languages of the major target markets.

## Marketing tools used by the ecotourism industry

McKercher (1998: 89) champions the idea of strategic marketing of ecotourism businesses. He suggests that it is a process of formulating long-term objectives about the positioning of the business and how it is differentiated from other businesses. In order to formulate the plan it is necessary to undertake situational analysis comprising external and internal elements. The external factors lie outside the direct control of the business and include analyses of competitors, markets, customers and the environment. The internal analysis focuses on oneself and those features of the business over which the owner has direct control. It encompasses analyses of business performance, the product portfolio and the available resources. Once the external and internal analyses have been completed then the data is presented as a SWOT analysis outlining the business's strengths, weaknesses, opportunities and threats. For example, operators need to recognise the challenge of seeking out the ecotourist, many of whom are active information seekers, who use a wide range of sources when planning their holiday. Thus, word of mouth and local information are important influences, as is the Internet as a key source of information and as a booking medium.

## SWOT analysis

As with tourism marketing generally, in ecotourism SWOT analysis is a widely used technique. Best practice goes beyond appreciation of the natural environment, to encompass an understanding of social activities, economic impacts on the facilities and region and spatial expression of community values. This may be achieved through a marketing audit and an associated statement of strengths, weaknesses, opportunities and threats (SWOT). As discussed earlier, the SWOT is an effective way to analyse the current status of ecotourism marketing and project future threats and opportunities likely to impact the ecotourism suppliers and managers and ecotourists themselves.

### Strengths

Effective market segmentation is a key to defining an appropriate user group for ecotourism as the section below will show. To market a genuine ecotourism venture, it is important to ensure the validity and legitimacy of the experience. Obtaining accurate statistics and a demographic and psychographic profile of potential consumers may go some way to doing this, by aligning perceived user wants with the product/service produced. Ecotourism is based on visitation and appreciation of the natural attributes of a region. It provides a low-cost attraction on which ecotourism products may be developed and moulded. The unique and varied nature of many protected natural areas provides an excellent basis for development of specialised services focusing on a limited geographic zone, which can be translated to an appropriate advertising campaign and areas for sustainable competitive advantage. Ecotourists are very discerning and take time to educate themselves about a destination prior to departure. This means that careful market research into the form of advertising most likely to attract the consumer by heightened involvement is liable to have a profound effect in achieving response, and produce a decision based on the characteristics of the target market. Thus, both operators and destination marketers need to build on the available strengths of the product (i.e. the environment and natural attributes) and to communicate them to the market.

## Threats

In the past few years, ecotourism has become a marketing buzzword and has been used to sell any number of products, and the 'eco' tag is no longer a real indication of the quality of the product on offer. One reason for the increasing proliferation of the 'ecotourism' label is because of the general lack of understanding as to what ecotourism is. Some of the products being marketed are totally unrelated to ecotourism, yet it is this label which is being used to sell them. As a result, many of the problems or negative trends which make ecotourism unsustainable relate to the fact that 'principles fundamental to ecotourism are not being incorporated into the conception, planning, design, development, operation or marketing of the product' (Wight 1993a: 3). As a result, operators and destination marketers need to ensure the ecolabel is used in sophisticated ways to communicate with consumers and not used as a catch-all term just to market a destination.

## Opportunities

There are numerous opportunities available to marketeers of ecotourism products/services that allow the goals of sustainability and profitability to be met simultaneously. The proliferation of interest groups, particularly nature-based organisations, provides an opportunity for direct marketing. As Kerr (1992) argued, ecotourism is not a product that should be aimed at the masses, but smaller groups of discerning visitors who will pay for an authentic experience. This small-group, intimate approach to crafting the tourism experience has great potential to generate high levels of visitor satisfaction, educational goals and create memorable and value-added products which generate profit.

Developing an image of a destination, or an image of the experience, is crucial in maximising involvement and influencing the decision-making behaviour of the intended audience. The creation of a strong image that is a realistic reflection of the product is extremely beneficial. In order to ensure the sustainability of the venture, and the area on which ecotourism is based, the managerial philosophy adopted should be holistic. The utilisation of an ecotourism opportunity spectrum (see Chapter 3 for more detail) presents a long-term opportunity to further segment the ecotourism market based on the degree of authenticity of the ecotourism experience by the potential client. Thus, ecotourism product marketing can be significantly improved through increasing analysis and study of carrying capacities and host communities

prior to the establishment of the operation; improved education and interpretive material; and a greater focus on providing a quality experience by
value-added attributes to the product (Wearing and Neil 1999: 109–14).

### Weaknesses

One of the fundamental weaknesses in ecotourism as a product and its marketing by operators and destinations is how the negative environmental impacts
are managed, mitigated and understood. The intended outcome of ecotourism
is the development of tourism as a sustainable economic resource for the
destination. Ecotourism must minimise negative impacts on the environment.
Many tour operators know how to minimise the detrimental impact of tourism on wildlife and they have to maintain rigorous standards as a result of
their love and respect for nature as ecotourism operators are often learned
naturalists. Ryel and Grasse (1991) state that travel companies contemplating
tours to exceptionally delicate areas may find that a particularly fragile condition exists, either in terms of the wildlife population or the indigenous human
population that would make visitation too harmful or corruptive. Regardless
of accessibility for tourism and its potential value to the travel company or
local economy, attracting travellers to such a destination would be irresponsible.
Thus, ethical issues and hard decisions need to be made, or poorly thought out
decisions on the products sold could detract from what one is seeking to achieve.

Ecotourism should stimulate among travellers and among the inhabitants
of the destination an awareness, appreciation and understanding of the ecosystem and the need for preservation. Many nature-oriented travel programmes

**Plate 9.1**  Iguazu Falls marks the intersection of Argentina, Brazil and Paraguay. It is natural
icons such as the falls which attract ecotourists who seek an encounter with both the natural
attraction as well as the local peoples.

tend to emphasise the overt spectacles of nature, such as watching sunrise over the African savannah, viewing the Iguazu Falls or diving the Great Barrier Reef. But what of the less apparent, equally fascinating wonders of nature? We need to examine the environment more completely. Ryel and Grasse (1991: 165) argued that

> ecotourism should redefine for the traveller what is sensational. Colonies of leaf cutter ants marching across the jungle floor holding high their leaf fragment as though it were a green parasol, an unfolding drama in a spider's web, or a flowering epiphyte precariously suspended from a towering mahogany tree should command equal time with vast herds of large mammals and thundering waterfalls.

In this respect, ecotourism is an inclusive activity that can be valuable to the visitor and host community alike.

## Market segmentation: its application to ecotourism

For the ecotourism industry, understanding the motivations for ecotourists' pursuit of nature-based activities is essential if they are to understand the reasons for seeking engagement in such experiences. As Chapter 4 highlighted, the ecotourist is a far from homogeneous market and its growing diversity and deepening (Epler Wood 1998a) have meant the ecotourism industry must be more sophisticated in how it identifies and designs products, and markets them to potential clients. The growing complexity within the ecotourism market means that certain approaches can be utilised to understand the more specific demands and needs of the ecotourist through the process of market segmentation. This process is explained succinctly by Palacio and McCool (1997: 236) from a marketing perspective where

> Market segmentation is a process by which a large, potentially heterogenous market is divided into smaller more homogenous components or segments. A number of methods exist to segment markets. These methods have been based on social–demographic characteristics (age, gender, income, etc), geography, behaviour and 'psychographics' or motivations. Benefit based segmentation, where market re-searchers examine the benefits of a product perceived by potential purchasers has become a powerful tool in determining what it is about the product that makes it attractive, useful and worth the price to consumers.

Yet segmentation is not just about grouping ecotourists into more discrete categories based on certain characteristics. Ziffer (1989) developed a segmenta-tion model of ecotourism suppliers according to their motivation and impact on the local community through involvement and the level of impact on ecotourism resources (see Figure 9.2). Although as Wight (1993a: 5) argued, 'This model is a simplification as there may in reality be a dynamic overlap in the motivations and activities of the sectors', it does illustrate the principle of segmentation in an attempt to understand how stakeholders and the ecotourism industry interact. Ultimately, the segmentation process is used to try and understand more clearly the complexity and amalgam of factors which inter-act to produce groups and activities focused around a range of identifiable

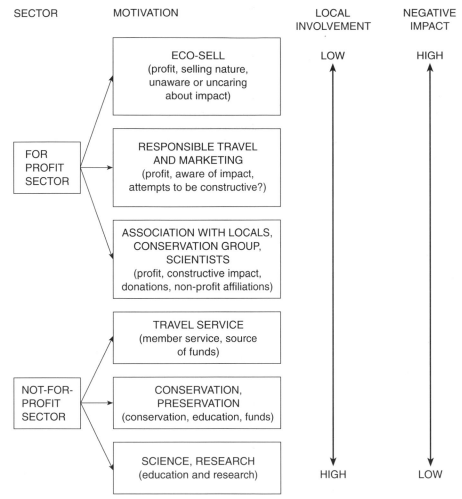

**Figure 9.2** Segmentation model of ecotourism suppliers, motivations, and impact
*Source*: Based on Wight (1993a: 5) and Ziffer (1989).

characteristics. As Palacio and McCool (1997: 237) recognised, segmentation is a critical method to employ from a marketing perspective because 'The ecotourism and sustainable tourism literature is increasingly aware that average "ecotourists" do not really exist.' What a great deal of debate has focused on is the criteria and segmentation bases used to devise categories of ecotourists. For example, Palacio and McCool (1997) question the validity of using recreation activity behaviour as the basis for differentiation among tourists. In their study of ecotourists in Belize, Palacio and McCool (1997) used a benefit segmentation technique to examine the relationship between market segments in relation to expected benefits.

## Palacio and McCool's benefit segmentation of ecotourists

From 206 interviews among tourists at Belize International Airport, respondents were asked to rate 18 items representing expected benefits of a visit to Belize. Following multivariate statistical analysis, using principal components analysis, four major expected benefit domains were derived. Factor 1 was interpreted as the desire to escape from the pressures of everyday life. Factor 2 was related to appreciation of/learning about the natural environment. Factor 3 was related to the health and well-being of the respondent and factor 4 was concerned with cohesiveness and the importance of sharing recreational experiences. From these four domains, a cluster analysis was used to identify four groups of visitors which are outlined in Table 9.1. The four segments which resulted were evaluated in terms of the scores in relation to the four expected benefit domains. The 'nature escapists' scored highly on their appreciation of and learning about nature but lower on the other two benefit domains. This group comprised 21.5 per cent of the sample. The second group was termed 'ecotourists' with consistently high scoring on the four domains which appeared to be consistent with Wight's (1996) characterisation of ecotourists. This group comprised 18 per cent of the sample. The third group, 'comfortable naturalists', comprised 33.3 per cent of the sample and scored more

**Table 9.1** Participation in selected recreation activities by tourists in Belize (particular rates in percentages)

| Activity | Tourist type | | | | |
|---|---|---|---|---|---|
| | Nature escapists | Ecotourists | Comfortable naturalists | Passive players | Significance* |
| Swimming | 75 | 77 | 71 | 60 | 0.31 |
| Hiking | 63 | 50 | 40 | 34 | 0.04 |
| Sailing | 23 | 35 | 13 | 16 | 0.06 |
| Canoeing | 18 | 21 | 11 | 12 | 0.56 |
| Photography | 73 | 79 | 63 | 66 | 0.36 |
| Snorkelling | 73 | 77 | 77 | 56 | 0.07 |
| Camping | 5 | 9 | 3 | 6 | 0.70 |
| Sunbathing | 70 | 71 | 57 | 44 | 0.03 |
| Viewing wildlife | 70 | 68 | 58 | 64 | 0.62 |
| Diving | 28 | 35 | 42 | 26 | 0.27 |
| Birding | 43 | 32 | 24 | 38 | 0.23 |
| Visiting ruins | 60 | 59 | 45 | 50 | 0.41 |
| Fishing | 35 | 38 | 36 | 30 | 0.88 |
| Activity index | 6.1 | 6.1 | 5.0 | 4.8 | 0.01 |

* Significance level based on chi-square for individual activity participation and analysis of variance for the activity index, which is computed by assigning a score of one to each activity in which a respondent participates.

*Source*: Palacio and McCool (1997: 241).

Table 9.2 Selected respondents' social-demographic and visit characteristics

| Variable | Tourist type | | | | |
| --- | --- | --- | --- | --- | --- |
| | Nature escapists | Ecotourist | Comfortable naturalists | Passive players | Significance* |
| Number of respondents | 40 | 34 | 62 | 50 | |
| Gender | | | | | |
| Male (%) | 54 | 41 | 50 | 68 | 0.09 |
| Female (%) | 46 | 59 | 50 | 32 | |
| Number of times visited Belize (mean) | 1.2 | 1.1 | 3.0 | 2.7 | 0.38 |
| Number of people in group (mean) | 2.4 | 3.0 | 4.9 | 5.7 | 0.04 |
| Duration of stay in Belize (mean days) | 7.7 | 6.5 | 10.1 | 8.5 | 0.31 |
| Age of respondents (mean years) | 39.3 | 40.0 | 43.1 | 48.8 | 0.0004 |

* Significance level based on analysis of variance or chi-square as appropriate.

*Source*: Palacio and McCool (1997: 240).

Table 9.3 Mean scores for segments on extracted factors

| Segment | Factor | | | |
| --- | --- | --- | --- | --- |
| | Escape | Learn about nature | Healthy activity | Cohesive |
| Nature escapists | 4.02 | 4.05 | 2.32 | 2.05 |
| Ecotourists | 4.52 | 4.64 | 3.99 | 4.27 |
| Comfortable naturalists | 3.26 | 3.46 | 2.65 | 3.62 |
| Passive players | 2.03 | 3.13 | 1.69 | 2.08 |
| Significance | 0.00 | 0.00 | 0.00 | 0.00 |

Statistical significance based on analysis of variance.

*Source*: Palacio and McCool (1997: 239).

moderately on the escape and learning domains yet lower than the nature escapists and ecotourists. This group were interested in nature and escape functions but wanted to pursue it in comparative comfort. Lastly, the 'passive players' comprised 26.9 per cent of the sample since they scored low on all the benefit domains. In terms of the socio-demographic and visit characteristics of these visitors (see Table 9.2), notable differences assisted in segmenting the market. For example, nature escapists had small group size and visited Belize alone. In contrast, the ecotourists were relatively young, had little experience of Belize and may have been 'country hopping', while passive players and comfortable naturalists were revisiting and had the largest length of stay. The recreational activities which the visitors engaged in are shown in Table 9.3, with highest rates of participation recorded by nature escapists and ecotourists. These two groups also participated in the greatest range of activities, reflected in the activity index calculated in relation to the number of activities in which individuals participated.

This study adopted a somewhat different approach to segmentation from other studies through the benefit method, but it showed that one can devise products for ecotourists and other groups with an interest in nature in very precise ways to reflect the attitudes, desires and activities which each group seeks out. The research indicated that in devising products for nature-based visitors and ecotourists in particular, it was useful to base the definition of 'ecotourists' on 'motivations or benefits expected than *a priori* statements of what ecotourists should be doing or defining ecotourists based on where sampling occurs' (Palacio and McCool 1997: 242) In addition, the benefit segmentation approach may be useful in understanding how to construct specific ecotourism experiences, since 'the data also suggest that the ecotourist experience results in a wide variety of social–psychological benefits built upon the recreational engagement' (Palacio and McCool 1997: 242). One further example of the application of the segmentation process can be found in the following case study of Quebec.

---

## CASE STUDY   Market segmentation and marketing ecotourism in the Lower North Shore of Quebec

In an interesting study by Hull (1998), the Lower North Shore of Quebec, a remote area of the Gulf of St Lawrence, Canada, was examined in relation to ecotourism development. As the fishery industry has closed in the region, attention shifted to tourism to generate new employment opportunities, particularly ecotourists. Figure 9.3 shows the location of the Lower North Shore, which runs from Natashquan to Blanc Sablon, a distance of 380 km with a population of 5,200 in 15 communities. Within the region are English- and French-speaking residents and 14 per cent of the population comprised Montagnis, a Native American group. Rural depopulation has become a major problem since the fisheries closed in the late 1980s and early 1990s. The region's resource base is marine-related, with a world famous site for marine mammal and humpback whale watching. A large seabird population, of 100,000 nesting seabirds and migratory birds, was reflected in some of the oldest sanctuaries established in the region by the Canadian Wildlife Service in 1925.

Hull (1998) surveyed 538 visitors in 1995, a 6 per cent sample of all visitors to the region in that year, which was a fairly representative survey. Depending on the survey site, between 55 and 75 per cent of visitors were from Canada, with French and US visitors dominating the overseas markets. Hull (1998) reviewed marketing activities for ecotourism in the region to understand what attracted visitors and noted a four-step framework in the marketing activities:

- the initial awareness phase, where the traveller is made aware of the potential features and attractions in the destination;
- the travel planning phase, where the tourist contacts the organisation for information on the destination;

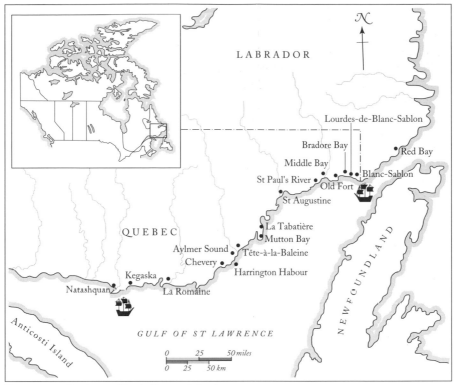

**Figure 9.3** The Lower North Shore of Quebec

- the commitment phase, where a booking is made;
- the experience phase.

In terms of the awareness phase, magazine and newspaper articles on the North Shore region were published in the Quebec newspaper *La Presse*. In Europe, a French travel magazine *La Mer & Océan* and *Photodigest*, *L'actualité* and *Montoniege* in Canada ran feature articles with visual images of nature and the environment. In the analysis of reasons for visiting two areas in the Lower North Shore region, Hull (1998) found that landscape, nature and culture were important attractions (see Table 9.4).

During the travel planning phase, visitors rated the sources of information used to plan their trip (Table 9.5). This revealed that government information, guides and word of mouth were important information sources. In the commitment phase, it was evident that some visitors booked a long time in advance and some made much shorter decisions to visit in the summer months. This is important given the diversity of the market and with between 70 and 80 per cent of visitors first-time visitors. In the experience phase, infrastructure (i.e. ferry services) influenced the amount of time visitors spent in the region. In terms of visitor activities, Table 9.6 shows that nature, culture and passive activities (i.e. meeting locals and taking photographs) were dominant activities. Even so, Hull (1998) argued that between 64 and 72 per

**Table 9.4**  Initial reasons for coming to the Lower North Shore

| Kegaska | Rank | Blanc–Sablon | Rank |
|---------|------|--------------|------|
| Landscape | 1 | Landscape | 1 |
| Culture | 2 | Icebergs | 2 |
| Whales | 3 | Culture | 3 |
| Adventure | 4 | Residents | 4 |
| Residents | 5 | Adventure | 5 |
| Icebergs | 6 | Relaxation | 6 |
| Relaxation | 6 | Whales | 7 |
| Seabirds | 8 | Fishing | 8 |
| Hiking | 9 | Other | 9 |
| Arts/crafts | 10 | Hiking | 10 |

*Source*: Hunt (1998: 151).

**Table 9.5**  Sources of information used in planning trip

| Kegaska | Rank | Blanc–Sablon | Rank |
|---------|------|--------------|------|
| Tourist guide | 1 | Friends | 1 |
| Friends | 2 | Government | 2 |
| Government | 3 | Tourist guide | 3 |
| Newspaper | 4 | Magazine | 4 |
| Relatives | 5 | Relatives | 5 |
| Magazine | 6 | Other | 6 |
| Television | 6 | Television | 7 |
| Other | 8 | Travel agent | 8 |
| Travel agent | 9 | Newspaper | 9 |
| Tour operator | 10 | Tour operator | 10 |

*Source*: Hunt (1998: 152).

**Table 9.6**  Activities visitors engaged in while on Lower North Shore

| Kegaska | Rank | Blanc–Sablon | Rank |
|---------|------|--------------|------|
| Nature study | 1 | Visiting historic sites | 1 |
| Taking photos | 1 | Visiting parks | 2 |
| Meeting locals | 3 | Meet locals | 3 |
| Boat trip | 4 | Taking photos | 4 |
| Visiting historic sites | 5 | Purchasing arts/crafts | 5 |
| Birdwatching | 6 | Nature study | 6 |
| Hiking | 7 | Camping | 7 |
| Visiting parks | 8 | Fishing | 8 |
| Fishing | 9 | Birdwatching | 9 |
| Purchasing arts/crafts | 10 | Hiking | 10 |
| Camping | 11 | Boat trips | 11 |

*Source*: Hunt (1998: 154).

cent of visitors considered themselves to be ecotourists. Whether they conform with the strict principles devised for ecotourism is debatable. However, what the study illustrates for marketers in terms of segmentation is that a diverse group of visitors exists. The products and experiences they seek need to be framed in relation to the four-stage marketing process discussed by Hull (1998). This illustrates that destination and product marketing are vital at each stage of the tourist buying process, that marketing needs to focus on each market segment and the factors which influence their ecotourism market.

## Reaching the ecotourism market

According to the seminal study on marketing ecotourism by Ryel and Grasse (1991) there are a number of ways of reaching the consumer, including: choosing your advertising media carefully, crafting the message to communicate the product offering to the potential ecotourist, the use of traditional brochures and special promotional events. Their suggestions include the following.

### Choosing the advertising media

Once the characteristics of the target audience have been defined through segmentation, the company should determine which advertising media to utilise. A company and its product will immediately inherit a measurable degree of trust and acceptance among consumers simply by virtue of their presence in the right advertising medium. Specialised magazines that are well established and affiliated with highly respected, internationally recognised organisations such as the Australian Conservation Foundation are a prime source of advertising. Other magazines such as *Australian Geographic* and *Geo*, which are not affiliated with special institutions, can also target ecotourism products effectively within Australia, while similar publications such as *The Geographical Magazine* and *BBC Wildlife* in the UK can be used for overseas marketing. Identifying a key interest common to most ecotourism prospects can help a travel company find effective advertising channels. Special travel itineraries offered by the company may require targeting advertising to special interest magazines. For example, a coral reef diving expedition to the Ningaloo reef in Western Australia or the Great Barrier Reef in Australia could be effectively advertised in the international *Skin Diver* magazine.

Ecotourism companies need to realise maximum results from advertising by maintaining a constant presence in the primary media they use. Frequency leads to recognition and top-of-mind awareness. Nature travel companies should therefore invest in repeated advertising with their most productive advertising media. Frequency contracts with media also earn special discount rates. Cooperative marketing also pays dividends. Ecotourism operators do not always have to carry the full burden of advertising costs. Most airlines and many of the more established lodge operators will provide cooperative advertising funds to travel companies that feature their services in the advertisement.

Advertising that complements editorial content also enhances the effectiveness of advertising.

## Crafting the message

Financial constraints often limit nature travel companies to a relatively subtle presence in advertising media. In order to capture attention and induce action, ecotourism marketers must ensure that their advertisements are strategically placed both within the magazine and on the page, and that they are creatively designed and written. They should try to maintain a consistent positioning strategy advertisement design, use of colour and photographic or illustrative mood in order to draw attention and establish recognition. The most difficult challenge of advertising ecotourism is the development of effective copy. This is difficult to do within the confines of a tiny display advertisement, particularly because the inclusion of mandatory information often leaves little room for enticing prose. Consequently the primary advertising objective of most nature travel companies is to encourage their audience to request additional information about the featured destination by telephone or e-mail. If the advertisement successfully accomplishes that objective, captivating brochures describing the destination in detail, projecting vivid images of the wildlife and culture of the habitat, and expressly or implicitly addressing the concept of ecotourism can be mailed to the inquirer.

## Direct mail

A valuable outcome of well-targeted, direct response advertising is the creation of a strong mailing list. Mailing lists generated from response to the ecotourism company's own advertising generally means the names and addresses obtained are those of qualified ecotourism prospects. A mailing list is a powerful marketing tool. It allows the company to provide key prospects and past travellers with brochures, newsletters and updates on new destinations.

## Traditional brochures

Most traditional travel brochures are designed to awaken the reader's interest. They can be brilliantly contrived fables or lavish detail depicting breathtaking panoramas. Ecotourism takes a very different angle towards promotion. To appeal to their most desired prospects, ecotourism marketeers present the inherently astounding facts about the destinations they offer. The visual images within the brochures are never meticulously staged shots featuring voluptuous models and caviar moulds. Instead they are snapshots or nature frozen in time. Ecotourism operators use brochures in a variety of ways. The most effective method is to offer travel prospects a visually attractive annual travel catalogue or digest supplemented by more detailed destination specific brochures. The catalogue features all of the company's current destinations with a broad description of sights and activities. Brochures specific to each destination offered by the ecotourism operator could greatly enhance and supplement the annual catalogue.

## Group travel

Ecotourism has a special appeal for zoos, museums, aquariums, nature centres and environmental organisations. These institutions have begun to recognise the potential for educating their members about conservation issues through nature travel and many of them have full-time travel coordinators on their staff. The travel company can best demonstrate its overall quality and its commitment to environmentally sensitive ecotourism by offering familiarisation tours to group representatives. The ecotourism operator may also produce direct mail flyers for the institution to mail to its membership list.

## Special promotional events

Promotions such as radiothons, workshops and competitions are a unique cost-effective way to generate consumer excitement and expand the message of ecotourism to a wider audience. Ecotourism operators should select high-profile partners that have clients with similar demographics (for instance, a popular sport optics manufacturer). Through this cooperation, the ecotourism operator can gain credibility, enhance its image, and broaden awareness for its travel products. Marketing involves matching tourism products with peoples' needs. It recognises that people are different and desire different types of tourist experience (Selin 1994). It is much more than just promotion. It also includes finding out what clients want, identifying target markets, developing programmes, location and scheduling decisions, and pricing strategies. Marketing challenges natural resource managers to adopt a more client-centred management philosophy – managing people, not just rainforests, hiking trails or endangered wildlife. Numerous new ways exist for the marketing of ecotourism-accredited products. A number of new initiatives include the national marketing initiative for NEAP, e-commerce and ECoNETT.

## The Internet

An innovative option for reaching potential visitors in the competitive marketplace of the twenty-first century is through the Internet. The Internet offers small ecotourism companies the opportunity to reach visitors around the world; however, web marketing must be done well to be effective and should not be viewed as a panacea for attracting visitors (see Page *et al.* 2001 for more detail). McKercher (1998: 134) adopted a sceptical perspective about the benefits of the Internet to small-scale ecotourism operators. He likened the Internet to being in a great darkened hall filled with millions of tourism brochures, yet the searcher has only a small pocket torch to find his or her way around. The possibility of actually stumbling across a specified company is rather limited. McKercher (1998) added that in one search conducted in June

1997 over 666,000 ecotourism sites, 400,000 nature-based tourism sites and 3.6 million tourism sites were identified. This in itself poses problems for both the micro-operator and destination in getting their products showcased and highlighted innovatively by Internet search engines.

## ECoNETT

The World Travel and Tourism Council and the DGXXIII tourism unit of the European Commission undertook a joint project in December 1995 to develop an information network for tourism and the environment. The result was ECoNETT – the European Community Network for Environmental Travel and Tourism (Lipman 1998). The rationale behind ECoNETT was to increase awareness of sustainable travel and tourism, and in turn to stimulate changes in management practices, to achieve sustainable travel and tourism development worldwide. The ECoNETT Internet site currently has over 1,200 files including recent environmental projects, good practice examples, details of publications, details on environmental awards/labels and input from experts and leading organisations. Backing this is a regular newsletter, which is also available by post. Discussion groups will soon be launched on the site, and their interactive nature will allow users to keep in touch with the latest developments while making contact with like-minded professionals online. ECoNETT is an excellent resource that represents the most comprehensive database of environmental travel and tourism available on the Internet. The EcoNETT web site is designed to provide information for the travel industry, tourism destinations, governments, academics and media, as well as the general public. Its contents include environmental information on general guidance, legal obligations, approaches to water, waste and energy management, examples of best practice, how to establish environmental management systems, and techniques and technologies to reduce environmental impact (see http://www.wttc.org for more detail).

## E-commerce

Robinson (1998) suggested that worldwide electronic commerce (e-commerce) has developed to the point where it is predicted that the travel industry will now account for 35 per cent of all 'online' sales. Businesses are now confronting the realisation that their marketing and sales will need to be in a radically different form in the future. Ecotourism products are ideally suited to be marketed to niche markets through a highly efficient but new marketing distribution channel such as the Internet. However, Robinson (1998) suggested that in order to exploit this opportunity ecotourism operators will need to differentiate their products, re-examine their marketing strategies and become conversant with e-commerce. There is a substantial body of evidence to support the argument that the tourism industry is seriously embracing the notion of sustainable tourism. This apparent conversion, however, is regarded with suspicion by some observers, who claim that many businesses are climbing aboard the environmental bandwagon only to retain or increase their market share and their profitability, without either fully understanding or being fully committed to the principles of sustainability (Wheeller 1994). Yet it is not just a question of a shotgun approach to e-commerce as Lindberg and McKercher (1997: 68) argued; the size of the ecotourism market depends on how one defines ecotourism. For example, the percentage of all tourism that is ecotourism using nature tourism as a definition will be much larger than the percentage of all tourism that uses sustainable tourism as a definition. Thus the issue of market size cannot be separated from the issue of definition. For ecotourism operators, it requires clear definition of their product and market niche before engaging in e-commerce strategies.

## Critically evaluating ecotourism marketing: the language of marketing

The growing interest in the green labelling of tourism products, especially with the eco-prefix, has led critics to indicate that 'ensuring that the values and principles inherent in ecotourism are incorporated into ecotourism products and activities is the challenge for marketers who wish to tap consumer interest in ecotourism' (Wight 1993a: 4). Wight (1993a) suggested that a range of marketing language has emerged with ecotourism (Figure 9.4), ranging from eco-sell through to values-oriented perspectives. The spectrum of language was seen to parallel the motivation of stakeholders identified by Ziffer (1989) (see Figure 9.2). Wight (1993a) maintained that the varied perspectives and motivations need to be structured around the principles of responsible marketing. In fact, Wight (1993a) identified three positions where companies and agencies can engage in environmental marketing: balance, eco-exploitation or neglect. Ideally, ecotourism should be sold to consumers in a sensitive manner, with sustainability a key element of the marketing message, together with clear conservation goals. In Europe, the Association of Independent Tour Operators' (AITO) more far-sighted members 'have begun to realise that it is time . . . to protect the product on which businesses depend . . . if we do not help conserve the very places which our clients clamour to see, in five years time, we shall have no clients at all' (Wood and House 1991: 8). Marketers need to be ethical in their marketing efforts as increasingly consumers are being discerning about the green products offered in the marketplace. Indeed, it has been argued that the language of promotion does not necessarily support the intentions of the person or organisation using it. As Muhlhausler and Pearce (2000: 138) argued, 'in the case of ecotourism [on Fraser Island, Queensland, Australia], this means that poorly used language is reducing the quality and performance of ecotourism activity'. This may expand the gap between what the tourist expects from the ecotourism experience and what is delivered.

In Dann's (1996: 248) analysis of the language of ecotourism, the promotional messages sought to contrast the

**NON-SPECIFIC, SELL-ORIENTED PHRASES**

Eco-Sell Oriented
- we just offer the best, most affordable and largest variety of 'classic and unusual' ecotourism one can find, anywhere
- rainforest ecology tours
- budget travel to 'untouristed' destinations
- areas generally neglected by the teeming tourist masses
- destinations untouched by mass tourism
- off the beaten track

Generic Language
- environmental awareness, self-discovery and personal exchange with exotic cultures or enchanted adventures to classic destinations
- ecologically sensitive
- cross-cultural focus
- environmentally friendly
- sensitive to both the physical environment and to local culture
- spirited adventures for the responsible traveller
- sustainable ecological development
- people-conscious nature tours
- nature travel

Science/Conservation Oriented
- one-week volunteer work
- visit the world's natural environments while you help preserve them. Trip proceeds support environmental and cultural preservation
- some trips involve travellers in conservation projects
- scientific expeditions
- restoration projects
- tours support jungle conservation and Peruvian children's foundation

Explanatory/Values Oriented
- small groups (8–10)
- Maximum group size 12
- Worker-owned transport companies
- Locally owned hotels
- Gives 1 per cent of profits to peace and environmental groups
- Newsletter prior to departure and lectures through tour
- Woman- and indigenous-owned business
- Supporting local economic development
- Your guide is a naturalist, tour parties are small

**SPECIFIC, VALUES-ORIENTED PHRASES**

**Figure 9.4**   Spectrum of language used to market ecotourism
*Source*: Wight (1993a: 5).

complexities of urban existence (attributed to the target audience) and the bucolic, pristine and uncomplicated life of the vacation area . . . Second, the liberating act of travel is described as one of escape . . . Third, by replacing a mere house with a 'home', the tourist is afforded the opportunity for 'real living' . . . Fourth, the escape to the simple life, the green grass of a new 'home', and gentle art of living, collectively emphasise the need to distance oneself from others – the golden hordes of mass tourism . . . Fifth, in the act of locating the individual far from the madding crowd, the whole world is preserved as an indefinite domain with limitless possibilities . . . Sixth, this odyssey becomes analogous to a pilgrimage with the realisation that it is a voyage of discovery.

Eco-explicit messages conceal the profit motives of operators as Dann (1996) found, using a promotional discourse as 'greenspeak'. What existed, as Dann (1996) argued, was a multilayered language, used to convert consumers from low-spending mass tourists to high-spending green tourists, using some of the principles of ecotourism in this conversion process. This certainly confirmed many of Wight's (1993a) earlier concerns on the tourism industry's use of ecolabelling to sell holiday experiences which adversely impacts upon the bona fide ecotourism businesses.

## Conclusion

Ecotourism marketing is about building relationships between the ecotourism industry and the people they want to attract. Communicating the product offering is becoming a complex process for operators now that the market for ecotourism has deepened and broadened. Market segmentation techniques may offer a number of opportunities to better understand the market and its needs. In terms of marketing issues for the future development of the ecotourism industry, there is a clear need to improve cooperative partnerships to communicate more efficiently to potential clients. At the same time, ensuring the integrity of the ecotourism product is maintained is vital as the product becomes more competitive and demand expands. One useful area of action for regulatory bodies to focus on is the development of training and accreditation to ensure quality standards are maintained, especially so that environmental ethics and commitment are enshrined in business operations.

What appears to plague the small ecotourism operator, in contrast to the larger nature tour operator, is raising awareness of their product through regular and consistent media exposure. Here, the marketing mix needs to be utilised within the confines of the advertising budget to achieve a profile, although cooperative marketing is invaluable in this context. However, the simple use of 'greenspeak' is inadequate for the large nature-based operators in the destination countries, since it will inevitably compromise the integrity and values of the scrupulous ecotourism operators. This reinforces the need for ecotourism operators to set themselves apart from green marketing and shallow experiences, to focus on the deep markets where value-added experiences will yield higher returns.

Green marketing has certainly become a persuasive tool in the selling of holidays, but it is clear that the committed ecotourist will seek out quality experiences and see through the hype and glossy images to question what is being sold. Marketing has a major role to play in ecotourism and its further development, but operators and destinations need to be aware of the competition for the green consumer who is naively being confused with the ecotourist.

## Questions

1. Why is marketing important to ecotourism operators?
2. What is meant by the term 'marketing mix' in ecotourism?

3. Why do ecotourism businesses and destination marketers need to use segmentation techniques?
4. As an ecotourism operator, how would you go about marketing a new venture?

## Further reading

For a good review of the marketing context which ecotourism operators need to work within see:

McKercher, B. (1998) *The Business of Nature Based Tourism*, Melbourne, Australia: Hospitality Press.

Eagles, P. (2001) 'Information sources for planning and management', in D. Weaver (ed.), *Encyclopedia of Ecotourism*, Wallingford: CAB International, 611–26.

For a more specific review of the problems of marketing ecotourism operations in Australia see:

McKercher, B. and Robbins, B. (1998) 'Business development issues affecting nature-based tourism operators in Australia', *Journal of Sustainable Tourism*, **6** (2): 173 – 88.

A detailed analytical approach to ecotourist segmentation can be found in:

Palacio, V. and McCool, S. (1997) 'Identifying ecotourists in Belize through benefit segmentation: a preliminary analysis', *Journal of Sustainable Tourism*, **5** (3): 234–43.

The debate over the way ecotourism is sold to tourists can be found in:

Wight, P. (1993) 'Ecotourism: ethics or eco-sell', *Journal of Travel Research*, **31** (3): 3–9.

For a discussion of the value of web sites in ecotourism see:

Mader, R. (1999) 'Ecotourism research and promotion on the web: experiences and insights', *International Journal of Contemporary Hospitality Management*, **11** (2/3): 78–9,

and on tourism marketing ethics see:

Wheeler, M. (1995) 'Tourism marketing ethics: an introduction', *International Marketing Review*, **12** (4): 38–49.

# Chapter 10

# Future issues and prospects for ecotourism

Ecotourism has assumed a global presence as a broad all-encompassing term that has come to represent a spectrum of tourism activities in natural areas. In its purest form, it represents a phenomenon which can add understanding and a rich experience to the visitors' knowledge, beliefs and attitude to the environment. In its crudest form, it is represented by the 'green' operators seeking to utilise the latest buzzword to market new products. Ecotourism is as much a frame of mind, a way of thinking about human interaction with the natural environment and local people, where conservation ethics are vigorously promoted from the biocentric perspective. One of the principal conflicts which ecotourism faces is its commodification, reframing and utilisation by the anthropocentric business interests which dominate the global tourism industry. What ecotourism has witnessed over the last 20 years is the classic symptom of the mass production and packaging of the tourism experience as a commodity to be traded and exchanged for commercial gain. To the purists, this crass commercialisation of the natural assets of regions of the world, often untouched by tourism, represents an enormous threat to biodiversity, cultural integrity and local communities as Western commercial values follow in the wake of the tourist. Many of the basic tenets of ecotourism as a small-scale, sensitive, unobtrusive and environmentally respectful activity may be adhered to by operators, but it is the sheer volume of pressure posed by the demand for such products in specific areas that induces controversial impacts.

It is ironic that the United Nations designated the year 2002 as the International Year of Ecotourism (IYE), with regional meetings coordinated by the WTO and a World Ecotourism Summit in Quebec in 2002. It is interesting to observe that the first regional seminar to be held in 2002 in Mozambique on ecotourism in Africa identifies many of the themes which this activity needs to consider and address both now and in the future, including:

- the development of ecotourism in national and wildlife parks, protected and other natural areas;
- the involvement of local communities;
- the management of facilities, visitors and activities related to ecotourism.

These three themes and the associated issues have been raised and critically evaluated in this book. The importance of the ecotourism stakeholders (i.e. public sector agencies, private companies, tourism trade associations, communities living within and nearby natural areas that are ecotourism attractions, NGOs, community associations and research/educational institutes) understanding the integrated nature of ecotourism and its impacts and challenges cannot be underestimated. This has to be set against existing concerns that 'Ecotourism has become the most rapidly growing and most dynamic sector of the tourism market' (Honey 1999: 390). At the same time, there has been a clear paradigm shift in the way conservation and nature-based tourism interacts. As Honey (1999: 390) recognised,

> Effective conservation now includes involving and benefiting the people living nearest the protected areas – finding harmony between people and parks – and nature tourism has come to mean not just wilderness experiences but also activities that minimize visitor impact while benefiting both the protected areas and the surrounding human populations. This shift in consciousness and understanding has led to a great deal of experimentation and creativity, most often at the local level.

Yet as this book has shown, a wide spectrum of activities try to label themselves as 'ecotourism' when in fact they do not meet the stringent criteria applied by researchers such as Fennell (1999). Indeed, Fennell (1999) believed that retaining lofty ideals, to set high standards and immovable benchmarks, is vital if ecotourism is to survive as an activity in the tourism industry. The alternative is that it simply becomes swamped by the global tour operators who integrate vertically and horizontally and commodify the product at high prices to meet demand. What concerns many commentators is that the growing interest in more green forms of tourism which are environmentally focused, is adding to what Epler Wood (1998a) saw as the deepening and broadening of ecotourism as an activity. This has led researchers such as Fennell (1999: 278–9) to devise a broad agenda to ensure that the socio-ecological goals of a pure ecotourism culture are retained as the area expands, which include:

1. Minimising the number of operators and tourists within ecotour regions in line with the capacity of the environment to absorb the impacts of ecotourism.
2. Conducting further research on the business philosophies of ecotour operators in understanding how they adhere to regional land-use strategies.
3. Insisting that operators maintain a specified level of competence, through accreditation.
4. Insisting that governments and industry work together to institute fair and equitable guidelines to regulate and/or guide the ecotourism industry.
5. Research that supports the notion that the development of an ecotourism industry should not be imposed on a community, but rather should start from the ground up.
6. Insisting that international agencies be encouraged to coordinate research.
7. Establishing stronger linkages between educational institutions and local people by providing such people with the tools (e.g. diploma, degree) to work in the industry.
8. Working to provide a definition of ecotourism and ecotourists which is acceptable to the international community.

9. Developing a template to determine the percentage of ecotourism revenues that should go to local populations.
10. Placing more emphasis on addressing the critical absence of focus in ecotourism research, including research theory and methodologies.
11. Examining international models where trusts have been established from tourism or other types of developments.

A more specific range of issues which the ecotourism industry and stakeholders will need to consider include sustainability, ethics, the trend towards greening in all tourism experiences, the inclusion of indigenous people in ecotourism development and community benefits.

## Sustainability

Environmental, ecological, cultural and economic sustainability are among the cornerstones of any viable form of ecotourism activity now and in the future. Since the natural environment underpins ecotourism it is essential that it be protected and conserved. However, in the pursuit of profit some entrepreneurs operating in natural environments under the banner of 'ecotourism', particularly

**Plate 10.1**   Zoos have seized upon the growing interest in wildlife for day trips and tourist visits and to see many forms of wildlife up close which may be endangered or hard to see, as is the case with this otter in Wellington Zoo, New Zealand. This may extend the conservation goals of wildlife tourism to a wider audience in the first instance and could gather momentum in the future.

in the less developed world, are simply not adhering to principles of stewardship of the environment. Yet tourism activity that degrades the environment,
adversely affects the local community or fails to return worthwhile economic
benefits is not sustainable in the long term. Thus, it is important that ecotourism
operators undertake best-practice methods to minimise adverse environmental
impacts caused by visitor activity, transport and facility use. In addition, the
need for environmental protection provides a compelling argument for governments to devote more money and resources into nature conservation and
protected area management.

Tourism and the natural environment can form a symbiotic relationship
(Dowling 1991, 1996d, 1997b, 2000c). This can be achieved by developing
purpose-built tourist resort complexes; investment in and careful design of
tourism infrastructure; and the hardening of sites to carry more tourists while
conserving the natural environment. Thus, there is a strong case for promoting 'sustainable' forms of tourism such as 'ecotourism', as a way of fostering
harmony between people and nature through tourism. Unfortunately, such
principles would often appear to be at variance with the economic arguments
in favour of mass tourism.

McLaren (1998: 98) noted that ecotourism's popularity is actually magni-
fying the negative impacts upon the earth, since it promotes development of
natural areas, arguing that

**Plate 10.2**   Tourists in the Antarctic in February 2001. While there are strict rules regarding
the minimum distance tourists are allowed to approach the wildlife, the reverse does not
apply. This can result in some close human – wildlife interactions.

for a tourist to have truly minimal impact, she would have to walk to the destination, use no natural resources, and bring her own food that she grew and harvested. She would also have to carry along her own low-impact accommodations (a tent) or stay in a place that is locally owned and use alternative technologies and waste treatment. Of course she would also leave the destination in no worse or perhaps in even better condition than she found it and contribute funds to local environmental protection and community development.

Wearing and Neil (1999) suggest that if the ecotourism industry should regard the use of protected areas as a resource of immense privilege, it should adapt itself to the constraints necessary to protect these areas in perpetuity. Likewise Wall (1994) argued that if ecotourism is to thrive, then it should be based upon a balanced understanding of both ecosystems and tourism systems. In a similar vein Fennell (1999: 270) argued for a more protectionist approach to ecotourism, since 'such a view is based on the belief that if ecotourism is to survive it will have to do so by reverting back to or adopting a "greener" agenda'. However, it has been suggested that the best thing the tourism industry can do for the environment is not necessarily to foster the development of ecotourism but to make mass tourism developments more sustainable.

## Ethics and ecotourism

An emerging issue in ecotourism generally is that of ethics in the advertising and delivery of the tourism product. At a Western Australia (WA) State Tourism Conference held on 7 June 1996 in Perth, Mr Terry McVeigh, General Manager, Industry Development, WA Tourism Commission noted the emerging trend in Australian tourism of litigation for non-performance in the tourism product. A year later, at a meeting of FACET, WA, the then Chief Executive of the WA Tourism Commission, Mr Shane Crockett, also raised the issue as one for tourism companies to be concerned about in lieu of two German inbound tour operators being sued by clients for misrepresenting the WA outback product. Obviously 'truth in the advertising and delivery' of products is going to be an important element of the business of ecotourism in the future and hence the need for accreditation of operators. But more profound issues related to codes of conduct, appropriate forms of ecotourism development and impacts on the resource base pose major ethical problems for the industry, if it seeks to recognise them.

## The greening of tourism

Ecotourism has widespread application and it can act as an exemplar for other forms of environmentally responsible tourism through the promotion of best practice in planning, design, management and operations. Lessons learned in the ecotourism industry can be applied to all types of tourism, for example through the greening of hotels and resorts. However, not all would agree. According to Honey (1999), mainstream ecotourism or 'ecotourism lite' is often described with catchy phrases such as 'treading lightly on the earth' and 'taking only photos, leaving only footprints'. The advertisements, brochures and publications contain buzzwords such as *quiet, rainforest, clean air, pure, lush, unspoiled, nature, breathtaking, bio-, eco-* and *green*. In recent years, much of the mass tourism industry has adopted this type of 'green' language or even established environmental departments, but it has made only superficial changes in conventional tour packages, such as offering a brief walk in the rainforest or not changing guests' sheets and towels each day. In one respect, it may prove difficult for the ecotourism industry in the future to differentiate its products and ecologically sustainable principles if the mass tourism industry is already fringing upon this niche in its use of language in its advertising.

The effectiveness of ecotourism in the future will ultimately depend on who will benefit, as well as where, when and how it can be appropriately implemented: all of which is dependent on a wide range of actions which are underpinned by the philosophical approaches we have discussed, particularly in relation to their implementation, planning and management frameworks.

Honey (1999: 21) suggested that ultimately, the goal must be to move ecotourism beyond simply a new niche within nature travel. It must become a vehicle for significantly transforming the way tourism itself is carried out, for 'greening', not merely 'greenwashing', the entire industry. Fennell (1999: 244) surmised that 'one of the unfortunate realities of ecotourism is that despite its altruistic intentions, to date there is little evidence that it is less intrusive than other types of tourism development'. He added that a regional ecotourism development problem is the fact that there seems to be a feeling of unlimited assurance that ecotourism will ultimately resolve any tourism dysfunctions within a region. Tourism decision-makers and planners, perhaps on the basis of overly optimistic forecasts of management consultants, often inherently believe that their jurisdictions will be competitive in a highly competitive global eco-tourism market. This has currently become an issue in Canada, where provinces – owing to their geological and natural features – have unbridled optimism for the sector. Fennell (1999: 274) rightly argued that 'in my estimation, the real job that lies ahead is not in writing off ecotourism (this is too easy), but rather in striving to build clarity and meaning into the concept through some funda-mental restructuring. Perhaps we just need to play better by the rules, but in the case of ecotourism the rules have yet to be fully agreed upon'.

## The inclusion of indigenous people

One highly contentious key issue facing ecotourism is the place of indigenous people and culture, particularly in developing countries (Johnston 2000). A key characteristic of the Australian definition of ecotourism is that it is based on cultural as well as natural values. In this regard, the Australian National Ecotourism Strategy advocated that cultural involvement requires consultation and negotiation with local communities (particularly indigenous communit-ies) and organisations responsible for the management of cultural heritage values (Commonwealth Department of Tourism 1994: 18). However, rhetoric aside, the reality is that there is minimal involvement in ecotourism by indigenous people in many countries despite the often strong demand for it by international visitors. Yet to leave people out of the equation in the visitation by tourists to natural areas is merely to replicate the Western view that wilderness areas must be areas where humans do not live. As Chapter 8 emphasised, a key element of overcoming these perceptions is through empowering and encouraging local people to engage in ecotourism to harness community benefits (Timothy and White 1999).

Without a sound product which is well managed, and a consumer focus, any ecotourism business will struggle to survive. One of the basic tenets of ecotourism is that it should not only be economically viable for the business owners but that it should also provide material well-being to local communities. By extension this should also bring greater regional benefits and should also provide finances for resource conservation. The profitability of ecotourism and flow of money and resources back to a local area and its community is axiomatic to the development of ecotourism. Utilising models of good practice, such as the Capirona example, needs to gain a wider dissemination to promote such deals.

## Ecotourism trends: future prospects

There are a number of trends which are impacting upon ecotourism now, and will do so in the future. They include the strong market demand, its high-profile nature, its increasing professionalism, widespread application of techniques, and the fact that it is a growth industry. There is strong market demand for ecotourism as evidenced by the worldwide growth of tourism by 8 per cent per annum with the growth in ecotourism, as discussed in Chapters 3 and 4. Ecotourism is a high-yield industry for the successful operators. Ecotourists are usually older, educated and more affluent visitors who do not mind paying for the high costs associated with ecotourism and are used to using technology, so many of their ecotour enquiry bookings are transacted via the Internet and e-mail (see Bristow 1999 for the example of Belize and its presence on the world wide web). This has been accompanied by increasing professionalism within the ecotourism sector. Many codes of ethics for tourists and codes of practice for operators exist although there is still a long way to go in their development and refinement. In addition, schemes such as the Australian National Accreditation Scheme provide an opportunity for tourists and operators to promote bona fide ecotourism operations to uphold quality experiences and to avoid rogue operators tarnishing the sector's image. This may be viewed as a natural maturing of the ecotourism industry. Christ (1998: 193) noted that 'if ecotourism is an experiment, and it still is, there are now enough positive results to take it very seriously. The days are gone when one wondered whether adopting the principles of ecotourism could make tourism become a catalyst for nature conservation and community development. There is, finally, ample evidence that this is true.'

In fact, Ceballos-Lascurain (1999: 9) argued that ecotourism has now moved into a phase of maturity but noted that 'hopefully, the coming years will confirm a productive and propitious maturity'. McKercher (1998: 202) agreed with this assessment and argued that as ecotourism moves into a phase of maturity the competition will intensify as existing businesses grow and new ones become established. Thus, in order to survive in the future, ecotourism businesses will have to differentiate their products more precisely, especially as the market is being broadened with the emergence of a range of soft to hard products.

## Ecotourism at a crossroads

Ecotourism is now at a crossroads (Dowling 2000c). This is supported by a survey of literature on ecotourism which reveals a number of current and emerging trends and issues. Books, reports and papers which support this notion include ecotourism in the less developed world (Weaver 1998), Asia (Lindberg *et al.* 1998b), the USA (Lew 1998a), Australia (Dowling 1998b), Costa Rica (Lumsdon and Swift 1998) and Ecuador (Epler Wood 1998b). Christ (1998: 193) stated that

> In order to move ecotourism successfully forward in the years ahead, we must try to apply the same criteria which have shown results at the small-scale level, to the large-scale commercial nature-based tourism sector. This will encourage a growing number of private-sector, nature based tourism companies, who have shown a willingness to become more sensitive to ecotourism issues, to get involved not only with ecologically friendly operations but to extend their commitment into the most challenging arena of ecotourism practice today – successful community development.

The Ministerial Conference on Oceans and New Tourism Dimensions held on 3–4 June 1998 in connection with the Expo '98 World Fair in Lisbon, Portugal, identified the emergence of products which will dominate the tourism market in the new millennium (WTO 1998). Mr Francesco Frangialli, WTO Secretary-General, stated that 'this conference served to spotlight certain products which are emerging today such as nature and ecotourism products, cruises, water sports, and tourism in the polar regions, the deserts and the great tropical forests' (WTO 1998: 1). The WTO reported that ecotourism is now one-fifth of the global market, accounting for approximately 20 per cent of total international travel and is now worth US$20 billion a year (WTO 1998).

With such assessments, it could be argued that ecotourism has moved, or is moving, from a small, narrow niche market into mainstream tourism. However, we would argue that the case is overstated and that tourism to natural areas, including ecotourism, nature-based tourism and/or adventure tourism, still represents a relatively small element of the overall industry and that the rhetoric about its explosive growth is yet to be met in reality. However, the warnings held by recent commentators, as outlined in this chapter, need to be heard, otherwise ecotourism's appeal as a trendy consumer product and marketing label will rapidly wane as tourists become more discerning, leading to a possible backlash effect whereby ecotourism products, whether genuine or not, are bypassed for another new fad.

## The International Year of Ecotourism 2002

The United Nations (UN) designation is aiming to encourage cooperation among governments, international and regional organisations and NGOs to achieve the aims of Agenda 21 in promoting development and the protection of the environment. In recognition of the economic and environmental benefits of sustainable tourism, the UN General Assembly stressed the need to integrate sustainable development in the tourist industry, and invited states, intergovernmental and governmental organisations to exert all possible efforts on behalf of the success of the Year. This has come about by the recognition of the:

- need for full integration of sustainable development in the tourism industry in order to ensure, *inter alia*, that travel and tourism contribute to the conservation, protection and restoration of the earth's ecosystem; that international trade in travel and tourism services takes place on a sustainable basis; and that environmental protection is an integral part of tourism development;
- need to promote the implementation of international conventions on the environment and development, including those on biodiversity and climate change;
- need for international cooperation in promoting tourism within the framework of sustainable development so as to meet the needs of present tourists and host countries and regions while protecting and enhancing opportunities for the future, managing resources to fulfil economic, social and aesthetic needs, and maintaining cultural integrity, essential ecological processes, biological diversity and life-support systems;
- support of the WTO for the importance of ecotourism, and particularly of the designation of the year 2002 as the International Year of Ecotourism, in fostering better understanding among peoples everywhere, in leading to greater awareness of the rich heritage of various civilisations and in bringing about a better appreciation of the inherent values of different cultures, thereby contributing to the strengthening of world peace.

## Implications

Potts and Harrill (1997) suggest that the stage is set for a form of tourism beyond ecotourism called 'travel ecology', since the strategy for ecotourism or sustainable tourism is minimal negative impact whereas the overall strategy for travel ecology would be community enhancement. Travel ecology is the study of ecological impacts of travel and humankind–nature interactions of community tourism. It differs from ecotourism, nature-based and sustainable tourism in its emphasis on ecology and community. The concept of travel ecology has evolved in recent years with an emphasis on community planning carried out by local citizens. Place discovery, quality of life goals, Environmental Assessment that includes resource identification and enhancement need to occur prior to setting action plans for tourism. This approach provides empowerment for local communities to become more environmentally responsible as well as to retain more ownership over their destiny. This is also likely to be accompanied by a growing interest among researchers on the diversity of ecotourism as an experience, particularly the social psychology of the tourist experience and the importance of the ecotourism element. Ryan *et al.* (2000: 161) highlight a growing awareness that

> ecotourism has its own anthropology of symbols and signifiers . . . [so that] . . . ecotourism is not simply another form of consumerism whereby the tourist legitimizes the act of consumption . . . in a nutshell, to return to an earlier statement, tourists tour for reasons of change and relaxation – rarely are they lay anthropologists, botanists or environmental scientists. As consumers of tourism, their choice of the tourist product is akin to the consumption of other products.

While it is widely accepted among tourists that being an ecotourist is a trend-driven process for the environmentally aware visitor, this is a superficial interpretation that needs to be challenged by further research as ecotourism continues to mature and develop as a form of tourism that continues to grow in the new millennium. However, as the recent outbreak of foot-and-mouth disease in the UK has shown, the future growth and development of ecotourism require man–nature relationships to be fully understood and more biocentric perspectives are needed to nurture and manage the tourist–nature relationship. Ecotourism, if harnessed and managed in a progressive and sensitive way, can be both a sustainable and extremely enriching and rewarding form of tourist experience in the new millennium.

## Questions

1. How will the future development of ecotourism be shaped by global consumer tastes for tourism?
2. Why is ecotourism such a popular form of holiday experience?
3. How far will the International Year of Ecotourism influence the future development and focus of ecotourism?
4. What future role should NGOs such as The International Ecotourism Society play in influencing industry trends and consumer tastes?

## Further reading

See the following for a useful overview of global issues affecting the future development of ecotourism:

Dowling, R. (2000) 'Global ecotourism at the start of the new millennium', *World Leisure Journal*, **42** (2): 11–19.

On future developments in the ecotourism industry see:

Issaverdis, J. (2001) 'The pursuit of excellence: benchmarking, accreditation, best practice and auditing', in D. Weaver (ed.), *Encyclopedia of Ecotourism*, Wallingford: CAB International, 579–94.

Higginbottom, K. and Thwaites, R. (2001) 'Education and Training', in D. Weaver (ed.), *Encyclopedia of Ecotourism*, Wallingford: CAB International, 627–38.

Fennell, D. (2001) 'Areas and needs in ecotourism research', in D. Weaver (ed.), *Encyclopedia of Ecotourism*, Wallingford: CAB International, 639–56.

# Ecotourism Internet sites

## International

The *Green Globe 21* website provides information on the Green Globe world certification programme for sustainable travel and tourism for twenty-first-century consumers, companies and communities.
www.greenglobe.org

*ECoNETT* is part of World Travel and Tourism Council's homepage. It comprises over 1,200 files, giving comprehensive coverage of sustainable tourism initiatives, as well as providing contacts and links to other sources.
www.wttc.org
(http://195.212.4.4/ – this address is direct to ECoNETT)

*GreenTravel.com* is an interactive site allowing destinations from all around the world to be selected and a choice of trips available is displayed. A large selection of adventure tourism activities are provided, as well as information on books and gear, ideas and resources.
www.greentravel.com

The *Green-Travel Home Page* provides a global perspective of ecotourism and many ecotourism links around the world.
www.green-travel.com

*The Ecotourism Society's (TES) Ecotourism Explorer* homepage is a 'site for the discovery of the ecotourism path'. Designed for researchers, conservationists and business people it provides a wide range of information on the topic of ecotourism. TES is an international, non-profit membership organisation.
http://www.ecotourism.org

The *United Nations Commission on Sustainable Development* website provides a wide range of information on topics such as Agenda 21, events, news and publications, major groups and national information. Nothing on ecotourism but all about sustainable development . . .
www.un.org/esa/sustdev/

The *Eco-Source Network* homepage is a compilation of information and services regarding ecotourism and sustainable development. Its aim is 'to connect eco-minded travel and tourism professionals, consumers, students, teachers and policy makers around the globe'. It is extremely comprehensive and includes topics such as research, jobs and careers, statistics, an eco-gallery and related links.
www.ecosourcenetwork.com

The *Ecotravel Center* is an ecotourism resource from Conservation International. It offers information on travel that benefits conservation and local communities.
www.ecotour.org/

# National

## Australia

*Ecotourism Association of Australia (EAA)*. Formed, in 1991, the EAA is a non-profit organisation. This site is still under construction.
www.ecotourism.org.au/

*Ecotourism Resource Centre*. This site features an index to ecotourism resources and promotes local sites around the world. Very detailed with lots of Australian content.
www.bigvolcano.com.au/ercentre/ercpage.htm

The *Ecotourism Information Centre* website is developed by Charles Sturt University in collaboration with the Ecotourism Association of Australia, and supported by the Commonwealth Government's Office of National Tourism. It is intended for ecotourism professionals and has a number of databases and search options on a range of topics.
life.csu.edu.au/ecotour/EcoTrHme.html

The *Queensland Environmental Tourism* homepage includes information on research, the Queensland Ecotourism Plan, the National Accreditation Programme, a newsletter, related links and a holiday planner.
www.qttc.com.au/qep/index.htm

*Nature Base* is a website developed by Western Australia's Department of Conservation and Land Management. It is very well laid out and includes a section on tourism and recreation. There is also a pdf file included on the Nature Based Tourism Strategy, found in the 'New Projects' link.
www.calm.wa.gov.au/index.html

*Twinshare: Tourism Accommodation and the Environment* is a site developed by Australia's Office of National Tourism, Department of Industry, Science and

Resources. Provides valuable information for developers, design professionals, natural resource managers, tourism operators, government agencies and students. Information provided on the latest construction materials, design features, energy and waste technologies, and water management approaches. Also includes 12 case studies from around Australia.
http://twinshare.crctourism.com.au/

The Office of National Tourism has its *Best Practice Ecotourism Guide* which provides current industry practices in energy and waste management. A good site for people wanting to make their operations more environmentally friendly.
http://www.tourism.gov.au/publications/BPE/Start.html

## Hawaii

*Hawaii Ecotourism Association.* This website provides information on ecotourism issues and concerns in Hawaii, ecotourism links, a guide to activities and attractions offered, and latest news updates. The association's goal is to protect Hawaii's unique environment and culture through responsible travel.
http://www.planet-hawaii.com/hea

## Canada

The Green Tourism Association in Ontario, Canada has a good website which has a focus on urban green tourism and the role of ecotourism in cities as well as many links to other information sources.
www.greentourism.on.ca

## Estonia

The *Estonian Ecotourism* website contains extensive information on Estonia, and also listings of ecotourism organisations, programmes, articles and papers.
www.ecotourism.ee

## Latin America

*Ecotravels in Latin America* is a site dealing with environmental travel and ecotourism in the Americas. It also includes an exploring ecotourism section which is very comprehensive.
www.planeta.com/

*Exploring Ecotourism* is an extremely comprehensive site providing current resources on ecotourism. Includes an ecotourism bibliography, bulletin board and online forum.
www2.planeta.com/mader/ecotravel/ecotour.html

*BETA – the Belize Eco-Tourism Association* site includes a code of ethics, goals and objectives, future plans and member listing.
www.belizenet.com/beta.html

## Alaska

The *Alaska Wilderness Recreation and Tourism Association* is a non-profit organisation that works to protect Alaska's natural resources and to promote a responsible travel ethic in the state. They represent tourism businesses, guides and other people working towards a healthy and sustainable tourism industry in Alaska.
www.awrta.org

## UK

The *Hebridean Whale and Dolphin Trust* has a wealth of data and research reports on its website and is a major player in the ecotourism sector in Scotland.
www.hwdt.org

*Tourism Concern* is a pressure group which works for responsible tourism and its website has a wealth of information, particularly in relation to community tourism to ensure local people benefit from ecotourism and other forms of tourism.
www.tourismconcern.org.uk

## Miscellaneous

*JourneyQuest.Com* – a North American site listing special interest and adventure travel operators. It also has a number of Australian operators listed.
http://journeyquest.com/

*Eco-Orbit* is an online magazine sponsored by Orbit International which focuses on ecotourism and sustainable development. Contains travel articles and solicits visitor input.
http://public-www.pi.se/~orbit/eco.html

*Conservation Corporation Africa.* This site includes a portfolio of CCA's safari lodges.
www.ccafrica.com

# Bibliography

A and M Training and Development (1997) *Review of Wildlife Tourism in Scotland*, A report for the Scottish Tourism and Environment Initiative, Inverness.

Acernaza, M.A. (1985) 'Planification estrategica del turismo: esquema methodologico', *Estudios Turisticos*, **85**: 45–70.

Acott, T.G. and La Trobe, H. (1998) 'An evaluation of deep ecotourism and shallow ecotourism', *Journal of Sustainable Tourism*, **6** (3): 238–53.

Acott, T.G., La Trobe, H.L. and Howard, S.H. (1998) 'An evaluation of deep ecotourism and shallow ecotourism', *Journal of Sustainable Tourism*, **6** (3): 238–53.

Addison, L. (1996) 'An approach to community-based tourism planning in the Baffin Region, Canada's far north', in L.C. Harrison and W. Husbands (eds), *Practising Responsible Tourism: International Case Studies in Tourism Planning, Policy and Development*, New York: John Wiley and Sons, 296–312.

Affeld, H. (1975) 'Social aspects of the development of tourism', in UN, *Planning and Development of the Tourist Industry in the ECE Region*, New York: United Nations.

Agarwal, R.X. and Nangia, S. (1974) *Economic and Employment Potential of Archaeological Monuments in India*, New Delhi: Asia Publishing House.

AIMAC and Fisheries WA (1998a) *Management Plan for Sustainable Tourism at the Houtman Abrolhos Islands*, Fisheries Management Paper No. 120, Perth, Western Australia: Abrolhos Islands Management Advisory Committee and Fisheries Western Australia.

AIMAC and Fisheries WA (1998b) *Future Directions for Tourism at the Houtman Abrolhos Islands*, Fisheries Management Paper No. 121, Perth, Western Australia: Abrolhos Islands Management Advisory Committee and Fisheries Western Australia.

Akama, J.S. (1996) 'Western environmental values and nature–based tourism in Kenya', *Tourism Management*, **17** (8): 567–74.

Akoglu, T. (1971) 'Tourism and the problem of environment', *Tourist Review*, **26**: 18–20.

An Foras Forbatha (1973) *Brittas Bay: A Planning and Conservation Study*, Dublin: An Foras Forbatha.

Andersen, D.L. (1993) 'A window to the natural world: the design of ecotourism facilities', in K. Lindberg and D.E. Hawkins (eds), *Ecotourism: A Guide for Planners and Managers*, Vermont, USA: The Ecotourism Society, 116–33.

Andersen, D.L. (1994) 'Ecotourism destinations: a conservation from the beginning', *Trends*, **31** (2): 31–8.

Annals of Tourism Research (1987) Special Issue: Tourism and the Environment, *Annals of Tourism Research*, 14(1).

Ap, J. (1990) 'Residents' perceptions research on the social impacts of tourism', *Annals of Tourism Research*, **17** (4): 610–16.

Ap, J. and Crompton, J.L. (1993) 'Residents' strategies for responding to tourism impacts', *Journal of Travel Research*, **32** (1): 47–50.

Archer, B. (1982) 'The value of multipliers and their policy implications', *Tourism Management*, **3**: 236–41.

Archer, B. (1987) 'Demand forecasting and estimation', in J.R.B. Ritchie and C.R. Goeldner (eds), *Travel, Tourism and Hospitality Research: A Handbook for Managers*, New York: Wiley, 77–85.

Argyle, M. (1996) *The Social Psychology of Leisure*, London: Penguin.

Ashley, C. and Roe, D. (1998) *Enhancing Community Development in Wildlife Tourism: Issues and Challenges*, IIED Wildlife and Development Series No. 11, London: International Institute for Environment and Development.

Ashton, R. and Ashton, P. (1993) 'An introduction to sustainable tourism (ecotourism) in Central America', Paper prepared for Paseo Pantera: Regional Wetlands Management in Central America project. Gainsville, USA: Wildlife Conservation International.

Ashworth, G. (1992) 'Planning for sustainable tourism: slogan or reality?', *Town Planning Review*, **63** (3): 325–30.

Australian Conservation Foundation (1994) *Tourism and Ecological Sustainable Development in Australia*, Fitzroy, Australia: Australian Conservation Foundation.

Australian Department of Tourism (1994) *National Ecotourism Strategy*, Canberra: Australian Government Publishing Service.

Ayala, H. (1995) 'From quality product to eco-product: will Fiji set a precedent?', *Tourism Management*, **16** (1): 39–47.

Ayala, H. (1997) 'Resort ecotourism: a catalyst for national and regional partnerships', *Cornell Hotel and Restaurant Administration Quarterly*, **38** (4): 34–45.

Aylward, B., Allen, K., Echeverria, J. and Tosi, J. (1996) 'Sustainable ecotourism in Costa Rica: the Monteverde Cloud Forest Reserve', *Biodiversity and Conservation*, **5** (3): 315–43.

Backman, K., Wright, B. and Backman, S. (1994) 'Ecotourism: a short descriptive exploration', *Trends*, **31** (2): 23–7.

Bacon, P.R. (1987) 'Use of wetlands for tourism in the insular Caribbean', *Annals of Tourism Research*, **14** (1): 104–17.

Ballantine, J. (1991) 'An analysis of the characteristics of a population of Canadian tourists to Kenya', Masters' thesis, Department of Recreation and Leisure Studies, University of Waterloo, Ontario.

Ballantine, J. and Eagles, P. (1994) 'Defining Canadian ecotourists', *Journal of Sustainable Tourism*, **2** (4): 210–14.

Ballantine, W.J. and Gordon, D.P. (1979) 'New Zealand's first marine nature reserve, Cape Rodney to Okakari Point, Leigh', *Biological Conservation*, **15**: 273–80.

Balmer Crapo and Associates (1977) *A Review of Existing Tourism Zones and Suggested Primary Tourism Destination Zones*, Ontario: Canadian Government Office of Tourism.

Basel, J. (1993) 'An excellent example of ecotourism', in The Adventure Travel Society, *1993 World Conference on Adventure Travel and Eco-tourism*, Manaus, Brazil, Englewood, Colorado, USA: The Adventure Travel Society, 203–7.

Baud Bovy, M. (1964) *Tourism Planning in the Canary Islands*, Paris: OECD.

Baud Bovy, M. (1982) 'New concepts in planning for tourism and recreation', *Tourism Management*, **3** (4): 308–13.

BC Forest Service (1995) *The 1993 North-Eastern British Columbia Recreation Survey*, British Columbia: Recreation Section, Range Recreation and Forest Practices Branch, Ministry of BC Forests.

BC Ministry of DIT (1991) *Developing a Code of Ethics: British Columbia's Tourism Industry*, Victoria, British Columbia: Ministry of Development, Trade and Tourism.

Beaumont, N. (1998) 'The meaning of ecotourism according to . . . is there now consensus for defining this "natural" phenomenon? An Australian perspective', *Pacific Tourism Review*, **2** (3/4): 239–50.

Beck, B. and Bryan, F. (1971) 'This other Eden: a study of tourism in Britain', *The Economist*, **240**: 66–83.

Beed, T. (1961) 'Tahiti's recent tourist development', *Geography*, **46**: 368.

Beeh, J. (1999) 'Going green. Adventure vs ecotourism – Can the road less travelled get trampled too often?', *The Environmental Magazine*, **10** (3): 46–7.

Beeton, S. (1998) *Ecotourism: A Practical Guide for Rural Communities*. Collingwood: Landlinks Press.

Beeton, S. (1999) 'Hoof prints on the mind: an exploration of attitudinal relationships between bushwalkers and commercial horseback tours', *Tourism Management*, **20** (2): 255–9.

Bentley, T.A. and Page, S.J. (2001) 'The cost of adventure tourism accidents to the New Zealand tourism industry', *Annals of Tourism Research*, **28** (3): 705–26.

Bentley, T.A., Page, S.J. and Laird, I.S. (2000) 'Safety in New Zealand's adventure tourism industry: the client injury experience of adventure tourism operators', *Journal of Travel Medicine*, **7** (5): 239–46.

Bentley, T., Meyer, D., Page, S.J. and Chalmers, D. (2001a) 'The role of adventure tourism in injuries among visitors to New Zealand: an exploratory analysis using hospital discharge data', *Tourism Management*, **22** (4): 373–81.

Bentley, T., Page, S.J., Meyer, D., Chalmers, D. and Laird, I. (2001b) 'How safe is adventure tourism in New Zealand: an exploratory analysis', *Applied Ergonomics*, **32** (4): 327–38.

Berno, T. and Moore, K. (1996) 'The nature of the adventure tourism experience in Queenstown', Paper presented at the Tourism Down Under Conference, Centre for Tourism, University of Otago, December 1996.

Bisset, R. (1987) 'Methods for environmental impact assessment: a selective survey with case studies', in A. Biswas and Qu. Geping (eds), *Environmental Impact Assessment for Developing Countries*, London: Tycolly International.

Bisset, C., Perry, L. and Zeppel, H. (1998) 'Land and spirit: Aboriginal tourism in New South Wales', in S. McArthur and B. Weir (eds), *Australia's Ecotourism Industry: A Snapshot in 1998*, Brisbane: Ecotourism Association of Australia, 6–8.

Bjork, P. (2000) 'Ecotourism from a conceptual perspective, an extended definition of a unique tourism form', *International Journal of Tourism Research*, **2** (3): 189–202.

Blake, G. and Lawless, R. (1972) 'Algeria's tourist industry', *Geography*, **57** (2): 148–51.

Blamey, R. (1995) *The Nature of Ecotourism*, BTR Occasional Paper No. 21, Canberra: Bureau of Tourism Research.

Blamey, R. (1997) 'Ecotourism: the search for an operational definition', *Journal of Sustainable Tourism*, **5** (2): 109–30.

Blamey, R. and Braithwaite, V. (1997) 'A social values segmentation of the potential ecotourism market', *Journal of Sustainable Tourism*, **5** (1): 29–45.

Blamey, R. and Hatch, D. (1998) *Profiles and Motivations of Nature-Based Tourists Visiting Australia*, BTR Occasional Paper No. 5, Canberra: Bureau of Tourism Research.

Blangy, S. (1999) 'Ethical charters and other codes of conduct: recommendations for their implementation' [French], *Cahiers Espaces*, **61**: 122–32.

Blangy, S. and Kouchner, F. (1999) 'Quality label for the national park of Guadeloupe', *Cahiers Espaces*, **61**: 94–103.

Blangy, S. and Nielsen, T. (1993) 'Ecotourism and minimum impact policy', *Annals of Tourism Research*, **20** (2): 357–60.

Blank, U. and Gunn, C.A. (1965) *Guidelines for Tourism-Recreation in Michigan's Upper Peninsula*, Michigan, USA: Cooperative Extension Service, Michigan State University.

Boeger, E. (1991) 'Ecotourism/the environment: or the immense potential and import-ance of ecotourism', *Travel and Tourism Research Association Newsletter*, **12** (3): 2, 5–6.

Boniface, C. and Cooper, C. (1987) *The Geography of Travel and Tourism*, London: Heimenann.

Boo, E. (1990) *Ecotourism: The Potentials and Pitfalls*, Washington, DC: World Wild-life Fund.

Boo, E. (1992) *The Ecotourism Boom: Planning for Development and Management*. Washington, DC: World Wildlife Fund.

Borg, J. van der. and Costa, P. (1993) 'The management of tourism in cities of art', *Revue de Tourisme*, **48** (2): 2–10.

Bosselman, F. (1978) *In the Wake of the Tourist: Managing Special Places in Eight Countries*, Washington: The Conservation Foundation.

Bottrill, C. and Pearce, D. (1995) 'Ecotourism: towards a key elements approach to operationalising the concept', *Journal of Sustainable Tourism*, **3** (1): 45–54.

Bouchard, A. (1973) 'Carrying capacity as a management tool for national parks', *Park News (Journal of the National and Provincial Parks Association of Canada)*, October: 39–51.

Boyd, S. and Butler, R. (1995) *Development of an Ecotourism Opportunity Spectrum (ECOS) for Sites Identified Using GIS in Northern Ontario*. NODA/NFP Technical Report, Great Lakes Forestry Centre, Sault Ste. Marie, Ontario, No. TR-11.

Boyd, S. and Butler, R. (1996) 'Managing ecotourism: an opportunity spectrum approach', *Tourism Management*, **17** (8): 557–66.

Boyd, S. and Butler, R. (1999) 'Definitely not monkeys or parrots, probably deer and possibly moose: opportunities and realities of ecotourism in Northern Ontario', *Current Issues in Tourism*, **2** (2/3): 123–37.

Braddon, C.J.H. (1982) *British Issues Paper: Approaches to Tourism Planning Abroad*, London: British Tourist Authority.

Brake, L. (1988) 'Tourism as a tool for conserving arid lands', *Australian Parks and Recreation*, **24** (3): 37–40.

Brandon, K. (1996) *Ecotourism and Conservation: A Review of Key Issues*. Washington, DC: World Bank.

Brandt Commission (1980) *North–South: A Programme for Survival*, London: Pan Books.

Brannan, L., Condello, C., Stuckum, N., Vissers, N. and Priest, S. (1992) 'Public perceptions of risk in recreational activities', *Journal of Applied Recreation Research*, **17** (2): 144–57.

Bristow, R. (1999) 'Commentary: virtual tourism – the ultimate ecotourism', *Tourism Geographies*, **1** (2): 219–25.

Britton, S. (1982) 'The political economy of tourism in the Third World', *Annals of Tourism Research*, **9** (3): 331–58.

Brockelman, W. and Dearden, P. (1990) 'The role of nature trekking in conservation: a case study of Thailand', *Environmental Conservation*, **17** (2): 141–8.

Brown, F. (1998) *Tourism Reassessed: Blight or Blessing*, Oxford: Butterworth-Heinemann.

Brown, P.J., Driver, B.L. and McConnell, C. (1978) 'The opportunity spectrum concept and behavioural information in outdoor recreation resource supply inventories: background and application', in G.H. Lund, V.J. La Bau, P.F. Folliott and D.W. Robinson (technical co-ordinates), *Integrated Inventories of Renewable Natural Resources: Proceedings of the Workshop*, Fort Collins, Colorado: USDA Forest Service General Technical Report RM-55, 73–84.

Brown, K., Turner, K., Hameed, H. and Bateman, I. (1997) 'Environmental carrying capacity and tourism development in the Maldives and Nepal', *Environmental Conservation*, **24** (4): 316–25.

Brugger, E.A. and Messerli, P. (1984) 'The problem', in E.A. Brugger and P. Messerli (eds), *The Transformation of the Swiss Mountain Regions*, Berne: Verlag Paul Haupt, 21–30.

Brundtland, G. (1987) 'Our common future – call for action', *Environmental Conservation*, **14** (4): 291–4.

Bryden, J. (1973) *Tourism and Development: A Case Study of the Commonwealth Caribbean*, Cambridge: Cambridge University Press.

Buckley, P.J. (1987) 'Tourism – an economic transaction analysis', *Tourism Management*, **8** (3): 190–40.

Buckley, P.J. and Casson, M. (1987) *The Economic Theory of the Multinational*, London: Macmillan.

Buckley, R. (1987) 'A framework for ecotourism', *Annals of Tourism Research*, **21** (3): 661–9.

Buckley, R. and Pannell, J. (1990) 'Environmental impacts of tourism and recreation in national parks and conservation reserves', *The Journal of Tourism Studies*, **1** (1): 24–32.

Budowski, G. (1976) 'Tourism and conservation: conflict, coexistence or symbiosis', *Environmental Conservation*, **3**: 27–31.

Bull, A. (1995) *The Economics of Travel and Tourism*, 2nd edn, Harlow: Longman.

Burnett, G.W. and Rowntree, K. (1990) 'Agriculture, research and tourism in the landscape of Lake Baringo, Kenya', *Landscape and Urban Planning*, **19**: 159–72.

Burnett, G.W. and Uysal, M. (1991) 'Dominica – geographic isolation and tourism prospects', *Tourism Management*, **12** (2): 112–18.

Burns and Associates (1989) *Paper and Proceedings of a Seminar of the Environmental Impacts of Travel and Tourism*, Canberra: Australian Government Publishing Service.

Burton, R. (1974) *The Recreational Carrying Capacity of the Countryside*, Occasional Publication No. 11, Keele University Library, Keele.

Burton, R. (1998) 'Maintaining the quality of ecotourism: ecotour operators' responses to tourism growth', *Journal of Sustainable Tourism*, **6** (2): 117–42.

Butler, R. (1980) 'The concept of the tourist area cycle of evolution: implications for management of resources', *Canadian Geographer*, **24**: 5–12.

Butler, R. (1990) 'Alternative tourism: pious hope or trojan horse', *Journal of Travel Research*, **28** (3): 40–5.

Butler, R. (1991) 'Tourism, environment, and sustainable development', *Environmental Conservation*, **18** (3): 201–9.

Butler, R. (1992) 'Alternative tourism: the thin edge of the wedge', in V.L. Smith and W.R. Eadington (eds), *Tourism Alternatives: Potentials and Problems in the Development of Tourism*, Philadelphia: University of Pennsylvania Press, 31–46.

Butler, R. (1998) 'Sustainable tourism – looking backwards in order to progress?', in C.M. Hall and A. Lew (eds), *Sustainable Tourism: A Geographical Perspective*, Harlow: Addison-Wesley Longman, 25–34.

Butler, R. (2000) 'Tourism and the environment: a geographical perspective', *Tourism Geographies*, **2** (3): 337–59.

Butler, R. and Hall, C.M. (1998) 'Conclusion: the sustainability of tourism and recreation in rural areas', in R. Butler, C.M. Hall and J. Jenkins (eds), *Tourism and Recreation in Rural Areas*, Chichester: John Wiley & Sons, 249–58.

Butler, R. and Waldbrook, L. (1991) 'A new planning tool: The Tourist Opportunity Spectrum', *Journal of Tourism Studies*, **2** (1): 2–14.

Campbell, L.M. (1999) 'Ecotourism in rural developing communities', *Annals of Tourism Research*, **26** (3): 534–53.

Canadian Environmental Advisory Council (1991) *A Protected Areas Vision for Canada*, Ottawa: Ministry of Supplies and Services.

Cannon, T. (1989) *Basic Marketing Principles and Practice*, 3rd edn, London: Holt, Rinehart and Winston.

Careless, R. (1990) *Tourism Resource Sustainable Development Planning: the Whistler Case Study*. Paper presented to the Globe '90 Conference on Global Opportunities for Business and the Environment – Tourism Stream, Vancouver: 19–23 March.

Carlozzi, C. and Carlozzi, A. (1968) *Conservation and Caribbean Regional Progress*, New York: The Antioch Press.

Carson, R. (1962) *Silent Spring*, Greenwich, Conn.: Fawcett.

Carter, R. and Davie, J. (1996) '(Eco)tourism in the Asia Pacific Region', in H. Richins, J. Richardson and A. Crabtree (eds), *Ecotourism and Nature-Based Tourism: Taking the Next Steps*, Proceedings of the Ecotourism Association of Australia National Conference 1995, Brisbane: Ecotourism Association of Australia, 67–72.

Carter, R. and O'Reilly, P. (1999) 'A rapid appraisal methodology for environmental auditing', *Journal of Tourism Studies*, **10** (2): 14–22.

Cater, E. (1993) 'Ecotourism in the third world – problems for sustainable tourism development', *Tourism Management*, 85–90.

Cater, E. (1994) 'Introduction', in E. Cater and G. Lowman (eds), *Ecotourism: A Sustainable Option?*, Chichester: John Wiley & Sons, 3–17.

Cater, E. (1997) 'Ecotourism or ecocide?', *People and the Planet*, **6** (4): 9–11.

Cater, E. and Lowman, G. (eds) (1994) *Ecotourism: A Sustainable Option?* Chichester: John Wiley & Sons.

CEAC (1992) *Ecotourism in Canada*, Ottawa: Canadian Environmental Advisory Council, Ministry of Supply and Services.

Ceballos-Lascurain, H. (1987) *Estudio de prefactibilidaad socioeconomica del turismo ecologico y anteproyecto asquitectonico y urbanistico del Centro de Turismo Ecologico de Sian Ka'an, Quintana Roo*. Study completed for SEDUE, Mexico.

Ceballos-Lascurain, H. (1991) 'The potential of ecotourism' [Spanish], *Revista Intercontinental de Turismo*, **2** (1): 107–10.

Ceballos-Lascurain, H. (1996) *Tourism, Ecotourism and Protected Areas*, Gland: International Union for Conservation of Nature and Natural Resources.

Ceballos-Lascurain, H. (1998) 'Introduction', in K. Lindberg, M. Epler Wood and D. Engeldrum (eds), *Ecotourism: A Guide for Planners and Managers*, vol. 2, Vermont: The Ecotourism Society, 7–10.

Ceballos-Lascurain, H. (1999) 'The future of ecotourism into the millennium: an international perspective', in S. McArthur and R. Dowling (eds), *Australia – the World's Natural Theme Park*, Proceedings of the Ecotourism Association of Australia 7th National Conference Kingfisher Bay Resort and Village, 14–17 October 1999. Canberra: Bureau of Tourism Research, 1–9.

Chadwick, G. (1971) *A Systems View of Planning*, Oxford: Pergamon Press.

Chalker, L. (1994) 'Ecotourism: on the trail of destruction of sustainability? A Minister's view', in E. Cater and G. Lowman (eds), *Ecotourism: A Sustainable Option?*, Chichester: John Wiley & Sons, 87–99.

Chape, S. and Chalmers, C.E. (1984) 'Tourism and the role of coastal management planning in Western Australia', *Australian Ranger Bulletin*, **2** (4): 111–13.

Charters, T., Gabriel, M. and Prasser, S. (eds) (1996) *National Parks: Private Sector's Role*, Toowoomba: University of Southern Queensland Press.

Chase, L.C., Lee, D.R., Schulze, W.D. and Anderson, D.J. (1998) 'Ecotourism demand and differential pricing of national park access in Costa Rica', *Land Economics*, **74** (4): 466–82.

Chester, G. (1997) 'Australian ecotourism accreditation off and running', *The Ecotourism Society Newsletter*, Second Quarter: 9.

Chin, C. (1997) 'Ecotourism in Bako National Park, Borneo', BSc. (Hons) thesis, Perth, Western Australia: Murdoch University.

Chin, C., Moore, S., Wallington, T. and Dowling, R. (2000) 'Ecotourism in Bako National Park, Borneo: visitors' perspectives on environmental impacts and their management', *Journal of Sustainable Tourism*, **8** (1): 20–35.

Chirgwin, S. and Hughes, K. (1997) 'Ecotourism: the participants' perceptions', *Journal of Tourism Studies*, **8** (2): 2–7.

Choongki, L., Juhee, L. and Sangyoel, H. (1998) 'Measuring the economic value of ecotourism resources: the case of South Korea', *Journal of Travel Research*, **36** (4): 40–6.

Choy, D.J.L. (1991) 'Tourism planning: the case for market failure', *Tourism Management*, **12**: 313–30.

Choy, D.J.L. (1998) 'Changing trends in Asia – Pacific tourism', *Tourism Management*, **19** (4): 381–2.

Christ, C. (1998) 'Taking ecotourism to the next level', in K. Lindberg, M. Epler Wood and D. Engeldrum (eds), *Ecotourism: A Guide for Planners and Managers*, Vol. 2, Vermont: The Ecotourism Society, 183–95.

Christian, C., Potts, T., Burnett, W. and Lacher, T. (1996) 'Parrot conservation and ecotourism in the Windward Islands', *Journal of Biogeography*, **32** (3): 387–93.

Christiansen, D.R. (1990) 'Adventure tourism', in J.C. Miles and S. Priest (eds), *Adventure Education*, Pennsylvania: Venture Publishing.

Clare, P. (1971) *The Struggle for the Great Barrier Reef*, London: Collins.

Clark, R.N. and Stankey, G.H. (1979) *The Recreation Opportunity Spectrum: A Framework for Planning, Management and Research*, General Technical Report PNW-98, Portland, Oregon: Department of Agriculture, Forest Service, Pacific Northwest Forest and Range Experiment Station.

Clark, R.N., Hendee, J.C. and Campbell, F. (1971) 'Values, behaviour, and conflict in modern camping culture', *Journal of Leisure Research*, **3** (3): 143–59.

Cloke, P. and Perkins, H. (1998) 'Pushing the limits: place promotion and adventure tourism in the South Island of New Zealand', in H. Perkins and G. Cushman (eds), *Time Out? Leisure, Recreation and Tourism in New Zealand and Australia*, Auckland: Addison Wesley Longman, 271–87.

Cohen, E. (1972) 'Towards a sociology of international tourism', *Social Research*, **39**: 164–82.

Cohen, E. (1978) 'The impact of tourism on the physical environment', *Annals of Tourism Research*, **5** (2): 215–37.

Cohen, E. (1979) 'A phenomenology of tourist experiences', *Sociology*, **13**: 179–202.

Cohen, E. (1989) 'Alternative tourism – a critique', in T.V. Singh, L. Thenus and F.M. Go (eds), *Towards Appropriate Tourism: The Case of Developing Countries*, Frankfurt am Main: Peter Lang, 127–42.

Colvin, J. (1994) 'Capirona: a model of indigenous ecotourism', *Journal of Sustainable Tourism*, **2** (3): 174–7.

Commonwealth Department of Tourism (1993) *Draft National Ecotourism Strategy*, Canberra: Commonwealth of Australia.

Commonwealth Department of Tourism (1994) *National Ecotourism Strategy*, Canberra: Australian Government Publishing Service.

Commonwealth Department of Tourism (1995) *Best Practice Ecotourism: A Guide to Energy and Waste Minimisation*, Canberra: Commonwealth Department of Tourism.

Commonwealth of Australia (1996a) *National Ecotourism Accreditation Program*, Canberra: The Department of Industry, Science and Tourism.

Commonwealth of Australia (1996b) *Projecting Success: Visitor Management Projects for Sustainable Tourism Growth*, Canberra: The Department of Industry, Science and Tourism.

Commonwealth of Australia (1997) *Ecotourism Snapshot: A Focus on Recent Market Trends*, Canberra: The Department of Industry, Science and Tourism.

Cooper, C., Fletcher, J., Gilbert, D. and Wanhill, S. (1998) *Tourism: Principles and Practice*, 2nd edn, London: Pitman.

Cotterill, D. (1996) 'Developing a sustainable ecotourism business', in H. Richins, J. Richardson and A. Crabtree (eds), *Ecotourism and Nature-Based Tourism: Taking the Next Steps*, Proceedings of the Ecotourism Association of Australia National Conference 1995, Brisbane: Ecotourism Association of Australia, 135–9.

Coventry, N. (1993) 'New Zealand eco-tourism under international spotlight', *Accountants Journal*, March, 55–6.

Crabtree, A. (2000) 'Interpretation: ecotourism's fundamental, but much neglected tool', *The International Ecotourism Society Newsletter*, Third Quarter: 1–3.

Crabtree, J., Leat, P., Sartarossa, J. and Thomson, K. (1994) 'The economic impact of wildlife sites in Scotland', *Journal of Rural Studies*, **10** (1): 61–72.

Craig-Smith, S.J. (1994) 'Pacific Island tourism – a new direction or a palimpsest of western tradition?' *Australian Journal of Hospitality Management*, **1** (1): 23–6.

Craig-Smith, S.J. and Fagence, M. (1992) *Sustainable Tourism Development in Pacific Island Countries*, New York: United Nations.

Craig-Smith, S.J. and Fagence, M. (1994) A critique of tourism planning in the Pacific, in C. Cooper and A. Lockwood (eds) *Progress in Tourism, Recreation and Hospitality Management*, Vol. 6, Chichester: John Wiley & Sons, 92–110.

Crittendon, A. (1975) 'Tourism's terrible toll', *International Wildlife*, **5** (3): 412.

Crotts, J. (1994) 'Taking the hype out of ecotourism', *Trends*, **31** (2): 2–3.

Crozier, M., Marx, S. and Grant, J. (1978) 'Off-road vehicle recreation: the impact of off-road motor cycles on soil conditions', in *Proceedings of the 9th New Zealand Geographical Conference*, New Zealand Geographical Society, University of Otago, Dunedin, 76–9.

Cullen, R. (1986) 'Himalayan mountaineering expedition garbage', *Environmental Conservation*, **13** (4): 293–7.

Curry, S. (1982) 'Wildlife conservation and game viewing tourism in Tanzania', Discussion paper No. 81, Project Planning Centre, University of Bradford.

Curry, S. (1985) 'Tourism circuit planning: carrying capacity at Ngorogoro Crater, Tanzania', in *The Impact of Tourism and Recreation on the Environment: A*

*Miscellany of Readings*, Selected papers from a Seminar at the University of Bradford, 27 June–1 July 1983, Occasional paper No. 8, University of Bradford.

Daeng, K. (1990) 'Alternative tourism', *Alternative Tour Thailand*, **2**: 3.

Dahl, A.L. and Lamberts, A.E. (1977) 'Environmental impact on a Samoan coral reef: a resurvey of Mayor's 1917 transect', *Pacific Science*, **31** (1): 309–19.

Daly, A. and Ralston, L. (1996) 'The importance of land use planning and zoning to the ecotourism industry', in *It's Showtime for Tourism: New Products, Markets and Technologies*, Proceedings of the 27th Travel and Tourism Research Association Conference, Las Vegas, 260–5.

D'Amore, L. (1993) 'A code of ethics and guidelines for socially and environmentally responsible tourism', *Journal of Travel Research*, **31** (3): 64–6.

Dann, G. (1996) 'Greenspeak: an analysis of the language of ecotourism', *Progress in Tourism and Hospitality Research*, **2** (3): 247–59.

Darling, F. and Eichhorn, N. (1967) 'The ecological implications of tourism in national parks', in *Ecological Impact of Recreation and Tourism upon Temperate Environments*, IUCN Proceedings and Papers, New Series No. 7, Morges, Switzerland, 98–101.

Dasmann, W. (1945) 'A method for estimating the carrying capacity of range lands', *Journal of Forestry*, **43**: 400–2.

Dasmann, R., Milton, J. and Freeman, P. (1973) *Ecological Principles for Economic Development*, London: John Wiley & Sons.

David, F.R. (1989) 'How companies define their mission statements', *Long Range Planning*, **22** (1): 90–7.

de Kadt, E. (ed.) (1979) *Tourism: Passport to Development*, Oxford: Oxford University Press.

de Kadt, E. (ed.) (1990) 'Making the alternative sustainable: lessons from development for tourism', in *Environment, Tourism and Development: An Agenda for Action? A Workshop to Consider Strategies for Sustainable Development*, 4–10 March. Valetta, Malta: Centre for Environmental Management and Planning, Old Aberdeen.

De Lacy, T. (1998) 'Using tourism as a conservation tool in protected areas in China', Paper presented at Ecotourism Association of Australia Conference, 28–31 October.

Deming, A. (1996) 'The edges of the civilised world: tourism and the hunger for wild places', *Orion*, **15** (2): 28–35.

Department of Employment/English Tourist Board (1991) *Tourism and the Environment: Maintaining the Balance*, London: HMSO.

Devall, B. and Sessions, G. (1985) *Deep Ecology: Living as if Nature Mattered*, Salt Lake City: Gibbs Smith.

DFID (n.d.) *Changing the Nature of Tourism: Developing an Agenda for Action*, London: Environment Policy Department, Department for International Development.

Diamantis, D. (1999) 'The concept of ecotourism: evolution and trends', *Current Issues in Tourism*, **2** (2/3): 93–122.

Diamantis, D. and Ladkin, A. (1999) 'The links between sustainable tourism and ecotourism: a definitional and operational perspective', *Journal of Tourism Studies*, **10** (2): 35–46.

Dieke, P. (1995) 'Tourism and structural adjustment programmes in the African economy', *Tourism Economics*, **1** (1): 71–93.

Dieke, P. (ed.) (2000) *Tourism in Africa*, New York: Cognizant Communications.

Din, K.H. (1982) 'Tourism in Malaysia: competing needs in a plural society', *Annals of Tourism Research*, **9** (3): 453–80.

DIST (1998) 'Latest inbound visitor movements', *Impact*, October. A monthly fact sheet on the economic impact of tourism and the latest visitor arrival trends published by the Australian Department of Industry, Science & Resources, Sport and Tourism Division.

DIST (2001) 'Latest inbound visitor movements', *Impact*, February. A monthly fact sheet on the economic impact of tourism and the latest visitor arrival trends published by the Australian Department of Industry, Science & Resources, Sport and Tourism Division.

Doggart, C. and Doggart, N. (1997) 'Environmental impacts of tourism in developing countries', *Travel and Tourism Analyst*, **2**: 71–86.

Douglas, A. and Taylor, J. (1998) 'Riverine based ecotourism: Trinity River non-market benefit estimates', *International Journal of Sustainable Development and World Ecology*, **5** (2): 136–48.

Douglas, J. (1992) 'Ecotourism: the future for the Caribbean?', *UNEP Industry and Environment*, **15** (3–4): 64–6.

Dower, M. (1974) 'Tourism and conservation: working together', *The Architects' Journal*, **18** (159): 939–63.

Dowling, R.K. (1976) 'Environmental education', *New Zealand Environment*, **16**: 24–6.

Dowling, R.K. (1990) 'Integrating tourism and conservation', in S.R. Verma, S. Singh and S. Kumar (eds), *Environmental Protection – A Movement*, New Delhi: Nature Conservators, 5–25.

Dowling, R.K. (1991) 'Tourism and the natural environment: Shark Bay, Western Australia', *Tourism Recreation Research*, **16** (2): 44–8.

Dowling, R.K. (1992a) 'Tourism and environmental integration: the journey from idealism to realism', in C. Cooper and A. Lockwood (eds), *Progress in Tourism, Recreation and Hospitality Management*, Vol. 4, Chichester: John Wiley & Sons, 33–44.

Dowling, R.K. (1992b) 'The ecoethics of tourism: guidelines for developers, operators and tourists', in B. Weiler (ed.), *Ecotourism: Incorporating the Global Classroom – 1991 International Conference Papers*, Canberra: Bureau of Tourism Research, 237–41.

Dowling, R.K. (1993a) 'Tourism planning, people and the environment in Western Australia', *Journal of Travel Research*, **31** (4): 52–8.

Dowling, R.K. (1993b) 'Tourist and resident perceptions of the environment–tourism relationship in the Gascoyne Region, Western Australia', *GeoJournal*, **29** (3): 243–51.

Dowling, R.K. (1993c) 'An environmentally based planning model for regional tourism development', *Journal of Sustainable Tourism*, **1** (1): 17–37.

Dowling, R.K. (1995) 'Ecotourism development: regional planning and strategies', in S. Hiranburana, V. Stithyudhakarn and P. Dhamabutra (eds), Proceedings of the International Conference *Ecotourism: Concept, Design and Strategy*, Institute of Eco-Tourism, Srinakharinwirot University, Bangkok, Thailand, 6–8 February 1995. Bangkok: Srinakharinwirot University Press, 84–114.

Dowling, R.K. (1996a) 'Ecotourism in Thailand', *Annals of Tourism Research*, **23** (2): 488–90. USA.

Dowling, R.K. (1996b) 'The Australian Ecotourism Conference: "Taking the Next Steps"', *Journal of Sustainable Tourism*, **4** (1): 53–4.

Dowling, R.K. (1996c) 'Ecotourism: the rising star of Australian tourism', in T. Gardner (ed.), Compiled Conference Papers of the Ecotourism Association of Australia National Conference, *Strategic Alliances: Ecotourism Partnerships in Practice*, Kangaroo Island, South Australia, 14–17 November 1996. Brisbane: Ecotourism Association of Australia, 19–24.

Dowling, R.K. (1996d) 'Visitor management in Shark Bay, Western Australia', in C.M. Hall and S. McArthur (eds), *Heritage Management in Australia and New Zealand: The Human Dimension*, 2nd edn, Melbourne: Oxford University, 160–9.

Dowling, R.K. (1997a) 'Plans for the development of regional ecotourism: theory and practice', in C.M. Hall, J. Jenkins and G. Kearsley (eds), *Tourism Planning and Policy in Australia and New Zealand: Cases, Issues and Practice*, Sydney: Irwin Publishers, 110–26.

Dowling, R.K. (1997b) *The Explosive Growth of Ecotourism in Australia*. Proceedings of World Ecotour '97, Rio de Janiero, Brazil, 15–18 December 1997, 152–63.

Dowling, R.K. (1998a) 'Global ecotourism – an alternative form of tourism or a new form of mass tourism?', in J. Kandampully (ed.), *Proceedings of New Zealand Tourism and Hospitality Research Conference 'Advances in Research'*, Part 2, Hosted by Lincoln University, Akaroa, Canterbury, New Zealand, 1–4 December 1998.

Dowling, R.K. (1998b) 'The growth of Australian ecotourism', in J. Kandampully (ed.), *Proceedings of New Zealand Tourism and Hospitality Research Conference 'Advances in Research'*, Part 1, Hosted by Lincoln University, Akaroa, Canterbury, New Zealand, 1–4 December 1998.

Dowling, R.K. (1998c) 'Ecotourism planning and development', *Indian Journal of Travel & Tourism*, **2** (1): 57–70.

Dowling, R.K. (1999a) 'Harnessing the benefits of regional ecotourism development: lessons from Western Australia's nature-based tourism strategy', in B. Weir, S. McArthur and A. Crabtree (eds), *Developing Ecotourism into the Millennium*, Proceedings of the Ecotourism Association of Australia 6th National Conference, Margaret River, Western Australia, 29–31 October 1998. Canberra: Bureau of Tourism Research, 31–5. <www.btr.gov.au/conf_proc/ecotourism>

Dowling, R.K. (1999b) 'Developing tourism in the environmentally sensitive north west Cape Region, Western Australia', in T.V. Singh and S. Singh (eds), *Tourism Development in Critical Environments*, New York: Cognizant Communication Corporation, 163–75.

Dowling, R.K. (2000a) 'Ecotourism in South East Asia: a golden opportunity for local communities', in K.S. Chon (ed.), *Tourism in Southeast Asia: Opportunities and Challenges*, New York: The Haworth Hospitality Press.

Dowling, R.K. (2000b) 'Ecotourism at the dawn of the new millennium: some thoughts for the southern hemisphere', *Proceedings of World Ecotour '97*, Bahia, Brazil, 5–8 April.

Dowling, R.K. (2000c) 'Global ecotourism at the start of the new millennium', *World Leisure Journal*, **42** (2): 11–19.

Dowling, R.K. (2000d) 'Visitors' views of an icon ecotourism site', *Proceedings of the Ecotourism Association of Australia 8th National Conference 'Ecotourism – Changing the Nature of Australia'*, Lorne and Phillip Island, Victoria, 2–5 November.

Dowling, R.K. and Alder, J. (1996) 'Shark Bay Western Australia: managing a coastal world heritage area', *Coastal Management in Tropical Asia: A Newsletter for Practitioners*, No. 6: 17–21.

Dowling, R.K. and Charters, T. (2000) 'The planning and development of ecotourism in Queensland', in T. Charters and K. Law (eds), *Best Practice Ecotourism in Queensland*, Brisbane: Tourism Queensland, 1–16.

Dowling, R.K. and Field, G. (1999) 'Guiding initiatives in Western Australia', in B. Weir, S. McArthur and A. Crabtree (eds), *Developing Ecotourism into the Millennium*, Proceedings of the Ecotourism Association of Australia 6th National Conference, Margaret River, Western Australia, 29–31 October 1998. Canberra: Bureau of Tourism Research, 54–7. <www.btr.gov.au/conf_proc/ecotourism>

Dowling, R.K. and Hardman, J. (1996) 'Ecotourism in Asia: the Thailand experience', in H. Ritchins, J. Richardson and A. Crabtree (eds), *Proceedings of the Ecotourism Association of Australia National Conference 'Taking the Next Steps'*, Alice Springs, 18–23 November 1995. Brisbane: Ecotourism Association of Australia, 73–8.

Dowling, R.K. and James, K. (1996) 'The south west ecotourism strategy', in H. Ritchins, J. Richardson and A. Crabtree (eds), *Proceedings of the Ecotourism Association of Australia National Conference 'Taking the Next Steps'*, Alice Springs, 18–23 November 1995. Brisbane: Ecotourism Association of Australia, 25–32.

Doxey, G.V. (1975) 'A causation theory of visitor resident irritants: methodology and research inferences', in *The Impact of Tourism*, San Diego: Proceedings of the Sixth Annual Conference of The Travel Research Association, 195–8.

Driver, B.L. (1975) 'Quantification of outdoor recreationists' preferences', in B. van der Smissen and J. Myers (eds), *Research: Camping and Environmental Education*, Pennsylvania: HPEP series no. 11, The Pennsylvania State University, 165–87.

Driver, B.L. and Tocher, S.R. (1970) 'Toward a behavioural interpretation of recreational engagements, with implications for planning', in B.L. Driver (ed.), *Elements of Outdoor Recreation Planning*, Ann Arbor, Michigan: University of Michigan Press, 9–13.

Driver, B.L., Brown, P.J., Stankey, G.H. and Gregoire, T.G. (1987) 'The ROS planning system: evolution, basic concepts, and research needed', *Leisure Sciences*, **9** (3): 201–12.

Drumm, A. (1998) 'New approaches to community-based ecotourism management. Learning from Ecuador', in K. Lindberg, M. Epler Wood and D. Engeldrum (eds), *Ecotourism: A Guide for Planners and Managers*, Vol. 2, Vermont: The Ecotourism Society, 197–213.

Dudenhoefer, D. (1991) *Ecotourism Boom Forces Nation to Seek New Alternatives, 1991–1992 Guide to Costa Rica*, San Jose: Tico Times.

Duenkel, D. (1984) 'Tourism and the environment: a review of the literature and issues', *Environmental Sociology*, **37**: 5–18.

Duenkel, D. and Scott, H. (1994) 'Ecotourism's hidden potential – altering perceptions of reality', *Journal of Physical Education Research and Dance*, October: 40–4.

Duffus, D. and Dearden, P. (1990) 'Non-consumptive wildlife-oriented: a conceptual framework', *Biological Conservation*, **53**: 213–31.

Durst, P. and Ingram, C. (1988) 'Nature-oriented tourism promotion by developing countries', *Tourism Management*, **9** (1): 39–43.

Dutton, I. and Hall, C.M. (1989) 'Making tourism sustainable: the policy/practice conundrum', in *Proceedings of the Environment Institute of Australia Second National Conference*, Melbourne: Environment Institute of Australia, 196–296.

Dyess, R. (1997) 'Adventure travel or ecotourism?', *Adventure Travel Business*, April: 2.

Dyson, J. (1998) 'From poachers to protectors', *Reader's Digest*, June: 58–65.

EAA (1998) 'Sydney Olympics to get world's first "green" hotel', *Ecotourism Association of Australia Newsletter*, March: 7.

EAA (1999) 'Couran Cove Resort – an example of best practice environmental management', in the *Australian Ecotourism Guide 2000*, Brisbane: Ecotourism Association of Australia, 9.

EAA (1999b) *NEAP National Accreditation Program*, Brisbane: Ecotourism Association of Australia.

EAA and ATOA (1997) *National Ecotourism Accreditation Program*, Brisbane: Ecotourism Association of Australia and Australian Tourism Operators Network.

Eadington, W.R. and Redman, M. (1991) 'Economics and tourism', *Annals of Tourism Research*, **18** (1): 41–56.

Eagles, P. (1992) 'The travel motivations of Canadian ecotourists', *Journal of Travel Research*, **31** (2): 3–7.

Eagles, P. (1995) 'Tourism and Canadian parks: fiscal relationships', *Managing Leisure*, **1**: 16–27.

Eagles, P., Ballantine, J. and Fennell, D. (1992) 'Marketing to the ecotourist: case studies from Kenya and Costa Rica', Paper presented at the International Union for Conservation of Nature and Natural Resources (IUCN) IVth World Congress on National Parks and Protected Areas, Caracas, Venezuela, 10–12 February.

Eagles, P., Ballantine, J.L. and Fennell, D.A. (1995) *Marketing to the Ecotourist: Case Studies from Kenya and Costa Rica*. Ontario: University of Waterloo.

Eagles, P. and Cascagnette, J. (1995) 'Canadian ecotourists: who are they', *Tourism Recreation Research*, **20** (1): 22–8.

Eagles, P. and Higgins, B. (1998) 'Ecotourism market and industry structure', in K. Lindberg, M. Epler Wood and D. Engeldrum (eds), *Ecotourism: A Guide for Planners and Managers*, Vol. 2. Vermont: The Ecotourism Society, 11–43.

Eagles, P. and Wind, E. (1994) 'Canadian ecotours in 1992: a content analysis of advertising', *Journal of Applied Recreation Research*, **19** (1): 67–87.

Eagles, P. *et al.* (eds) (1995) *Ecotourism: Annotated Bibliography for Planners and Managers*, 3rd edn, Vermont: The Ecotourism Society.

Echtner, C. (1999) 'Tourism in sensitive environments: three African success stories', in T.V. Singh and S. Singh (eds), *Tourism Development in Critical Environments*, New York: Cognizant Communication Corporation, 149–62.

Economist Intelligence Unit (1989) 'The Pacific islands', *International Tourism Report*, **4**: 70–99.

Edington, J. and Edington, M. (1977) *Ecology and Environmental Planning*, London: Chapman & Hall.

Edington, J. and Edington, M. (1986) *Ecology, Recreation and Tourism*, Cambridge: Cambridge University Press.

Edwards, I.J. (1977) 'The ecological impact of pedestrian traffic on alpine vegetation in Kosciusko National Park', *Australian Forestry*, **40**: 108–20.

Ehrlich, P., Ehrlich, A. and Holdren, J. (1970) *Ecoscience: Population Resources and Environment*, San Francisco: W.H. Freeman.

ENETC (1973) *Tourism and Conservation – Working Together*, Copenhagen: Europa Nostra and the European Travel Commission.

ENVIREG (1994) *Economic Development and Environmental Protection in Coastal Areas: A Guide to Good Practice*, ENVIREG, Brussels: Commission of the European Communities, DG XVI.

Epler, B. (1991) *An Economic and Social Analysis of Tourism in the Galapagos Islands*, Providence: University of Rhode Island, Coastal Resources Center.

Epler Wood, M. (ed.) (1997) *Final Report, Ecotourism at a Crossroads: Charting the Way Forward*, A Summary of Conference Results and Recommendations held in Nairobi, October 1997, Vermont: The Ecotourism Society.

Epler Wood, M. (1998a) 'New directions in the ecotourism industry', in K. Lindberg, M. Epler Wood and D. Engeldrum (eds), *Ecotourism: A Guide for Planners and Managers*, Vol. 2, Vermont: The Ecotourism Society, 45–61.

Epler Wood, M. (1998b) 'Meeting the global challenge of community participation in ecotourism: case studies and lessons from Ecuador'. America Verde Working Papers, No. 2.

Epler Wood, M. (1999a) 'Do ecotours help or hurt? Ecotourism society founder talks about responsible tourism'. http://abcnews.go.com/ABC2000/abc2000travel/chat_wood.html

Epler Wood, M. (1999b) 'The Ecotourism Society – an international NGO committed to sustainable development', *Tourism Recreation Research*, **24** (2): 119–23.

ERM Mitchell McCotter (1995a) *South West Regional Tourism Strategy,* Vol. 1, prepared for the South West Development Commission, ERM Mitchell McCotter Perth.

ERM Mitchell McCotter (1995b) *South West Regional Tourism Strategy,* Vol. 2, prepared for the South West Development Commission, ERM Mitchell McCotter Perth.

Fagence, M. (1997) 'Ecotourism and Pacific Island countries: the first generation of strategies', *The Journal of Tourism Studies*, **8** (2): 26–38.

Farrell, B. (ed.) (1977) *The Social and Economic Impact of Tourism on the Pacific Communities*, Santa Cruz: Centre for South Pacific Studies, University of California.

Farrell, B.H. (1982) *Hawaii, The Legend that Sells*, Honolulu: University Press of Hawaii.

Farrell, B.H. (1986) *Difficult Choices in Pacific Development.* Paper presented to the Islands '86 Conference on Islands of the World, University of Victoria, Canada.

Farrell, B. and McLellan, R. (1987) 'Tourism and physical environment research', *Annals of Tourism Research*, **14** (1): 1–16.

Farrell, B. and Runyan D. (1991) 'Ecology and tourism', *Annals of Tourism Research*, **18** (1): 41–56.

Feizkhah, E. (1998) 'Tourism on thin ice', *Time*, 4 May: 40–2.

Fennell, D. (1990) 'A profile of ecotourists and the benefits derived from their experience: a Costa Rican case study', Master's thesis, University of Waterloo, Ontario.

Fennell, D. (1994) 'Tourism industry and tourism destinations: predator, competitor, neutral and symbiotic relationships', paper presented at the Annual Meeting of the Canadian Association of Geographers, Wilfrid Laurier University, May 1994.

Fennell, D. (1999) *Ecotourism: An Introduction.* London: Routledge.

Fennell, D. (2000) 'What's in a name? Conceptualizing natural resource-based tourism', *Tourism Recreation Research*, **25** (1): 97–100.

Fennell, D. and Eagles, P. (1990) 'Ecotourism in Costa Rica: a conceptual framework', *Journal of Park and Recreation Administration*, **8** (1): 23–34.

Fennell, D. and Malloy, D. (1995) 'Ethics and ecotourism: a comprehensive ethical model', *Journal of Applied Recreation Research*, **20** (3): 163–83.

Fennell, D.A. and Malloy, D.C. (1999) 'Measuring the ethical nature of tourism operators', *Annals of Tourism Research*, **26** (4): 928–43.

Fennell, D.A. and Weaver, D.B. (1997) 'Vacation farms and ecotourism in Saskatchewan, Canada', *Journal of Rural Studies*, **13** (4): 467–75.

Fernie, J. and Pitkethly, A. (1985) *Resources: Environment and Policy*, London: Harper and Row.

Ferrario, F.F. (1981) *An Evaluation of the Tourist Potential of KwaZulu and Natal*, Durban: KwaZulu Development Corporation.

Field, G. (1998) *Best Recipes for Interpreting Our Heritage: Activities for Ecotour Guides and Others*, Perth: Department of Conservation and Land Management

Finney, B. and Watson, A. (1977) *A New Kind of Sugar: Tourism in the Pacific*, Honolulu: East-West Technology and Development Institute, East-West Centre.

Finucane, S. and Dowling, R. (1995) 'The perceptions of ecotourism operators in Western Australia', *Tourism Recreation Research*, **20** (1): 14–21.

Forster, R.R. (1973) *Planning for Man and Nature in National Parks*, No. 26, Morges: IUCN.

Fox, M. (1977) 'The social impact of tourism: a challenge to researchers and planners', in B.R. Finney and A. Watson (eds), *A New Kind of Sugar: Tourism in the Pacific*, Honolulu: East-West Technology and Development Institute, East-West Centre: 27–48.

France, L. ed. (1998) *Earthscan Reader in Sustainable Tourism*, London: Earthscan Publications.

Francillon, G. (1975) 'Tourism in Bali and its economic and socio-cultural impact: three points of view', *International Social Science Journal*, **27**: 723–52.

Frangialli, F. (1998) 'Tourism: 2020 vision', *World Travel and Tourism Development*, **3**: 93–7.

Funding Proposal for the Development of a National Strategy to Outline Australia's Contribution to the 'International Year of Ecotourism in 2002'. Proposal prepared by The Ecotourism Association of Australia, October 1999.

Fries, P. (1998) 'Purists take on the profiteers in a battle for the great outdoors', in *Profits in the Wilderness: The Ecotourism Industry's Identity Crisis*, The Weekend Australian Financial Review, 11–12 July.

Gajraj, A.M. (1981) 'Threats to the terrestrial resources of the Caribbean', *Ambio*, **10** (6): 307–11.

Gajraj, A.M. (1988) 'A regional approach to environmentally sound tourism development', *Tourism Recreation Research*, **13** (2): 5–9.

Gale, F. and Jacobs, J. (1987) *Tourists and the National Estate*, Canberra: AGPS.

Galloway, J. (1999) 'A partnership for progress', *World Travel and Tourism Development*, **5**: 120–1.

Garland, B.R. and West, S.J. (1985) 'The social impact of tourism in New Zealand', *Massey Journal of Asian and Pacific Business*, **1** (1): 34–9.

Garrison, R.W. (1997) 'Sustainable nature tourism: California's regional approach', in *World Ecotour '97 Abstracts Volume*, Rio de Janeiro: BIOSFERA, 180–2.

Genot, H. (1995) 'Voluntary environmental codes of conduct in the tourism sector', *Journal of Sustainable Tourism*, **3** (3): 166–72.

Georgulas, N. (1970) Tourist destination features. *Journal of the Town Planning Institute* **56** (10): 442–6.

Getz, D. (1986) 'Models in tourism planning towards integration of theory and practice', *Tourism Management*, **7** (1): 21–32.

Getz, D. (1987) *Tourism Planning and Research: Traditions, Models and Futures*. Paper presented to the Australian Travel Research Workshop, Bunbury, Western Australia, 3–6 November.

Getz, D. (1994) 'Residents' attitudes towards tourism: a longitudinal study in Spey Valley, Scotland', *Tourism Management*, **15** (4): 247–58.

Giannecchini, J. (1993) 'Ecotourism: new partners, new relationships', *Conservation Biology*, **7** (2): 429–32.

Gilbert, J. (1997) *Ecotourism Means Business*, Wellington: GP Publications.

Gilpin, A. (1990) *An Australian Dictionary of Environment and Planning*, Melbourne: Oxford University Press.

Girardin, M. (1999) 'Sabi Sabi – a working example of ecotourism', Johannesburg: Sabi Sabi Private Game Reserve, 9.

GLOBE '90 (1990) *An Action Strategy for Sustainable Tourism*, Ottawa: Tourism Canada.

Godfrey, P.J. and Godfrey, M.M. (1980) 'Ecological effects of off-road vehicles on Cape Cod', *Oceanus*, **23** (4): 56–67.

Godschalk, D.R. and Parker, F.H. (1975) 'Carrying capacity: a key to environmental planning', *Journal of Soil and Water Conservation*, **30**: 160–75.

Goldsmith, E., 1974, 'Pollution by tourism', *The Ecologist*, **48** (1): 47–8.

Gonzalez, M. (1998) 'Ecuador's tourism "Eggs" are mostly found in one basket', *Intercoast Network*, Spring: 15.

Good, L. (1988) *Bako National Park: A Management Plan*, Kuching, Malaysia: Sarawak Forest Department.

Goodwin, H. (1996) 'In pursuit of ecotourism', *Biodiversity and Conservation*, **5** (3): 277–91.

Goodwin, H., Kent, I., Parker, K. and Walpole, M. (1998) *Tourism, Conservation and Sustainable Development: Case Studies from Asia and Africa*, IIED Wildlife and Development Series No. 12, London: International Institute for Environment and Development.

Goudberg, N., Cassells, D. and Valentine, P. (1991) 'The prospects for an ecotourism industry in northern Queensland wet tropical rainforests', in N. Goudberg, M. Bionnell and D. Benzaken (eds), *Tropical Rainforest Research in Australia*, Proceedings of a Workshop held in Townsville, 4–6 May 1990, Townsville: Townsville Institute of Tropical Rainforest Studies.

Gould, J. (1995) 'Protecting Pacific forests', *Habitat Australia*, **23** (5): 14–15.

Graefe, A.R. and Vaske, J.J. (1987) 'A framework for managing quality in the tourist experience', *Annals of Tourism Research*, **14**: 389–404.

Greenwood, D. (1972) 'Tourism as an agent of change: a Spanish Basque case study', *Ethnology*, **11**: 80–91.

Groetzbach, E. (1985) 'The Bavarian Alps: problems of tourism, agriculture, and environment conservation', in T.V. Singh and J. Kaur (eds), *Integrated Mountain Development*, New Delhi: Himalayan Books, 141–55.

Gunn, C. (1972) *Vacationscape: Designing Tourist Regions*, New York: Van Nostrand Reinhold.

Gunn, C. (1973) Tourism and the environment – five special studies, in *Destination USA, Report of the National Tourism Resources Review Commission*, Washington, DC: US Government Printing Office.

Gunn, C. (1977) 'Industry pragmatism *v.* tourism planning', *Leisure Sciences*, **1**: 85–94.

Gunn, C. (1978) 'Needed: an international alliance for tourism–recreation–conservation', *Travel Research Journal*, **2**: 3–9.

Gunn, C. (1979a) *Tourism Planning*, New York: Crane-Russak.

Gunn, C. (1979b) *Tourism Development: Assessment of Potential in Texas*, Bulletin MP-1416, Texas Agricultural Experiment Station and Recreation and Parks Department, College Station, Texas: Texas A&M University.

Gunn, C. (1982) *Tourism Development Potential in Canada*, Ottawa: Canadian Government Office of Tourism.

Gunn, C. (1987) 'Environmental designs and land use', in J.R.B. Ritchie and C.R. Goeldner (eds), *Travel, Tourism and Hospitality Research: A Handbook for Managers and Researchers*, New York: John Wiley & Sons, 229–47.

Gunn, C. (1988) *Tourism Planning*, London: Taylor and Francis.

Gunn, C. (1991) *Redefining the Tourism Product – The Environmental Experience*. Paper presented to the 22nd Annual Conference of the Travel and Tourism Research Association, Long Beach, California.

Gunn, C. (1994) *Tourism Planning: Basics, Concepts, Cases*, 3rd edn, Washington, DC: Taylor & Francis.

Gurung, C.P. and de Coursey, M. (1994) 'The Annapurna Conservation Area Project: a pioneering example of sustainable tourism?', in E. Cater and G. Lowman (eds), *Ecotourism: A Sustainable Option?*, Chichester: John Wiley & Sons, 177–94.

Haenn, N. (1994) 'A new tourist, a new environment: can ecotourism deliver?', *Trends*, **31** (2): 28–30.

Halbertsma, N.F. (1988) 'Proper management is a must', *Naturopa*, **59**: 23–4.

Hall, C.M. (1991) *Introduction to Tourism in Australia: Impacts, Planning and Development*, Melbourne: Longman Cheshire.

Hall, C.M. (1993a) 'Ecotourism in Antarctica and adjacent sub-Antarctic islands: development, impacts, management and prospects for the future', *Tourism Management*, **14** (2): 117–22.

Hall, C.M. (1993b) 'Ecotourism in the Australian and New Zealand sub-Antarctic islands', *Tourism Recreation Research*, **18** (2): 13–21.

Hall, C.M. (1994) 'Ecotourism in Australia, New Zealand and the South Pacific: appropriate tourism of a new form of ecological imperialism?', in C. Cater and G. Lowman (eds), *Ecotourism: A Sustainable Option*, Chichester: John Wiley & Sons, 137–57.

Hall, C.M. (1995) *An Introduction to Tourism in Australia: Impacts, Planning and Development*, 2nd edition, Melbourne: Longman.

Hall, C.M. (1998) 'Historical antecedents of sustainable tourism and ecotourism: new labels on old bottles', in C.M. Hall and A. Lew (eds), *Sustainable Tourism: A Geographical Perspective*, Harlow: Addison-Wesley Longman, 13–24.

Hall, C.M. (2000) *Tourism Planning: Policies, Processes and Relationships*, Harlow: Pearson Education Limited.

Hall, C.M. and Butler, D. (1995) 'In search of common ground: reflections on sustainability, complexity and process in the tourism system', *Journal of Sustainable Tourism*, **3** (2): 99–105.

Hall, C.M. and Jenkins, J. (1995) *Tourism and Public Policy*, London: Routledge.

Hall, C.M. and Lew, A. (eds) (1998) *Sustainable Tourism: A Geographical Perspective*, Harlow: Addison-Wesley Longman.

Hall, C.M. and McArthur, S. (1991) 'Commercial white water rafting in Australia', *Australian Journal of Leisure and Recreation*, **1**: 25–30.

Hall, C.M. and McArthur, S. (1996) 'Natural places: an introduction', in C.M. Hall and S. McArthur (eds), *Heritage Management in Australia and New Zealand: The Human Dimension*, 2nd edn, Melbourne: Oxford University Press, 128–34.

Hall, C.M. and McArthur, S. (1998) *Integrated Heritage Management*, London: HMSO.

Hall, C.M. and Page, S.J. (eds) (1996) *Tourism in the Pacific: Issues and Cases*, London: ITBP.

Hall, C.M. and Page, S.J. (1999) *The Geography of Tourism and Recreation: Environment, Place and Space*, London: Routledge.

Hall, C.M. and Page, S.J. (2001) *The Geography of Tourism and Recreation: Environment, Place and Space*, 2nd edn, London: Routledge.

Hall, D. (1984) 'Conservation by ecotourism', *New Scientist*, **101** (1399): 38–9.

Hall, D. and Kinnaird, V. (1994) 'Ecotourism in Eastern Europe', in E. Cater and G. Lowman (eds), *Ecotourism: A Sustainable Option?*, Chichester: John Wiley & Sons, 111–36.

Hamill, L. (1975) 'Analysis of Leopold's quantitative comparisons of landscape esthetics', *Journal of Leisure Research*, **7**: 16–28.

Hammitt, W. and Cole, D. (1987) *Wildland Recreations Ecology and Management*, New York: John Wiley & Sons.

Hardin, G. (1968) 'The tragedy of the commons', *Science*, **162**: 1243–8.

Harris, R., Heath, E., Toepper, L. and Williams, P. (1999) *Sustainable Tourism: A Global Perspective*. Oxford: Butterworth-Heinemann.

Harris, R. and Leiper, N. (eds) (1995) *Sustainable Tourism: An Australian Perspective*, Chatswood, Australia: Butterworth-Heinemann.

Harrison, D. (1997) 'Ecotourism in the South Pacific: the case of Fiji', in *World Ecotour '97 Abstracts Volume*, Rio de Janeiro: BIOSFERA, 75.

Harrison, L. and Husbands, W. (eds) (1996) *Practising Responsible Tourism: International Case Studies in Tourism Planning, Policy and Development*, New York: John Wiley & Sons.

Hatch, D. (1997) 'Understanding the ecotourism market', Paper presented at the Ecotourism Association of Australia Conference, Port Stephens, Bureau of Tourism Research.

Hatch, D. (1998) 'Understanding the Australian nature based tourism market', in S. McArthur and B. Weir (eds), *Australia's Ecotourism Industry: A Snapshot in 1998*, Brisbane: The Ecotourism Association of Australia, 1–5.

Haulot, A. (1974) *Tourisme et environnement: la recherche d'un équilibre*, Verviers: Marabout Monde Moderne.

Hawkins, D. (1994) 'Ecotourism: opportunities for developing countries', in W. Theobald (ed.), *Global Tourism: The Next Decade*, Oxford: Butterworth-Heinemann, 261–73.

Hawkins, E.D., Shafer, C.L. and Rovelstad, J.M. (eds) (1980) *Tourism Planning and Development Issues*, Washington, DC: George Washington University.

Hawkins, D.E., Epler Wood, M. and Bittman, S. (eds) (1995) *The Ecolodge Sourcebook: For Planners and Developers*. Vermont: The Ecotourism Society.

Hay, J. (ed.) (1992) *Ecotourism Business in the Pacific: Promoting a Sustainable Experience*, Conference Proceedings, Environmental Science Occasional Publication No. 8, Environmental Science, University of Auckland, New Zealand and the East-West Center, University of Hawaii, USA.

Haywood, K. and Walsh, L. (1996) 'Strategic tourism planning in Fiji: an oxymoron or providing for coherence in decision making?', in L. Harrison and W. Husbands (eds), *Practising Responsible Tourism: International Case Studies in Tourism Planning, Policy, and Development*, New York: John Wiley & Sons, 103–25.

Healy, R. (1989) *Economic Consideration in Nature-Oriented Tourism: The Case of Tropical Forest Tourism*, Durham, North Carolina: Southeastern Center for Forest Economic Research.

Healy, R. (1994) '"Tourist merchandise" as a means of generating local benefits from ecotourism', *Journal of Sustainable Tourism*, **2** (3): 137–51.

Heeley, J. (1981) 'Planning for tourism in Britain', *Town Planning Review*, **52**: 61–79.

Helleiner, F.M. (1997) 'Was Sir Edmund Hillary an ecotourist? The essence of ecotourism', in *World Ecotour '97 Abstracts Volume*, Rio de Janeiro: BIOSFERA, 78–82.

Helu-Thaman, K. (1992) 'Ecocultural tourism: a personal view for maintaining cultural integrity in ecotourism development', in J. Hay (ed.), *Ecotourism Business in the Pacific: Promoting a Sustainable Experience*, Conference Proceedings, Environmental Science Occasional Publication No. 8, Environmental Science, University of Auckland, New Zealand and the East-West Center, University of Hawaii, USA.

Henning, D. (1993) 'Nature-based tourism can help conserve tropical forests', *Tourism Recreation Research*, **18** (2): 45–50.

Hetzer, N. (1965) 'Environment, tourism, culture', LINKS (July): reprinted in *Ecosphere*, 1970, **1** (2): 1–3.

Higginbottom, K., Rann, K., Moscardo, G., Davis, D. and Muloin, S. (2001) *Status of Wildlife Tourism in Australia: An Overview*, Wildlife Tourism Report Series: Report No 1, Status Assessment of Wildlife Tourism Series, CRC for Sustainable Tourism Research Report Series, Gold Coast University, Brisbane, Australia.

Higgins, B. (1996) 'The global structure of the nature tourism industry: ecotourists, tour operators, and local businesses', *Journal of Travel Research*, **35** (2): 11–18.

Hiranyakit, S. (1984) 'Tourism planning and development', *UNEP Industry and Environment Newsletter*, **7** (1): 2–3.

Hjalager, A.-M. (1996) 'Tourism and the environment: the innovation connection', *Journal of Sustainable Tourism*, **4** (4): 201–18.

Hjalager, A.-M. (1999) 'Consumerism and sustainable tourism', *Journal of Travel and Tourism Marketing*, **8** (3): 1–20.

Hogarth, M. (1999) 'Clean games get the green light', *The West Australian*, 15 September: 6.

Holden, A. (2000) *Environment and Tourism*, London: Routledge.

Holden, A. and Kealy, H. (1996) 'A profile of UK outbound "environmentally friendly" tour operators', *Tourism Management*, **17** (1): 60–4.

Holder, J. (1988) 'Pattern and impact of tourism on the environment of the Caribbean', *Tourism Management*, **9** (2): 119–27.

Holland, S.M., Ditton, R. and Graefe, A. (1998) 'An ecotourism perspective on billfish fisheries', *Journal of Sustainable Tourism*, **6** (2): 979–116.

Holloway, J.C. (1989) *The Business of Tourism*, 3rd edn, London: Pitman.

Holloway, J.C. and Plant, R.V. (1988) *Marketing for Tourism*, London: Pitman.

Holloway, J.C. and Robinson, A. (1995) *Marketing for Tourism*, Harlow: Longman.

Holmes, B.F. (1980) 'On blending tourism with natural beauty', in D.E. Hawkins, E.L. Shafer and J.M. Rovelstad (eds), *Tourism Planning and Development Issues*, Washington, DC: George Washington University.

Honey, M. (1999) *Ecotourism and Sustainable Development: Who Owns Paradise?*, Washington, DC: Island Press.

Hong, E. (1985) *See the Third World While It Lasts: The Social Environmental Impact of Tourism with Special Reference to Malaysia*, Consumers' Association of Penang, Malaysia.

Hoole, A.F. and Downie, B.K. (1978) *Zoning in National Parks*, Winnipeg: Prairie Region, Parks Canada.

Horner, S. and Swarbrooke, J. (1996) *Marketing Tourism, Leisure and Hospitality in Europe*, London: ITBP.

Hoyt, E. (2000) *Whale Watching 2000: Worldwide Tourism Numbers, Expenditures and Expanding Socioeconomic Benefits*, Crowborough: International Fund for Animal Welfare, UK.

Hudman, L.E. (1978) 'Tourism's role and response to environmental issues and potential future effects', *Annals of Tourism Research*, **5** (1): 112–25.

Hudman, L.E. (1991) 'Tourist impacts: the need for regional planning', *The Tourist Review*, **4/91**: 17–21.

Hughes, G. (1995) 'The cultural construction of sustainable tourism', *Tourism Management*, **16** (1): 49–59.

Hugo, M. (1999) 'A comprehensive approach towards the planning, grading and auditing of hiking trails as ecotourism products', *Current Issues in Tourism*, **2** (2/3): 138–73.

Hull, J. (1998) 'Market segmentation and ecotourism development on the Lower North Shore of Quebec', in C.M. Hall and A. Lew (eds), *Sustainable Tourism: a Geographical Perspective*, Harlow: Addison-Wesley Longman, 146–58.

Hummel, J. (1994) 'Ecotourism development in protected areas of developing countries', *World Leisure and Recreation*, **36** (2): 17–23.

Hunter, C. and Green, H. (1995) *Tourism and the Environment: A Sustainable Relationship?* London: Routledge.

Hvenegaard, G. (1994) 'Ecotourism: a status report and conceptual framework', *Journal of Tourism Studies*, **5** (2): 24–35.

Hvenegaard, G., Butler, J. and Krystofiak, D. (1989) 'Economic values of bird watching at Point Pelee National Park, Canada', *Wildlife Social Bulletin*, **17** (4): 526–31.

Hvenegaard, G. and Dearden, P. (1998) 'Ecotourism versus tourism in a Thai national park', *Annals of Tourism Research*, **25** (3): 700–20.

Hviding, E. and Bayliss-Smith (2000) *Islands of Rainforest: Agroforestry, Logging and Ecotourism in Solomon Islands*, Aldershot: Ashgate Publishing Ltd.

Hyma, B. and Wall, G. (1979) 'Tourism in a developing area: the case of Tamil Nadu, India', *Annals of Tourism Research*, **6**: 338–50.

Industry and Environment (1984) *Tourism*, Special Issue of UNEP's Industry and Environment Newsletter, Volume 7 (1), Paris: United Nations Environment Programme.

Industry and Environment (1986) *Carrying Capacity for Tourism Activities*, Special Issue of UNEP's Industry and Environment Newsletter, Volume 9 (1), Paris: United Nations Environment Programme.

Ingram, D. and Durst, P. (1987) 'Nature-oriented travel to developing countries', FPEI Working Paper No. 28, Research Triangle Park, Washington, DC: Southeastern Centre for Forest Economics Research.

Ingram, C.D. and Durst, P.B. (1989) 'Nature-oriented tour operators: travel to developing countries', *Journal of Travel Research*, **28** (2): 11–15.

Inskeep, E. (1987) 'Environmental planning for tourism', *Annals of Tourism Research*, **14** (1): 118–35.

Inskeep, E. (1988) 'Tourism planning: an emerging specialisation', *Journal of the American Planning Association*, **54** (3): 360–72.

Inskeep, E. (1991) *Tourism Planning: An Integrated and Sustainable Development Approach*, New York: Van Nostrand Reinhold.

Inskeep, E. (1992) 'Sustainable tourism development in the Maldives and Bhutan', *Industry and Environment*, **15** (3/4): 31–6.

Inskeep, E. (1994) *National and Regional Tourism Planning: Methodologies and Case Studies*, London: Routledge.

IUCN (International Union for the Conservation of Nature and Natural Resources) (1967) *Ecology, Tourism and Recreation*, proceedings of the Tenth Technical Meeting, Morges, Switzerland: IUCN.

IUCN (1975) *World Directory of National Parks and Other Protected Areas*, Gland, Switzerland: IUCN.

IUCN (1978) *Categories, Objectives and Criteria for Protected Areas*, A Final Report prepared by Committee on Criteria and Nomenclature Commission on National Parks and Protected Areas (CNPPA), Morges, Switzerland: IUCN.

IUCN (1980) *World Conservation Strategy*, Gland, Switzerland: IUCN.

Ivanko, J. (1997) 'Conservation meets community development – ecotourism and microenterprise ventures that produce local livelihoods', *The Rotarian*, 30–33.

Jaakson, R. (1997) 'Exploring the epistomology of ecotourism', *Journal of Applied Recreation Research*, **22** (1): 33–47.

Jackson, I. (1986) 'Carrying capacity for tourism in small tropical Caribbean islands', *UNEP's Industry and Environment Newsletter,* **9** (1): 7–10.

Jafari, J. (1974) 'The socio-economic costs of tourism to developing countries', *Annals of Tourism Research,* **1**: 227–59.

Jafari, J. (1990) 'Research and scholarship: the basis of tourism education', *Journal of Tourism Studies,* **1** (1): 33–41.

Jafari, J. (ed.) (2000) *Encyclopedia of Tourism,* London: Routledge.

James, M. (1993) 'Tribes and tourists', *Inside Indonesia,* December: 23–4.

Jansen-Verbeke, M. and Ashworth G.J. (1990) 'Environmental integration of recreation and tourism', *Annals of Tourism Research,* **17** (4): 618–22.

Järviluoma, J. (1992) 'Alternative tourism and the evolution of tourist areas', *Tourism Management,* **13** (1): 118–20.

Jaura, R. (1998) 'Tourism: developing nations expect big cut from tourism income', *Inter-Press Service,* 11 March.

Jefferies, B. (1982) 'Sagamartha National Park: the impact of tourism in the Himalayas', *Ambio,* **11** (5): 274–82.

Jefferson, A. and Lickorish, L. (1988) *Marketing Tourism: A Practical Guide,* Harlow: Longman.

Jie, Z., KeZun, Z. and GuiQin, J. (2000) 'Forest parks and sustainable development of ecotourism in China', *Journal of Forestry Research,* **11** (1): 63–8.

Jim, C.Y. (1987) 'Trampling impacts of recreationists on picnic sites in a Hong Kong country park', *Environmental Conservation,* **14** (2): 117–27.

Jim, C.Y. (1989) 'Visitor management in recreation areas?, *Environmental Conservation,* **16** (1): 19–32, 40.

Johnston, A. (2000) 'Indigenous peoples and ecotourism: bringing indigenous knowledge and rights into the sustainability equation', *Tourism Recreation Research,* **25** (2): 89–96.

Johnston, M. (1989) 'Accidents in mountain recreation: the experiences of international and domestic visitors in New Zealand', *GeoJournal,* 19: 323–8.

Johnston, M. and Viken, A. (1997) 'Tourism development in Greenland', *Annals of Tourism Research,* **24** (4): 978–82.

Jones, A. (1992) 'Is there a real "alternative" tourism?', *Tourism Management,* **13** (1): 102–3.

Jordan, C.F. (1995) *Conservation: Replacing Quantity with Quality as a Goal for Global Management,* New York: John Wiley & Sons.

Kangas, P., Shave, M. and Shave, P. (1995) 'Profile: economics of an ecotourism operation in Belize', *Environmental Management,* **19** (5): 669–73.

Karan, P.P. and Mather, C. (1985) 'Tourism and environment in the Mount Everest region', *Geographical Review,* **75** (1): 93–5.

Karwacki, J. and Boyd, C. (1995) 'Ethics and ecotourism', *Business Ethics,* **4** (4): 25–232.

Kay, J. (1980) 'Evaluating environmental impacts of off-road vehicles', *Journal of Geography,* **80** (1): 10–18.

Kelleher, G.G. (1987) 'Management of the Great Barrier Reef', *Australian Parks and Recreation,* **23** (5): 27–33.

Kelleher, G.G. (1990) 'Sustainable development of the Great Barrier Reef Marine Park', Paper presented to the Globe 90 Conference on Global Opportunities for Business and the Environment–Tourism Stream, Vancouver, Canada, 19–23 March.

Kelleher, G.G. and Kenchington, R. (1982) 'Australia's Great Barrier Reef Marine Park: making development compatible with conservation', *Ambio,* **11** (5): 262–7.

Keller, C. (1987) 'Stages of peripheral tourism development – Canada's Northwest Territories', *Tourism Management*, **8** (1): 20–32.

Kenchington, R. (1989) 'Tourism in the Galapagos Islands: the dilemma of conservation', *Environmental Conservation*, **16** (3): 227–36.

Kerr, J. (1992) 'Making dollars and sense out of ecotourism/nature tourism', in B. Weiler (ed.), *Ecotourism: Incorporating the Global Classroom – 1991 International Conference Papers*, Canberra: Bureau of Tourism Research, 248–52.

Khan, M. (1997a) 'An examination of the relationship between service quality expectations of ecotourists and their environmental attitude and behaviour, travel motivation, and value dimension', in *The Evolution of Tourism: Adapting to Change*, Proceedings of the 28th Annual Travel and Tourism Association (TTRA) Conference, Lexington, USA: TTRA, 60–4.

Khan, M. (1997b) 'Tourism development and dependency theory: mass tourism vs ecotourism', *Annals of Tourism Research*, **24** (4): 988–91.

Khan, M. and Hawkins, D. (1997) 'American ecotourists: an empirical evaluation of their characteristics', in *The Evolution of Tourism: Adapting to Change*, Proceedings of the 28th Annual Travel and Tourism Association (TTRA) Conference, Lexington, USA: TTRA, 388–95.

Khatri, T. (1994) 'Tourism and corals in the Bay of Bengal islands', *Environmental Conservation*, **21** (1): 81.

King, B. (1992) 'Cultural tourism and its potential for Fiji', *Journal of Pacific Studies*, **16**, 74–89.

Klopper, R. (1976) 'Physical planning and tourism in the Federal Republic of Germany', in *ECE Planning and Development of the Tourist Industry in the ECE Region*, New York: United Nations, 50–6.

Kotler, P. and Armstrong, G. (1991) *Principles of Marketing*, 5th edn, New Jersey: Prentice Hall.

Kousis, M. (2000) 'Tourism and the environment: a social movements perspective', *Annals of Tourism Research*, **27** (2): 468–89.

Kozlowski, J.M. (1984) 'Threshold analysis to the definition of environmental capacity in Poland's Tatry National Park', in J. McNeely and J. Miller (eds), *National Parks, Conservation and Development*, Proceedings of the World Congress on National Parks, Bali Indonesia, 11–22 October 1982, Washington, DC: Smithsonian Institution Press, 450–62.

Kozlowski, J.M. (1986) *Threshold Approach in Urban, Regional and Environmental Planning*, St Lucia: University of Queensland Press.

Kozlowki, J.M. (1990) 'Sustainable development in professional planning: a potential contribution of the EIA and UET concepts', *Landscape and Urban Planning*, **19** (4): 307–32.

Kozlowski, J.M., Rosier, J. and Hill, G. (1988) 'Ultimate environmental threshold (UET) method in a marine environment (Great Barrier Reef Marine Park in Australia)', *Landscape and Urban Planning*, **15**: 327–36.

Kretchmann, J. and Eagles, P. (1990) 'An analysis of the motives of ecotourists in comparison to the general Canadian population', *Society and Leisure*, **13** (2): 499–507.

Krippendorf, J. (1975) *Die Landschaftsfresser*, Berne: Hallwag Verlag.

Krippendorf, J. (1984) 'The capital of tourism in danger', in E.A. Brugger and P. Messerli (eds), *The Transformation of the Swiss Mountain Region*, Berne: Verlag Paul Haupt, 429–50.

Krippendorf, J. (1987) *The Holidaymakers*, Oxford: Butterworth-Heinemann.

Kundaeli, J. (1983) 'Making conservation and development compatible', *Ambio*, **12** (6): 326–31.

Kusler, J. (1991) 'Ecotourism and resource conservation: introduction to issues', in J. Kusler (ed.), *Ecotourism and Resource Conservation: A Collection of Papers*, Vol. 1, Madison, Wisconsin: Omnipress.

Kutay, K. (1989) 'The new ethic in adventure travel', *Buzzworm: The Environmental Journal*, **1** (4): 31–4.

Kutay, K. (1993) 'Brave new role: ecotour operators take centre stage in the era of green travel', *Going Green: The Ecotourism Research for Travel Agents*, Supplement to *Tour and Travel News*, 25 October, 80.

Laarman, J.G. and Durst, P.B. (1987) *Nature Travel and Tropical Forests*, FPEI Working Paper Series, Southeastern Center for Forest Economics Research, Raleigh, USA: North Carolina State University.

Laarman, J.G. and Durst, P.B. (1993) 'Nature tourism as a tool for economic development and conservation of natural resources', in J. Nenon and P.B. Durst (eds), *Nature Tourism in Asia: Opportunities and Constraints for Conservation and Economic Development*. Washington, DC: US Forest Service.

Laarman, J.G. and Gregersen, H. (1996) 'Pricing policy in nature tourism', *Tourism Management*, **17** (4): 247–54.

Landals, A. (1986) 'The – tourists are ruining the parks', in *Tourism and the Environment: Conflict or Harmony?* Proceedings of a Symposium sponsored by the Canadian Society of Environmental Biologists, Alberta Chapter, Calgary, Canada, 18–19 March 1986, CSEB, Alberta, 89–99.

LaPlanche, S. (1995) *Stepping Lightly on Australia – A Travelling Guide to Ecotourism*. Melbourne: Angus and Robertson.

Lawrence, T., Wickins, D. and Phillips, N. (1997) 'Managing legitimacy in ecotourism', *Tourism Management*, **18** (5): 307–16.

Laws, E. (1991) *Tourism Marketing: Service and Quality Management Perspectives*, Cheltenham: Stanley Thornes.

Lawson, F. and Baud Bovy, M. (1977) *Tourism and Recreation: A Handbook of Physical Planning*, London: The Architectural Press.

Lawton, L. and Weaver, D. (2000) 'Nature-based tourism and ecotourism', in B. Faulkner, G. Moscardo and E. Laws (eds), *Tourism in the Twenty First Century*, London: Continuum, 34–48.

Lee, D. and Snepenger, D. (1992) 'An ecotourism assessment of Tortuguero, Costa Rica', *Annals of Tourism Research*, **19** (2): 367–70.

Lee, L. (1996) 'A long way to go', *PATA Travel News*, May, 12.

Lees, H. (1992) 'Ecotourism: retraining the big promise', in J. Hay (ed.), *Ecotourism Business in the Pacific: Promoting a Sustainable Experience*, Conference Proceedings, Environmental Science Occasional Publication No. 8, Environmental Science, University of Auckland, New Zealand and the East-West Center, University of Hawaii, USA, 61–4.

Leiper, N. (1981) 'Towards a cohesive, curriculum in tourism, the case for a distinct discipline', *Annals of Tourism Research*, **8** (1): 69–84.

Leiper, N. (1990) *Tourism Systems: An Interdisciplinary Perspective*, Palmerston North: Massey University, Department of Management Systems, Occasional Paper 2.

Leslie, D. (1986) 'Tourism and conservation in national parks', *Tourism Management*, **7** (1): 52–6.

Lew, A. (1998a) 'Ecotourism trends', *Annals of Tourism Research*, **25** (3): 742–6.

Lew, A. (1998b) 'The Asia-Pacific ecotourism industry: putting sustainable tourism into practice', in C.M. Hall and A. Lew (eds), *Sustainable Tourism: A Geographical Perspective*, Harlow: Addison-Wesley Longman, 92–106.

Liddle, M. (1975) 'A selective review of the ecological effects of human trampling on natural ecosystems', *Biological Conservation*, **7**: 17–36.

Liddle, M. (1997) *Recreation and the Environment: The Ecological Impact of Recreation and Ecotourism*, London: Chapman and Hall.

Lieberknecht, K., Papazian, J. and McQuay, A. (1999) 'Balancing conservation and economics: the development of an ecotourism plan for Panama', *Journal of Sustainable Forestry*, **8** (3/4): 107–26.

Lime, D. and Stankey, G.H. (1972) 'Carrying capacity: maintaining outdoor recreation quality', in *Northeastern Forest Experiment Station Recreation Symposium Proceedings*, Upper Darby, USA: Northeastern Forest Experiment Station, 174–83.

Lindberg, K. (1991) *Policies for Maximising Nature Tourism's Ecological and Economic Benefits*, Washington, DC: World Resources Institute.

Lindberg, K. (1996) 'Does ecotourism achieve its conservation and development objectives?', in H. Richins, J. Richardson and A. Crabtree (eds), *Ecotourism and Nature-Based Tourism: Taking the Next Steps*, Proceedings of the Ecotourism Association of Australia National Conference 1995, Brisbane: Ecotourism Association of Australia, 85–91.

Lindberg, K. (1998) 'Economic aspects of ecotourism', in K. Lindberg, M. Epler Wood and D. Engeldrum (eds), *Ecotourism: A Guide for Planners and Managers*, Vol. 2, Vermont: The Ecotourism Society, 87–117.

Lindberg, K. and Enriquez, J. (1994) *An Analysis of Ecotourism's Economic Contribution to Conservation and Development in Belize*, Vol. 2, Washington, DC: World Wildlife Fund.

Lindberg, K., Enriquez, J. and Sproule, K. (1996) 'Ecotourism questioned: case studies from Belize', *Annals of Tourism Research*, **23** (3): 543–62.

Lindberg, K., Epler Wood, M. and Engeldrum, D. (eds) (1998a) *Ecotourism: A Guide for Planners and Managers*, Vol. 2, Vermont: The Ecotourism Society.

Lindberg, K., Furze, B., Staff, M. and Black, R. (1998b) *Ecotourism in the Asia–Pacific Region: Issues and Outlook*, Vermont: The Ecotourism Society.

Lindberg, K. and Hawkins, D. (eds) (1993) *Ecotourism: A Guide for Planners and Managers*, Vol. 1, Vermont: The Ecotourism Society.

Lindberg, K. and McKercher, B. (1997) 'Ecotourism: a critical overview', *Pacific Tourism Review*, **1** (1): 65–79.

Lindsay, J.J. (1980) 'Compatibility planning for different types of outdoor recreation and natural resources', in D.E. Hawkins, E.L. Shafer and J.M. Rovelstad (eds), *Tourism Planning and Development Issues*, Washington, DC: George Washington University, 139–47.

Lipman, G. (1998) 'Making the net work', *World Travel and Tourism Development*, Issue 4: 138–41.

Loverseed, H. (1997) 'The adventure travel industry in North America', *Travel and Tourism Analyst*, **6**: 87–104.

Lucas, P.H.C. (1992) *Protected Landscapes: A Guide for Policy-Makers and Planners*. The IVth World Congress on National Parks and Protected Areas, Caracas, Venezuela, IUCN–The World Conservation Union. London: Chapman and Hall.

Lucas, R. (1964) 'Wilderness perception and *use*: the example of the Boundary Waters Canoe Area', *Natural Resources Journal*, **3** (1): 394–411.

Lucas, R.C. (1990) 'Wilderness use and users: trends and projections in wilderness recreation management: an overview', in J.C. Hendee, G.H. Stankey and R.C. Lucas (eds), *Wilderness Management*, Golden: North American Press.

Lumsden, L. (1997) *Tourism Marketing*, London: ITBP.

Lumsden, L. and Swift, J. (1998) 'Ecotourism at a crossroads: the case of Costa Rica', *Journal of Sustainable Tourism*, **6** (2): 155–72.

Lundberg, D. (1974) 'Caribbean tourism: social and racial tensions', *Cornell Hotel and Restaurant Administration Quarterly*, **15** (1): 82–7.

Lusigi, W. (1981) 'New approaches to wildlife conservation in Kenya', *Ambio*, **10** (2–3): 87–92.

Luzar, E., Diagne, A., Gan, C. and Henning, B. (1995) 'Evaluating nature-based tourism using the new environmental paradigm', *Journal of Agricultural and Applied Economics*, **27** (2): 544–55.

Luzar, E., Diagne, A., Gan, C. and Henning, B. (1998) 'Profiling the nature-based tourist: a multinomial logit approach', *Journal of Travel Research*, **37** (1): 48–55.

McArthur, S. (1997) 'Introducing the national ecotourism accreditation programme', *Australian Parks and Recreation*, **33** (2): 30–4.

McArthur, S. (1998) 'Introducing the undercapitalized world of interpretation', in K. Lindberg *et al.* (eds), *Ecotourism: A Guide for Planners and Managers*, Vol. 2. Vermont: The Ecotourism Society, 63–85.

McArthur, S. and Weir, B. (eds) (1998a) *Ecotourism Through to the Year 2000*, Proceedings of the Ecotourism Association of Australia National Conference 1997, Port Stephens, New South Wales. Brisbane: The Ecotourism Association of Australia.

McArthur, S. and Weir, B. (eds) (1998b) *Australia's Ecotourism Industry: A Snapshot in 1998*, Brisbane: The Ecotourism Association of Australia.

McCabe, C. (1998) 'True-blue green', *The Weekend Australian*, 14–15 February.

McCabe, J. (1979) 'The Iwasaki proposal – some background on a conservation resource', *Habitat Australia*, **7** (1): 16–17.

MacCannel, D. (1976) *The Tourist: A New Theory of the Leisure Class*, London: Macmillan.

McCool, S.F., Martin, S.R. and Yuan, M. (1990) *The 1989 Bear Trap Canyon Visitor Study*, School of Forestry Research Report No. 13, Missoula: Institute for Tourism and Recreation Research.

McDougall, G. and Munroe, H. (1994) 'Scaling and attitude measurement in travel and tourism research', in J.R.B. Ritchie and C.R. Goeldner (eds), *Travel, Tourism and Hospitality Research: A Handbook for Managers*, 2nd edn, New York: John Wiley & Sons, 115–30.

McFarlane, B. and Boxall, P. (1996) 'Participation in wildlife conservation by birdwatchers', *Human Dimensions of Wildlife*, **1** (3): 1–14.

McIntosh, I. (1999) 'Ecotourism: a boon for indigenous people?', *Cultural Survival Quarterly*, Summer: 3.

Mackay Consultants (1989) *Jobs and the Natural Heritage in Scotland*, A Report for Scottish Natural Heritage, Edinburgh: Scottish Natural Heritage.

MacKay, K. and McVetty, D. (1996) 'An ecotourism focus for destination marketing in the Canadian North', in *It's Showtime for Tourism: New Products, Markets and Technologies*, Proceedings of the 27th Travel and Tourism Research Association Conference, Las Vegas, 254–9.

McKean, P. (1976) 'Tourism, culture change and culture conservation in Bali', in D. Banks (ed.) *Changing Identities in Modern South East Asia and World Anthropology*, The Hague: Mouton, 237–45.

McKercher, B. (1993) 'The unrecognised threat to tourism: can tourism survive "sustainability"?', *Tourism Management*, **14**: 131–6.

McKercher, B. (1996) 'Perceived differences between "tourism" and "recreation" in parks', *Annals of Tourism Research*, **23** (3): 563–76.

McKercher, B. (1998) *The Business of Nature Based Tourism*, Melbourne: Hospitality Press.

McKercher, B. and Robbins, B. (1998) 'Business development issues affecting nature-based tourism operators in Australia', *Journal of Sustainable Tourism*, **6** (2): 173–88.

Mackie, I. (1986) 'Tourism and the environment: a natural partnership', in *Tourism and the Environment: Conflict or Harmony?*, Proceedings of a Symposium sponsored by the Canadian Society of Environmental Biologists, Alberta Chapter, Calgary, Canada, 18–19 March 1986, CSEB, Alberta, 17–22.

McLaren, D. (1998) *Rethinking Tourism and Ecotravel: The Paving of Paradise and What You Can Do to Stop It*, West Hartford, Connecticut: Kumarian Press.

McLennan, R., Inkson, K., Dakin, S., Dewe, P. and Elkin, G. (1987) *People and Enterprises: Human Behaviour in New Zealand Organisations*, Auckland: Holt, Rinehart and Winston.

McNeely, J. (1990a) 'How conservation strategies contribute to sustainable development', *Environmental Conservation*, **17** (1): 9–13.

McNeely, J.A. (1990b) 'The future of national parks', *Environment*, **32** (1): 16–20, 36–41.

McNeely, J. and Thorsell, J. (1989) 'Jungles, mountains and islands: how tourism can help conserve the natural heritage', *World Leisure and Recreation*, **31** (4): 29–39.

McSweeney, G. (1992) 'Observing nature in action in the Pacific', in J. Hay (ed.), *Ecotourism Business in the Pacific: Promoting A Sustainable Experience*, Conference Proceedings, Environmental Science Occasional Publication No. 8, Environmental Science, University of Auckland, New Zealand and the East-West Center, University of Hawaii, USA.

Maile, P. and Mendelsohn, R. (1993) 'Valuing ecotourism in Madagascar', *Journal of Environmental Management*, **38**: 213–18.

Makame, H. (1968) 'Tourism', *African Development*, **2** (3): 3–5.

Malisz, B. (1963) *Threshold Theory*, Warsaw: Biuletyn IUA, 16/7.

Malloy, D. and Fennell, D. (1998a) 'Codes of ethics and tourism: an exploratory content analysis', *Tourism Management*, **19** (5): 453–61.

Malloy, D. and Fennell, D. (1998b) 'Ecotourism and ethics: moral development and organizational cultures', *Journal of Travel Research*, **36** (4): 47–56.

Manyani, A. (1998) 'Optimal management of ecotourism', *Tourism Economics*, **4** (2): 147–69.

Mann, M. (2000) *The Community Tourism Guide: Exciting Holidays for Responsible Travellers*, London: Tourism Concern.

Manning, E.W. and Dougherty, T.D. (1995) 'Sustainable tourism: preserving the golden goose', *Cornell Hotel and Restaurant Administration Quarterly*, **36** (2): 29–42.

Marion, J.L. and Farrell, T.A. (1998) 'Managing ecotourism visitation in protected areas', in K. Lindberg *et al.* (eds), *Ecotourism: A Guide for Planners and Managers*, Vermont: The Ecotourism Society, 155–81.

Marsh, J.S. (1986a) 'National parks, tourism and development: Easter Island and the Galapagos Islands', in J.S. Marsh (ed.), *Canadian Studies of Parks, Recreation and Tourism in Foreign Lands*, Occasional Paper No. 11, Department of Geography, Trent University, Ontario, 215–40.

Marsh, J.S. (1986b) 'Wilderness tourism', in *Tourism and the Environment: Conflict or Harmony?* Proceedings of a Symposium sponsored by the Canadian Society of Environmental Biologists, Alberta Chapter, Calgary, 18–19 March 1986, Alberta Chapter, Alberta: CSEB, 47–60.

Marsh, J.S. (ed.) (1986c) *Canadian Studies of Parks, Recreation and Tourism in Foreign Lands*, Proceedings of a special session of the Canadian Association of Geographers Working Group on Parks, Recreation and Tourism at the Annual Meeting of the Canadian Association of Geographers, Calgary, 19–22 June, Occasional Paper No. 11, Department of Geography, Trent University, Ontario.

Marshall, D. (1998) 'A profile of the region's ecotourism operators – Shortland Wetlands Centre?', in S. McArthur and B. Weir (eds), *Ecotourism Through to the Year 2000*, Proceedings of the Ecotourism Association of Australia National Conference 1997, Port Stephens, New South Wales. Brisbane: The Ecotourism Association of Australia, 7–8.

Mason, P. (1994) 'A visitor code for the Arctic', *Tourism Management*, **15** (2): 93–7.

Mason, P. and Leberman, S. (1998) 'Managing mountain biking in the Manawatu region of New Zealand', in J. Kandampully (ed.), *Advances in Research, New Zealand Tourism and Hospitality Research Conference 1998, Part II*, 1–4 December 1998, Akaroa, New Zealand. Lincoln University: Canterbury, New Zealand.

Mason, P. and Mowforth, M. (1995) *Codes of Conduct in Tourism*, Department of Geographical Sciences Occasional Paper No. 1, Plymouth: University of Plymouth.

Mason, P., Johnston, M. and Twynam, D. (2000) 'The World Wide Fund for Nature Arctic Tourism Project', *Journal of Sustainable Tourism*, **8** (4): 305–23.

Mason, S. and Moore, S. (1998) 'Using the Sorensen network to assess the potential effects of ecotourism on two Australian marine environments', *Journal of Sustainable Tourism*, **6** (2): 143–54.

Master, D. (1998) *Marine Wildlife Tourism: Developing a Quality Approach in the Highlands and Islands*, A report for the Tourism and Environment Initiative and Scottish Natural Heritage, Inverness.

Mathieson, A. and Wall, G. (1982) *Tourism: Economic, Physical and Social Impacts*, Harlow: Longman.

Mehta, H. (1998) 'Here be ecolodges!', *The Ecotourism Society Newsletter*, Second Quarter: 1–3.

Menkhaus, S. and Lober, D. (1996) 'International ecotourism and the valuation of tropical rainforests in Costa Rica', *Journal of Environmental Management*, **47** (1): 1–10.

Middleton, V.T.C. (1988) *Marketing in Travel and Tourism*, London: Heinemann.

Middleton, V.T.C. and Hawkins, R. (1998) *Sustainable Tourism – A Marketing Perspective*, Oxford: Butterworth-Heinemann.

Mieczkowski, Z. (1995) *Environmental Issues of Tourism and Recreation*, Lanham: University Press of America.

Mill, R.C. and Morrison, A.M. (1985) *The Tourism System: An Introductory Text*, New Jersey: Prentice Hall.

Millar, S. (1989) 'Heritage management for heritage tourism', *Tourism Management*, **10** (1): 9–14.

Miller, G. Jr (1994) *Living in the Environment: Principles, Connections, and Solutions*, 8th edn, Belmont, Calif.: Wadsworth Publishing Company.

Miller, K. (1978) *Planning National Parks for Ecodevelopment: Methods and Cases from Latin America*, Ann Arbor, Mich.: University of Michigan, Centre for Strategic Wildland Management Studies.

Miller, M.L. (1987) 'Tourism in Washington's coastal zone', *Annals of Tourism Research*, **14** (1): 58–70.

Miller, M.L. and Auyong, J. (1991) 'Coastal zone tourism: a potent force affecting environment and society', *Marine Policy*, March: 75–99.

Miller, M.L. and Ditton, R.B. (1986) 'Travel, tourism and marine affairs', *Coastal Zone Management Journal*, **14** (12): 1–20.

Millman, R. (1989) 'Pleasure seeking v. the "greening" of world tourism', *Tourism Management*, **10** (4): 275–8.

Milne, S. (1992a) 'Tourism and economic development in South Pacific island microstates', *Annals of Tourism Research*, **19** (1): 191–212.

Milne, S. (1992b) 'Tourism development in Niue', *Annals of Tourism Research*, **19** (3): 565–9.

Ministry of Commerce (1996) *Safety Management in the Adventure Tourism Industry: Voluntary and Regulatory Approaches*, Wellington: Ministry of Commerce.

Mishan, E. (1969) *The Costs of Economic Growth*, Harmondsworth: Penguin.

Mitchell, B. (1979) *Geography and Resource Analysis*, New York: Longman.

Mitchell, L.S. and Murphy, P.E. (1991) 'Geography and tourism', *Annals of Tourism Research*, **18** (1): 51–70.

Mlinaric, I. (1985) 'Tourism and the environment: a case for Mediterranean cooperation', *International Journal of Environmental Studies*, **25** (4): 239–45.

Morin, S.L. (1995) 'Defining indicators and standards for recreation impacts in Nuyts wilderness area in Walpole–Nornalup National Park, Western Australia', Master of Science thesis, School of Biological and Environmental Sciences, Murdoch University, Perth.

Morin, S.L., Moore, S.A. and Schmidt, W. (1997) 'Defining indicators and standards for recreation impacts in Nuyts Wilderness, Walpole-Nornalup National Park, Western Australia', *CALM Science*, **2** (3): 247–66.

Morrison, A., Hsieh, S. and Wang, C.Y. (1992) 'Certification in the travel and tourism industry: the North American experience', *The Journal of Tourism Studies*, **3** (2): 32–40.

Morrison, D. (1995) *Wildlife Tourism in the Minch: Distribution, Impact and Development Opportunities*, A report for the Minch Project partnership, Stornaway.

Motavalli, J. (1998) 'Conservations: Paul and Anne Erlich', *E: The Environmental Magazine*, November–December 1996.

Mountfort, G. (1974) 'The need for partnership: tourism and conservation', *Development Forum*, April: 6–7.

Mountfort, G. (1975) 'Tourism and conservation', *Wildlife*, **17**: 30–3.

Mowforth, M. (1993) *Ecotourism: Terminology and Definitions*, Occasional Paper Series, Plymouth: Department of Geographical Sciences, University of Plymouth.

Mowforth, M. and Munt, I. (1998) *Tourism and Sustainability: New Tourism in the Third World*, London: Routledge.

Muhlhausler, P. and Peace, A. (2000) 'Mind your language: ecolinguists as a resource for ecotourism', in S. McArthur and R.K. Dowling (eds), *Australia – the World's Natural Theme Park*, Proceedings of the Ecotourism Association of Australia 7th National Conference, Kingfisher Bay Resort and Village, Queensland, 14–17 October 1999. Canberra: Bureau of Tourism Research, 138–43. <www.btr.gov.au/conf.proc/ecotourism>

Munt, I. (1994) 'Eco tourism or ego-tourism?', *Race and Class*, **36**: 1.

Muqbil, I. (1994) 'Lessons from the Lisu', *PATA Travel News*, March: 12–15.

Murphy, K. (1997) 'The Ecotourism Society', *Annals of Tourism Research*, **24** (2): 483–4.

Murphy, P. (1983) 'Tourism as a community industry: an ecological model of tourism development', *Tourism Management*, **4** (3): 180–93.

Murphy, P. (1985) *Tourism: A Community Approach*, London: Routledge.

Murphy, P. (1986a) 'Tourism as an agent for landscape conservation: an assessment', *The Science of the Total Environment*, **55**: 387–95.

Murphy, P. (1986b) 'Conservation and tourism: a business partnership', in I.B. Mackie (ed.), *Tourism and the Environment: Conflict or Harmony?* Proceedings of a Symposium sponsored by the Canadian Society of Environmental Biologists, Alberta Chapter, Calgary, 18–19 March 1986, CSEB, Alberta, 117–27.

Murphy P. (1988) 'Community driven tourism planning', *Tourism Management*, **9** (2): 96–104.

Myers, N. (1972) 'National parks in savannah Africa', *Science*, **178**: 1255–63.

Myers, N. (1973a) 'The people crunch comes to Africa', *Natural History*, **82**: 10–15.

Myers, N. (1973b) 'Impending crisis for Tanzanian wildlife', *National Parks and Conservation Magazine*, **47** (8): 18–23.

Neale, G. (1998) *The Green Travel Guide*, London: Earthscan Publications.

Nelson, J.G. (1974) 'The impact of technology on Banff National Park', in *Impact of Technology on Environment: Some Global Examples*, Studies in Land Use History and Landscape Change No. 6, London, Ontario: University of Western Ontario.

Nelson, J.G. (1988) 'National parks and protected areas, national conservation strategies and sustainable development', *Geoforum*, **18** (3): 291–319.

Nelson, J. (1994) 'The spread of ecotourism: some planning implications', *Environmental Conservation*, **21** (3): 248–55.

Nelson, J. (2000) 'Tourism and national parks in North America: an overview'. Tourism and national parks: issues and implications. In R. Butler and S. Boyd (eds), *Tourism and National Parks*, Chichester: John Wiley & Sons, 303–21.

*New Wave Magazine* (1998a) 'Coco Beach Hotel, Mauritius becomes environmentally friendly', *New Wave Magazine*, December, No. 8: 21.

*New Wave Magazine* (1998b) 'Protocol of agreement for Southern African tourism', *New Wave Magazine*, December, No. 8: 16.

New Zealand Tourism Board (1993) *New Zealand International Visitor Survey 1992/3*, Wellington: New Zealand Tourism Board.

Newsome, D., Moore, S.A. and Dowling, R.K. (2001) *Natural Area Tourism: Ecology, Impacts and Management*, Bristol: Channel View Publications.

Nicholson, M. (1970) *The Environmental Revolution*, London: Hodder and Stoughton.

Nicholson-Lord, D. (1997) 'The politics of travel: is tourism just colonialism in another guise?', *The Nation*, 6 October: 18.

Nixon, R. (1999) 'Green travel', *Hispanic*, **12** (5): 43–6.

Nolan, H.J. (1980) 'Tourist attractions and recreation resources providing for natural and human resources', in D.E. Hawkins, E.L. Shafer and J.M. Rovelstad (eds), *Tourism Planning and Development Issues*, Washington, DC: George Washington University, 272–82.

Nor, S.M. (1992) 'Eco-tourism: opportunities, challenges and responsibilities', Paper presented to the Asean Conference on Asean Heritage, Penang, Malaysia, 19 January.

Norris, R. (1992) 'Can ecotourism save natural areas?', *Parks*, January/February: 31–4.

Notzke, C. (1999) 'Indigenous tourism development in the Arctic', *Annals of Tourism Research*, **26** (1): 55–76.

OAS (1984) 'Reference guidelines for enhancing the positive socio-cultural and environmental impacts of tourism', Vol. 5, *Enhancing the Positive Impact of Tourism on the Built and Natural Environment*, Washington, DC: Organization of American States.

Obua, J. and Harding, D. (1996) 'Visitor characteristics and attitudes towards Kibale National Park, Uganda', *Tourism Management*, **17** (7): 495–505.

Obua, J. and Harding, D. (1997) 'Environmental impact of ecotourism in Kibale national park, Uganda', *Journal of Sustainable Tourism*, **5** (3): 213–23.

OECD (1980) *The Impact of Tourism on the Environment*, Paris: Organization for Economic Co-operation and Development.

Office of National Tourism (1996) *Projecting Success: Visitor Management for Sustainable Tourism Growth*, Canberra: Department of Industry, Science and Tourism.

Olokesusi, F. (1990) 'Assessment of the Yankari Game Reserve, Nigeria: problems and prospects', *Tourism Management*, **11** (2): 153–63.

Oppermann, M. (ed.) (1997) *Pacific Rim Tourism*, Wallingford: CAB International.

Orams, M. (1995) 'Towards a more desirable form of ecotourism', *Tourism Management*, **16** (1): 3–8.

Orams, M.B. (1996) 'A conceptual model of tourist-wildlife interaction: the case for education as a management strategy', *Australian Geographer*, **27** (1): 39–51.

Orams, M. (1997) 'Historical accounts of human–dolphin interaction and recent developments in wild-dolphin based tourism in Australasia', *Tourism Management*, **5**: 317–26.

Orams, M. (1999) *Marine Tourism: Development, Impacts and Management*, London: Routledge.

Orams, M. (2000) 'Towards a more desirable form of ecotourism', in C. Ryan and S.J. Page (eds), *Tourism Management: Towards the New Millennium*, Oxford: Pergamon, 315–23.

Orams, M. and Neil, D. (1998) *Dolphin and Whale Research at Tangalooma 1989–1998*, Centre for Tourism Research, Massey University at Albany, Auckland.

O'Reilly, P., Weir, B. and Plumridge, T. (1998) 'How should the ecotourism industry contribute to conservation?', in S. McArthur and B. Weir (eds), *Ecotourism Through to the Year 2000*, Proceedings of the Ecotourism Association of Australia National Conference 1997, Port Stephens, New South Wales. Brisbane: The Ecotourism Association of Australia, 23.

O'Riordan, T. (2000) *Environmental Science for Environmental Management*, Harlow: Prentice Hall.

Ouma, J. (1970) *Evolution of Tourism in East Africa*, Nairobi: East African Literature Bureau.

Ovington, J., Groves, K., Stevens, P. and Tanton, M. (1973) *A Study of the Impact of Tourism at Ayers Rock–Mt Olga National Park*, Environmental Consultant Group, Department of Forestry, Australian National University, AGPS, Canberra.

Page, S.J. (1992) 'Perspectives on the environmental impact of the Channel Tunnel on tourism', in C.P. Cooper and A. Lockwood (eds), *Progress in Tourism, Recreation and Hospitality Management*, Vol. 4, London: Belhaven, 82–102.

Page, S.J. (1994) *Transport for Tourism*, London: Routledge.

Page, S.J. (1995) *Urban Tourism*. London: Routledge.

Page, S.J. (1997) *The Cost of Accidents in the Adventure Tourism Industry*, Consultants report for the Tourism Policy Group, Wellington: Ministry of Commerce.

Page, S.J. (1999) *Transport and Tourism*, Harlow: Addison-Wesley Longman.

Page, S.J. (2000) 'Tourism in natural environments', in C. Ryan and S.J. Page (eds), *Tourism Management: Towards the New Millennium*, Oxford: Pergamon, 273–8.

Page, S.J., Brunt, P., Busby, G. and Connell, J. (2001) *Tourism: A Modern Synthesis*. London: Thomson Learning.

Page, S.J. and Getz, D. (eds) (1997) *The Business of Rural Tourism: International Perspectives*, London: ITBP.

Page, S.J. and Meyer, D. (1996) 'Tourist accidents: an exploratory analysis', *Annals of Tourism Research*, **23**: 666–90.

Page, S.J. and Meyer, D. (1997) 'Injuries and accidents among international tourists in Australasia', in S. Clift and P. Grabowski (eds), *Health and Tourism*, Cassell: London: 61–80.

Page, S.J. and Thorn, K. (1997) 'Towards sustainable tourism planning in New Zealand: public sector planning responses', *Journal of Sustainable Tourism*, **5**: 59–77.

Page, S.J., Forer, P. and Lawton, G. (1999) 'Small business development and tourism: terra incognita', *Tourism Management*, **20** (4): 435–60.

Palacio, V. and McCool, S. (1997) 'Identifying ecotourists in Belize through benefit segmentation: a preliminary analysis', *Journal of Sustainable Tourism*, **5** (3): 234–43.

Parkes, J. (1999) 'Island in danger of being loved to death', *The Australian*, 12 May.

Parks Canada (1983) *Parks Canada Policy*, Ottawa: Parks Canada.

Parliamentary Commissioner for the Environment (1997) *Management of the Environmental Effects Associated with the Tourism Sector, Summary*, Wellington: Office of the Parliamentary Commissioner for the Environment, 8 pp.

Parsons, D.J. and MacLeod, S.A. (1980) 'Measuring impacts of wilderness use', *Parks*, **5** (3): 8–12.

Paul, B.K. and Rimmawi, H.S. (1992) 'Tourism in Saudi Arabia: Asir National Park', *Annals of Tourism Research*, **19** (3): 501–15.

Pawson, I., Stanford, D. and Adams, V. (1984) 'Effects of modernization on the Khumbu region of Nepal: changes in population structure, 1970–82', *Mountain Research and Development*, **4** (1): 73–81.

Payne, D. and Dimanche, F. (1996) 'Towards a code of conduct of the tourism industry: an ethics model', *Journal of Business Ethics*, **15**: 997–1007.

Payne, R. and Graham, R. (1993) 'Visitor planning and management in parks and protected areas', in P. Dearden and R. Rollins (eds), *Parks and Protected Areas in Canada*, Toronto: Oxford University Press.

Pearce, D.G. (1978) 'A case study of Queenstown', in *Tourism and the Environment*, New Zealand: Department of Lands and Survey, 23–45.

Pearce, D.G. (1980) *Tourism in the South Pacific: the Contribution of Research to Development and Planning*, Proceedings of UNESCO Tourism Workshop, Rarotonga, 10–13 June, NZ Man and Biosphere Report No. 6, NZ National Commission for UNESCO/Department of Geography, University of Canterbury, Christchurch.

Pearce, D.G. (1985) 'Tourism and environmental research: a review', *International Journal of Environmental Studies*, **25** (4): 247–55.

Pearce, D.G. (1988) 'The spatial structure of coastal tourism: a behavioural approach', *Tourism Recreation Research*, **13** (2): 11–14.

Pearce, D.G. (1989) *Tourist Development*, 2nd edn, London: Longman.

Pearce, D.G. (1995) *Tourism Today: A Geographical Analysis*, 2nd edn, London: Longman.

Pearce, P. (1982) *The Social Psychology of Tourist Behaviour*, Oxford: Pergamon.

Pearce, P. (1990) 'Farm tourism in New Zealand: a social situation analysis', *Annals of Tourism Research*, **17** (3): 337–52.

Pearce, P. (1993) 'The fundamentals of tourist motivation', in D. Pearce and R. Butler (eds), *Tourism Research: Critique and Challenges*, London: Routledge, 113–34.

Perez, L. (1975) 'Tourism in the West Indies', *Journal of Communications*, **25**: 136–43.

Peterson, G.L. (1974) 'Evaluating the quality of the wilderness environment: congruence between perceptions and aspirations', *Environment and Behaviour*, **6**: 169–93.

Phillips, A. (1985) 'Opening address', in *Tourism, Recreation and Conservation in National Parks and Equivalent Reserves*, a European Heritage Landscapes Conference, Peak National Park Centre, Peak Park Joint Planning Board, Derbyshire, 9–14.

Philpott, N. (1998) 'Jersey – green for go!', *World Travel and Tourism Development*, Issue 4: 144–7.

Pigram, J.J. (1980) 'Environmental implications of tourism development', *Annals of Tourism Research*, **7**: 554–83.

Pigram, J.J. (1983) *Outdoor Recreation and Resource Management*, Beckenham: Croom Helm.

Pigram, J.J. (1985) *Outdoor Recreation and Resource Management*, 2nd edn, London: Croom Helm.

Pigram, J.J. (1986) 'Regional resource management: a case for development', paper presented to the Conference on Planning and Development on the North Coast, Valla Park, New South Wales, August 1986.

Pigram, J.J. (1990) 'Sustainable tourism: policy considerations', *Journal of Tourism Studies*, **1** (2): 2–9.

Pigram, J. and Jenkins, J. (1999) *Outdoor Recreation Management*, London: Routledge.

Pimbert, M. and Pretty, J. (1995) 'Parks, people and professionals: putting "participation" into protected area management', Discussion Paper No. 57, Geneva, Switzerland: United Nations Research Institute for Social Development.

Pizam, A. (1978) 'Tourism's impacts: the social costs to the destination community as perceived by its residents', *Journal of Travel Research*, **16** (4): 8–12.

Place, S. (1991) 'Nature tourism and rural development in Tortuguero', *Annals of Tourism Research*, **18** (2): 186–201.

Place, S. (1995) 'Ecotourism for sustainable development: oxymoron or plausible strategy', *GeoJournal*, **35** (2): 161–73.

Place, S.E. (1998) 'How sustainable is ecotourism in Costa Rica?' in C.M. Hall and A.A. Lew (eds), *Sustainable Tourism Development: Geographical Perspectives*, Harlow: Addison-Wesley Longman, 107–18.

Plimmer, N. (n.d.) 'Antarctic tourism: issues and outlook', Paper No. 10, Pacific Asia Travel Association.

Plog, S.C. (1973) 'Why destination areas rise and fall in popularity', *Cornell Hotel and Restaurant Administration Quarterly*, November: 13–16.

Poh Kwee, T. (1995) 'A case for ecotourism development in Brunei Darussalam', *Malaysian Journal of Tropical Geography*, **26** (2): 143–9.

Pollock, N. (1971) 'Serengeti', *Geography*, **56** (2): 145–7.

Poon, A. (1989) 'Competitive strategies for a new tourism', in C.P. Cooper (ed.), *Progress in Tourism, Recreation and Hospitality Management*, Vol. 4, London: Belhaven, 91–102.

Poon, A. (1993) *Tourism, Technology and Competitive Strategies*, Wallingford: CAB International.

Potter, A.F. (1978) 'The methodology of impact analysis', *Town and Country Planning*, **46** (9): 400–4.

Potts, T. and Harrill, R. (1997) 'In search of a travel ecology paradigm', in *The Evolution of Tourism: Adapting to Change*, 28th Annual Conference Proceedings, Lexington, Kentucky: Travel and Tourism Research Association, 186–208.

Pretty, J. and Primbert, M. (1995) 'Trouble in the Garden of Eden', *The Guardian*, 13 May, Section D.

Prosser, G. (1986) 'The limits of acceptable change: an introduction to a framework for natural area planning', *Australian Parks and Recreation*, **22** (2): 5–10.

'Protocol of Agreement for Southern African Tourism' (1998) *New Wave Magazine*, December, No. 8: 16.

Prunier, E. and Sweeney, A. (1993) 'Case study. Tourism and the environment: the case of Zakynthos', *Tourism Management*, April: 137–41.

Reyes Rodriquez, J.A. (1980) 'Tourism development and natural resources conservation', in D.E. Hawkins, E.L. Shafer and J.M. Rovelstad (eds), *Tourism Planning and Development Issues*, Washington, DC: George Washington University, 73–85.

Reynolds, P. and Braithwaite, D. (2001) 'Towards a conceptual framework for wildlife tourism', *Tourism Management*, **22** (1): 31–42.

Richardson, J. (1993) *Ecotourism and Nature-Based Holidays*, Choice Books, Sydney: Simon & Schuster Australia.

Richins, H., Richardson, J. and Crabtree, A. (eds) (1996) *Ecotourism and Nature-Based Tourism: Taking the Next Steps*, Proceedings of the Ecotourism Association of Australia National Conference, Alice Springs, Northern Territory, 18–23 November 1995. Brisbane: Ecotourism Association of Australia.

Riley, R. and Turco, D. (1994) 'Ecotourism: where business and the environment meet', *Visions in Leisure and Business*, **13** (3): 14–28.

Robertson, R., Dawson, C., Kuentzel, W. and Selin, S. (1996) 'College and university curricula in ecotourism and nature-based tourism', *Journal of Natural Resources and Life Sciences Education*, **25** (2): 152–5.

Robinson, A.M. (1998) 'Changing business practices to capitalise on the marketing opportunity "E commerce"', Paper presented at the Ecotourism Association of Australia National Conference, Margaret River, Western Australia, 28–31 October 1998.

Rodriguez, A. (1999) 'Kapawi: a model of sustainable development in Ecuadorean Amazonia', *Cultural Survival Quarterly*, Summer: 43–4.

Rodriquez, F. (1978) 'Tourism and the environment: an interview by the World Travel Organization', *World Travel*, **143**: 49–51.

Rodriquez, S. (1987) 'The impact of the ski industry on the Rio Hondo watershed', *Annals of Tourism Research*, **14** (1): 88–103.

Rogers, C. (1981) 'Caribbean – coral reefs under threat', *New Scientist*, 5 November: 382–7.

Romeril, M. (1983) 'A balanced strategy for recreation, tourism and conservation: the case of Les Mielles, Jersey', *Tourism Management*, **4**: 126–8.

Romeril, M. (1984) 'Coastal tourism – the experience of Great Britain', *Industry and Environment*, **7** (1): 4–7.

Romeril, M. (1985a) 'Tourism and conservation in the Channel Islands'. *Tourism Management*, **6** (1): 43–9.

Romeril, M. (1985b) 'Tourism and the environment – towards a symbiotic relationship (introductory paper)', *International Journal of Environmental Studies*, **25** (4): 215–18.

Romeril, M. (1988) 'Coastal tourism and the Heritage Coast programme in England and Wales', *Tourism Recreation Research*, **13** (2): 15–19.

Romeril, M. (1989a) 'Tourism and the environment – accord or discord?', *Tourism Management*, **10** (3): 204–8.

Romeril, M. (1989b) 'Tourism – the environmental dimension', in C.P. Cooper (ed.), *Progress in Tourism, Recreation and Hospitality Management*, Vol. 1, London: Belhaven, 103–13.

Romsa, G. (1981) 'An overview of tourism and planning in the Federal Republic of Germany', *Annals of Tourism Research*, **8** (3): 333–56.

Rosier, J., Hill, G. and Kozlowski, J.M. (1986) 'Environmental limitations: a framework for development on Heron Island, Great Barrier Reef', *Journal of Environmental Management*, **23**: 59–73.

Ross, S. and Wall, G. (1999a) 'Evaluating ecotourism: the case of North Sulawesi, Indonesia', *Tourism Management*, **20** (6): 673–82.

Ross, S. and Wall, G. (1999b) 'Ecotourism: towards congruence between theory and practice', *Tourism Management*, **20** (2): 123–32.

Ross, W.A. (1987) 'Evaluating environmental impact statements', *Journal of Environmental Management*, **25**: 137–47.

Rothman, R.A. (1978) 'Residents and transients: community reaction to seasonal visitors', *Journal of Travel Research*, **16** (3): 8–13.

Ruschmann, D.M. (1992) 'Ecological tourism in Brazil', *Tourism Management*, **13** (1): 125–8.

Russell, D., Botterill, C. and Meredith, G. (1995) 'International ecolodge survey', in *The Ecolodge Sourcebook – for Planners and Managers*, Vermont: The Ecotourism Society.

Ryan, C. (1997) 'Rural tourism in New Zealand: rafting at River Valley Ventures in the Rangitikei', in S.J. Page and D. Getz (eds), *The Business of Rural Tourism: International Perspectives*, London: ITBP, 162–87.

Ryan, C. (1998) 'Saltwater crocodiles as tourist attractions', *Journal of Sustainable Tourism*, **6** (4): 314–27.

Ryan, C. (1999) 'Issues of sustainability in tourism', *Tourism Management*, **20** (2): 177.

Ryan, C. (2000) 'Selecting holidays: the purchase decision and its antecedents', in C. Ryan and S.J. Page (eds), *Tourism Management: Towards the New Millennium*, Oxford: Pergamon: 1–8.

Ryan, C., Hughes, K. and Chirgwin, S. (2000) 'The gaze, spectacle and ecotourism', *Annals of Tourism Research*, **27** (1): 148–63.

Ryan, C. and Montgomery, D. (1994) 'The attitudes of Bakewell residents to tourism and issues in community responsive tourism', *Tourism Management*, **15** (5): 358–69.

Ryel, R. and Grasse, T. (1991) 'Marketing ecotourism: attracting the elusive ecotourist', in T. Whelan (ed.), *Nature Tourism Managing for the Environment*, Washington, DC: Island Press, 164–86.

Rymer, T. (1992) 'Growth of US ecotourism and its future in the 1990s', *Hospitality Review*, **10** (1): 1–10.

Saenger, P. (1990) 'Environmental impacts of coastal tourism: an overview and guide to relevant literature', in I. Dutton and P. Saenger (eds), *Environmental Management of Tourism in Coastal Areas*, Proceedings of a Training Workshop held in Bogor and Bali, Indonesia, Vols 1 and 2, Workshop Reports and Papers, Southeast Asian Regional Centre for Tropical Biology, 18–45.

Salm, R. (1985) 'Coral reef and tourist carrying capacity: the Indian Ocean experience', *Industry and the Environment*, **9** (1): 11–13.

Schänzel, H.A. and McIntosh, A.J. (2000) 'An insight into the personal and emotive context of wildlife viewing at the Penguin Place, Otago Peninsula, New Zealand', *Journal of Sustainable Tourism*, **8** (1): 36–52.

Scheyvens, R. (1999) 'Ecotourism and the empowerment of local communities', *Tourism Management*, **20** (2): 245–9.

School of Travel Industry Management (1987) *The Impact of Tourism on the Commonwealth of the Northern Mariana Islands*, The School of Travel Industry Management, University of Hawaii at Manoa, Hawaii.

Schreyer, R. and Roggenbuck, J.W. (1978) 'The influence of experience expectations on crowding perceptions and social-psychological carrying capacity', *Leisure Sciences*, **1**: 373–94.

Scottish Development Department (1973) *Threshold Analysis Manual*, Edinburgh: HMSO.

Seaton, A. and Bennett, M. (eds) (1996) *Marketing Tourism Products*, London: ITBP.

Seibert, J.C. (1973) *Concepts of Marketing Management*, New York: Harper Row.

Selengut, S. (1996) 'Maho Bay, Harmony, Estate Concordia and the Concordia Eco-Tents', in H. Richins, J. Richardson and A. Crabtree (eds), *Ecotourism and Nature-Based Tourism: Taking the Next Steps*, Proceedings of the Ecotourism Association of Australia National Conference 1995, Brisbane: Ecotourism Association of Australia, 311–14.

Selin, S. (1994) 'Marketing protected areas for ecotourism: an oxymoron?', *Trends*, **31** (2): 19–22.

Seth, P. (1985) *Successful Tourism Management*, New Delhi: Sterling Publishers.

Shackleford, P. (1985) 'The World Tourism Organisation: thirty years of commitment to environmental protection', *International Journal of Environmental Studies*, **25** (4): 257–64.

Shackley, M. (1996) *Wildlife Tourism*, London: ITBP.

Shackley, M. (1998a) ' "Stingray City" – managing the impact of underwater tourism in the Cayman Islands', *Journal of Sustainable Tourism*, **6** (4): 328–38.

Shackley, M. (ed.) (1998b) *Visitor Management – Case Studies from World Heritage Sites*, Oxford: Butterworth-Heinemann.

Shafer, E.L. Jr, Hamilton, J.F. and Schmidt, E. (1969) 'Natural landscape preferences: a predictive model', *Journal of Leisure Research*, **1**: 1–9.

Shelby, B. and Heberlein, T.A. (1984) 'A conceptual framework for carrying capacity determination', *Leisure Sciences*, **6** (4): 433–51.

Shephard, K. and Royston-Airey, P. (2000) 'Exploring the role of part-time ecotourism guides in central southern England', *Journal of Sustainable Tourism*, **8** (4): 324–32.

Silverberg, K., Backman, S. and Backman, K. (1996) 'A preliminary investigation into the psychographics of nature-based travellers to the Southeastern United States', *Journal of Travel Research*, **35** (2): 19–28.

Simmons, I.G. (1981) *The Ecology of Natural Resources*, London: Edward Arnold.

Sinclair, M. and Stabler, M. (1997) *The Economics of Tourism*, London: Routledge.

Sindiga, I. (1999) 'Alternative tourism and sustainable development in Kenya', *Journal of Sustainable Tourism*, **7** (2): 108–27.

Sindiyo, P.M. and Pertet, F.N. (1984) 'Tourism and its impact on wildlife conservation in Kenya', *UNEP Industry and Environment Newsletter*, March: 14–19.

Singh, T. and Singh, S. (eds) (1999) *Tourism Development in Critical Environments*, New York: Cognizant Communication Corporation.

Singh, T.V. and Kaur, J. (eds) (1985a) *Integrated Mountain Development*, New Delhi: Himalayan Books.

Singh, T.V. and Kaur, J. (1985b) 'In search of holistic tourism in the Himalaya', in T.V. Singh and J. Kaur (eds), *Integrated Mountain Development*, New Delhi: Himalayan Books, 365–401.

Singh, T.V. and Kaur, J. (1988) 'Tourism in the mountains', *Tourism Recreation Research*, **13** (1): 3–5.

Sirakaya, E. and McLellan, R. (1998) 'Modelling tour operators' voluntary compliance with ecotourism principles: a behavioral approach', *Journal of Travel Research*, **36** (3): 42–55.

Sirakaya, E., Sasidharan, V. and Sönmez, S. (1999) 'Redefining ecotourism: the need for a supply-side view', *Journal of Travel Research*, **38** (2): 168–72.

Sirakaya, E. and Uysal, M. (1997) 'Can sanctions and rewards explain conformance behaviour of tour operators with ecotourism guidelines?', *Journal of Sustainable Tourism*, **5** (4): 322–32.

Slaughter, C.W., Racine, C.H., Walker, D.A., Johnson, L.A. and Abele, G. (1990) 'Use of off-road vehicles and migration of effects in Alaska permafrost environments: a review', *Environmental Management*, **14** (1): 63–72.

Slinger, V. (2000) 'Ecotourism in the last indigenous Caribbean community', *Annals of Tourism Research*, **27** (2): 520–3.

Smith, C. and Jenner, P. (1989) 'Tourism and the environment', *Travel and Tourism Analyst*, **5**: 68–86.

Smith, P.G.R., Nelson, J.G. and Theberge, J.B. (1986) *Environmentally Significant Areas, Conservation, and Land Use Management in the Northwest Territories: A Method and Case Study in the Western Arctic*, Technical Paper No. 1, Heritage Resources Centre, University of Waterloo, Waterloo.

Smith, V. (ed.) (1977) *Hosts and Guests: The Anthropology of Tourism*, Philadelphia: University of Pennsylvania Press.

Smith, V. (ed.) (1989) *Hosts and Guests: The Anthropology of Tourism*, 2nd edn, Philadelphia: University of Pennsylvania Press.

Smith, V. (1994) 'An ecotourism case study in sub-Antarctic islands', *Annals of Tourism Research*, **21** (2): 344–54.

Smith, V.L. and Eadington W.R. (eds) (1992) *Tourism Alternatives: Potential and Problems in the Development of Tourism*, Philadelphia: Pennsylvania University Press.

Sofield, T. (2000) 'Rethinking and reconceptualising social and cultural issues in South East and South Asian tourism', in C.M. Hall and S.J. Page (eds), *Tourism in South and South East Asia: Issues and Cases*, Oxford: Butterworth-Heinemann, 45–57.

Sorensen, R. (1991) 'Overseas Adventure Travel Inc., Case Study 9-391-068', Boston: Harvard University, Harvard Business School.

Spanoudis, C. (1982) 'Trends in tourism and development', *Tourism Management*, **3** (4): 314–18.

*Spiegel, Der* (1972) 'In zelm Jahren sind das hier Slums', *Der Spiegel*, 3 July, **26** (28): 56–64.

Sproule, K. and Suhandi, A. (1998) 'Guidelines for community-based ecotourism programs: lessons from Indonesia', in K. Lindberg, M. Epler Wood and D. Engeldrum (eds), *Ecotourism: A Guide for Planners and Managers*, Vol. 2, Vermont: The Ecotourism Society, 215–35.

Stabler, M.J. (ed.) (1997) *Tourism and Sustainability – Principles to Practice*, Wallingford: CAB International.

Stankey, G.H. (1978) 'Wilderness carrying capacity', in J.C. Hendee, G.H. Stankey and R.C. Lucas (eds), *Wilderness Management*, Miscellaneous Publication No. 1365, Washington, DC: USDA Forest Service.

Stankey, G.H. (1988) 'Issues and approaches in the management of recreational use in natural areas', *Recreation Australia*, **8** (3): 1–6.

Stankey, G.H. (1989) *Conservation, Recreation and Tourism*. Paper prepared for the Institute of Australian Geographers 23rd Conference, The University of Adelaide, 13–16 February.

Stankey, G.H. and Lime, D.W. (1973) *Recreational Carrying Capacity: An Annotated Bibliography*, General Technical Report INT-3, Ogden, Utah: US Department of Agriculture, Forest Service, Intermountain Forest and Range Experiment Station.

Stankey, G., Cole, D., Lucas, R., Petersen, M. and Frissell, S. (1984) *The Limits of Acceptable Change (LAC) System for Wilderness Planning*, General Technical Report INT-176, Ogden, Utah: US Forest Service.

Steele, P. (1995) 'Ecotourism: an economic analysis', *Journal of Sustainable Tourism*, **3** (1): 29–44.

Stevens, B. (1994) 'An analysis of corporate ethical code studies: "where do we go from here?"', *Journal of Business Ethics*, **13**: 63–9.

Stewart, W. (1994) 'Disentangling ecotourism', *Annals of Tourism Research*, **21** (4): 840–1.

Streiffert, K. (n.d.) 'Birding and ecotourism: the lure of birding dollars is creating a strong incentive to save bird-rich habitats worldwide', *Living Bird*, 28–32.

Stronza, A. (1999) 'Learning both ways: lessons from a corporate and community ecotourism collaboration', *Cultural Survival Quarterly*, Summer: 36–9.

Stynes, D.J. (1977) *Recreational Carrying Capacity and the Management of Dynamic Systems*. Paper presented to the National Recreation and Park Association Congress, Las Vegas, 2–6 October.

Stynes, D.J. (1979) *A Simulation Approach to the Determination of Recreation Carrying Capacity*. Proceedings of the National Workshop on Computers in Recreation and Parks, National Recreation and Parks Association, St Louis.

Subedi, B. and Devlin, P. (1998) 'Wildlife viewing tourism: impacts of elephant safaris in the Royal Chitwan National Park, Nepal' in J. Kandampully (ed.), *Advances in Research, New Zealand Tourism and Hospitality Research Conference 1998, Part I*, 1–4 December 1998, Akaroa, New Zealand. Canterbury, New Zealand: Lincoln University.

Swarbrooke, J. (1999) *Sustainable Tourism Management*, Wallingford: CAB International.

Tangi, M. (1977) 'Tourism and the environment', *Ambio*, **6** (6): 336–41.

TCA (1998) *Being Green Keeps You Out of the Red – An Easy Guide to Environmental Action for Accommodation Providers and Tourist Attractions*, Tourism Council Australia, Sydney.

TDC-SGV (1976) *National Plan on Tourism Development, Final Report*, Bangkok: Tourist Organisation of Thailand.

Telfer, D. and Wall, G. (1996) 'Linkages between tourism and food production', *Annals of Tourism Research*, **23** (3): 635–53.

Tershy, B., Bourillon, L., Metzler, L. and Barnes, J. (1999) 'A survey of ecotourism on islands in northwestern Mexico', *Environmental Conservation*, **26** (3): 212–17.

*The Australian* (1998) 'Olympics try sunny side up', *The Weekend Australian*, 6–7 June.

The Canadian Tourist Commission (1995) *Adventure Travel in Canada: An Overview of Product, Market and Business Potential*, Ottawa: Tourism Canada.

The Ecotourism Society (1993) *Ecotourism Guidelines: For Nature Tour Operators*, Vermont: The Ecotourism Society.

The Ecotourism Society (1995) *Ecotourism: An Annotated Bibliography for Planners and Managers*, Vermont: The Ecotourism Society.

The Ecotourism Society (1997) *Membership Directory*, Vermont: The Ecotourism Society.

The Ecotourism Society (1998) *Ecotourism Statistical Fact Sheet*, Vermont: The Ecotourism Society.

The Ecotourism Society (2000) *The Business of Ecolodges*, Vermont: The International Ecotourism Society.

The Ecotourism Society (n.d.) *A Collection of Ecotourism Guidelines*, Vermont: The Ecotourism Society.

Thomas, T. (1994) 'Ecotourism in Antarctica. The role of the naturalist-guide in presenting places of natural interest', *Journal of Sustainable Tourism*, **2** (4): 204–9.

Thomason, P., Crompton, L. and van Kamp, B. (1979) 'A study of the attitudes of impacted groups within a host community toward prolonged staying tourist visitors', *Journal of Travel Research*, **18** (3): 2–7.

Thomlinson, E. and Getz, D. (1996) 'The question of scale in ecotourism: case study of two small ecotour operators in the Mundo Maya region of Central America', *Journal of Sustainable Tourism*, **4** (4): 183–8.

Tiansheng, P. (1992) 'The ecological environment of Mt. Huangshan Scenic Area and its protection strategy', *UNEP Industry and Environment*, **15** (3–4): 28–30.

Tilden, J. (1977) *Interpreting Our Heritage*, 3rd edn, Chapel Hill, NC: University of North Carolina Press.

Timothy, D. and White, K. (1999) 'Community-based ecotourism development on the periphery of Belize', *Current Issues in Tourism*, **2** (2/3): 226–42.

Toplis, S. (1994) 'The environmental tourist', *Habitat Australia*, **22** (3): 16–19.

Tourism Queensland (1997) *Queensland Ecotourism Plan*, Brisbane: Tourism Queensland, Small Business and Industry.

Tourism Queensland (1999) 'Olympic spotlight on environmental tourism', *Ecotrends*, September: 7.

Travis, A.S. (1980) 'Tourism development and regional planning in east Mediterranean countries', *International Journal of Tourism Management*, **1** (4): 207–18.

Travis, A. (1982) 'Managing the environment and cultural impacts of tourism and leisure development', *Tourism Management*, **3** (4): 256–62.

Tribe, J. (1995) *The Economics of Leisure and Tourism*, Oxford: Butterworth-Heinemann.

Turnbull, R.G.H. (1990) 'Coastal planning in Scotland: a framework for tourism', in *Environment, Tourism and Development: An Agenda for Action*, Proceedings of a Workshop to Consider Strategies for Sustainable Tourism Development, Scotland: Centre for Environmental Management and Planning, 1–10.

Turner, J. (1997) 'The policy process,' in B. Axford, G. Browning, R. Huggins, B. Rosamond and J. Turner, *Politics: An Introduction*, London: Routledge, 409–39.

Turner, L. and Ash, J. (1975) *The Golden Hordes: International Tourism and the Pleasure Periphery*, London: Constable.

Turton, M. (1999) 'Greenies guard Greece', *The West Australian – Big Weekend*, 7 August.

Tyler, D. and Dangerfield, J.M. (1999) 'Ecosystem tourism: a resource-based philosophy for ecotourism', *Journal of Sustainable Tourism*, **7** (2): 146–58.

Ulack, R. (1993) 'The impact of tourism in Fiji: a comparison of two villages', *The American Geographical Society*, **43** (2), 1–7.

UNDP and WTO (1986) *Bhutan Tourism Development Master Plan*, Madrid: United Nations Development Programme and the World Tourism Organisation.

UNEP (1995) *Environmental Codes of Conduct for Tourism*, United Nations Environmental Program, Technical Report No. 29, Paris: UNEP.

UNEP and WTO (1982) *Joint Declaration Between the United Nations Environmental Programme and the World Tourism Organisation*, Madrid: WTO.

UNEP and WTO (1983) *Workshop on the Environmental Aspects of Tourism*, Madrid: WTO.

UNESCO (1976) 'The effects of tourism on socio-cultural values', *Annals of Tourism Research*, November/December: 74–105.

United Nations (1977) *Threshold Analysis Handbook*, Document No. ST/ESA/64, New York: United Nations Department of Economic and Social Affairs.

United Nations (1998) 'Declaring the year 2002 as the International Year of Ecotourism', Resolution 1998/40, 46th Plenary Meeting, 30 July 1998, New York: United Nations General Assembly.

United States Congress Office of Technology Assessment (1993) 'Science and technology issues in coastal ecotourism', *Tourism Management*, **14** (4): 307–15.

United States Travel Data Center (1991) *Discover America: Tourism and the Environment: A Guide to Challenges and Opportunities for Travel Industry Business*, Washington: Travel Industry Association of America.

University of Hawaii (1987) *The Impact of Tourism on the Commonwealth of the Northern Mariana Islands*. School of Travel Industry Management, University of Hawaii at Manoa, Hawaii, USA.

Urry, J. (1990) *The Tourist Gaze: Leisure and Travel in Contemporary Societies*, London: Sage.

US Department of the Interior (1993) *Guiding Principles of Sustainable Design*, Denver, Colorado: Denver Service Center.

Valentine, P. (1992) 'Review. Nature-based tourism', in B. Weiler and C.M. Hall (eds), *Special Interest Tourism*, London: Belhaven, 105–28.

Valentine, P. (1993) 'Ecotourism and nature conservation: a definition with some recent developments in Micronesia', *Tourism Management*, **14** (2): 107–16.

van Oosterzee, P. (1984) 'The recreation opportunity spectrum: its use and misuse', *Australian Geographer*, **16** (2): 97–104.

van Riet, W.F. and Cooks, J. (1990) 'An ecological planning model', *Environmental Management*, **14** (3): 339–48.

Veal, A.J. (1992) *Research Methods for Leisure and Tourism: A Practical Guide*, London: Longman.

Victurine, R. (2000) 'Building tourism excellence at the community level: capacity building for community-based entrepreneurs in Uganda', *Journal of Travel Research*, **38** (3): 221–9.

Wagar, J. (1964) *The Carrying Capacity of Woodlands for Recreation*, Society of American Foresters, Forest Service Monograph 7: 23.

Wall, G. (1982) 'Cycles and capacity: incipient theory or conceptual contradiction?', *Tourism Management*, **3** (3): 188–92.

Wall, G. (1994) 'Ecotourism: old wine in new bottles?', *Trends*, **31** (2): 4–9.

Wall, G. (1996) 'One name, two destinations', in L. Harrison and W. Husbands (eds), *Practising Responsible Tourism: International Case Studies in Tourism Planning, Policy and Development*, New York: John Wiley & Sons, 41–57.

Wall, G. (1997) 'Is ecotourism sustainable?', *Environmental Management*, **21** (4): 483–91.

Wall, G. and Wright, C. (1977) *The Environmental Impact of Recreation*, Publication Series No. 11, Department of Geography, University of Waterloo, Ontario.

Wallace, G. and Pierce, S. (1996) 'An evaluation of ecotourism in Amazonas, Brazil', *Annals of Tourism Research*, **23** (4): 843–73.

Walpole, M. and Goodwin, H. (2000) 'Local economic impacts of dragon tourism in Indonesia', *Annals of Tourism Research*, **27** (3): 559–76.

Walter, R.D. (1975) *The Impact of Tourism on the Environment*, ARRA Monograph 7, Melbourne: Australian Recreation Research Association.

Walther, P. (1986) 'The meaning of zoning in management of natural resource lands', *The Journal of Environmental Management*, **22**: 331–4.

WATC (1997) *A Nature Based Tourism Strategy*, Perth: Western Australia Tourism Commission and the Department of Conservation and Land Management.

WATC (1989) *Western Australia, Australia's Golden West: Gascoyne, A Comprehensive Guide for Holiday Makers*, Perth: Western Australia Tourism Commission.

WATC/EPA (1989) *The Eco Ethics of Tourism Development*, prepared by B.J. O'Brien for the Western Australia Tourism Commission and the Environmental Protection Authority, Perth.

Waters, S. (1966) 'The American tourist', *Annals of the American Academy of Political and Social Sciences*, **368**: 109–18.

Wathern, P. (1990) *Environmental Impact Assessment: Theory and Practice*, London: Unwin Hyman.

WCED (1987) *Our Common Future*, Report of the World Commission on Environment and Development (The Brundtland Commission), Oxford: Oxford University Press.

Wearing, S. (1995) 'Professionalism and accreditation of ecotourism', *Leisure and Recreation*, **37** (4): 31–6.

Wearing, S. and Harris, M. (1999) 'An approach to training for indigenous ecotourism development', *World Leisure and Recreation*, **41** (2): 9–17.

Wearing, S. and Neil, J. (1999) *Ecotourism Impacts, Potentials and Possibilities*, Melbourne: Butterworth-Heinemann.

Weaver, D. (1991) 'Alternative to mass tourism in Dominica', *Annals of Tourism Research*, **18**: 414–32.

Weaver, D. (1998) *Ecotourism in the Less Developed World*, Wallingford: CAB International.

Weaver, D.B. (1999) 'Magnitude of ecotourism in Costa Rica and Kenya', *Annals of Tourism Research*, **26** (4): 792–816.

Weaver, D. (ed.) (2001) *Encyclopedia of Ecotourism*, Wallingford: CABI Publishing.

Weaver, D. and Oppermann, M. (2000) *Tourism Management*, Brisbane: John Wiley & Sons.

Weber (1986) 'Trekking (wrecking?) in Nepal', *Habitat Australia*, **14** (4): 29–31.

Weiler, B. (1993) 'Nature-based tour operators: are they environmentally friendly or are they faking it?', *Tourism Recreation Research*, **18** (1): 55–60.

Weiler, B. (ed.) (1992) *Ecotourism: Incorporating the Global Classroom – 1991 Conference Papers*, Proceedings of the Inaugural International Ecotourism Symposium, University of Queensland, Brisbane, 25–27 September. Canberra: Bureau of Tourism Research.

Weiler, B. and Davis, D. (1993) 'An exploratory investigation into the roles of the nature-based tour leader', *Tourism Management*, **14** (2): 91–8.

Weiler, B. and Hall, C. (eds) (1992) *Special Interest Tourism*, London: Belhaven.

Weiler, B. and Richins, H. (1995) 'Extreme, extravagant and elite: a profile of ecotourists on Earthwatch Expeditions', *Tourism Recreation Research*, **20** (1): 29–36.

Wellings, P.A. and Crush, J.S. (1983) 'Tourism and dependency in southern Africa: the prospects and planning of tourism in Lesotho', *Applied Geography*, **3**: 205–23.

Wells, M. and Brandon, K. (1992) *People and Parks: Linking Protected Area Management with Local Communities*, Washington, DC: World Bank, World Wildlife Fund and US Agency for International Development.

Western, D. (1993) 'Defining ecotourism', in K. Lindberg and D. Hawkins (eds), *Ecotourism: A Guide for Planners and Managers*, Vermont: The Ecotourism Society.

Westman, W.E. (1985) *Ecology, Impact Assessment, and Environmental Planning*, Environmental Science and Technology Series, New York: John Wiley & Sons.

Wheeller, B. (1991) 'Tourism: troubled times', *Tourism Management*, **12** (2): 91–6.

Wheeller, B. (1992a) 'Is progressive tourism appropriate?', *Tourism Management*, **13** (1): 104–5.

Wheeller, B. (1992b) 'Alternative tourism – a deceptive ploy', in C. Cooper (ed.), *Progress in Tourism, Recreation and Hospitality Management*, Vol. 4, Chichester: John Wiley & Sons, 140–6.

Wheeller, B. (1994) 'Ecotourism, a ruse by any other name', in C. Cooper and A. Lockwood (eds), *Progress in Tourism, Recreation and Hospitality Management*, Vol. 5, Chichester: John Wiley & Sons, 3–11.

Whelan, T. (ed.) (1991) *Nature Tourism: Managing for the Environment*, Washington, DC: Island Press.

Whelan, T. (1997) *Nature Tourism*, London: Earthscan Publications Ltd.

Wight, P. (1993a) 'Ecotourism: ethics or eco-sell', *Journal of Travel Research*, **31** (3): 3–9.

Wight, P. (1993b) 'Sustainable ecotourism: balancing economic, environmental and social goals within an ethical framework', *Journal of Tourism Studies*, **4** (2): 54–66.

Wight, P.A. (1995) 'Sustainable ecotourism: balancing economic, environmental and social goals within an ethical framework', *Tourism Recreation Research*, **20** (1): 5–13.

Wight, P. (1996) 'North American ecotourists: market profile and trip characteristics', *Journal of Travel Research*, **34** (4): 2–10.

Wight, P. (1997a) 'Ecotourism accommodation spectrum: does supply match the demand?', *Tourism Management*, **18** (4): 209–19.

Wight, P. (1997b) 'Ecotourist market research: a user-oriented approach', *The Evolution of Tourism: Adapting to Change*, Proceedings of the 28th Annual Travel and Tourism Association (TTRA) Conference, Lexington, USA: TTRA, 156–65.

Wight, P.A. (1998) 'Tools for sustainability analysis in planning and managing tourism and recreation in the destination', in C.M. Hall and A. Lew (eds), *Sustainable Tourism Development: A Geographical Perspective*, Harlow: Addison-Wesley Longman, 75–91.

Wild, C. (1994) 'Issues in ecotourism', in C. Cooper and A. Lockwood (eds), *Progress in Tourism, Recreation and Hospitality Management*, Vol. 6, Chichester: John Wiley & Sons, 12–21.

Williams, M.C. (1988) 'Coastal zone management strategies: the Caribbean experience', in F. Edwards (ed.), *Environmentally Sound Tourism in the Caribbean*, Proceedings of the Workshop on Environmentally Sound Tourism Development held in Barbados 6–10 April 1987, Alberta: The Banff Centre School of Management, University of Calgary Press, 23–37.

Wilson, M. (1987) 'Nature-oriented tourism in Ecuador: assessment of industry structure and development needs', North Carolina State University, Raleigh, North Carolina, No. 20.

Wiszka, A. and Hindson, J. (1991) 'Protecting a Polish paradise', *Geographical Magazine*, **60** (6): 1–3.

Witmer, V. (1998) 'Ecotourism in Virginia, USA: how can we ensure its success?', *Intercoast Network*, Spring: 19.

Witt, S.F., Brooke, M.Z. and Buckley, P.J. (1991) *The International Management of Tourism*, London: Unwin Hyman.

Witt, S. and Gammon, S. (1991) 'Sustainable tourism development in Wales', *Revue de Tourisme*, **46** (4): 32–6.

Witt, S. and Moutinho, L. (eds) (1989) *Tourism Marketing and Management Handbook*, Hemel Hempstead: Prentice Hall.

Wood, K. and House, S. (1991) *The Good Tourist*, London: Mandarin.

Woods, B. and Moscardo, G. (1998) 'Understanding Australian, Japanese and Taiwanese ecotourists in the Pacific Rim region', *Pacific Tourism Review*, **1** (4): 329–39.

World Bank (1972) *Tourism – Sector Working Paper*, Washington, DC: World Bank.

World Resources Institute (1993) 'Ecotourism: rising interest in nature vacations has mixed results for host countries and the resources they promote', in *Environmental Almanac*, Boston: Houghton Mifflin.

WTO (1980) *Manila Declaration on World Tourism*, Madrid: World Tourism Organisation.

WTO (1997) *Yearbook of Tourism Statistics*, Madrid: World Tourism Organisation.

WTO (1998) 'Ecotourism – now one-fifth of market', *World Tourism Organisation News*, January–February: 6.

WTO (1999) *Tourism: 2020 Vision – Executive Summary*, Madrid: World Tourism Organisation.

WTO and UNEP (1992) *Guidelines: Development of National Parks and Protected Areas for Tourism*, Madrid: World Tourism Organisation.

Wunder, S. (2000) 'Ecotourism and economic incentives – an empirical approach', *Ecological Economics*, **32** (3): 465–79.

Wylie, J. (1994) *Journey Through a Sea of Islands: a Review of Forest Tourism in Micronesia*, Honolulu, Hawaii: USDA Forest Service.

Yee, J. (1992) *Ecotourism Market Survey: A Survey of North American Ecotourism Tour Operators*, 2nd edn, Bangkok: Pacific Asia Travel Association.

Yeoman, J. (2000) 'Achieving sustainable tourism: a paradigmatic perspective', in M. Robinson, J. Swarbrooke, N. Evans, P. Long and R. Sharpley (eds), *Reflections on International Tourism: Environmental Management and Pathways to Sustainable Tourism*, Sunderland: Business Education Publishers, 311–27.

Young, B. (1985) 'Tourism and conservation workshop: Nova Scotia, Canada', *Journal of Rural Studies*, **1** (1): 97–100.

Young, G. (1973) *Tourism: Blessing or Blight*, Harmondsworth: Penguin.

Zeiger, B. (1997) 'Ecotourism: wave of the future', *Parks and Recreation*, **32** (9): 84–92.

Zierer, C. (1952) 'Tourism and recreation in the west', *Geographical Review*, **42**: 462–81.

Ziffer, K. (1989) *Ecotourism: The Uneasy Alliance*, Washington, DC: Conservation International and Ernst & Young.

# Subject Index

# Place Index